Island C___

French Settlers in Grenada

1498 - 1763

John Angus Martin

The Grenada National Museum Press
St. George's, Grenada

Other books by John Angus Martin:
A-Z of Grenada Heritage (Macmillan Caribbean)

Dedicated to

Yeredh, Liam, Jason, Haroun

Venis Malcolm Martin
(1925-2012)

and

The rest of the family

Contents

Acknowledgements

Island Caribs and French Settlers in Grenada began many years ago when I stumbled across census data for Grenada dating from 1669. Recognizing its importance, I decided to analyze it as the basis for my masters' thesis in history titled "L'Isle de la Grenada: French Settlement and Development, 1649-1762." Since 1999 when I completed that thesis, I have been occupied with writing a detailed history of Grenada under the French, of which this is the result. To provide a more complete pre-1763 history of the islands, details of the Amerindian occupation and European invasions are chronicled, including the British attempt to settle the island in 1609.

Many people have contributed in various ways to the research, writing and publication of this book, and I would like to express my gratitude to them all. I would especially like to thank my brother Liam Martin for his continued support, guidance and encouragement; without his constant prodding this book would not have made it this far this soon. Elizabeth Kennedy has been supportive of my efforts and I thank her very much. Of the many others I would like to acknowledge the following: the members of my History thesis committee Drs. Susan Sinke, Alan Grubb and Joseph Arbena, the History Department at Clemson University, my sister Janice and her husband Gregory Williams, Jason Burns, Haroun Hallack and Chris Mathews, Wahid and Zaineb Hallack, Germain and Fiona Knight, and the many who have assisted with the translations of French and Spanish words and passages, including Melanie Hill, Rolande Lewis, Sophie Lamesre, Raphael Sanchez-Sola, Sandra Russo, Jill Brayshaw and Jean-Marc David. Thanks to the folks at the Grenada National Museum who have provided a wonderful home, especially Jean Pitt, Elizabeth Raffety, Oliver Pilgrim, Robert Pierre, Spencer Francis and John Pitt, and others in the Spice Isle who have been very supportive, including Meg Conlon, Erik Johnson, David Lord, Suelin Low Chew Tung and Bertha Pitt-Bonaparte. I owe a great debt of gartitude to Jonathan Hanna for the wonderful discourse and friendship, and especially his commitment to reading the entire manuscript and suggesting necessary changes. I especially thank my son Yeredh for being patient with me as I was often consumed with the writing of this book, and may have been less than attentive to his needs. For the love and support of family and friends I am forever grateful.

List of Illustrations

List of Tables

(see Appendix I)

x

Introduction

This period of its history is rather obscure.[1]

On 10 February 1763 the French colony of Grenada and the Grenadines, captured by the British in March 1762, officially became a British colony after 113 years of French colonisation. It remained a British colony for the next 211 years, except between July 1779 and December 1783 when it was recaptured by the French during the War of American Independence.[2] In the decades following its initial cession Grenada quickly began to rival those of the established British colonies, following the creation of "an island economy which stood second only to that of Jamaica," England's largest and richest colony in the region at the time.[3] Over the next two centuries of British colonisation Grenada experienced the explosion of its slave population following large imports of captive Africans, political and religious conflicts that led to the bloody revolt of its French subjects and their slaves in 1795-96, the end of the Transatlantic Slave Trade in 1808, the end of slavery and apprenticeship in 1834 and 1838 respectively, social revolution and universal adult suffrage in 1951, and finally independence in 1974. Despite its long and continuous British occupation, Grenada exhibits a conspicuous French presence even after 230 years since the departure of the last French colonial governor. While Grenada's rich history under British colonial occupation since 1763 has been documented and analyzed in some detail, much of its history prior to that date remains rather deficient.[4] The discussion of the history of the Island Caribs in the Lesser Antilles is mired in debate, and little analysis has been done on their occupation of Grenada following European incursion into the region.[5] Except for the arrival and hasty retreat of the British in 1609, little is known of their failed attempt to establish a tobacco colony in Grenada. Of the French period, the details remain to be told.

Like its post-1763 history, the early modern history of Grenada is quite intriguing and offers fascinating insights into the indigenous Amerindian populations in the region and their reactions to Spanish incursions, early European colonization of the Caribbean with the failed British attempt in 1609 and the successful French settlement in 1649, wars of subjugation and ultimately decimation of the indigenous populations, privateering and colonial wars among the Europeans, the establishment of plantation agriculture, and the corresponding creation and expansion of African chattel slavery and its impact on economic and social institutions. It is a testament to the French and the foundation they had built between 1649 and 1762 that the British were able to create a prosperous colonial economy in the decades after its cession.

Much of the early modern history of Grenada after the arrival of Europeans in the Caribbean relates to the French, who in their 113 years occupation, saw the island traverse a long, sometimes difficult road to the realization of a successful colonial economy.[6] Its fifteen years under proprietary rule resulted in the subjugation of the indigenous population, but accomplished little else in terms of development, consumed as it was with internal political conflicts. Another ten years of administration by the Crown-sponsored Compagnie des Indies occidentales françaises (French West India Company) had little impact on the island's economy, though it remained an interest of French minister Jean-Baptiste Colbert because of its proximity to South America. French colonial status, instituted in 1674, only continued Grenada's neglect in the face of growing colonial conflicts in the region and limited resources. The island was neglected as the French concentrated their investments in the development of the larger and more valuable colonies of Martinique, St. Domingue, and to a lesser extent Guadeloupe. It was not until the first quarter of the eighteenth century and the period of a prolonged peace in the region that Grenada began to show signs of steady growth. That growth was brought about by the widespread economic expansion in the French Antilles and the growing trade, despite colonial restrictions, in the Atlantic economy. Indigo, the primary crop in Grenada until the 1720s, was gradually replaced by sugar cane, reflecting the common feature throughout the region. Thereafter, Grenada experienced measured economic growth as sugar production steadily increased, alongside the continued cultivation of secondary staples like indigo, cocoa, cotton, and especially coffee. Paralleling this growth was significant population changes as imported African slaves came to overwhelmingly dominate the labor force and production. The changes in the physical environment were evident in the growing infrastructure as well. The social stratification of the society—a small number of wealthy sugar planters and merchants (*grand blancs*) at the top of the social and political order, followed by a larger group of small white coffee farmers and skilled workers (*petit blancs*), then a small freedman non-white class (*affranchis*), and the majority slave population (*esclaves or Nègres*) at the bottom—gradually reflected that of the other Caribbean colonies. At mid-eighteenth-century Grenada had achieved a political and economic stability that was the basis of plantation economies throughout the region.

Historiography of French Grenada

The historiography of the Caribbean region, especially of the French Antilles, has all but ignored colonial French Grenada, except in passing references. The meager historical analyses to date on French colonial Grenada have been undertaken by historians of the French Antilles. Of particular note is James Pritchard's *In Search of Empire: The French in the Americas, 1670-1730*, which provides notable references to Grenada's early colonial development. A number of others that deal with aspects of Grenada's French history include Pierre Margry, who in his 1878 article "Origines Françaises des pays d'Outre-Mer," examines the settlement of Grenada under du Parquet[7]; Nellis M. Crouse, in his *French Pioneers in the West Indies*, also documents the initial French settlement of Grenada[8]; A. Latron, in his article "Les mésaventures d'un gentilhomme colonial," provides an examination of the Comte de Sérrilac and his ownership of Grenada,[9] and Henri Malo, in his article "La perte et prise de la Grenade (mars 1675)," discusses the unsuccessful attempt by Dutch privateers to capture the island.[10] All of these are primarily political histories concerned with personalities or events of the mid-seventeenth century French Antilles. As a result of the meager historical analysis to date, the historiography of French colonial Grenada is very incomplete, especially in English-language histories of Grenada. Of the three general histories of Grenada, the 113 years of French occupation are only superficially examined, incorporating little economic and social analysis beyond the Island Carib-French conflict.[11] This is due most assuredly to Grenada's subsequent British occupation, association and aggregation with the British possessions in the region, and its minimal economic value within the early French Antilles. For British and Caribbean historians, the absence of original documents in either British or Grenadian archives concerning the islands' French colonization, remain the primary reason for that period's neglect.[12] The French language, of which all the original documents were written in, most probably made in-depth analysis of Grenada difficult for many students of its history.[13]

For this study a variety of sources, primarily French, are of the greatest importance. Original documents in the Archives Nationales, Paris form the most important source of information on this period.[14] Many of these documents have been overlooked or ignored, especially by English-language historians of Grenada.[15] Extensive use has been made of the general correspondences between the governors and other government officials at Grenada to the governor-general and intendant at Martinique between 1664 and 1762.[16] These documents concern the administration of the government of Grenada and reveal much about the important issues and events affecting the colony on a daily basis. Supplementing the correspondences are census data between 1669 and 1761.[17] This data form the basis for much of the quantitative analysis undertaken as they are absolutely essential in analyzing the economic and demographic changes, and illustrate the role of the various groups in orchestrating the economic and social development of the island.

Though the above documents reveal much of the initial French occupation of Grenada, gaps remain. The fire of December 1771 has been identified as the cause of the destruction of valuable records that could have provided a great deal of insights into the island's social development under the French. Few, if any, personal correspondences and diaries have been found to date to add to the stories of families and their everyday survival. One of the important areas that remains ambiguous is slavery and plantation life. Much of what is presented here about the slave trade and slavery have been gleaned from censuses and other records, particularly statistical data. Specific plantations' records like account books or inventories are totally lacking, thus making any detailed analysis of everyday life, especially for the slaves, difficult. Another problem has to do with Grenada's status as a colony of Martinique. Investigating the commercial history of the French in Grenada is problematic because Grenada was administered from Martinique, and as such much of its economy was channeled through there, especially prior to the 1730s. As a result there is a lack of production and trade data for exports from the seventeenth and eighteenth centuries to analyze its economy. There is also an absence of data concerning the slaves imported to Grenada directly from Martinique.

Extensive use is made of the contemporary accounts by Jean-Baptiste Dutertre and Jean-Baptiste Labat, and particularly the anonymous 17th-century French manuscript *Histoire de l'isle de Grenade en Amérique* that chronicles the first ten years of the French settlement on Grenada and published in 1975. The anonymous manuscript was first used by Pierre Margry in his 1878 article "Origines Françaises des pays d'Outre-Mer," which he considered more reliable than Dutertre's *Histoire générale des Antilles habitées par les François* concerning the initial French settlement on Grenada. The anonymous manuscript and its possible author were investigated by Jacques de Dampierre in 1904 and Joseph Rennard in 1931, both attributing it to Bénigne Bresson, a Dominican priest resident in Grenada between 1656 and 1659.[18] According to Petitjean-Roget, Bresson "has written here, in great haste, a text obviously meant to justify those who were accused of murdering du Bu.... However he had not been satisfied with the usual plea for mercy; using older settlers, his friends as witnesses, he gives us a rich and precise chronicle of the little known beginnings of one of the small French Caribbean islands."[19]

Jean-Baptiste Dutertre's *Histoire générale* provides many details from the island's settlement to around 1667. Until the widespread availability of *Histoire de l'isle de Grenade*, Dutertre's *Histoire générale* represented the sole chronicle of French Grenada's early history. Though some specific details of Grenada's settlement and conquest have been called into question, *Histoire générale* nonetheless provides valuable information, especially on Dutertre's visit to Grenada in 1656, the Comte de Sérillac's purchase of

Grenada from Governor du Parquet, and his unsuccessful attempts to colonize it. Used in conjunction with *Histoire de l'isle de Grenade*, it remains an important source for the study of Grenada's early history under the French, and of northern European settlement and expansion in the Caribbean in the seventeenth century.[20]

Jean-Baptiste Labat's *Nouveau voyages aux isles de l'Amerique, 1693-1705* provides one of the few eyewitness accounts of the struggling French colony around 1700, some fifty years after its initial colonization.[21] Though he does not provide a detailed analysis of the economy or society, Labat provides descriptions of the fortifications of the island, some census data, and a valuable map of the layout of the colony to date. There is, however, discrepancy in the date of Labat's visit. He claims that he met Governor de Bellair, but the governor had already departed Grenada for France by September 1700. Chatillon, in his study of Labat's *Nouveau voyages*, identifies the problem of the dates of his entire trip between 3-28 September 1700 to Barbados, Grenada and St. Vincent.[22] It is most likely that Labat recorded incorrect dates, and his trip took place the previous year, but definitely by January 1700 and not September 1700.

A number of secondary sources on the French Antilles were helpful in the placement of Grenada within the French colonial experience. Primary among these are James Pritchard's *In Search of Empire*, Philip P. Boucher's *France and the American Tropics to 1700* and *Cannibal Encounters*, Jean-Pierre Moreau's *Les Petites Antilles de Christophe Colomb à Richelieu*, Stewart L. Mims's *Colbert's West India Policy*, Liliane Chauleau' *Dans les îles du vent: La Martinique*, Louis-Philippe May's *Histoire économique de la Martinique*, and Gabriel Debien's *Les Esclaves aux Antilles (xviie-xviiie siècles)* and "Les Engagés pour les Antilles, 1634-1715."[23]

Of immense value to this study is an *Explication du plan de l'isle de la Grenade*, the survey of the island carried out by Jean-Baptiste Pinel at the request of the incoming British government; Paterson's *A Topographical Description of the Island of Grenada* provided additional information.[24] The accompanying map, with the numbered estates, their sizes and types of crops produced, provides valuable information about the French colony and property ownership at the end of their rule (see Illustration 10.2). The map, showing the road network and towns, illustrates the extent of infrastructural development under the French. Complimenting this is the *Extracts From the Capitation Rolls for the Quarters of Basse-Terre, Maigrin, Marquis, Sauteurs, Grand Pauvre and Goyave, Grenada, and the Island of*

Carioacou (sic) which provide more details on the French residents (by name) and their ownership of moveable property, particularly slaves.[25] The *Registers of Records*, particularly the French language series that date to the British period, but include interesting information on the history of the French in Grenada, were only examined superficially for this study because extensive work needs to be done to reconstruct that data.[26]

This history of early Grenada comprises twelve chapters. Chapter 1 ("The Island Caribs of Grenada") examines the indigenous population, particularly the debates on their origin and cannibalism, some aspects of their culture, and the available data on their occupation of Grenada on the eve of European invasion. Chapter 2 ("Prologue to Settlement") looks at the conflicts of the 1500s and early 1600s between the Island Caribs of Grenada and Europeans, particularly the Spanish. Chapter 3 ("The 1609 British Attempt to Settle Grenada") chronicles the first European attempt to settle the island to establish a tobacco producing colony. Chapter 4 ("French Settlement and Island Carib Resistance") looks at French plans to settle Grenada, the successful foothold gained by Governor du Parquet, and the Island Caribs' attempt to thwart that invasion. Chapter 5 ("Comte de Sérillac's Colonial Misadventures") focuses on the failure of Governor de Sérillac to create his dream colony in Grenada. Chapter 6 ("A Tenuously Held Colony") details Grenada from its administration under the Compagnie des Indes occidentales françaises and struggles to defend itself against the Dutch, to colonial conflicts in the late 1600s, and the emergence of stability in the early 1700s. Chapter 7 ("Peopling Grenada's Slave Society") analyzes the available census data to illustrate the growth of the colony, as well as details of the various populations and their impact in shaping French Grenadian society. Chapter 8 ("Production in Grenada's Slave Society") utilizes census and other data to chart the development of export and subsistence agriculture. Chapter 9 ("Plantation Society") details the overall development of the island, its place in the French Antilles, its infrastructure, society, defenses, and the colonial conflicts that threatened its development. Chapter 10 ("An End and a Beginning") looks at the capture of the islands by the British and the beginning of their rule. Chapter 11 ("... and the Grenadines") provides a history of the archipelago of small islands, particularly the largest Carriacou and Bequia, up to partition between Grenada and St. Vincent. Chapter 12 ("Legacy of the Island Caribs") looks at the surviving memory of the Island Caribs.

1

The Island Caribs of Grenada

*'We find some difficulty to know ourselves, so
different are we grown from what we were here-to-fore.'*[1]

Though much has been written about the Island Caribs in the over
500 years since they encountered European invasion on their shores,
Island Carib identity remains an enigma.[2] Despite extensive research,
Caribbean scholars "are not at all agreed about what constitutes Island
Carib ceramics as opposed to that of prehistoric island inhabitants."[3] The
debate is further complicated by the fact that for over one hundred and
fifty years after European contact, Island Carib culture remained
unrecorded, leaving a huge gap in the historical and ethnographic data. It
was not until the mid-1600s when northern Europeans came to colonize
the Lesser Antilles that the details of the historical Island Carib culture
became well known. It is rather ironic, then, that the era in which so
much was learned about them also witnessed the destruction of their way
of life and the decimation of their populations.

Until the late twentieth century the questions of who the Island
Caribs were and where they originated were widely accepted based on the
historical evidence. But as scholars began reexamining the historical,

1

linguistic, ethnographic and archaeological data in greater detail, the accepted answers to the questions of Island Carib identity appeared deficient. It became clear that the historical representation of the Island Caribs was much more complex than previously portrayed, and requires extensive interdisciplinary analysis before some kind of consensus can be reached. Presently, almost every aspect of Island Carib identity, including their name, remains part of an ongoing debate.

"Those of Caniba, Whom They Call Caribes"

The history of the Carib name is a classic lesson in colonialism and the need by its proponents to name and redefine. The name Carib dates back to when Europeans first arrived in the Americas, and even before they encountered the people subsequently known as (Island) Caribs. Christopher Columbus, on his initial voyage to the region in 1492, recorded a number of words in his journal–caniba, canima and canibales– that the Tainos, the Amerindians he encountered in the Bahamas and Cuba, identified as referring to lands and peoples to the southeast who were their enemies and supposedly consumed human flesh.[4] In a later entry Columbus records what he believes is a description of these cannibals, given by the Tainos he "rescued" from the Caribs, as having "only one eye and the face of a dog."[5] Las Casas adds that "the admiral thought they were lying and felt that those who captured them must have been under the Great Khan."[6] In yet another entry in his journal Columbus refers to "those of Caniba, whom they call Caribes…"[7]

When, on the second voyage in 1493, Columbus and his crew came in contact with the Amerindians of the Lesser Antilles, they immediately labeled them Caribs. Diego Chanca, the ships' physician, on landing on Guadeloupe and "rescuing" a number of Amerindian captives, describes articles found in the huts: "he brought away four or five bones of the arms and legs of men. When we saw this, we suspected that the islands were those of Caribe, which are inhabited by people who eat human flesh."[8] Chanca continues that "We asked the women who were captive on this island what these people were; they replied that they were caribes."[9] The name persisted, from then associated with the consumption of human flesh, and spread "like a kind of linguistic weed" throughout the region and beyond.[10] These islands would become well known as the Caribbee or Cannibal Islands, and represented as such on early maps of the region, evoking fear among weary travelers.

The Spanish demand for slave labor inevitably led to the Carib designation being arbitrarily applied to all allegedly unfriendly, uncooperative and cannibalistic peoples in the region, as Spain granted its colonists legal sanction to enslave anyone so labeled.[11] The name Carib survived into the twentieth century until anthropologists added the "Island" modifier to avoid confusion between these former occupants of the Lesser Antilles or Insular Caribs, and the present Cariban-speaking Galibis of northern South America who are also referred to as Caribs.[12]

The debate surrounding the Island Carib name is further complicated by the fact that the historical Island Caribs in the mid-1600s were recorded as speaking two "languages," and having multiple self-derivations.[13] In the so-called "men's language," a pidgin with "mainland Cariban lexical elements," but with a "largely Arawakan character,"[14] the Island Caribs are recorded by Father Raymond Breton (who published the only dictionary of the Island Carib languages) as referring to themselves as Callinago/Kalinago. This term (Kalina, plus suffix –go) identifies the Island Carib with the Cariban-speaking Galibi or Kalina of northeastern South America among whom they claimed origin.[15] This has led Louis Allaire to suggest that based on self-ascription, the Island Caribs should be called "island Kalinas."[16] Davis and Goodwin, however, disagree, insisting that it is "not justified and creates a misleading suggestion that they shared the cultural heritage of the mainland Kalina.[17]

In the second language, one belonging to the Arawakan family of languages and designated "women's language" by Breton, the Island Caribs called themselves Callipuna/Kalipuna, a term also "used to designate several Arawakan-speaking groups in South America."[18] Allaire, however, argues that Kalina is a shortened form deriving from Kalipuna, "the original ethnic denomination."[19] One of the problems, according to Allaire, is that Breton did not provide a more precise definition of Kalinago and thus "historians and anthropologists have been at wits' end trying to figure out the relationship among these words."[20]

The Carib/Island Carib designation, which Davis and Goodwin view as a "legacy of Columbus's original hearsay evidence from Española [and] reinforced by the exigencies of sixteenth-century Spanish slave policy,"[21] is by far the most widespread because of its historicity. Recently, following Allaire's lead, many have begun referring to the Island Caribs as

Kalinago, preferring to use a name believed to be self-ascribed. Rather than resolving the contentious issue surrounding their name, it has added to the complexity. The debate surrounding these various names—Carib, Island Carib, Kalinago, Kalipuna, Kalina—continue, but is only one piece of the larger debate on Island Carib identity.

Except for the reports of encounters between the Island Caribs and Europeans, primarily the Spanish, there is little information on Island Carib culture in the first 150 years of contact. What the Spanish did establish, correctly or incorrectly, was that the Caribbean archipelago comprised two exclusively distinct ethnic groups—Tainos in the Greater Antilles (who supposedly responded peacefully towards the Spanish), and the Island Caribs in the Lesser Antilles (who supposedly acted hostile towards the Spanish). This dichotomy, long accepted by scholars of Caribbean history and culture, remains at the heart of the ongoing debates on Island Carib origin and identity.[22] The primary focus of the debate is whether the people called Island Caribs were an entity unto themselves, and/or, in any way, directly related to the Tainos of the Greater Antilles or the Galibis/Kalina of the South American mainland?

When northern Europeans first began recording details of Island Carib culture in the mid-1600s, Europeans had already been interacting with the Lesser Antillean populations for four to five generations and initiated changes that profoundly impacted these populations. These changes, caused by Spanish slave raids, reprisals, trade and foreign diseases, along with the forced migration and assimilation of possibly diverse Amerindian groups, Africans and Europeans into Lesser Antillean communities, greatly affected Island Carib culture.[23] In ongoing attempts to understand Island Carib origin and identity, a number of models, utilizing various facets of the available data, have been advanced. There are notable variations to these models, and some raise more questions than they answer, while others present intriguing hypotheses.

The oldest and most widely held theory of Island Carib origin is that they were the descendants of Cariban speakers from northern South America. Known popularly as the "Carib invasion" model, it maintains that Cariban speakers from the mainland invaded the Lesser Antilles and captured the islands from the less-aggressive Tainos, killing the men and abducting the women as slaves and wives.[24] The historical Island Caribs themselves, in retelling their origin myths to seventeenth-century French missionaries, seemed to corroborate the invasion model.[25] Though there

4

are variations on the myths recorded in Dominica, St. Vincent and Guadeloupe, all seem to point to "an invasion of either Galibi or Kalina peoples from the South American mainland."[26] Analyses of the myths told by the Island Carib informants have produced conflicting results. Though the Island Caribs may have related their own stories of origin, they also seemed to have accepted European views of their culture and incorporated them into their origin myths; they were also known to boast about their mercurial exploits. Gullick concludes that "at a theoretical level these traditions [of origin] can be shown to be suspect, and at a more pragmatic one some aspects can be shown to be false."[27]

The peculiarity of the various languages spoken among the Island Caribs, especially the men's language, with its Cariban elements, appears to some scholars to strongly support the myths recorded by Breton. Numerous scholars have since used the men's language and myths to support the Carib invasion model. Taylor (noted linguist of the Island Caribs) and Hoff "believe that it is impossible to explain the available linguistic data unless one accepts the native tradition that there has been such an invasion.[28] Opponents, however, argue that the men's language was simply "a lingua franca used for trade with mainland peoples,"[29] a fact Taylor and Hoff agree, believing that "once the former had lost their full command of the common ancestral language" they relied upon the men's language for their communication.[30] Davis and Goodwin argue that it is unlikely "that a pidgin would develop among descendants of immigrants who had been speakers of the 'donor' language."[31]

When Ripley Bullen undertook archaeological fieldwork in Grenada in 1962, he believed he had unearthed evidence to support the invasion model.

> This gradual replacement of one ceramic series by another would seem to fit the historically reported conquest of the Lesser Antilles by the Caribs. They are said to have attacked a settlement, to have killed the men and married the women or to have taken them as concubines or second wives, and then to have lived in the new area. They must have brought some [Carib] women with them—assuming women to be the pottery makers—to have introduced the Suazey series.[32]

The break in the ceramic chronology as represented by the Suazey series with that preceding it, appeared to Bullen to support the conquest scenario, associating Suazoid ceramics with the historical Island Caribs.

5

Yet, Bullen admits that there are some elements of continuity with the previous Calivigny series, which he explained by suggesting that the Island Carib subjugation of Taino women resulted in their continued contributions to pottery manufacture.[33] Bullen's thesis, however, has been challenged by a number of scholars, even proponents of the invasion model. As Allaire notes, Suazey ceramic "development [is] unique to the Lesser Antilles…, and is totally lacking in Trinidad and everywhere on the mainland."[34] Also, its production, confined to the Windward Islands, ceased somewhere between 1300 and 1450 CE, while the historical Island Caribs continued to inhabit the region for over two centuries. Allaire believes that Amerindians who preceded the Island Caribs, the Igneri, "left the islands before the [Island] Caraibe entered," and manufactured Suazey pottery.[35] Research is ongoing, and Boomert suggests that Suazoid ceramics was replaced by the Cayo series, and linked to the historic Island Caribs, but its associations require further research, particularly in Grenada.[36]

Although the Island Carib men's language and their myths of origin appear to support the Carib invasion model, one major problem remains. There is a lack of archaeological evidence to support an invasion scenario, especially since Bullen's Suazey thesis has been discredited. Thus a number of scholars have proposed interesting modifications to the invasion model. One such modification by Allaire proposes that Cariban speakers from South America arrived in the Lesser Antilles either a generation or two just prior to European arrival (as opposed to around 1100 CE and the appearance of Suazey ceramics), or that Kalina warriors and traders rapidly acculturated the resident Taino population.[37] These scenarios are not without their problems. As Davis and Goodwin point out, there is no archaeological or linguistic evidence for a proto-historic or late prehistoric (i.e. post-CE 1200) migration into the Lesser Antilles.[38]

Another popular theory of Island Carib origin is the "Arawakan continuity" model. It proposes that the Island Caribs and the Tainos shared a common ancestor, a pre-historic Arawakan migrant from South America. Peter Hulme is of the view that the Island Caribs "did not differ ethnically from their 'Arawak' enemies," the differences being primarily economic and political.[39] Others go even further, suggesting that the Spaniards exaggerated the differences and created peaceful Tainos and warlike Island Caribs to enslave and exterminate the latter when they resisted Spanish colonization.[40] Proponents of the Arawakan continuity model argue that the Island Caribs were long-time residents of the Windward Islands, having derived from ceramic Saladoids, and are culturally distinct from mainland populations, despite their Carib or Kalinago designations.[41] Gullick hypothesizes "that the Caribs were derived from the Arawak [i.e. Taino] does agree with linguistic and genetic studies of the [Island] Caribs' descendants."[42] It is widely accepted that one of the languages spoken by the Island Caribs is a member of the Arawakan family of languages. He goes on to offer the hypothesis that "a small number of Carib speakers intermarried with the Arawak inhabitants of the Lesser Antilles" and were rejected by the Arawaks, but accepted by the Galibis, "producing a people who, while genetically and linguistically mainly Arawak, called themselves Carib."[43]

These various models illustrate the complexity of the incomplete archaeological, ethnographical, historical and linguistic evidence, and their analyses and interpretations to date. Holdren, however, believes that researchers "have begun to recognize the impossibility of fitting a homogeneous Caraibe identity into either the Arawakan continuity or Cariban invasion models," and that the "study of the [Island] Caraibe has undergone an intrinsically revolutionary process."[44] This paradigm shift "views the Lesser Antilles as composed of a changing mosaic of cultures."[45] Some scholars, like Samuel Wilson, observe that the "historical and archaeological evidence from the Lesser Antilles suggest that there is more heterogeneity than has been recognized."[46] He adds that "the prehistoric and early historic Lesser Antilles contained a complex of ethnic groups which had considerable interaction with each other, the mainland, and the Greater Antilles."[47]

Views like Wilson's have led to the proposal of a third model, the "reticulate model," which suggests that the complexity of the evidence supports the opinion that the people which history identifies as Island Caribs were in fact a heterogeneous mix "composed of multiple ethnic groups with more than one contributing ancestor."[48] It further contends that they were neither unitary nor "arrived at the same time or in the same place," and "varied in source between the islands.[49] In the case of Grenada, they were in fact at least two groups of Amerindians, one group the French labeled "Caraïbe" and the other "Galibi," which Holdren uses to support the reticulate model.[50]

Caribbean scholars remain far apart in their views on the origin and identity of the Island Caribs. The complexity of the historical and physical data, and the dearth of archaeological evidence associated with the historical Island Caribs make the debate more complex. Yet scholars are coming up with new ways of looking at the evidence and creating innovative hypotheses that are breaking with the primary models and re-examining much of what was historically accepted, and hopefully will arrive at a consensus on Island Carib identity.

The Persistent Charge of Cannibalism

For almost five centuries it was widely accepted as an historical fact that the inhabitants of the Lesser Antilles, the (Island) Caribs, were cannibals. What that meant ranged from the ritualistic mastication or consumption of "choice" pieces of human flesh from a dead enemy to customary, lavish, barbecued, gustatory feasts, sometimes involving Europeans as the main course–the delicate French were reportedly more desirable to the tough English or indigestible Spanish (Illustration 1.2). This, more than any other characteristic of their recorded culture captivated the imagination of Europeans and received much attention in their reporting on the Island Caribs. It came to define the Island Caribs for centuries, leaving them a legacy of fierce cannibalism that continues to gnaw at their memory.[51] Though there were those who discredited the charge of habitual cannibalism, others often repeated the cannibalistic tales, many with embellishments. The debate, begun centuries ago, still rages.

Like their name (Island) Carib, the indigenous inhabitants of the Lesser Antilles received the infamous title anthropophagy even before Europeans set eyes upon them. The word cannibal, which came to replace anthropophagy in common usage, was derived from one of the words that Columbus interpreted from the Tainos as referring to the Island Caribs and their supposed anthropophagy. In the inevitable shock of contact with previously unknown peoples, cultures and languages, Columbus and his crew made interpretations that appeared based more on their own expectations of what these lands and people were than on actual communication and observations. Others have argued that it was a deliberate branding as a basis for exploitation. Columbus believed that he had in fact reached Asia and expected to find much of what Europeans had believed and mythologized about the East. For example, he expected to find the Great Khan from Marco Polo's journey to China, and thought

8

he had reached India, hence Indians and the Indies, and later West Indies to differentiate it from the actual (East) Indies.

It is quite evident that Columbus' descriptions of the "cannibals," even before he met them, "reflected inherited classical and medieval notions about anthropophagi inhabiting the far ends of the earth."[52] There was considerable mythology surrounding cannibalism in Europe at the time, for example Christian accusations of blood libel against the Jews, the use of human body parts in medicine, and Christians themselves were ritualistically consuming the body and blood of Jesus Christ.[53] Cannibals were only one of a number of mythological monstrosities that the Spaniards expected to find and which the Tainos supposedly informed them existed in the Lesser Antilles. In his journal of the first voyage, Columbus recorded that "there are men with one eye and others with dogs' snouts who eat men. On taking a man, they beheaded him, drink his blood, and cut off his genitals" (Illustration 1.2).[54] Another tale was of Amazon women who mated with cannibals. Though the outlandish tales quickly disappeared, the charge of cannibalism persisted.

It is of interest to note that a number of early writers, including Bartolomé Las Casas (who used Columbus' original journals), acknowledged that Columbus was skeptical about the stories of Island Carib cannibalism. Yet, it was not long before Columbus began spreading the tales across Europe of bloodthirsty cannibals inhabiting the Lesser Antilles. A number of writers, including William Arens, have argued that the charge of cannibalism, begun by Columbus, and popularized by European travelers and writers, survived solely to justify the enslavement of the Island Caribs.[55] Arens continues, "Resistance and cannibalism became synonymous and also legitimized the barbaric Spanish reaction."[56] The view that the charge of cannibalism may have been used solely to sanction slavery has become quite popular, and a prominent argument against the historically accepted charge of Island Carib cannibalism.

Cultural bias of materially less developed peoples has been a facet of European colonialism, dating back to the tales of cannibalism by the Greek historian Herodotus and others. It is quite evident, that upon encountering new and different peoples, be they African, Amerindian or Asian, Europeans used myths and misunderstanding to create stereotypes that were often later accepted as historical facts; the history of European Jewry is a prime example.[57] In the case of the Island Caribs, the Spanish misunderstood burial and warrior customs, or ancestral worship customs that utilized the bones or remains of their dead and that of their enemies; they were reported to partake of "Preserved fat and bones of defeated enemies [which] were apparently gnawed in rage."[58] Some have argued that the charge of cannibalism was purely political or based on cultural bias, but what is the evidence for or against Island Carib cannibalism?

Though Columbus gradually accepted the existence of Island Carib cannibalism, he had no credible "evidence" to substantiate the charge he introduced across Europe in his 15 February 1493 letter to Luis de Santángel.[59] That soon changed in November 1493 when Columbus made landfall in the Lesser Antilles. It was on Guadeloupe, according to the ships' physician, Diego Chanca, that the Spaniards witnessed "evidence" of Island Carib cannibalism when "we saw those bones we immediately suspected we were then among the Caribbee islands whose inhabitants eat human flesh."[60] Chanca's letter continues:

> In one house they found the head of a man cooking. The boys whom they capture young, they are said to castrate and keep them as servants until they are full grown, or until they wish, and then they make a feast and kill them and eat them, and they say that the flesh of the boys and women is not good, nor like that of men. Three of these boys fled to the fleet, all of whom had been castrated.[61]

The customary form of cannibalism consumed many of the early accounts like Chanca's above, but they eventually developed into the ritualistic accounts, like those related by Fathers Raymond Breton and Jean-Baptiste Dutertre, who lived among the Island Caribs in the first half of the 1600s.[62] A seventeenth-century commentator describes the Island Caribs on Grenada celebrating their victory over their enemies, by

> eat[ing] part of the prisoners of war, while they were in triumph, which they rather did out of malice, chewing only one mouthful and spitting it out again, and animating one another thereby to be fierce and cruel to their enemies, as a thing pleasing to their gods, and it hath been a great mistake in those that have reported the Southern Indians ate one another as food, for its performed rather as a religious injunction, although the custom be barbarous.[63]

Chanca and the early Spanish were ignorant of Island Carib practices that involved the remains of their enemies: "Caribs killed male enemies in elaborate rituals, burned their flesh and carried the ashes in small calabashes around their necks, ate the fat on certain occasions, and finally, used human bones to make flutes. They also preserved the bones of their dead relatives."[64]

Thus the reports of Island Carib cannibalism began, and continued with numerous variations for the next century and a half. In the case of Grenada, accounts of Island Carib cannibalism date to the Spanish, and included accounts by travelers who stopped to either trade or refresh. Many of the celebrated eyewitness accounts, however, turned out to be second-hand, copied from published accounts, or altogether fabricated. André Thevet, though he did not travel to the Caribbean, reported in 1560 that "on Grenada there are a hundred strong, powerful cannibals who eat what they catch—for the most part, they eat birds, human flesh, fish, and some fruits. The island is full of these people and is therefore not a port for ships."[65] In 1565 John Hawkins related the story of a captain who stopped at Grenada to refresh and "could not doe the same for the canybals, who fought with him very desperately two days."[66] As late as 1614 Nicolás de Cardona sailed past the island and repeated the tales of Island Carib cannibalism.

> They are big thieves and do battle continuously with the Christian Indians of the Paria [Trinidad] Mission and coastal mainland and at times they reach all the way to the island of Margarita, killing and taking prisoners the Christians whom they call 'Cacona', meaning slaves, whose hair they shave and they fatten them, and at certain times of festivities and drunkenness that they have, they kill them and they roast and eat them as they build barbeques, tall from the ground, which are like beds of thin sticks and on top of them they place the human body cleaned and gutted and washed, and underneath they light up a great amount of firewood, and after they are roasted a great number of them get together in a big hut where they eat and get drunk, and they do the same thing with the Christians they kill.[67]

Grenada's unfavorable reputation in the early 1600s was widespread among Europeans in general, but trading ships also frequented the island to cut timber and trade for tobacco with the Island Caribs. It was reportedly a favorite port of the Dutch, but in 1629, a Dutch ship, under Loncq, "was to try and capture some Grenada natives who posed a powerful threat since they regularly killed members of Dutch crews sent to that island for water and wood."[68] An incident with French traders described the Island Caribs as devious, promising "a shipment of

11

tobacco, but they would delay and delay until the opportunity arose to kill and eat the French crew."[69] It is rather interesting, however, that during the period the British and French carried out their colonization activities (which presented the opportunity for closer observation), there was not one report of Island Carib cannibalism. In the violent confrontations with the French between 1649 and 1659 as related in the *Historire de l'isle de Grenade en Amérique*, there is no mention of cannibalism, as if the practice never existed at all, having faded away like the other incredible tales popularized by the Spanish. It seems that ignorance and unfamiliarity were partly responsible for the elaborate tales, but some might argue that with conquest there was no need for propaganda.

Robert Myers scrutinizes the "few reports of Carib cannibalism," dating from Columbus to the seventeenth-century French missionaries who lived among the historical Island Caribs. Myers reviews the primary accounts, but finds only one of these supposed firsthand reports to be reliable, that of Father Raymond Breton who lived among the historical Island Caribs on Dominica for many years and said he witnessed a cannibal feast. Despite Breton's use of terms like "I think" and "I heard it said," Myers believes his observation cannot be dismissed without due analysis. Yet Myers' overall conclusion, like that of a number of modern scholars, is that "all the evidence is weak, circumstantial, and largely secondhand." Myers concludes that "if the Caribs were on trial for cannibalism, they would be acquitted."[70]

If the lack of evidence against the charge of Island Carib cannibalism renders an acquittal as Myers concludes, can it go even further and exonerate the Island Caribs from such a damning stereotype, if that's all it is? William Arens has probably made the most compelling argument to do exactly that. In 1979 Arens published *The Man-Eating Myth*, a study in which he dismisses the very notion of cannibalism as a myth generated to enslave or otherwise oppress a hostile 'other.'"[71] Arens' view, though widely criticized, is championed by many and has led to a reexamination of the evidence on cannibalism, especially in the case of the Island Caribs.[72] In reviewing the accounts of Island Carib cannibalism Arens concludes, "They may have been hostile to their neighbors, aggressively resisted Spanish imperialism, and preferred their culture to the European, but that is as much as can be said."[73] Despite the views of Arens and others, there is evidence that the Island Caribs participated in rituals involving human remains that was exaggerated by Europeans, especially the Spanish, due to their cultural biases and used as a reason to exploit and wage war against them.[74]

The Island Caribs of Camàhogne[75]

Grenada, unlike Barbados and a number of the Leeward Islands, had a settled Amerindian population on the eve of the failed British colonization attempt in 1609 and the successful French colonization in 1649. Though that population may have been large relative to the other islands in the pre-contact period because of Grenada's proximity to the mainland, it probably suffered from frequent Spanish raids, reprisals and diseases, and, as a result, may have witnessed a decrease by the early 1600s. Estimates of that population, for any period, are nonexistent. The indigenous population seemed to have exhibited some degree of flux by the 1600s because of movement among the islands and relocation caused by European intrusion. Bouton's explanation for Martinique probably holds true for Grenada: "It is not possible to state the true number of the Caribs on Martinique because they are continually and actively visiting and passing among those of Dominica and other islands. Sometimes they are many Caribs there and sometimes fewer."[76] Since no contemporary estimates are available, any attempt to calculate figures presents a problem because the only available data are descriptive phrases like "many" and "numerous" when numbers of Island Caribs are identified.[77]

The debate over population numbers for any of the indigenous groups in the Americas is contentious and very problematic. Most of the available historical data are biased, or no more than guesses. The case of the Tainos in the Greater Antilles is illustrative of this complex problem.[78] Yet, despite the inherent difficulties, it is important to have an idea of the extent of Grenada's indigenous population because it helps set the stage for the confrontation with the invading French colonists.

It is possible to produce a vague estimate of the Grenada indigenous population by using population formulas based on, for example, density per area. Steward has estimated that the population density per 100 square kilometers for the Lesser Antilles, i.e. Island Carib populations, is around 500.[79] With a total area of 312 square kilometers, Grenada could probably support a population of roughly 1,550. The available information from the historical period does not appear to support this large number, so the figure of 1,550 is therefore taken as an upper limit for Grenada on the eve of colonization.[80]

The Amerindian population at that time would have been scattered on the north and east coasts, having possibly retreated from Spanish slave raids to more defensible positions. It is quite possible that Amerindian settlements were scattered across the island prior to the advent of Europeans in the region in the 1490s, occupying the less defensible west and southwest.[81] Based on evidence in the *Histoire de l'isle de Grenade en Amérique*, the Island Caribs and Galibis in the late 1640s and 1650s had approximately ten permanent villages on Grenada. Some of these were located at Grand Pauvre and Duquesne on the northwest coast, Sauteurs and Levara in the north, Grand Marquis in the east, and Galibis Bay and Bacolet in the southeast. The Island Caribs often occupied the settlements in the north and northwest, while the Galibis occupied those in the east and southeast.[82] It is not clear what the extent of ethnic exclusivity was among the villages, but the Galibis and Island Caribs often cooperated in their attacks against the French; the French settlers in the 1650s often identified them as one and the same.[83]

The Island Caribs and Galibis lived in relatively autonomous groups or villages, comprising between 30 and 40 extended families and led by a patriarchal headman.[84] In many cases he was related to everyone in his village, though he may have wives in other villages or islands. At the time of French colonization a number of these headmen were identified, and included both Galibis and Island Caribs. Among these were "Captains" Cairouane, Grand Pauvre, Marquis, Duquesne, Dubuisson, Antoine and Bacolos, many of the names presently associated with current place names in Grenada (Illustration 6.1).[85] They lived in settlements situated near the seashore on headlands, generally near rivers and streams, as the above settlements reveal. These small clearings contained a *karbay* (popular Fr. *cabet*) or long house where the men slept and congregated for, among other things, eating and drinking. The oval-shaped long houses, built of sticks and covered with leaves of thatch, held as many as 120 hammocks or beds.[86] Numerous small huts, which housed the women and children, surrounded the large *karbay*.

According to Rochefort, a new *karbay* is established "when a man hath a numerous family and retires with it at a certain distance from others, and builds houses or huts for to lodge it in, and a *cabet*, where all of the family meets to be merry, or to treat of the affairs which concern it

14

in common."[87] If, on average, a village comprised 100 plus individuals, the Island Carib population on Grenada in the mid-1600s can be estimated at approximately 1,000 plus. Though it still appears high based solely on the reading of the information of interactions between the Island Caribs and the French settlers, the population estimate helps create a picture of the indigenous population on the eve of colonization, and enhances the understanding of Island Carib culture in Grenada and their response to the French attempt to settle on the island.

A great deal is known about the culture of the seventeenth-century inhabitants of the Lesser Antilles. This is in no small measure due to the writings of French Catholic missionaries like Raymond Breton and Jean-Baptiste Dutertre who accompanied the European settlements that subsequently took possession of the Island Carib-occupied territories.[88] Breton's work is by far the most informative because of his almost twenty years residence among the Island Caribs of Dominica and Guadeloupe.[89] These contemporary accounts help paint a picture of the peoples of the Lesser Antilles and further the understanding of who they were, despite the fact that the narratives reflect European cultural biases and ignorance.

Politically and socially, Island Carib society showed less complexity than the better-known Taino culture, not exhibiting its multifaceted hierarchical structure. Each Island Carib village was largely self-governing and under the authority of a "captain" or headman.[90] The captain (*tuibutuli hauthe*) supervised the economic activities of his community. Though villages and even various groups from one island cooperated with villages from other islands, observers described the Island Caribs as possessing a strong sense of political independence. Labat observed that "there are no people in the world so jealous of their liberty, or who resent more the smallest check to their freedom."[91] Wilson sees this as the reason for the "disintegrative forces [that] kept multi-village polities from becoming permanent."[92] Yet, that independent spirit and decentralization may have aided the Island Carib in their fight against the Europeans and enabled them to survive as long as they did, unlike the Tainos who were practically wiped out within the first fifty years of European invasion.

Island Carib leadership was not hereditary like those of the Tainos, but elected based on their knowledge and powers of endurance. An individual could be chosen to lead a war party comprising hundreds of Island Caribs from many villages and various islands. Though a war chief held the position for life, he "enjoyed no special treatment during feasts and times of war."[93] He was able to exact obedience during wartime, but relinquished that power upon the conclusion of the war or raid.[94] The war chief (*ubutu*) "appears to have been more polygamous than the typical village head, yet did not seem to enjoy an extraordinary economic position, nor did he receive extraordinary mortuary treatment in death."[95] One of those leaders on Grenada was the Galibi Captain Cairouane, whom the French colonists recognized as being the "father savage Galibis," and treated him as the "leader" of the Amerindians on the island.[96] It becomes clear that his position was not without challenge as his life was threatened as a result of his allowing the French to "settle" in Grenada and thereafter tolerated them; as a result he was forced to leave the island, possibly for the mainland.[97]

It is not clear whether the Island Carib villages on Grenada were part of a larger socio-political unit as was evident on Dominica, with villages either part of the east or west and under a geographical leader.[98] Some leaders do appear to have been more prominent, but that may have been as a result of the French selecting cooperative leaders to achieve their goals. There does seem, however, to have been a separation between the so-called Carib and the Galibi villages. Though they lacked a unitary government, the Amerindians on Grenada and throughout the Windward Islands often cooperated for various activities, particularly wars or raids, against the Amerindians of Trinidad and the Venezuelan coast, and later the Europeans. From the arrival of Europeans in the region, Island Carib attacks and reprisals have been reported as comprising groups from various islands. Island Caribs from Grenada, St. Vincent and Dominica were often recorded as staging attacks against the Spanish at Trinidad and the islands off the Venezuelan coast. It is quite likely that the Amerindians on Grenada followed the lead of those on St. Vincent and Dominica, as Taylor suggests, "the forces of Dominica were said to take the lead in such campaigns."[99] During the Island Carib-French wars in Grenada, the Island Caribs from St. Vincent led the attacks against the French in Grenada, and instigated the Grenada Island Caribs to resist the French. Oftentimes, the Island Caribs on Grenada would blame those of St. Vincent for attacks against the French.

The Island Caribs immediately earned the reputation (among Europeans) as a belligerent people, beginning with Columbus' interpretation of the Tainos' fear of the Island Caribs who supposedly waged frequent raids against them. The oldest hypothesis of Island Carib origin, the Carib invasion model, is premised on their supposed war-like nature. They were reported to have captured the Lesser Antilles by attacking the "peaceful" Tainos, killing the men and taking the women as slave wives. Like much else in the region, the Island Carib was seen as the antithesis of the peaceful Taino, earning the reputation as the "bad boys of the Indies" who were feared by many.[100] Yet, war for the Island Caribs "was an element of their social structure, a condition without which the network of kinship relations and alliances, residence patterns, exchange of goods, and rituals of initiation and accession to chiefship, would not exist."[101] Much of the culture revolved around raids, reprisals and war.

The Taino, in describing the Island Caribs, identified them as carrying bows and arrows. This weapon was a particular menace to the Tainos. The arrows were often tipped with poison made from the manchineal tree, or sometimes carried fire if the situation warranted it. For close combat the Island Carib utilized a *boutou* (Illustrations 1.3 and 4.1). These two weapons, though appearing inferior to the European sword and musket, were a menace to the Spanish and other Europeans who oftentimes witnessed the consequences first hand. The Island Caribs could fire about ten arrows, accurate at a distance of forty yards, in the time it took to reload a musket. The Island Caribs were also known for using hot peppers as a form of "biological weapon," and were adept stone throwers. Another important piece in their artillery was the pirogue or canoe, which were of superior design and quality than that of the Taino, and were capable of holding between forty and fifty warriors. It facilitated their numerous raids, and enabled them to quickly come to the assistance of each other. By the time of European occupation of their islands, the Island Caribs had became known for their guerilla tactics, with their ambush attacks the usual response to European invasion.

The economy of the Island Caribs was quite similar to that of the Tainos and the other indigenous peoples throughout the region, with minor differences. The Island Caribs depended on both the land and sea for their livelihood. Fishing and hunting seemed to have been as important as farming, possibly more so, especially in times of war. Though they lived on the larger islands they also "cultivated" and collected plants and hunted animals from the many small islands and islets like the Grenadines, hence their desire to defend "unoccupied" territory; Boucher termed it a "commuter economy."[102] Like the Tainos, they practiced a slash-and-burn or shifting cultivation, though Watts thought the Carib practice of conuco agriculture more haphazard.[103]

Crops cultivated by the Island Caribs included manioc or cassava (*Manihot esculenta*), sweet potato (*Ipomea batatas*), corn or maize (*Zea mays*), arrowroot (*Maranta arandinacea*), banana (*Musa* sp.), the tubers yam (*Discorea trifida*) and tannia (*Xanthosoma* spp.), and a variety of local vegetables and fruits. Cassava, both bitter and sweet varieties, was the most important part of the Island Carib diet. The bitter variety contained a small quantity of prussic acid and required preparation to neutralize the mild poison before consumption. Cassava flat cake production required a number of utensils, including a stone-chipped grater or *matoutou*, a basket squeezer that expelled the caustic juice, a sifter, and cassava griddle for making bread(Illustration 1.4); the European iron griddle replaced the Island Carib stone griddle soon after contact. The grated cassava was then dried to produce flour from which bread was made. The juice of the cassava was used to make *tamali*, a cooked sauce used to dip foods. *Ouicou*, a fermented beer made from masticated cassava, enjoyed widespread use as identified by seventeenth-century observers who often reported that the Island Caribs indulged in drinking orgies. Corn was secondary, utilized primarily as a roasted treat.

The Island Caribs used a number of fishing techniques, including crabbing, plant poisons to stun fish, fishing lines and harpoons. They relished the land crab (*Cardisoma guanhumi*), found in large quantities in mangrove swamps across the islands. It formed part of the main dish that was complimented with cassava and *tamali* sauce, made from pepper and the green meat of the crab found near to its shell. They hunted, with bow and arrows and dogs, the agouti (*Dasyprocta aguti*), opossum or *manicou* (*Didelphis marsupialis insularis*), and the green iguana (*Iguana iguana*). These were boiled in manioc water, roasted or smoked on a boucan grill. Birds like the semi-domesticated muscovy duck (*Cairina moschata*), and an assortment of fish made up the rich and diverse diet of the Island Caribs.

For the Island Caribs trade or barter with Europeans soon became important by the time the French and British entered the region as colonizers. The Island Caribs had become accustomed to a number of European goods–iron tools, copper, knives, guns, axes, fishhooks, cloth, glass beads and other trinkets–incorporating them into their everyday chores. Though they manufactured their own alcoholic beverages they came to relish European manufactured rum and wines. In exchange for these goods the Island Caribs offered an assortment of produce, including tobacco, bush meat, cassava and other tuber crops. These exchanges led some historians and commentators, intentionally or not, to conclude that Amerindians gave away their lands for mere trinkets. In many cases, Island Caribs welcomed European colonists because of their desire to trade with them, but would subsequently expel them once they realized they were a threat to their continued existence.

The European observers of the Island Caribs, particularly the French missionaries, were very harsh in their condemnation of the belief system practiced by the Island Caribs. They regarded these beliefs and ceremonies as barbaric. Their bias may have had more to do with the negligible success they had in converting the Island Caribs, which they also blamed on "the poor impression the savages have formed of the bad things of the Christians," particularly the cruelty towards the Island Caribs.[104] Dutertre, however, believed that the Island Caribs "would make their way to Heaven if they were illuminated by the Light of Faith… [because] they undertake such frightful austerities, such painful fasts, such strange mortifications, such cruel bloodlettings, that many Saints in possession of glory could not have undertaken so many in this life."[105]

The belief system of the Island Caribs revolved around the principle of good (icheriri) and evil (mapouya) spirits that affected every aspect of their lives. They had many rituals and ceremonies that were officiated by the shaman (boyez). Though Breton argues that "they have no words to express the powers of the soul, such as the will, the understanding, nor that which concerns religion,"[106] the Island Caribs did believe that each person possessed three "souls." One resided in the head and was felt beating in the temple, a second in the arm and felt in the pulse, and the third in the heart. Upon death the soul in the heart flew into the sky to be happy, while the other two become mapouyas or evil spirits that tormented the living. These were so prevalent they even invaded their sleep in the form of nightmares, which could cause its victims to suddenly awaken, screaming in hopes of chasing off the evil spirit.

The mapouya is manifested in sickness, fear, death, failure and natural disasters like hurricanes, hence their worship of the god Huracan. They believed that each person possessed a mapouya and that any sickness was caused by a spell placed on the victim by another's mapouya. If someone was suspected of causing another's illness, that person, usually a woman, was put to death. The ceremonies to cure illnesses were performed by the shaman who, using tobacco smoke as incense, made the good spirits assemble to combat the presence of the *mapouyas*. When someone recovered from an illness s/he would perform a feast to the *mapouya*. The shaman also performed rituals and ceremonies to aid the success of a village in agriculture and raids. Because of his powers of medicine and divination he was well respected. They may also have performed sacrifices to appease the *mapouya*. They often wore the *mapouya's* "hideous and horrible image around their neck" to appease it.[107]

While *mapouyas* were everywhere, the *icheriri* resided in the home where it offered protection. The Island Carib also keep the hair and some bones of their dead relatives in their homes as their spirits helped protect them by warning them of dangers.[108] Offerings of cassava and *ouicou* were made to their *icheriri*, as well as the first fruits from the garden. They did not kill bats because they believed that they were good spirits and guarded the home; to kill one meant death.

A number of other cultural practices among the Island Caribs captivated European observers. None was more fascinating than the couvade or sympathetic labor that involved the practice of prolonged fasting by a father for forty days following the birth of a child, especially if it was a first-born male. Though the explanation given was that the child might take on the appearance of the animal that the parents consumed, it probably had more to do with making sure that there was enough for the baby to eat. Another was the practice of flattening the forehead of a newborn baby, a physical characteristic desired among the Island Carib.

The clothing of the Island Carib was minimal, in "puris naturalis," except for a small "band of cotton" strung around the waist to cover their private parts. They decorated their bodies with a mixture of oil and a red dye from the annatto (*Bixa orellana*) plant, which may have also served as an insect repellent. A blue-black dye from the fruit of the genep tree (*Melicocca bijuga*) was used by the men to tattoo "bands on the body, and rings of the same glaze around the eyes." As described by the French colonists in 1649: "[The men] all freshly painted, armed with arrows and clubs, their usual weapons, their hair neatly tied on the back, decorated on the top with parrot feathers of many different colors, adorned with a *caracoli* in the nose, white trade beads around the neck, rings on their fingers…"[109] They also practiced scarification to demonstrate their strength and endurance. These scars were inflicted with the agouti's teeth at various occasions like the birth of a first son, when a father symbolically transferred his courage to his newborn. The women were often described as wearing a *rosada* or bracelet around their arms and legs made of "basket-work."

The year 1492 was a significant one in the history of the world, with the European invasion of the Americas and determined attempts to colonize this "new world." It marked a turning point in the history of the Amerindian peoples of the Americas, but immediately the Caribbean. It had far-reaching consequences for the Tainos who greeted Columbus on his arrival, and the Island Caribs who were confronted by him on his second voyage in 1493. The Tainos, whom Columbus had labeled peaceful and servile, succumbed from Spanish enslavement and diseases within fifty years. The so-called fierce and war-like Island Caribs were able to mount a spirited defense of their territories and scored victories that earned them respect as warriors and short-term survival. Yet their ultimate fate was probably a foregone conclusion in light of the fact that the Europeans had a devastating advantage of "guns, germs and steel," and a population willing to brave the odds to occupy these far-off islands.[110] For the Island Caribs, the 1600s would present the greatest challenge to their polity, but they first had to survive the Spanish invasion in the 1500s.

2

Prologue to Settlement

For most of the sixteenth century, however, Island Caribs had to deal with a most difficult European people, the Spaniards.[1]

On his third voyage to the Americas in 1498, Christopher Columbus is believed to have sighted the island of Grenada. That event, as well as the name he evidently gave Grenada, La Concepción, have been debated ever since.[2] According to Las Casas, Columbus, on his way west from la Boca del Drago, Trinidad, sighted two peaks to the north of that island.[3] Since it was the eve of the annual Christian feast of the Assumption of the Virgin Mary on 15 August, he named one peak Asunción and the other Concepción. Las Casas believed, and many have since accepted, that Columbus named Tobago, the island closest to Trinidad, Asunción, and Grenada Concepción.[4] Yet confusion over the names Columbus may or may not have given each island has led a number of writers to label Grenada Asunción or Assumption.[5] Despite the academic debates, however, Columbus' 1498 sighting of Grenada has been implanted into memory as the island's genesis into modern history.

On the island that Columbus named La Concepción and which Spain subsequently claimed, lived populations of Amerindians who had made it their home for quite some time.[6] To most of its inhabitants, the island was known as Camáhogne, or a variant of that name.[7] Neither Columbus nor any member of his crew approached or landed on the island as is often cited in popular travel magazines. If in fact the island was sighted as is accepted, only its highest peaks were discernible by Columbus and his crew sailing scores of miles away.

Columbus, by default, has been accorded the recognition as the European "discoverer" of Grenada. When the modern state came into being with its independence from the United Kingdom on 7 February 1974 Columbus' sighting of Grenada was enshrined on the islands' new coat of arms: the *Santa María de Guía* on which Columbus sailed on his third voyage and a gold cross represent the 1498 sighting, and a Madonna lily attests to the island's original namesake and dedication to Mary of the Immaculate Conception.[8] In 1898, to mark the 400th anniversary of the sighting by Columbus, Grenada issued a postage stamp commemorating that event and its naming "La Concepción." There have been many other Grenadian stamps issued since celebrating Columbus; others have also celebrated the islands' Amerindian heritage. Despite all of these, however, the recognition may be misplaced. According to Roukema, it was Vicente Yañez Pinzón, the Spanish navigator and explorer who sailed with Columbus on earlier voyages, who actually was the first European to visit Grenada only a year and nine months after Columbus' believed sighting. Much of the evidence is from Juan de La Cosa's c. 1500 world map, which was the first to depict the Caribbean. The information for this map of the Lesser Antilles was, according to Roukema, derived from Pinzón's map which he made following his exploration of the Americas in 1499-1500. Concerning Grenada on Cosa's map, Roukema insists that Mayo or Isla de Mayo "unquestionably indicates Grenada"; some have incorrectly identified Ascension on that map as Grenada following the believed Columbus designation of Grenada as Asunción. He continues that "the details of the La Cosa map allow us to go even farther. They allow the inference that Pinzón left the Gulf of Paria [Trinidad] at the end of April [1500], discovered the island of Grenada early in May and presumably on May 1, visited St. George's Harbour on the island's western side...." This, identified on Cosa's map as "*pº yna*," is "a corruption of *Puerto de la Reyna* (in modern Spanish *Puerto de la Reina*) or Queen's Harbour.... In any case the port referred to was the present St. George's Harbour in Grenada."[9]

Columbus' journey through the southern Caribbean opened the area and its inhabitants to Europeans. Thus began the encounters between Grenada's Amerindian populations and Europeans, especially the Spanish, who traveled throughout the region in ever increasing numbers. Far from the often-cited belief that Grenada's indigenous populations were left undisturbed following Columbus' believed sighting of the island, there were in fact numerous encounters and frequent bloody confrontations between the two beginning soon thereafter.

The first of these encounters occurred in 1499 when Alonzo de Ojeda, Juan de la Cosa and Amerigo Vespucci were exploring South America and the Caribbean. Pursuing a request by friendly Amerindians from the South American coast, the Spanish explorers reportedly sailed to the Antilles where these fierce enemies resided and attacked Island Caribs at either Grenada or St. Vincent, killing and capturing many.[10] This violent encounter signaled the beginning of a belligerent relationship between the Island Caribs and the Spanish that continued throughout the next century (Illustration 2.1). A more enduring consequence of that voyage, however, was Juan de la Cosa's *mappa mundi* which contained the first representation of the Caribbean islands on a world map. On Cosa's 1500 map, the island Columbus reportedly named La Concepción was identified as Mayo, though its association with Grenada is not without debate.[11] The name Mayo lasted for only a few years, disappearing entirely by 1523 when the island became exclusively known as La Granada.[12]

Spanish colonists, beginning in 1492, took up residence in the Greater Antilles, first on the island of Hispaniola. Their quest for precious metals, particularly gold, food and other resources quickly led to the subjugation of the resident Island Arawaks or Tainos as forced laborers.[13] The Tainos made frequent attempts to resist the cruel treatment by the Spanish, but newly introduced diseases and the establishment of the *repartimiento-encomiendo* system of land settlement that institutionalized forced labor resulted in a precipitous decline in their populations. The Spanish settlers, desiring to replenish the rapidly declining labor force on Hispaniola, made slave raids against the Amerindians of the Bahamas and the other islands of the Greater Antilles.[14] These raids had the similar effect of depleting the Amerindian populations in the western Caribbean. However, the continued enslavement and mistreatment of the Tainos brought pleas on their behalf, forcing the colonists to seek new sources of labor.[15] Yet, as the destruction of the Tainos of the Bahamas between 1509 and 1513

24

illustrated, their decline in the Greater Antilles was inevitable, primarily as a result of Spanish slave raids and enslavement, and introduced diseases.

The destruction of the Taino populations in the Spanish colonies created a shortage of labor. The colonists responded by petitioning for the conscription of "unfriendly" Amerindians in the region.[16] In 1503 Queen Isabella of Spain, while prohibiting the conscription of peaceful and friendly Indians, i.e. the Tainos, allowed the capture and enslavement of "a people called Cannibals," the Island Caribs. In early 1511 the Tainos on Puerto Rico rebelled and were assisted by Island Caribs from St. Croix. Though it was unsuccessful, the revolt led to the Spanish Crown legally granting its settlers the right to wage war on the "cannibals." The 23 December 1511 decree on the Caribs, titled "Royal decree authorizing the taking as slaves of the Caribs...," granted the right to Spanish colonists to enslave the occupants of the islands of "Trinidad, San Bernardo, Fuerte, Los Barbudos, Dominica, Matenino, Santa Lucia, San Vicente, La Asunción, Tobaco, Mayo y Barú" and the port of Cartagena.[17] As the need for labor increased, so too did the area from where they could be taken, which by 1520 included Florida, Mexico and the South American mainland, as far south as Brazil.[18] These laws were further reaffirmed in 1525, but in 1542 the Spanish Crown prohibited the enslavement of the Island Caribs. Only five years later, however, due to the persistent demands of the Spanish colonists in the Caribbean, adult male Island Carib warriors were exempted from the 1542 prohibition, and in 1569 so too were female Island Caribs. As late as 1608 the Spanish were given license by the Crown to carry out raids against the Amerindians of the eastern Caribbean, including Grenada.

Grenada was a strategically important island of the Amerindians in the Lesser Antilles. It was located at the southern extreme of the Caribbean archipelago and lay within 100 miles of Trinidad, which itself was a mere ten miles from the South American mainland. Grenada was thus a primary rendezvous for Amerindians making the journey to and from the continent, using it "as a place to stop and refresh."[19] According to a seventeenth-century commentator: "This place was formerly a great account with the Carib Indians for at their return from the wars on Trinidada and with the Arawacacs, Nepoyes, Warooes, and other nations of Indians, if they had successe, they stay'd there until the old men and women brought their daughters from St. Vincents and other islands to congratulate their return with songs and dances."[20]

As a stopover Grenada was home to a "large," if transitory, community of Amerindians, including a population of Cariban-speaking Galibis from the continent by the 1500s.[21] Europeans too, beginning with the Spanish, would stop at the island because it was heavily wooded and possessed many rivers and streams, though it is not clear to what extent Grenada was used by these more recent visitors as a place to refresh.[22] Traders, especially northern Europeans, later frequented the island because of its reputed high-quality tobacco and tropical timbers. Its proximity to the Spanish settlements at Trinidad, Margarita, Cumana and on the continent made it a suitable place from which northern Europeans could engage the Spanish in illicit trade or plunder.

There are only a few reports that chronicle encounters between Island Caribs on Grenada or the neighboring islands and the Spanish, who came on slaving raids or stopped to trade or refresh on their journeys. Though the Island Caribs sometimes traded with the Spanish for ironware and manufactured goods that they had come to desire, they oftentimes attacked the Spaniards as retaliation for attacks committed against them by Europeans. Before long, an atmosphere of open hostility became the norm between the two, as the one fought for the preservation of his way of life, and the other for a foothold and dominance in the region.

From the first decade of the sixteenth century, the Island Caribs on Grenada (and the rest of the Lesser Antilles) encountered Spanish slave raiders from the Greater Antilles and the "pearl islands" of Margarita and Cubagua off the Venezuelan coast. There are little or no details to shed light on the extent and impact of these raids on Island Carib populations, but by 1520 a number of the islands in the Lesser Antilles was probably depopulated as a result.[23] Only the densely populated, heavily fortified and strategically located islands of Dominica, St. Vincent, Guadeloupe, Martinique, St. Lucia and Grenada were able to resist these devastating raids. Exactly how the raids affected the Grenadian population is unknown, but they must have suffered tremendously from the relentless harassment. One direct consequence must have been the depletion of the population through deaths as a result of resistance to capture and capture itself, as Island Caribs later related stories to the early French missionaries of Spanish massacres of their populations on various islands. Another was the retreat into the island and along the inaccessible Atlantic coast by the Island Caribs in order to better protect and defend themselves.

Contact with Europeans and African slaves also led to the spread of hitherto unknown diseases, especially smallpox, which inevitably took other lives, though the evidence of this is debatable.

Evidence from Spanish sources indicates that the Amerindians in the Lesser Antilles were a formidable force and resisted Spanish attempts to take control of any of the islands. The 1525 Spanish attempt to colonize Guadeloupe, then occupied by the Island Caribs, failed, as did the attempts to colonize Trinidad in the 1530s and 1560s. The Spanish settlements on Puerto Rico were often targeted by the Island Caribs who raided and destroyed plantations, and abducted Spaniards and African slaves. The Spanish, with their array of weaponry and ships, were oftentimes defeated or suffered heavy human and material losses at the hands of the Island Caribs, who employed guerilla-war tactics, and were equipped with dugout canoes which they skillfully maneuvered, poison-tipped arrows, and the feared *boutou* or war club.

By the second half of the 1500s, as more Spanish colonists entered the region along with an increase in maritime traffic, there was an escalation in the confrontations between the Spanish and the Island Caribs. As Antonio Vazquez de Espinosa notes:

> The island of Granada... is thickly peopled with Carib Indians called Camajuyas, which means lightening from heaven, since they are brave and warlike....[24]
> They [Tainos] live remote from the Spaniards, a fact which has induced the Camajuyas Caribs of the Windward Islands to fall upon them frequently with cannibal intent.[25]
> These Grenada Indians start out every year in late July or early August with their dugout navies on robbing expeditions along the whole coast of the Spanish Main, the islands of Trinidad and Margarita and others, and they have carried off many Christian Indians from them, eaten them up and devastated their land. These savages are so cruel that there is no mercy for those who fall into their hands, for they kill and eat them. And it will aid the service of God and His Majesty to conquer them, bringing them under subjection or killing the male Indians, by giving the commission to some powerful citizen of that country, and thus getting rid of that pirates' nest of savage cannibals; with them there, no security is possible in all the surrounding territories and islands; their conquest would bring quiet and tranquility.[26]

The Island Caribs did not only attack other native settlements, but staged coordinated attacks on Spanish settlements. One such raid by the Island

Caribs of Grenada was reported as having taken place in 1569 against the Spanish settlement of Carabelleda, Venezuela.[27] Some 300 Island Caribs in fourteen canoes landed during the night to prepare for an early morning assault on both the town and port. The Spanish were "informed by some Indian allies of the Caribs' proximity, [but] they gave scant credence to the warning, doing nothing more than station a sentinel."[28] The Island Caribs, "with their accustomed ferocity they went destroying with blood and fire everything before them, satiating their bestial appetite with the flesh of the Indians they were able to capture at the ports."[29] The attack on the city, with its armed Spaniards, proved far less successful. The sound of the approaching Island Caribs aroused the sentinel who sounded the alarm, and in the confusion caused by the assault some twenty armed Spaniards were able to unite and mount a defense of the town. The attackers, confronted with armed opposition and "realizing that their most valiant worriors were now dead, they began to retire toward the shore to seek the protection of their pirogues."[30]

These confrontations were also aggravated by the Spanish attempts to occupy Trinidad and their befriending of the resident Amerindians with whom the Island Caribs often fought. The Island Caribs are portrayed as attackers, creating tremendous problems for the Spanish in the region. They especially disrupted Spanish trade, often being accused of attacking ships at sea or anchored, sometimes causing them to wreck, and plundering the ships and killing or enslaving the crews and passengers. There are more often reports of groups of Island Caribs from Grenada, St. Vincent and Dominica making raids against the indigenous populations of Trinidad who aided the Spanish.[31]

Island Carib attacks on Spanish shipping and settlements, and Spanish wrecks in the area produced European and African slaves. The Island Caribs put many of them to work in their tobacco fields and gardens, contrary to Espinosa's belief that they were eaten. In 1561 alone, the Island Caribs on Grenada held at least 30 Spaniards, mainly women and children, following the wreck of a Spanish ship along the coast of Grenada.[32] Fifty Spanish colonists from Margarita, aided by friendly Amerindians, failed in their attempt to free the Spanish prisoners on Grenada.[33] The number of these captives and the extent of their treatment are unknown, but they may have accounted for a sizeable population. This is substantiated by Francisco de Vides' 1592 contract to colonize Trinidad, wherein it states that in order to populate that island he should pacify the Island Caribs on Grenada and liberate their Spanish and African captives.[34] The many captives held by the Island Caribs included Spanish, Portuguese and African slaves. Some were able, through various means, to escape as did the "three Christians (a Portuguese prisoner of five years, and two Spaniards who had been prisoners for two years)" in 1567; in 1578 a Spaniard tricked his captors into releasing him; and in 1593 an African slave escaped.[35] In 1614 Nicolás de Cardona, sailing near Grenada (Illustration 2.1), reported that

> From this island [of Grenada] I took out two black women that were their prisoners and had had their ears amputated and their nostrils perforated to mark them as slaves, and two children, sons of Dutchmen or Frenchmen and Caribe women, as well as a Christian Indian, the brother of another Indian from the mission of Paria whom they had eaten eight days ago, and this one, because he was thin, had been kept for another festivity.[36]

These tales of capture and escape of Europeans and Africans were quite common throughout the region until the mid-1600s as the well-known capture of Garcia Troche, grandson of Ponce de Leon, in 1569, and the escape of the free black Luisa Navarret in 1580 illustrate.[37]

Beginning in the 1520s the French entered the Caribbean as usurpers of the Spanish trade monopoly in the region (the British followed by the 1560s and the Dutch by the 1590s).[38] The legendary riches of Spain's American colonies and the homeward-bound fleets enticed those Europeans who were excluded from this trade. The following century is a litany of exploits by men like Jean Fleury, Jambe de Bois, Jacques de Sors, François Le Clerc, Jean Bontemps, Francis Drake, John Hawkins and Piet Heyn who plundered Spanish ports and shipping.[39] Many came in search of riches as merchants invested in what appeared to be very lucrative ventures. In the course of their piracy, the northern Europeans encountered the Island Caribs and traded with them, ultimately replacing the Spanish. Some of these sailors would establish temporary shelters in the Lesser Antilles that would subsequently pave the way for permanent settlements in the mid-1600s by the northern Europeans.

Contacts with the Island Caribs produced both favorable and unfavorable accounts, the latter being the most often recorded. André Thévet, in the 1550s, described Grenada as unapproachable because of the large numbers of Island Caribs settled there.[40] In 1565, the infamous John Hawkins related the tale of the French privateer and slaver Captain

Jean Bontemps of the ship *Dragon Vert* of Le Havre who in March 1565 "came to one of those Islands, called Granada, and being driven to water, could not doe the same for the canybals, who fought with him very desperatly two dayes."[41]

Spanish attempts to establish themselves in the Lesser Antilles proved futile, as the failure to settle Guadeloupe and Trinidad illustrated. Yet, it is quite evident that relative to the rest of Spain's empire in the Americas, the Lesser Antilles offered very little of value, except possibly a defensive one. As a matter of fact, when a permanent Spanish settlement did occur on Trinidad, it was only as a base for expeditions to the continent.

The Spanish explorer Don Antonio de Berrio y Oruña, as a base for his expeditions to discover the rumored golden city of El Dorado on the continent, initiated the settlement of San José de Oruña, Trinidad in May 1592. At the entrance to the Orinoco River, Berrio saw Trinidad as ideal for his exploration plans, establishing the island as a "depot and entrance to these great provinces."[42] The Island Caribs, however, created tremendous problems for the Spanish colonists at Trinidad, and in 1593 alone, reportedly attacked 44 Spanish canoes bound for Guiana from Trinidad and loaded with cassava and hammocks.[43] In 1594, Governor Berrio, in a letter to the king of Spain, complained that "the Caribs of the islands of Dominica, Granada, and other neighboring places harass and injure me."[44] Yet, Berrio did not attempt to settle any of the other islands or pacify the Island Caribs in Grenada or its northern neighbors.[45] Governor Berrio, like Walter Ralegh and many others, failed to locate the mythical riches of El Dorado; in fact Berrio's preoccupation with El Dorado led to his death, and ultimately Ralegh's too.

Though the Spanish colony at Trinidad remained neglected for over a century, its tobacco trade attracted northern Europeans, especially the British, and the Spanish colonists engaged them in contraband trade (*rescate*) between the 1590s and around 1612.[46] It was the profitable and illicit trade in tobacco that created the impetus for the first northern European settlement in the Lesser Antilles in 1609 when a "London-Dutch syndicate" sent over 200 English colonists to establish a tobacco-producing settlement on the island of Grenada.

3

The 1609 British Attempt to Settle Grenada

"...soe advantageous a designe..."[1]

In 1609 a "London-Dutch syndicate" sent over 200 English colonists to establish a settlement on the island of Grenada. This event is significant in the history of the colonization of the Lesser Antilles despite the fact that it is absent from most chronologies and discussions of northern European colonization in the region.[2] It was the first planned settlement by northern Europeans in the Caribbean archipelago and into Spanish claimed and occupied territory; the Spanish were only 100 miles away at Trinidad.[3] It was also probably the first agricultural or plantation colony attempted in the Caribbean by the British. Had this attempt proved successful it would have represented what St. Christopher (St. Kitts) represents, the first colony successfully settled by northern Europeans in the Lesser Antilles. The attempt in Grenada predates the St. Christopher settlements by fifteen years and is obscured by that success which became the incubator of many of the future settlements in the region by the French and the British.[4] The 1609 attempt remains obscure because it was unsuccessful, but also due to the dearth of historical sources and scant research into the venture to date.

The Grenada venture, nonetheless, should not be reduced to an historical footnote to the British (and French) colonizing activities in the region. It should be seen rather as an important prequel (as Roanoke is to Jamestown, Virginia in the US) to the major northern European colonization events in the Caribbean in the 1620s, and its possible aid to those later successful events because it was one of the building blocks of French and British colonization in the region. A better understanding of this seemingly insignificant event can provide more clarity when seen in the larger context of northern European intrusion into the Americas, particularly for the following reasons: (i) Its organizers defied the pro-Spanish policies of the British king, James I, (ii) It contested the Spanish colonization monopoly in the Americas, (iii) It was an outgrowth of privateering and the highly profitable contraband tobacco trade between the English (French and Dutch) and Spanish colonists in the early 1600s, (iv) It was outfitted by a group of London "merchant adventurers," (v) It was intended to circumvent high duties on imported tobacco from non-British territories, (vi) It was one of the first attempts to establish a plantation colony in the Americas by northern Europeans, (vii) It challenged the Island Caribs for possession of one of their islands, and (viii) Its failure led to the idea of producing "Spanish tobacco" in Jamestown, Virginia.

The cursory details of the 1609 British colonization attempt on Grenada can be extracted from a few passages in a seventeenth-century manuscript held in the British Library and credited to Major John Scott.[5] Though similar documents on Trinidad, Tobago, Guiana and Barbados are attributed to Scott, Holdren believes that the "section entitled 'The Description of Grenada'" is written in another hand.[6] Whether or not Scott penned the document is open for debate, but the author states that his account of the venture is derived from that of "Mr. Godfrey's," one of the expedition's sponsors. Godfrey supposedly wrote his account to express his dissatisfaction with the outcome of the venture and his unwillingness to support another.[7] The manuscript can be fairly dated to around 1665-67 based on the information and events referenced.

To date, the manuscript remains the principal and only known reference to the 1609 British colonization attempt on Grenada. It is rather disappointing that Spanish archival sources have so far remained silent on this event. This may be due to the short duration of the colony or a quid pro quo by renegade Spanish colonists at Trinidad who saw a British settlement close by as an economic asset, though the British thought otherwise. The lack of sources on the British side is probably a result of the secrecy surrounding the venture because its sponsors had defied their king, and the fear of possible repercussions if the scheme was uncovered.[8] Yet, a usual practice was to successfully establish a colony before seeking official recognition and a patent from the crown as were the later cases with St. Christopher and Barbados.

Despite this lack of information, a number of contemporary sources is available that can corroborate events surrounding the 1609 venture and some of the people who outfitted it, particularly their involvement in privateering and the contraband tobacco trade with the Spanish in the region. Though there are a few minor discrepancies with the manuscript, the supporting information furthers the understanding of the event and gives it greater historical precedence. It is clear that most of the details recorded in the manuscript are factual. As Andrews asserts, "...there is reason to accept the main burden of his account because we know from other evidence that the ships he mentions, promoted by these merchants, did make a voyage to the West Indies at this time and did visit Trinidad as he relates."[9] Andrews adds that the *Diana's* departure from Trinidad to collect the surviving colonists at Grenada, and arrival back in England, make chronological sense.[10]

No Peace Beyond the Line

Since its "discovery" in 1492, Spain tenuously controlled its papal-sanctioned claim to most of the Americas, monopolizing the colonization of the region, and attempted to maintain its exclusive trading zone with the use of force. Other European nations grudgingly acknowledged Spain's claims for most of the 1500s, even though their citizens, oftentimes with official support, took every opportunity to plunder Spanish ships and ports, or illegally trade with disgruntled Spanish colonists.[11] It is through these activities that northern "Europeans began cutting into the Spanish domain of the Isthmus of Panama and the Greater Antilles. They bartered their hardware, foodstuffs, clothing and shoes against ginger, indigo and later cacao and sugar from Spanish colonists."[12] Ongoing wars between Spain and the northern Europeans in the 1500s made their forays into the Caribbean justifiable, and created a situation where piracy reigned supreme. Men like Sir Francis Drake and Sir John Hawkins are legendary for the riches they amassed by preying on the Spanish.

By the beginning of the seventeenth century, "as the search for golden cities and easy plunder began to prove increasingly illusory," northern Europeans began to plan and attempt settlements in the Americas.[13] This colonial expansion by northern Europeans was a direct result of Spain's weakening economic and military power, signaled by the British defeat of the Spanish Armada in 1588. And as Newton so eloquently puts it, "swarms of English and French colonists poured like flies upon the rotting carcass of Spain's empire in the Caribbean."[14] Yet, it was not a foregone conclusion despite the prevailing view of the inevitable breach in Spain's Caribbean empire.

In August 1604 Great Britain and Spain signed the Treaty of London that ended the twenty-year Anglo-Spanish War. Negotiations had dragged on for months because neither wanted to surrender its position on access to the Americas. As such, the peace had failed to resolve the most contentious issues of free trade and colonization in the Americas, but guaranteed that "There ought to be free commerce where it existed before the war, in conformity with the use and observance of the ancient alliances and treaties before the war."[15] Both sides, thereafter, interpreted the treaty differently, Spain believing that the status quo of trade exclusion was maintained, and Great Britain believed that it had the right to pursue its aims in the Americas. For the British, the expression "No peace beyond the line" became the battle cry as they lobbied for and attempted to enforce free trade and colonization beyond Europe.[16]

Both the British and the French believed that their treaties with Spain allowed them to colonize territories in the Americas claimed by Spain but "unoccupied" by any Christian king, and the right to free trade with those territories; Spain, however, disagreed, but was not in a military position to dissuade them, though it tried. Since King James did not wish to disrupt the fragile peace with Spain, Britain's attention (and that of the French also) subsequently shifted to claims in the vast territory of North America where it had initially attempted to establish colonies and where the Spanish had no immediate interests. In 1497 John Cabot, an Italian mariner sailing for England, planted the British flag in Canada, establishing the later British claim to North America.[17] Other attempts included the French under Jacques Cartier in 1534, Jean-François de la Rocque de Roberval in 1541, and René de Laudonniè in 1564, and the English under Sir Humphrey Gilbert in 1583 and Sir Walter Ralegh's Roanoke settlements between 1584 and 1590. These settlements in North America, somewhat removed from Spanish reprisals, had proved unsuccessful because of the cold weather and Amerindian resistance. Attempts by the British, French and Dutch to establish colonies on the "wild coast" of Guiana after 1595, primarily in search of the golden city of Manoa and its fabled king El Dorado, but later to establish tobacco plantations, all proved unsuccessful because of Amerindian resistance and an "unhealthy environment."[18]

In pursuit of British North American claims King James I in April 1606 granted a royal charter to the Virginia Company of London, a joint stock company, to establish British settlements in Virginia. In May 1607 three ships, outfitted by the Virginia Company, landed at Jamestown, Virginia with 104 men and boys and began a settlement that was to become the first permanent English settlement in the Americas, though its survival was not evident in the first few years. The goal of the organizers in settling North America was the search for precious metals, a source for naval stores, and a passage to the Pacific. Not finding any, the colony suffered greatly in its first few years because of mismanagement, too little food, attacks from Native Americans and harsh winters. After the first five months at Jamestown, close to half of the original settlers were dead from diseases, starvation and attacks by the Native Americans. The winter of 1608 and the spring of 1609 were the harshest for the starving colonists, and the colony teetered on the brink of collapse. After much discussion, the survivors reluctantly decided to abandon the settlement and return to England. On their way out, ships with more colonists and supplies arrived, and the decision was made to return to Jamestown and make a second attempt. It was not, however, until Jamestown produced a crop of tobacco for the British market in 1613 that the colony found what would become its immediate salvation.

The British Crown's promotion of colonization in North America came at a cost to the small group of British merchants and traders engaged in the contraband tobacco trade; even Caribbean investors like Arnold Lulls bought shares in the Virginia venture and John Eldred was a member of the Virginia Company. Not only were resources redirected from the Caribbean to North America, but British citizens engaged in trade in the Caribbean faced double jeopardy.[19] King James I was adamant about preserving the fragile peace with Spain because of his greater political ambitions in Europe. While prior to the peace the illegal traders (*rescadores*) were supported by some at the British court as possible pressure on Spain to concede more at the bargaining table, that backing disappeared after the peace. Promoters traded under increased opposition from their own government, as the Spanish continued to prosecute them for piracy in British courts. The Spanish continued to deal harshly with any foreign shipping encountered in the region, though they lacked the resources to present a formidable deterrence. So in deciding to outfit the Grenada venture, the organizers were "covertly" defying the wishes of their King and taking great risks to themselves and property. Not only were they establishing a colony in territory occupied by Spain, which the British king had made clear could lead to charges of piracy, they were planning to set-up a tobacco-producing colony.

"Tobacco, That Outlandishe Weede"[20]

Europeans first observed the native Amerindians in the Caribbean, and later North America, using the tobacco plant for recreational as well as medicinal purposes—"drinking"/smoking or snorting it (Illustration 3.1). As the practice seemed rather unusual to the Europeans they were naturally curious, some suspiciously so. Soon, sailors and others returning from the Americas brought back tobacco and fascinated Europeans with their newfound smoking habit. But it was its possible medicinal uses that led to the introduction of tobacco seeds into Europe by the 1550s. Seeds were soon planted in Spanish and Portuguese gardens and thereafter spread throughout Europe as an exotic plant.

The British seemed to have developed a fondness for tobacco smoking, and following its introduction by adventurers like Sir John Hawkins and Sir Francis Drake by the 1560s, it became all the rage.[21] It came to represent the adventurism of the Elizabethan age, with Queen Elizabeth I herself supposedly persuaded to try the weed by her good friend Sir Walter Ralegh, one of its celebrated promoters. While many condemned it as the "Devil's weed," and others dubiously hailed its medicinal properties, it quickly grew in popularity and its use was widespread by the end of the 1500s.[22] Tobacco smoking soon became a craze among elements of British society who could afford it, and shops or dens sprang up all over London as "reeking gallants" went there to smoke expensive imported tobacco in trendy clay pipes.

The tobacco plant consumed in the Americas was of two varieties, *Nicotiana tobacum* and *Nicotiana rustica*, the former prevalent in South America and the Caribbean, with the latter common among the Native Americans in North America. Much of Europe got their tobacco from the Spanish who supplied the European market with *N. tobaccum*, the more desirable of the two; *N. rustica* was found to be rather harsh when smoked. This made tobacco very expensive and British merchants soon began to seek ways of procuring it cheaply. Its demand continued to increase, and led many of the privateers then operating in the Caribbean to begin trading for tobacco–among other things–with the Amerindians at Grenada and Trinidad in exchange for "weapons, alcohol, hardware tools and trinkets," and later with the Spanish at Cumana and Caracas."[23] Though many continued with privateering or a combination of privateering and illicit trade, a number of promoters concentrated on the tobacco trade as a clear indication that they "had begun to see the advantages of devoting the capital and organizational expertise gained in reprisals to commercial enterprises, and of establishing a strong claim to free trade in the Indies as the war entered its closing stages."[24] Though the ending of the war with Spain in 1603, and the peace in 1604, altered the political landscape and created greater risks for the promoters of these ventures, the contraband trade was very lucrative and continued to grow. By 1610 the trade was estimated at £60,000, and a year later at at £100,000.[25]

In 1604, when King James I anonymously published *A Counterblast to Tobacco*, the weed had become a valuable commodity in England, selling for as much as 35 pence (35d) to four shillings 10 pence (4s/10d) per pound. Notwithstanding his strong literary condemnation of tobacco, or because of it, the King added an impost or additional duty on tobacco imports, escalating the total duty from 2d to 6s/10d, an increase of 4,000 percent.[26] Tobacco merchants protested the rather exorbitant duties, and in 1607 John Eldred, a major tobacco trader, refused to pay the tax on a shipment of tobacco and encouraged others to do the same.[27] As a result, a suit was brought against Eldred by the "Farmers of Tobacco" (i.e. collectors of the duties), but the case may have been settled privately.[28]

The Farmers of Tobacco also protested the high impost because of the difficulty of collecting it from the reluctant traders. It wasn't until 1608 that the duty on imported tobacco was reduced to 1s 4d per pound for the leaf, and 1s 6d for "cane, pudding or ball" tobacco.

It seems that the high impost on foreign tobacco created the impetus to tobacco traders to establish a British tobacco-producing colony. It is also likely that tobacco production was on the minds of those who negotiated the second Virginia Company Charter in May 1609, some of whom were also involved in the Grenada venture. According to that charter, imports "were exempted from the payment of all customs duties for seven years, and in perpetuity from import duties in excess of the customary subsidy of five percent."[29] What that meant for the Grenada adventurers if they were successful was that they would not have to pay the exorbitant impost on tobacco from Grenada, a future British colony, as opposed to that from Spanish colonies when they negotiated a charter with similar conditions.

As with all American commodities produced by the Spanish, tobacco's production and sale were restricted and controlled by the Spanish authorities as much as they could. The same was true of tobacco seeds from Spanish territories, supposedly on the pain of death. Many Spanish colonists, impoverished and living on the fringes of the Spanish American empire, chose to disobey the authorities and sold or traded their crops of tobacco to the British, Dutch and French in direct violation of the Spanish Crown. As one Spanish official noted, the producers were "riff-raff who have no other source of income than the tobacco crop that is so esteemed in Flanders and England. I realize they will not reform, for they are people of small account, some of them doing it one year and another lot the next, so that the place is like a fair, by way of which contraband enters and reaches as far as Peru."[30] Beginning around the 1590s, this exchange evolved into a profitable contraband trade by the first decade of the 1600s, particularly at Trinidad and along the coast of northern South America.[31] The foreign traders risked their lives and possessions in engaging in the contraband trade, but their numbers increased in the first decade of the 1600s despite the Treaty of London in 1604, King James I's policy of pacification towards the Spanish, the high import taxes, and the Spanish authorities' efforts to suppress the trade.

The Spanish authorities made every effort to curtail the contraband tobacco trade with the northern Europeans, going so far as to outlaw the cultivation of the crop in many of its settlements along the South American coast and the Greater Antilles.[32] In 1603 Spanish authorities received approval to forcefully remove settlers from parts of Santo Domingo and Cuba where smuggling was rampant. The authorities did forcefully evacuate most of the settlers from the north and west of Santo Domingo, "taking away their women and belongings, compelling them to move with them to the new settlements and setting fire to their houses to make it clear that this had to be done."[33] In 1606 the Spanish authorities ordered a stop to the cultivation of tobacco at Venezuela, Nueva Andalucía and the Greater Antilles, and the forced removal of the population of Cumanagoto in order to disrupt the trade.[34] Yet, the illegal trade continued because marginalized Spanish colonists needed it to survive.

One of the most notorious offenders was the governor of the impoverished settlements of San Josef, Trinidad and San Tomé, Guiana, Fernando de Berrío. He was the son of Antonio de Berrío, the colonizer of Trinidad who had failed in his quest to find El Dorado, inheriting the governorship from his father upon his death in 1597; It was right around that time that the illegal trade began in earnest. As reports to Spain show, Fernando de Berrío openly supported the trade.

> At Trinidad Don Fernando Berrío conducts *rescates* publicly with the enemy, which is what your majesty has most tried to stop. And this is done so openly that by all accounts it is he who conducts the business and bargaining, divides the goods among his companions and pays for them... Throughout these provinces *rescates* have been done away with, but these territories take part in the Trinidad trade, because we can do nothing to prevent citizens of Caracas, Cumanagoto, Cumaná, La Margarita and even the New Kingdom of Granada from going there.[35]

The risks to both the foreigners and Spanish suppliers grew as the pressure to suppress the trade by the Spanish authorities increased. To deceivingly attempt to show Spanish officials that they were complying with the ban, colonists staged intermittent attacks against foreign ships. In 1608 Governor de Berrío hanged a number of British sailors from the *Ulysses*, who had come to trade for tobacco, after luring them ashore and despite receiving a ransom for their release.[36] Such indiscriminate attacks against the foreigners did not altogether end the trade, but the increasing risks to promoters and sailors created the impetus to pursue colonization in the region for the purpose of supplying tobacco to the lucrative European markets. The attempt to colonize Grenada in 1609 was motivated by the increasing risks to foreigners, and the belief that their access to Spanish-produced tobacco was coming to an end. The illegal trade, in fact, was practically ended around 1612 after Governor de Berrío was removed from his position by the Spanish authorities, closing the remaining markets. Just as the British tobacco traders had been forced to abandon Cumanagoto and Cumaná for San Josef and San Tomé because of the suppression of the trade, so too they were forced to attempt to establish tobacco colonies when the latter two outlets were threatened.[37]

April Fools

The idea of establishing a colony in the region for the sole purpose of producing tobacco was not at all new, "considering that sailors were used to establishing temporary camps to grow crops of tobacco."[38] As a matter of fact, the curtailing of the production of tobacco by Spanish authorities in 1606 saw northern Europeans seek out areas along the Wild Coast that Spain had only limited control over."[39] As one contemporary commented, "'setting forth a ship and men for ye design of tobaccos' on the margins of Spanish America-Guiana (between the deltas of the Orinioco and Amazon rivers), Virginia, Bermuda – caught the imagination of West European merchants as a possible investment." Pérotin-Dumon continues, that "Between the 1590s and 1610s, 'to settle a plantation to make tobacco,' to invest in sending settlers and ships, became a new type of project for joint-stock companies or merchants who had hitherto speculated on privateering or contraband-trading ventures."[40] One of those ventures was by a group of London-based merchant adventurers who embarked on a tobacco-producing colony on the island of Grenada.

According to the author of the Grenada manuscript, "Mr. Godfrey, Mr. [Richard] Hall, Mr. [Arnold] Lulls,[41] Mr. [William] Quarles, and Mr. Robinson," who formed themselves into a company, were the "Cheife undertakers" of the Grenada colony.[42] It is not clear what form the company took, but it was a common practice of the period for merchants to form themselves into companies to share the risks, especially of such a venture like this. One of the primary colonizing examples from this period was the Virginia Company of London which was orchestrating the settlement of Virginia. That company was a joint-stock company funded by investors who bought shares and expected to receive returns on their investments. The organizers believed that "settling Colonies is an Enterprise of too great Burthen and Expence for a few private Persons; and therefore after many vain Projects, they applied themselves to several of the Nobility, Gentry, and Merchants."[43] Unlike the Virginia Company, the Grenada merchants were not officially chartered or sanctioned, and probably could not attract investments beyond merchants who knew each other or had business dealings. The later successful colonies of St. Christopher and Barbados were financed by groups of merchants, many of whom had earlier financed privateering and trading ventures to the Americas. Being the first venture of its kind for the sponsors of the Grenada settlement, it was a very risky affair, considering that it was very different from their usual enterprise of contraband trade. The survival and profitability of agricultural colonies in the Americas remained untested, to say the least.[44] It would be five more years before John Rolfe (of Pocahontas fame) at Jamestown introduced Virginia-grown "Spanish tobacco" to the London market, thus ensuring the future profitability of plantation colonies, especially in the Caribbean.[45]

Of the five "chief undertakers" named, Richard Hall was probably the most prominent. He was a well-known London merchant and grocer. Lorimer describes him as a man of "real substance" and "with considerable resources and multifarious interests"; he was also a "farmer of the impost" on tobacco, an investor in Caribbean privateering and a Mediterranean trader.[46] Hall, and his partner John Eldred, were involved in privateering in the Caribbean since the 1590s. By the early 1600s he was involved with the contraband tobacco trade, and it was men from his ship, the *Ulysses*, who were hanged by Governor de Berrío in 1608.

Another partner in the Grenada venture was Arnold Lulls who was born in Antwerp and resident in 1600 in Billingsgate, London for over 20 years, having arrived in England sometime before 1585. He worked as a merchant grocer and jeweler. Based on his payments of the "Lay Subsidy," which stood at £40 in 1600, he was by this time "a man of some wealth."[47] Lulls is remembered more for his business, beginning around 1604, with jewels he provided the Royal Court; a number of designs he made for Queen Anne have survived.[48] He worked with John Spilman and William Herrick, jeweler to the King, and together they sold many expensive jewels to the royal family and foreign diplomats.

41

Arnold Lulls shared a genuine desire to support colonization in the Americas. He is listed in the Virginia Company of London as a stockholder in 1606, 1609, 1612 and 1620. He may have been involved in the contraband tobacco trade in the Caribbean as early as 1602 when his ship, the *Diana*, traded on the Orinoco for tobacco.[49] He may have been inspired by the establishment of the Virginia Company and by 1608 put forward the idea of colonization of Grenada to the other merchants in light of their involvement in the illegal tobacco trade.

William Quarles was a prominent "dealer in unusually expensive fabrics," and master of the Worshipful Company of Mercers, and Master of the Mercer in 1601, 1606 and 1617. He also served briefly as vice Alderman and Alderman of the City of London between 1599 and 1600. He was, with John Eldred, a contributor to the East India Company, and with Eldred and Lulls contributor to "A Charter Granted to the Company of the Merchants Discoverers of the North-West Passage." The other merchants—Godfrey and Robinson—remain unknown.

The information on the two prominent investors, Richard Hall and Arnold Lulls, shows a strong connection to King James' court. Their dealings with members of the royal court are rather interesting and could suggest a reason why they invested in the venture to establish a colony at Grenada. It is, however, very difficult to speculate on their relations at Court and whether these had anything to do with their Grenada venture. One would have to believe that some of their friends at Court knew of their planned venture and could have invested in it. Hall appeared to have connections to the Royal Court, particularly Sir Robert Cecil. The latter had a history of secretly investing in privateering in the Caribbean in the late 1500s and early 1600s.

The roles these merchants played in outfitting the Grenada venture are unclear, but Lorimer suggests that the *Diana* was trading for three London-based Flemish merchants—Arnold Lulls, John Abealls and Joos Croppenbury.[50] It is possible that they, together with Hall, were the primary outfitters of the Grenada colony, but that is also not clear. Arnold Lulls, or possible all three of the Flemish merchants, may have owned the *Diana*.[51] These three Dutchmen were resident in London for decades and were merchants of some means. Their role in the tobacco trade and the outfitting of the Grenada expedition is quite interesting. Lorimer, however, questions "whether the three Flemish merchants, who might claim to be Spanish subjects, served as front men to mask the dubious activities of their English associates."[52] The Northern Territories were at the time fighting against the Spanish for independence. This seems unlikely, though, because of Lulls' continued interests in colonization in the Americas. What is clear about some of the sponsors of the Grenada venture is that they had been involved in the contraband tobacco trade in the Caribbean for quite some time. In the same year as the venture all three Flemish "adventured" or invested in a voyage to Trinidad and the Orinoco in Sir John Watts' ship, the *Archangell*, which sailed in late 1609 or early 1610; the ship returned to London in July 1610.[53] The *Archangell* made another trip to the Orinoco in 1611 and brought back a shipment of tobacco for Arnold Lulls.[54]

As traders in the region, the sponsors of the Grenada colony would have been aware of the island's reputation for producing good quality tobacco. Grenada's abundance of trees, together with its many rivers and streams, made wooding and watering easy. But scores, possibly hundreds, of Amerindians who were noted for their hostility towards European interlopers, occupied Grenada, which was also in close proximity to the Spanish at Trinidad.[55] These two characteristics were far from advantageous to northern Europeans desiring to establish Caribbean plantation colonies. Amerindian resistance had forestalled all Spanish attempts to settle any of the islands of the Lesser Antilles. The Amerindians still occupied the majority, including Grenada, and vigorously defended them. The group of islands, as a whole, presented advantages to northern Europeans wishing to establish colonies in the region: isolation from outside interference, relative ease of protection, ability to confine the inhabitants or a captive labor force, and as "entrepôts for the economic penetration of Spanish holdings" in the Americas, if the Island Caribs were not a deterrent.[56]

When the promoters of the Grenada venture recruited 208 colonists and sent them to Grenada, what could have been their intentions? In the early 1600s, most ships that left British ports for the Americas were either involved in privateering or trade, or both. A few others, like Charles Leigh in 1604, journeyed to the Guianas in search of gold and other precious metals. In 1609 Robert Harcourt took thirty men to establish a colony on the Wiapoco, Guianas for the purpose of finding El Dorado; he would also trade with the Amerindians for tobacco and other crops.[57] Those leaving for North America were in search of gold and other precious metals, naval stores and a Pacific passage to the East. Clearly, the search for precious metals and trade were primary in the minds of those adventurers setting out in the first decade of the 1600s. The evidence on the Grenada mission is sparse, but all seem to indicate that the promoters intended to establish an agricultural colony for the purpose of producing tobacco.

The prevailing English view of planting a colony in the first decade of the 1600s still held to the Elizabethan views of the early adventurers like Sir Walter Ralegh, and that outlined in Richard Hakluyt's 1584 *A Discourse Concerning Western Planting*. These included the spreading of Christianity to the indigenous populations, accessing raw materials through trade, a vent for surplus British labor and manufactures, and finding a Pacific passage to Asia. Williamson believes that these views of colonization existed until 1613 and changed only as a result of experience gained from actual colonization like that of Jamestown, Virginia.[58] Watts agrees with Williamson that the change from the "plundering 'sea-dog'" to the "purse-adventurers," where "investors who were prepared to underwrite the immense complexities and expense of establishing permanent settlements in the Americas," occurred around 1613 when the Jamestown colony sent its first successful crop of tobacco to Britain.[59]

In discussing the 1609 Grenada venture, Williamson argues that the intention of the promoters of the Grenada venture "was to occupy Grenada as a base for trade with Trinidad and the adjoining coasts of the mainland, in much the same way as the Dutch used Curaçao and its neighbors [later on]."[60] Andrews, however, disagrees, insisting that it is quite evident that the sponsors of the venture "intended to found a tobacco producing colony: the 208 Londoners were surely not sent to set up a trading base."[61] The large number of colonists clearly indicates that the primary motive was more than just a trading base which could have been accomplished with far fewer men. The fact that the author of the manuscript discusses the difficulty of establishing new plantations in the West Indies and the unsuitability of the London colonists for such hard work indicate that they had intended to establish plantations.[62]

Grenada's proximity to South America most certainly presented an advantage to the promoters of the venture for further settlements on the mainland and/or to create a base for illegal trade with the Spanish at Trinidad and South America. It seems very likely that Grenada's proximity to South America made it rather attractive, and must have weighted heavily in its choice as the object of the first planned northern

European settlement in the Caribbean.[63] It could also simply mean that the promoters wanted to be close to the source of tobacco production to benefit from the knowledge and resources they needed to establish successful tobacco plantations.[64] Also, with an ongoing trade in the southern Caribbean, it would be easy to re-supply the Grenada colony when ships came to participate in the contraband tobacco trade at Trinidad or on the South American coast.

There is no information on the outfitting of the ships for the Grenada venture, leaving to speculation as to how the venture was supplied, colonists recruited, and who were to lead the colony and how. In researching the environment in which the venture was taking place, 1609 was a rather active one for British enterprises leaving to establish or resupply settlements in the Americas: Robert Harcourt took thirty men to establish a colony on the Wiapoco, Guiana, and a fleet of nine ships, packed with supplies, colonists, a new Virginia Company charter and newly appointed leaders, left England in June for Jamestown, Virginia to resupply the then struggling colony. How challenging would it have been to recruit the over 200 men for the Grenada expedition when the Virginia Company was also recruiting for its settlement? There was a great deal of negative publicity circulating in England about the Virginia settlement and its problems with starvation, diseases and attacks by the Native Americans. Having to supply an overseas colony was a very expensive undertaking, especially when various ventures had to compete for limited financial resources.

Probably in their favor was the fact that the Virginia Company was spearheading a massive advertising campaign for recruits and funding. In an attempt to dispel the rumors about the Virginia colony, it sought to reassure possible recruits that they will be supplied with food, clothing, tools, housing and free transportation to Virginia, and land once their seven years of service to the company was completed. The propaganda campaign included for the poor and upwardly mobile the promise of a bountiful land and riches to be had by all, and for others an appeal to their patriotism and seeing England become a colonial empire. The organizers of the Grenada venture could tailor their appeal for recruits with all of what Virginia had to offer, minus the harsh winters.

The only concrete piece of information concerning the journey from England to Grenada is that the three ships arrived in Grenada on 1 April 1609. Assuming that the ships took the customary route to the West

Indies, the journey took a month and a half to two months if the weather permitted. So Lulls' ship, the *Diana* (under Master William Thorn), and Hall's ship the *Penelope* and its pinnace the *Endeavour* left London around the beginning to the middle of February 1609. They made the two-week journey down the Thames and through the English Channel past the coast of France, Spain and Portugal before reaching the African coast and the Canary Islands. There they most probably stopped for a day or two, maybe more, to replenish their water supply and procure other needed food stuff; this was the final stop before crossing the Atlantic Ocean. From the Canary Islands they headed due west for the West Indies, aided by the northeasterly trade winds that had aided European ships beginning with Columbus in 1492. The four-week long journey has been described as the "closest thing to sailing downhill." They would have arrived in the Lesser Antilles in the vicinity of Barbados or Dominica where the ships would then sail south for Grenada, following the traditional route of the Spanish galleons going to South America.

The three ships, according to the author of the manuscript, sailed into "the great Bay of this Grenada," and the 208 colonists landed on 1 April 1609. Though the specific site of the settlement was not identified, it is almost certain that "the great Bay" refers to the natural harbor at what is presently called the Carenage, St. George's where the French colonists settled four decades later.[65] Initial European settlements in the Lesser Antilles were almost always situated on the leeward coast where they benefited from protected harbors, calm seas, and shelter from storms. The French also referred to the area in the south west of the island from Pointe Bois Maurice (presently Molinière Point) to Pointe Cabrit (presently Quarantine Point) as "La Grande Baye" (i.e. "Great Bay"), giving a possible clue as to the earlier British description. Within this "Great Bay" are three smaller bays—Grand Mal Bay, St. George's Bay and Grand Anse Bay—where settlements could have easily been established, though the area known today as the St. George's Harbour probably was the most ideal. It is the furthest point in from the coast, providing the most protection to ships and a settlement. On the other hand, it sits at the base of a filled-in, eroded volcanic crater that is ringed by hills that command all but the maritime approaches to any settlement situated along the bay. If the colonists did not construct adequate defenses to protect the settlement, they would be easy targets for the Island Caribs, even with their bows and poisoned arrows, and war clubs.

The tasks ahead for newly arrived colonists were many and most had to be completed quickly to ensure the success of the settlement. The first and foremost was choosing an appropriate site to establish the settlement. Some on the ships' crew would most likely have been familiar with the harbors surrounding the island, having used them for watering and wooding, or the expedition had already chosen the "great Bay" as the site based on an earlier survey. The bay was an attractive site because it afforded easy access from the sea and had many streams flowing into it. For protection from the Amerindians and possible Spanish retaliation, the colonists had to build a fort, most likely a palisade fort ringed with cannons. The next step would be to build basic shelters and begin the clearing of land for planting food crops and tobacco.

There is no information as to the reaction of the Amerindians to the appearance of the English and the establishment of their colony, except that the colonists "were often Disturbed by the Indians."[66] It is possible that the Island Caribs welcomed the British colonists, desiring to trade with them for European goods they desired. The Island Caribs were known to welcome Europeans to live and trade among them temporarily, but later turned against them due to the complexity of Island Carib relationships between the various groups scattered across the islands.

The author of the manuscript implies that it was primarily the instigation of two Spanish capuchin friars from Trinidad that caused the Island Caribs to destroy the British colony.[67] That the Spanish at Trinidad may have done everything in their power to bring about the failure of the English settlement at Grenada can be expected, but the absence of Spanish records to support that view creates some doubt. The historical relationship between the Spanish and the Island Caribs was one of enmity, and it is very unlikely that the Island Caribs would have aided the Spanish. The author's claim may be due more to national biases than reality; the historical response of the Island Caribs to attempted European settlements in the Lesser Antilles was to destroy them, as the Spanish were quite aware from their own experiences. Until the early 1600s there was not one permanent European colony in the Lesser Antilles, all attempts having been vigorously resisted by the Island Caribs.

Though the Island Carib attacks may have been the major cause of the settlement's demise, the colonists are described as persons not "fitt for the settling of Plantacions, being the Greater part the People of London, noe way inured to hardship and soe not Capeable of encountring the Difficulty that Attends new Plantations in the West-Indies."[68] If, as suspected, the expedition was to establish tobacco plantations, the tasks of clearing forests, planting subsistence and cash crops, and staying healthy and adequately fed were enormous. Forest clearing often led to the deaths of European colonists and African slaves alike because it was a difficult undertaking. The insufficient supply of food due to inadequate planning and/or spoilage and the inability to quickly produce food often led to conflicts with the Amerindians as the colonists resorted to raiding the Island Caribs' gardens, or making greater demands than trade could support. Exertion working in the hot tropical climate, especially wearing woolen clothing, also took its toll, as would diseases like malaria, typhoid fever and dysentery. This was the case with Jamestown, Virginia and many future colonial attempts in the Caribbean.

Arriving in April, the British colonists had roughly two months to establish themselves before the rainy season began in earnest in June.[69] With the rains came increased incidences of illnesses, and many could have suffered from exposure. If they were unable to construct adequate shelters and clear enough forests, especially to grow food, they could have suffered as a result. Many early European colonies in the Americas foundered due to the lack of food and the prevalence of tropical diseases. This was a significant problem for many of the colonizing ventures that set out from Europe in the early 1600s, and many suffered dearly.

After leaving the colonists at Grenada to their task of setting-up a colony, the three ships sailed on to illegally trade for tobacco with the Spanish colonists at Trinidad. Illicit trade was still profitable to the outfitters of the Grenada adventure. It is not clear when the ships departed Grenada, but they must have spent a few months there, helping the colonists establish the settlement. Robert Harcourt, who himself had only recently established a colony in Guiana, recorded seeing the three English ships in September 1609 at Punta de Galera, Trinidad where he had gone to trade for tobacco before returning to England for supplies for his colony.[70] He records interacting with the crews of the ships, the departure of Hall's two ships and the *Diana*, but mentions nothing about Grenada or the colony there. The manuscript's author provides some information as to what transpired while the ships were anchored off Trinidad: "the Spanish governor of that island, who wanted to ensure the failure of the English settlement by giving the Spanish friars enough time to instigate the Island Caribs, reportedly delayed them.[71] But Lorimer, citing another source, provides a different reason for the delay which was caused by Governor de Berrío, who in an attempt to show that he was observing the ban on tobacco trading with foreigners, "sent messages to La Margarita informing its governor that the English intended to cut wood at Cape Tres Puntas and advising him to set an ambush. Forewarned by a friendly Indian, Hall's men beat off the attack."[72] None of the ships were allowed to trade for tobacco as Mendoza informed the captains that "he could not Maintaine a Trade, without apparent hazard of his Life and Fortune."[73] The Spanish authorities were clamping down on the illegal trade and it was very difficult to procure a cargo of tobacco.

While attempting to trade, the British ships were told by Mendoza that the colony at Grenada was in distress, forcing an immediate return of the ships, according to the manuscript's author. On arriving in Grenada they found "their Coloniy the greatest part Destroyed those few that remayned they tooke with them for England," at the end of September 1609.[74] Andrews concludes "The *Diana* must have gone back alone to Grenada and taken off the survivors. We know from Spanish sources that the other two [ships] went on to a career of plunder."[75] It is possible that all three ships returned to Grenada, but after seeing the small size of the group that was left, Hall's ships decided to seek some profit by engaging in plunder. Exactly how many of the 208 colonists perished and under what circumstances are not known, but the survivors of the ill-fated attempt arrived back in England on 15 December 1609 "to ye great dissattisfaction of their Employers, who would [not] embarque any more, on soe advantageous a designe wherein they had once Miscarried."[76]

The British attempt to settle Grenada in 1609 failed after only six months, the immediate cause being attacks by the Amerindians. The inability to defend themselves against the Amerindians might be more a symptom of inferior planning, inadequate resources, poor management, or just bad luck. At almost the same time, the British colony at Jamestown, Virginia, with fewer men, confronted with harsh winters, attacks by Native Americans and incompetent leadership, was experiencing its most difficult period, but it was able to survive when a number of ships arrived with settlers to restock the settlement. The outfitters of the Grenada venture appeared not to have had a long-term plan for re-supplying the colony with colonists and food, believing that they would achieve immediate success. If the case of Jamestown is illustrative, where only 60 colonists out of 500 had survived after three years, the Grenada venture was doomed to failure due to inadequate planning. Its investors were shortsighted and should have heeded the advice, "Any colony that did not receive sufficient people and support from England could disappear, along with whatever resources investors had sunk into the project."[77] In the end, the Grenada venture failed like the first Roanoke settlement which had left England in April 1585 with 107 men, but survived to June 1586 when the remaining settlers were rescued by Sir Francis Drake and returned to England.

Andrews believes that the Grenada attempt "should have signaled a quite new message—the first indication [to the Spanish] that the northerners might develop an interest in the permanent occupation of some of the islands. However, the obvious answer to this alarming thought was that colonizers, if not already frightened off, would find it very hard to carry through any such attempt [because of the hostility of the Island Caribs]."[78] The British attempt to settle Grenada failed because of attacks by the Island Caribs, not the Spanish who, militarily, were in no position to deter the coming onslaught of northern Europeans serious about establishing tobacco colonies in the Lesser Antilles. These attempts would prove far more successful, especially the French and English colonies established in the northern Lesser Antilles and Barbados in the 1620s. European settlement of Grenada had to wait four more decades and the arrival of the French from Martinique, but the death of King James I of Great Britain and the ending of peace in Europe among the northerners ushered in the colonization of the Lesser Antilles by the British, French and Dutch beginning in 1624, and would eventually lead to the demise of the culture of its inhabitants, the Island Caribs.

"The Seed From Which Virginia Grew"[79]

There is evidence to support the view that the failure to establish a tobacco-producing colony in Grenada in 1609 led directly to the transfer of that idea to North America and the Jamestown settlement in Virginia. Grenada represented the last hope for free access to "Spanish tobacco" in the Caribbean, which by 1612 had all but closed to British traders. The strong connections between the individuals concerned in both projects may have led to the decision that "Spanish" tobacco, the more desirable and lucrative variety (*N. tabacum*), should be tried in Jamestown since the

Native Americans were cultivating another, but harsher variety (*N. rustica*) not fit for "drinking."

John Rolfe, a colonist who arrived in Jamestown in 1610, has been credited with experimenting with tobacco seeds that would become the basis for the establishment of large-scale production at Jamestown after giving some of his seeds to his friends "to make triall of." According to Ralph Humor, the then secretary of Virginia, "I may not forget the gentleman, worthie of much commendations, which first tooke the pains to make triall thereof, his name Mr. John Rolfe, Anno Domini 1612, partly for the love he hath a long time borne unto it, and partly to raise commodity to the adventurers..."[80] It has never been clear how John Rolfe procured the coveted seeds of "Spanish" tobacco with which he experimented. Though seeds were available in Europe, as it was grown in countries bordering the Mediterranean Sea, they were hard to come by because the Spanish prohibited its exportation on pain of death. Some, contending that Rolfe was an avid smoker back in England, originated the idea of growing Spanish tobacco in Virginia and brought the seeds with him from England. Woolley goes even further in speculating that Rolfe possibly "had some undocumented contact with the tobacco merchants [John] Eldred and [Sir John] Watts, which led to them pressing a sample of Trinidad tobacco seed into the palm of his hand with the suggestion that he try it in the Virginia soil."[81] It should be noted that Rolfe's ship was shipwrecked on Bermuda in July 1609 and spent months there before arriving at Jamestown in May 1610; supposedly his trunk containing the seeds survived intact? A more likely scenario is that Rolfe received the "Spanish" tobacco seeds sometime after he arrived at Jamestown. Some have speculated that he received the seeds directly from a ship's captain from whom he had requested them, who was trading between Jamestown and the southern Caribbean.

Woolley's suggestion, that the idea to grow Spanish tobacco in Jamestown, Virginia "began to germinate in the minds of the many merchants who shared an interest in both the tobacco trade and the Virginia venture," is supported by the evidence.[82] A look at two of these individuals involved with the tobacco trade and the Virginia Company supports this scenario. Sir John Watts was a London merchant and ship owner who figured prominently in the British privateering missions to the Caribbean in the late 1500s. His exploits were so well known that the Spanish considered him "the greatest pirate that has ever been in this kingdom."[83] He was a founding member of the East India Company and had served as its governor. He was an active member of the Virginia Company from its inception and served on its Royal Council. So successful was he as a privateer and merchant, "he had become, by the beginning of the seventeenth century, the leading merchant of London."[84] He was lord mayor of London and knighted by King James I.

John Eldred's involvement in Caribbean privateering is also legendary. A London merchant, he backed privateering missions to the Spanish Caribbean in the late 1500s and early 1600s, with his partner Richard Hall, a primary outfitter of the Grenada venture. Eldred was a prominent member of the Virginia Company and served as its deputy. Wooley speculates that "Through contacts with [Richard] Hakluyt, the idea may have already formed in his [Eldred's] mind of running trials to cultivate Spanish tobacco in Virginia."[85] Both John Eldred and Sir John Watts were major traders in Spanish Caribbean-grown tobacco.

The chief undertakers of the Grenada venture–Richard Hall, Arnold Lulls and Quales–were heavily involved with the tobacco trade, and most were investors in the Virginia Company. Richard Hall was a longtime trading partner of John Eldred in many voyages to the Caribbean. As mentioned, one of their ships encountered some problems in 1608 when it attempted to trade for tobacco at Trinidad.[86] Hall's trading partner, Eldred, most likely was a "silent investor" in the Grenada colony as well. It wasn't until 1612, the same year that Rolfe began his Spanish tobacco trials in Jamestown that Hall became an investor in the Virginia Company. Arnold Lulls had been an investor in the Virginia Company since its inception, and William Quarles became an "adventurer" in 1612.

The fact that Rolfe did not begin his trials until around 1612 possibly meant that he did not have the seeds when he arrived in 1610, and that the seeds arrived some time thereafter. If he did leave England with seeds in 1609 they most likely perished in the shipwreck. It seems quite likely that the idea of growing Spanish tobacco in Virginia did not take shape until after 1609 and the failure of the Grenada settlement. In looking at the possibility of when seeds could have been procured from Trinidad, the period 1610 to 1611 is probably the most opportune since Rolfe supposedly began his trials in 1612. A number of voyages by the ship the *Archangell* occurred around this time and one of its voyages most likely carried the seeds for the Jamestown trials from Trinidad to Jamestown via England. In "late 1609 or early 1610," the *Archangell* brought "back a cargo of tobacco for Sir John Watts and partners"; a second in the autumn of 1610 by the *Archangell*, now named the *John of London*, made a voyage to San Tomé for Watts and company and brought back tobacco; and in the spring of 1611 a third voyage brought back tobacco for Arnold Lulls. All three voyages occurred after the demise of the Grenada venture and were some of the last voyages by British traders to the region to trade for tobacco with the Spanish.

The failure of the Grenada colony and the worsening conditions procuring illicit tobacco from the Spanish at Trinidad and Guiana, forced the British adventurers to concentrate their efforts and resources at Jamestown just as similar conditions had created the impetus to establish the Grenada settlement. Though the colony was struggling at this point, the reorganization of the Virginia Company and concerted efforts to promote colonization in North America later proved successful. By the time the British had successfully established a tobacco colony in the Caribbean at St. Christopher in 1624, Jamestown was producing large quantities of tobacco for the British market and its growing success was an example for future agricultural settlements in the Caribbean.

4

French Settlement and Island Carib Resistance

This mobility, coupled with their secret and treacherous mentality, rendered them a formidable obstacle to the early [European] settlers, and the ultimate solution of the problem was provided only by a war of extermination.[1]

For over a century, the Island Caribs had successfully defended their islands against Spanish and other European aggression. They had retained the majority of them by the time northern Europeans entered the region as colonizers. The first six decades of the 1600s would prove to be the most difficult for the Island Caribs as the French, British and Dutch descended on the Lesser Antilles and challenged them for possession. The unsuccessful British attempt to settle Grenada in 1609 was an early indication that the northern Europeans were serious about occupying these islands, but the final struggle began in earnest in 1624/25 when the British and French successfully established settlements on the island of St. Christopher.

About October 1625 Pierre Belain d'Esnambuc, Urbain de Roissy and a small group of men arrived on the island of St. Christopher and established what would become the first permanent French foothold in the Caribbean.[2] They shared the island with the British who had established a colony there since January 1624, inaugurating permanent northern European settlement in the Lesser Antilles. The small Amerindian population there reportedly welcomed the Europeans to trade and coexisted with them for a while, but their resistance to expanding European settlements led to the British and French uniting to drive them off the island by 1627. This became an often-repeated response that threatened their very existence in the region.

Like the British, the French returned home and requested official sanction and financial support for their venture, and in October 1626 the Company of St. Christopher (Compagnie de Saint-Christophe) was established for the island's colonization. The young colony struggled to survive, coping with attacks by the Spanish, Island Caribs and its British neighbors, and had to endure the Company of St. Christopher's failure to supply it with desperately needed merchandise and colonists. Despite these difficulties it was able to continue, primarily because of the arrival of Dutch traders to supply goods and purchase its tobacco. The early success at St. Christopher led to a new charter in 1635 and the establishment of the Company of the Islands of America (Compagnie des Isles de l'Amérique) that pledged to colonize the islands of the Lesser Antilles in earnest.[3]

As the mid-1600s approached, the Amerindians in the Lesser Antilles found themselves besieged by advancing European intruders. These serious and incessant attempts by northern Europeans to colonize the islands of the Lesser Antilles led to the increasing loss of territory by the Island Caribs. Much of the islands in the northern Lesser Antilles, the islands later known as the Leeward Islands, were occupied by the British and French.[4] Even though the Island Caribs continued to live on Guadeloupe and Martinique alongside the French colonists since 1635, they were marginalized and subsequently driven off and/or left by 1660. Only a few significant islands–Dominica, St. Lucia, St. Vincent and Grenada–remained under complete Island Carib control by the mid-1600s. These were the remaining strongholds of the Island Caribs and were vital to them because they represented the vital link to South America where they traded and raided. Grenada appeared to be the weakest link in that chain, but it was a primary conduit to the continent that the Island Caribs were unwilling to give up without a fight. Thus Grenada represented the beginning of the final struggle for the Island Caribs for control of the Lesser Antilles, and ultimately the very existence of their way of life in the region.

French Plans and Attempts to Settle Grenada

There were no serious attempts to colonize Grenada in the three decades immediately following the failed British attempt in 1609, though both the French and British included it as part of their larger claims to the Lesser Antilles since the mid-1620s. In the late 1630s a French colonial official named de Bonnefoy, the procureur fiscal at St. Christopher, gave Grenada a glowing appraisal following a brief stop there on a trip from Guiana to St. Christopher.[5] He believed that Grenada possessed

> good land for the product of all kind[s] of provisions of that country; besides bringeth forth excellent crops of sugar-cane, ginger, and tobacco (but is not so proper for cotton and indigo), it hath the conveniency of excellent springs of fresh water, and some rivers, and in several places good anchorage for ships on the south and west parts, especially the Grand Bay; the timber very large and good for building and making casks; well stocked with fish in its several bays; and hath the conveniency of some small islands, a few leagues to the north east of it where there have excellent hunting.[6]

De Bonnefoy's flattering description of the island's potential for supporting a colony brought it to the notice of a number of French officials, some of whom made plans to colonize it, or seriously thought about the possibility of doing so.

In the 1640s discord among the several French governors surfaced and threatened to disrupt the governance of the islands under the Compagnie des Isles de l'Amérique. Many began to look beyond their respective islands in the hope of finding new territories to claim. At least two of these governors demonstrated their seriousness in colonizing Grenada, and unlike the English in 1609, had colonizing experience in the region and established colonies from which to launch expeditions. In late 1640, not 1638 as claimed by Dutertre, Philip de Lonvilliers de Poincy, governor of St. Christopher and governor-general of the French Antilles, planned taking possession of Grenada based on de Bonnefoy's earlier report.[7] However, the island's far distance from his base and the reported "numerous" Island Caribs settled there, made him abandon his plans due to these challenges.[8] In 1643 Governor Jean Aubert, fearing the loss of his position as governor of Guadeloupe, sent one Postel to reconnoiter Grenada, and was reportedly planning a settlement had not Charles Houël, his challenger for the governorship of that island, suddenly arrived, occupying all of his energies.[9] Though the island attracted attention, it remained unsettled by any European nation up to the mid-1600s. Despite its potential, Grenada was located beyond the general colonizing area of the northern Europeans throughout the first three decades of their activities in the region.

The most serious French attempt to colonize Grenada, interestingly, did not originate in the colonies, but from France by Philibert de Nouailly, Lord of Néron and gentleman of Burgundy.[10] De Nouailly, as a captain of one of the four militia companies, traveled to the West Indies in 1643 as part of Charles Poncet de Brétigny's expedition to colonize Cayenne, the "first major French colonial expedition to Guiana."[11] By late 1644 the colony had collapsed due to infighting and conflicts with the local Amerindians, de Brétigny among those killed in the conflicts. De Nouailly was among a group that abandoned the colony and took refuge in neighboring Surinam before returning to France via the French Caribbean where they told of the "terrible tales about Guiane."[12] During his time in the Caribbean de Nouailly heard of and/or possibly saw Grenada and developed an interest in it.[13]

Upon his return to France he negotiated with the Compagnie des Isles de l'Amérique, signing a contract on 10 July 1645 to "occupy and populate" Grenada and the Grenadines.[14] He was given a commission as governor for the period 1645 to 1650, and within the first year was required to build a fort, settle 200 men and women, and three clerics whose job it was to convert the Amerindians and minister to the settlers; colonists would be free of taxes for four years after which they would be taxed annually at fifty pounds of tobacco.[15] De Nouailly, in the search for capital and colonists to outfit his expedition, advertised for adventurers across Paris; the poster read in part: "The King commands, the lords of the island of Grenada in America announce that they will leave shortly, with several ecclesiastics and people of status to go to establish a colony in the aforementioned island with the glory of God, benefit of the King, and the conversion of the Savages. The profit is fifty percent each year..."[16] His publicity must have brought in the necessary resources because in June 1646 he arranged for de Beaumanoir to represent him as his lieutenant general, and the expedition left St. Nazaire on 18 July 1646, arriving at Martinique on 1 September that year.[17] Among the adventurers were two Carmelite priests Maurile de St. Michel and Ambroise de St. Anne who, as part of the contract, were going to establish "a mission to work with the conversion of a great number of Savages, who live there."[18] At Martinique the adventurers prepared to go to Grenada, but the island was reportedly plagued with conflict among the Amerindian groups. They described Grenada as "infested with Caribs," being divided between two warring parts that made it rather inaccessible to them at the time.[19] Having witnessed firsthand the destruction caused by attacks by unwelcoming Amerindians, it was decided to abandon the settlement of Grenada and return to France. Though many of his companions followed, a few, like de Beaumanoir and Father Maurile de St. Michel, remained in the French Antilles.[20]

Citing his dissatisfaction with the contract, de Nouailly had it modified in April 1647, and the following month made arrangements with Samuel Guesdon, his lieutenant general, to recruit twenty armed soldiers, fully equipped, and ready to embark before the end of August 1647 at either la Rochelle or Havre for the settlement of Grenada. Each of the men was to be paid 100 *livres* during the three years that they remained in the service of Guesdon, and would be allowed "the quantity of land that he was able to plow, sow and cultivate (on his own) as to the custom of the country."[21] Despite de Nouailly's preparation to confront the Island Caribs if the riotious situation prevailed, the expedition subsequently failed. On 8 May 1648 de Nouailly again had the contract modified a second time, promising to sail by 1 November 1648.[22] After every failed attempt de Nouailly had the contract altered, but to no avail. After three attempts in four years of trying he still had not occupied Grenada. Though claiming to have suffered losses of 300,000 *livres* in his failed attempts, he was still interested in making a fourth attempt and requested the assistance of the carmelite clergy to allow him to find priests willing to undertake the journey.[23] De Nouilly's delay was partially a result of the political unrest in France caused by the Fronde, but as his plans foundered, the French governor of Martinique set in motion his own plan to occupy Grenada.

Governor du Parquet Seizes an Opportunity

Mismanagement of the colonies and the discord among the governors resulted in the bankruptcy and subsequent collapse of the Compagnie des Isles de l'Amérique. Governor du Parquet was aware of the company's financial difficulties and the negotiations begun in November 1648 between Governor Houël of Guadeloupe and the company for the sale of that island to its governor. Du Parquet, who Boucher refers to as "the company's golden boy,"[24] had earned the respect of the directors of the company because of his successful administration of Martinique, and believed that they would give him the first opportunity to purchase any islands under his jurisdiction.[25] Knowing that the islands would be sold to their respective governors, du Parquet rushed into action plans to occupy as many of the "unoccupied" territories in the region, settling Grenada in March 1649 and St. Lucia in June 1650. Du Parquet, in taking possession of Grenada in 1649, did not do so in the name of the Compagnie des Isles de l'Amérique, but only in the name of the French King.

Jacques Dyle du Parquet was the French governor of Martinique when he initiated the colonization of Grenada. He was an officer in the regiment of Picardy, France, but left to join his uncle, Governor d'Esnambuc of St. Christopher, in 1634. Following the capture of Martinique's governor by the Spanish in 1636, du Parquet took over the administration of the island and was subsequently confirmed as governor by the Compagnie des Isles de l'Amérique.[26] Though well respected, he was considered inexperienced for the position of governor-general of the French Antilles following the death of his uncle in 1637. He was instrumental in the expansion of the colony on Martinique, establishing new settlements, constructing defenses and initiating sugar production.

Between 1640 and 1647 the French Antilles was in chaos as the governors, governors-general, and the Compagnie des Isles de l'Amérique were constantly at odds with each other over the administration of the islands. In 1646 the governors were waging a war against each other and Governor du Parquet was held hostage for over a year by Governor-General de Poincy because du Parquet had sided with de Poincy's rival.[27] Upon his release in January 1647 he concentrated on the development of Martinique, and soon set his sights on colonizing other territories.

In late 1648, or most probably early 1649, du Parquet sent Captain La Rivière to reconnoiter Grenada to locate a suitable site for settlement.[28] Accustomed to fishing around Grenada, La Rivière was to "build a makeshift hut close to the best harbor he could find, to shelter the arms and ammunition while awaiting the construction of a fort."[29] After sailing around the island, he settled on the spacious harbor on the southwest and constructed a shelter. His appearance on the island aroused the attention of some of the Amerindians who were concerned that an intruder had established himself on the island without their permission. La Rivière gave the excuse that the shelter was for his use while fishing.[30] The conversation shifted to the British who the Island Caribs exhibited much hostility towards, and La Rivière assured them that if "[du Parquet,] the great captain of Martinique" was allowed to live on their island he would protect them.[31] This response seemed enough to appease the Amerindians and "all other reason for discussion having been watered down by some good shots of liquor," laid the foundation for du Parquet's settlement of Grenada.[32] Dutertre, however, insists that it was the Island Caribs who "begged" du Parquet to come live among them, and seeing them so eager to receive him, he immediately prepared his expedition, fearing that they would change their minds and oppose his project.[33]

Though the Island Caribs had good reason to be hostile towards both the British and French, they seemed to have reserved more hostility for the British and developed a friendlier relationship with the French. It is possible that the Island Caribs' hostility towards the British stemmed from specific aggressions against them by early British privateers in the region, or maybe a direct response to their experiences with the English colonists in 1609. Despite the origin of the hurt, the Island Caribs had developed friendlier relationships with the French.[34] It may also have been some aspect of French culture and their willingness to engage the Island Caribs and sometimes live among them that made the French more likeable than the British. The French, as opposed to the British, seemed to have gained the respect of the Island Caribs across the region and Governor du Parquet was "greatly feared and respected" by them because of his command at Martinique.

Following La Rivière's return to Martinique, du Parquet set in motion his plans for Grenada. He recruited colonists, promising tax exemptions and land grants as incentives for those willing to go to Grenada to establish the colony. According to Labat, "Out of the large number who came forward he chose [those] whom he knew to be men of good stamina, well accustomed to the clearing of land and the cultivation of the soil for food for themselves and for trading."[35] Dutertre adds that they were also masons, carpenters, locksmiths, and other useful craftsmen among those chosen.[36] Du Parquet decided on forty-five men to begin his colony in Grenada and made the necessary preparations, including provisioning the expedition and the construction of a ship.[37] According to

Dutertre, du Parquet "prepared some cassava... so as to feed them during three months; without them having to hunt or fish, he added a supply of fat and salted meat, as if Grenada was the most deprived island in the world, from these convenient necessities of life; he gathered peas, Brazilian beans and all sorts of seeds to plant."[38] Among the other supplies were several barrels of gunpowder, "three casks of brandy, two casks of an excellent Madeira wine, and all the useful tools to cultivate the land; he also supplied a lot of glass beads and other trade goods, to trade with the savages," and "some timbers and planks already cut in sections for a lodge, so the building could be thrown together in a few days."[39]

On the afternoon of Sunday, 14 March 1649, the forty-five men, together with du Parquet, his chaplain, and a few prominent men on Martinique he trusted with the setting-up of the colony, gathered at Fort Saint-Pierre to begin the expedition. Labat adds that "To each of his men he gave a rifle, two belt pistols, a sword, a bayonet, and as much powder and shot as they could use in a day," making it quite clear that the French were prepared to use force if necessary.[40] Following a solemn mass by the chaplain, the party boarded the transports around six in the evening and departed Martinique for Grenada. The party, together with all their supplies, boarded the two ships captained by Lormier and Jean Pelletier, and two small boats or barks, belonging to du Parquet, with one captained by La Rivière.[41] The approximately 156 nautical miles journey along the leeward coast of St. Lucia, St. Vincent and the Grenadines was uneventful, and they dropped anchor in front of the Fond du Grand Pauvre, on the northwest coast of Grenada, three days later in the evening of 17 March 1649.[42] Early on the morning of Thursday, 18 March, as "the wind was favorable to their enterprise, they sailed straight into the first bay and they dropped anchor there around eight in the morning, and this was the most beautiful anchorage on the whole island... and as La Rivière had noticed."[43] As the leader of the enterprise, Governor du Parquet "landed first as this honor was due him" and gave thanks for the safe arrival of his enterprise.[44]

It is quite evident that there are discrepancies between the information in Dutertre and the Anonymous author concerning the expedition and its dates. Long accepted, because of its early publication, has been information from Dutertre that du Parquet outfitted 200 colonists and "sailed in June of the year 1650 and landed in Grenada four days later"; Labat added a more exact departure date of 16 June 1650.[45]

Petitjean Roget agrees with the Anonymous author, that in occupying Grenada, du Parquet did so "by force. With no previous authorization from the gentlemen of the Compagnie [des Isles de l'Amérique]," which had an outstanding contract for its colonization with Philibert de Nouailly. He further concludes that "When Father Dutertre states that possession of Grenada had been taken in June 1650, apparently he is only trying to hide the illegality of his friend du Parquet's act."[46] The date of June 1650 is therefore seen as a way to legitimize du Parquet's settlement of Grenada since by May 1650 he had begun arrangements to purchase Martinique, Grenada, St. Lucia and the Grenadines from the Compagnie des Isles de l'Amérique.[47] Governor du Parquet would have been aware of de Nouailly's existing contract and that his actions could be considered a violation. The question remains though, did Dutertre, who was fully aware of the situation when he was compiling his history, deliberately attempted a cover-up by altering the dates, or was it simply an error due to a mix up with the settlement date for St. Lucia which was June 1650? Dutertre's motives are definitely questionable as his early chronological history of Grenada shows that dates of events seemed to have been advanced at least a year to compensate for his initial "error."[48]

As soon as the party landed they immediately set about the task of establishing the settlement on the banks of the spacious harbor on the leeward coast, within a small lagoon, sometimes referred to as Étang d'eau saleé (Salt Water Lake). With the entire day ahead of them, the group gave thanks for their successful arrival, and du Parquet, taking the lead, "took a billhook himself, his men followed him, some taking one too, others an axe and all started to cut and work the woods."[49] They spent about three hours felling trees and clearing a space, then used the rest of the day to unload the supplies and equipment. The tree felling continued the next day until a large enough area was cleared upon which was constructed a small building with materials brought from Martinique. The next few days were spent constructing a palisade fort, which was completed on 25 March, the Christian Day of the Annunciation, hence the naming of the fort, Fort de l'Annonciation; it was armed with two cannons to protect the food supply and ammunition.[50] Governor du Parquet, in keeping with French tradition, performed the usual ceremony in taking possession of a new colony. On the shore of the lagoon, a rudely constructed cross, emblazoned with the coat of arms of His Majesty, was planted in the soil to the singing of the *Te Deum*, shouts of

"Long live the King and du Parquet!," and the firing of muskets and cannons; the latter also served as a warning to the Amerindians should they decide to disrupt the peace.[51] The celebrations continued for the remainder of the day, and du Parquet took the opportunity to appoint the leaders of the new settlement and had them swear loyalty to him.

Though the Island Caribs had observed the French from the moment they landed a week ago, they did not approach until the day after the celebrations, the Anonymous author mockingly adding that they must have "recovered from the fear caused by the noise of the cannon and musket shots."[52] About forty to fifty Amerindians arrived at the site by sea in a long boat, from the north,... all freshly painted, armed with arrows and *boutous*, their usual weapons (Illustrations 1.3 and 4.1).[53] Their chief, Kaïeroüanne, expressed his disapproval of the French settlement adding, "We do not want your land, why are you taking ours?"[54] The French swore that their settlement, with its cannons, was to provide protection to the Island Caribs because of an impending attack by the British who "intended to descend on their island to become masters of it and chase them off."[55] To show their goodwill, the colonists offered some gifts–billhooks, knives, axes, and sickles–and even "a beautiful red coat with silver braids and a gray hat trimmed with a bunch of red and white feathers" for the chief or captain.[56] The French ended the disquieting situation by providing their "guests" with whiskey and wine. In exchange for the gifts the Amerindians left some wild game and fruits.

It is this faithful exchange, or rather trade as the Island Caribs believed it to be, which contemporary writers like Dutertre and later writers and historians like Devas have misrepresented as the Island Caribs "heartily [handing over] every right they had in this island, holding back only their *cabets* and their dwellings."[57] It was the common "exchange" between Europeans and Amerindians across the region that the former would misrepresent as a contract, even if its terms were not understood as such by the Amerindians. In the case of Grenada, and recorded by the Anonymous author, the Island Caribs allowed the French to occupy a small piece of land, but there was absolutely no exchange of property rights to the island. The Island Caribs were known to welcome European settlements because of their desire for European trade goods. In exchange for the "gifts" they received from the French the Island Caribs had "left a few pigs, lizards and turtles that they had brought with them to trade on that first day."[58] The Island Caribs then made it absolutely clear to the French colonists that they could not settle anywhere else on the island, but had to content themselves with the land they currently occupied as this was a good enough spot to retreat on.[59]

French Struggles to Subjugate the Island Caribs

After initiating the settlement of Grenada, Governor du Parquet, before returning to Martinique, appointed Jean Le Comte to administer the colony. Like many of the early adventurers and colonists to the Antilles, Le Comte was from Normandy, France. He arrived in St. Christopher in the late 1630s and by 1645 was captain of a militia company there. In that same year he fled to Martinique following disagreements with Governor-General de Poincy over Poincy's refusal to accept the appointment of Patrocles de Thoisy, the newly designated governor-general of the French Antilles. Le Comte later joined du Parquet and the other governors in opposing de Poincy, leading an expedition to capture and ransom de Poincy's nephews, but also inadvertently resulted in du Parquet's capture. The Anonymous author describes Le Comte as "a man with good sense, judgment and behavior,"[60] but later chastises him for his "shameful" behavior and anger towards Father des Mares by barring him from saying mass at the Grand Fort chapel and forbidding others from giving him shelter.[61] Dutertre describes him favorably as "well shaped, of a martial appearance, of wit, of an affable mood, and who had all the needed qualities and experience to lead a colony."[62] As du Parquet's lieutenant general, Le Comte administered the Grenada colony and guided its initial establishment.[63]

In setting up the colony, Governor du Parquet created two militia companies, each comprising about twenty men, to protect and defend the settlement from the immediate threat of the Island Caribs, and possible attacks by other European nations, i.e. the Spanish located 100 miles south at Trinidad and the British situated 128 miles northeast at Barbados. Each company was commanded by a captain, with the aid of a lieutenant and a sergeant. Under Le Comte's command was Jean Lespron, also known as Le Marquis de Rheims or Le Marquis, who acted as his aid and lieutenant of the first militia company. Claude Maublant, alias Dubuisson, was lieutenant of the second company. The sergeants of the companies were Philippe Basil Normand and Thomas de la Cour.

64

The notary and clerk was Dominique de la Bedade who would play a prominent role in the first decade of the colony, and his records would become the basis for the detailed chronology of the island by the Anonymous author.

After deceptively acquiring the "concession" of land from the Island Caribs, du Parquet "ordered the land cleared, along the hill, near the pond, where he planned the arrangement of a large area, not with a view to establishing a market, but to ensure there being enough food for the support of the new settlers."[64] For the colonists who asked for plots du Parquet parceled out allotments "under the condition that those who had no servants were emmateloted, that means made an association of three together, or at least two, for fear of surprise from the Savages."[65] They embarked on the cultivation of regional staples, mainly food crops like cassava, sweet potato, maize, plantain and banana, all of these except the latter two were indigenous Caribbean/South American food crops then grown by the Amerindians. The settlers also planted a crop of *petun* or tobacco, the primary cash crop in the French Antilles at the time. The colonists supplemented their diet with abundant wild game like the agouti, armadillo, manatee or sea cow, sea turtles, mainly the green turtle, and a variety of birds and fishes.[66] The abundance of game on Grenada led to a number of "boats which went back and forth [from Martinique] for fishing and hunting."[67] The colonists also traded basic European manufactured goods, including wine, with the Amerindians for food crops, vegetables and wild meat.

Accommodated within the island's rugged coast are numerous bays. These provided anchorage and protection from violent weather like storms that often proved devastating when they struck. It was in one of these that the French established their first settlement, initially on the banks of a lagoon, part of an eroded water filled-in crater of an extinct volcano. The surrounding hills provided protection from storms, and the horseshoe bay proved ideal for careening ships, hence its later name Carenage. Small streams from the surrounding hills brought fresh water into the lagoon, thus providing the settlement with water. A number of salt ponds at the southern extreme at the Pointe des Salines provided salt for preserving food and daily nutrition. Water was in abundance because of the over fifty rivers and streams that crisscross the island, except the southern region which experience some dry conditions part of the year. The island's indented coast made travel easy and enabled the speedy

65

extension of the colony in a north-south direction, primarily along the leeward coast. However, there were many marshes and swamps, and because of insects like the mosquito, proved very unhealthy to the early colonists who nicknamed Grenada "the grave of the West Indies."[68] The island's rumored unhealthy atmosphere was variably cited as the reason for its slow economic development.[69]

For the initial eight months the French, under Le Comte, occupied a small part of the spacious natural harbor where they established the settlement of "Grand Fort." The fort and other structures were laid out on two sides of the lagoon at the far end of a horseshoe-shaped bay and across an isthmus that separated the lagoon from the entrance to the roadstead. Fort de l'Annonciation, described by Dutertre as "made strong enough not only to withstand against the Savages, in case they had the idea to come and attack it, but also to foreign countries who would undertake to drive him [du Parquet] away"[70] (Illustration 6.4).

In outfitting the Grenada colony, du Parquet was careful to avoid many of the problems that often afflicted new settlements. This adventure was well supplied with rations for three months, despite the fact that the colonists could procure food by hunting and gathering the fruits of the island. Also, the mother colony of Martinique was only a few days sail away and could help replenish stocks if the situation warranted. Before long the colonists were producing food for themselves and tobacco to sell via Martinique.

The cordial relationship between the Island Caribs and the French colonists allowed the colony to thrive, and the French decided to expand despite the Island Caribs' initial warning that they should not occupy land beyond the present settlement. Towards the end of September 1649 fifteen new colonists, including the first European woman and her husband, arrived in Grenada from Martinique. The increased population made the living conditions at Fort de l'Annonciation "greatly cramped and uncomfortable," and after receiving permission from Governor du Parquet, the colonists established a second settlement.[71] The Beau Séjour settlement, about three and a half miles to the north of the first, was situated along the western coast and located just south of a small bay, Petit Havre. The bay probably played an important part in the area being chosen as a suitable place to locate the second settlement. The Beau Séjour settlement comprised between 20 and 22 men under the command of Le Marquis, lieutenant of the militia company of the island. The rudely constructed Fort du Maquis, situated between the Beau Séjour River and the Anse du Corps de Garde (presently Flamingo Bay), housed the settlers and afforded them some protection. Outside of the fort the French cleared land to plant subsistence crops and tobacco. This expansion was an unmistakable sign to the Island Caribs that the French intended to stay, having enlarged their colony, built structures, cleared land and begun the cultivation of crops; this was no fishing expedition!

From his years of experience du Parquet had developed a strategy for dealing with the Island Caribs and had managed to maintain a guarded coexistence with them on Martinique. He believed he could do the same on Grenada, despite the fact that the Island Caribs in the area viewed him as a threat. In settling Grenada he brought enough trade goods that he instructed Le Comte to liberally distribute to the Island Caribs "to maintain the peace."[72] As the Anonymous author asserts, "They can be won over and kept by these means and their greater god is the one who gives them the most; mostly what they need desired.... Du Parquet had known this natural habit for a long time because he was used to dealing with them, and wishing their friendship, he wanted to keep them in this way."[73] But Le Comte had not followed du Parquet's instructions and had instead "traded" the goods with the Island Caribs, which du Parquet admonished and "had it not been for some small consideration extenuating his anger, he would have dismissed Le Comte from his office."[74]

Despite all his efforts to maintain the "peace" with the Island Caribs, du Parquet and his colony at Grenada were unsuccessful. The idea of peaceful coexistence was not a reality. The Island Caribs had seen the results of the advancing European settlements in the region and if they were not proactive they would be pushed out of their remaining islands just like St. Christopher, Guadeloupe and Martinique. When the French settled Grenada in 1649, they did so by deception, deliberately choosing not to disclose to the Island Caribs their plan to establish a colony there. Instead, they fabricated the story that they were there to protect the Island Caribs from the British who were planning to attack and occupy the island, hence the fort with its cannons. The clearing of the land to plant crops was necessary for their subsistence, as was the construction of houses. The Grenada Island Caribs accepted this reasoning and probably saw the French presence as beneficial to them, especially because of the easy access to European trade goods. However, they insisted that the

French remain on the lands already cleared, "without settling anywhere else."[75] The French were all too aware that the Island Caribs would challenge their colonial expansion as they had done in the other islands if their true intentions were immediately known. A ruse like this could provide enough time to fortify the colony, which would be better able to defend itself from the Island Caribs when they decided to attack. The deception worked and for almost eight months the French colonists peacefully coexisted with the Island Caribs. Once the French established a second settlement, however, the Island Caribs took notice, especially those on the island of St. Vincent. The intention of the French colonists was clear, especially since the rumored British attack never materialized.

Grenada was important to the Island Caribs because of its location and use as a transit point between the islands and northern South America. As such, it was linked with the other Carib-occupied islands through an intricate web of relationships and possibly a loose hierarchical military structure. When the French established a second settlement on Grenada the Island Caribs became alarmed because it was an all too familiar progression. Though Governor du Parquet was "greatly feared and respected" by them, Boucher believes that his settlement of Grenada was the event "that caused the great fissure with the Island Caribs."[76] Not necessarily with some of those on Grenada who ambivalently welcomed the French presence there, but with the other groups from the neighboring islands. The French settlements on Grenada became "a nightmare to St. Vincent [Island] Caribs because of its strategic potential to impede their free passage to the [Spanish] main, [and] would long poison [Island] Carib-French relations in the southern half of the Windwards."[77]

Yet, it was quite unexpected when the French colonists came under attack from the Island Caribs in November 1649, ending the detente that had persisted throughout the first eight months of their stay.[78] The two Grenada settlements came under attack, probably initiated more so by the Island Caribs on St. Vincent than those of Grenada. The first attack, according to the Anonymous author, was carried out by Island Caribs from Grenada who, like those of St. Vincent, wanted to see the French colony destroyed. Returning to Fort de l'Annonciation after collecting water from a nearby spring across the lagoon, a group of settlers was ambushed. The surprise attack left three settlers dead from poisoned arrows, the first to die, "who had soaked with their blood the first

68

settlement of Christianity on Grenada."[79] The survivors rushed back to the settlement to warn the others who quickly armed themselves, but the fight had already shifted to the second settlement at Beau Séjour.

About 500 Island Caribs from St. Vincent arrived in Grenada in their long boats and laid siege to the vulnerable settlement at Beau Séjour. The settlers had been forewarned by Chief Duquesne, "friend of the French [who] came quickly and secretly to advise those in Fort du Marquis to stand watch and store bread, meat, water and ammunition quickly because they were to be besieged by the people of St. Vincent."[80] The attack began with a ruse to draw settlers out of the fort. Three colonists took the bait and left the fort in pursuit of a pig running along the beach, but before they could catch it they were ambushed and killed. The initial attack of arrows, though killing some and wounding others, failed to dislodge the French from within Fort du Marquis. The Island Caribs tried to smoke them out by "setting fire to dry peppers so that the wind would carry the smoke in and smother them all."[81] Unfortunately the wind carried the peppers back onto the Island Caribs. The eight-day siege of Fort de Marquis, however, forced the French "sometimes to drink their own urine to wet their tongue" so they would not die of thirst.[82] The Island Caribs finally gave up the siege and the eight French survivors quickly retreated to the protection of Fort de l'Annonciation, thus abandoning the Beau Séjour settlement. In retaliation the French attacked and burned three Island Carib villages, ironically one belonging to the "friendly" Chief Duquense, but all had been vacated because they were expecting reprisals.

The surprise attacks by the Island Caribs, following the initial period of peace, was a usual response by them to prolonged European settlements among them. The French occupation of the strategically important island of Grenada and the expansion of their settlements there triggered the attacks, but the Grenada actions were part of the larger struggle between the two groups for dominance in the region. The months preceding the Grenada attacks witnessed a number of violent strikes by the French against the Island Caribs. In May 1649 the French from Martinique attacked the Island Caribs on St. Vincent, burning houses and destroying some villages because they had supported the Island Caribs of Martinique in their fight against the French. While fishing in the Grenadines three French sailors attacked and defeated the occupants of an Island Carib long boat and raided it. The Grenada attacks were in retaliation for those by the French, and because that colony's defences were weaker than Martinique, the Island Caribs felt confident in their abilities to destroy it.

The deadly attacks against the colony were a setback for the French, but they still possessed the military advantage over the Island Caribs as was evident in their ability to withstand the initial attacks. Seeing that their attacks had failed to displace the French, the Island Caribs initiated a guerrilla war against them, eliminating lone settlers one by one. The French colony was under siege, and

> From this time on, the war, the first one and lasting only about a year, was violent and bloody between us and them, they coming even within range of a pistol shot of the Grand Fort, stealing the food and making us very uncomfortable. Imagine all those barbarians without faith, or law, or king can inflict in pain and rage, and this is what they were doing to our poor settlers entrenched in their fort, not daring to go out without 'good foot, good eye, good defense.'[83]

In May 1650 the French welcomed an opportunity to exact revenge against the Island Caribs when an Island Carib named Thomas approached Governor du Parquet with a plan to ambush a gathering of warriors. Thomas, embroiled in a personal conflict with Chief Duquesne's family, killed Duquesne's son and escaped to Martinique to avoid retaliation.[84] When he approached du Parquet, he insisted that his life was threatened because of his friendship towards the French, failing to mention the murder he had committed. With a small force from Martinique, du Parquet joined the colonists on Grenada, and on 30 May staged a night assault against an unsuspecting group of Amerindians at a secluded site where they feasted. To the rallying cry of "There is no quarter, they must die," the French opened fire on the group. In the ensuing confusion caused by the surprised attack under the cover of darkness as many as forty Island Caribs were either massacred or "jumped" to their deaths from the cliff into the sea; the hill was later called le Morne des Sauteurs: "The Hill of Jumpers."[85] The village, after all its occupants were killed or scattered, was pillaged and burned. But the French, after blaming the incident on the "ones from Martinique," sued one of the Island Carib chiefs, Captain Antoine, for peace, which he seemed amenable to.

The attack at le Morne des Sauteurs was a devastating blow to the

Island Caribs, but they soon resumed their harassment of the French, especially those at the vulnerable settlement at Beau Séjour, which had been reoccupied. The French were forced to seek shelter in their fortified houses, and the guerilla attacks resulted in the colonists being afraid to venture beyond these except in well-armed groups. The cultivation of both subsistence and export crops suffered and the colony languished into 1651. It became common for du Parquet "to dispatch a bark, sometimes two, full of sailors and soldiers, which did nothing else but sail from Martinique to Grenada and back, to supply the inhabitants and the garrison with provisions, and to bring back whatever produce they had managed to collect."[86] The violent confrontations between the French and the Island Caribs created an almost unlivable environment for the former, but to the end of 1651 there was a lull in the attacks that afforded the settlers an opportunity to strengthen the colony.

Beginning with the attacks in November 1649 the French colonists were in a constant state of siege and fear for the next decade. There were periods of peace, but a state of war—a guerrilla war that proved almost impossible to defend against—persisted. Much of the colony's energies and resources were consumed by the war against the Island Caribs which had become for them one of extermination of the enemy. It was oftentimes very bloody, resulting in numerous violent deaths on both sides. To better protect against the attacks by the Island Caribs, attempts were made to strengthen the defensive position of the colony by continuing to bring in more settlers and building more fortifications. In June 1650, right after the ambush of the Island Caribs at Sauteurs, a third fort, Fort St. Jean, was built on the heights overlooking the Rivière St. Jean (the current St. John's River) about a half of a mile north of the Grand Fort. The fort, under the command of Le Fort, comprised some seventy men.[87] Located between the other two older settlements, it was well situated to provide support to both should the call go out for assistance.

In 1652 the French settlements on Grenada, experiencing some peace, received over 100 new settlers. A failed colony at Cayenne, South America stopped at Grenada and "left some seventy people."[88] Another "forty or so" had come from Martinique on two separate trips. Conflicts among the French, however, soon created internal divisions. A quarrel led to the governor barring the missionary, Desmières, from preaching in the make-shift chapel at Fort de l'Annonciation. He was practically thrown out of the settlement, and though all were forbidden to take him in, the settlers at Beau Séjour gave him accommodation; it wouldn't be the last time that this settlement stood in opposition to the administration at Grand Fort. They constructed a chapel and Desmières said mass there.[89] A chaplain, Aleaume, arriving from Cayenne, remained in the island about six months and said mass at the Grand Fort chapel. The influx of more settlers led to the rearrangement of the colony. Le Marquis was made a captain and assumed full command of the Beau Séjour militia, and Le Roy appointed his lieutenant. La Mere replaced Le Marquis as Le Comte's lieutenant and Charles Mariage replaced Normand as the sergeant who was probably killed by the Island Caribs. Le Fort was made a major and commanded the fort at the Rivière St. Jean. Colonists continued to arrive and in 1654 some 300 survivors of the 1652 Royville expedition to Cayenne "arrive[d] then to settle there [Grenada] with great quantities of fresh goods and ammunition."[90]

An unprovoked French attack on some St. Vincent Island Caribs' canoes returning from South America caused the Island Caribs to renew their attacks against the French, beginning "a second war, much bloodier and longer lasting than the first one."[91] On 15 April 1654, hundreds of Island Caribs, primarily from St. Vincent, attacked the colonists living outside of the fortified settlements. About fourteen colonists were killed, among them leading inhabitants and their families who had settled some distance north of Beau Séjour. The Island Caribs, after attacking the settlement at Beau Séjour, "grabbed anything they thought they could use and burnt everything else within the houses, a terror that ravaged about two leagues of country already well settled."[92] The renewed conflict did not only affect Grenada, but destroyed the French colony on St. Lucia and even threatened the French control of Martinique, which was saved by the arrival of some 300 Dutch soldiers from Brazil.[93]

On 11 June 1654 the Island Caribs returned "again in a rage,... they came down to Beau Séjour where they destroyed and burnt everything, even the chapel."[94] The opportune arrival of 64 soldiers, formerly with the Dutch in Brazil, meant protection for the fledgling colony when they offered their services, which the colonists contracted for a year. The soldiers were encamped in the Cabersterre among the Island Caribs at Fort d'Esnambuc at Morne des Sauteurs, making frequent raids on Island Carib settlements.[95] In July 1654 du Parquet, realizing the opportunity the presence of the 'soldiers of fortune' provided, ordered a comprehensive assault against the Island Carib settlements situated predominantly on the eastern coast or Cabesterre. His stated intent, written in a letter to Le Comte, was to rid the island of the Island Caribs from St. Vincent whom he believed were the ones responsible for the bloody attacks against the settlers; the lives of the Island Caribs from Grenada were to be spared.[96]

Realizing the dilemma created by du Parquet's orders and unable to carry them out, Le Comte and his militia attacked the Amerindian settlements.[97] He "orders everyone they find indiscriminately passed by the sword," leaving about eighty Amerindians dead, their *cabets* burned and gardens destroyed. To prevent escape and the spread of news of the raid to St. Vincent, the French destroyed all the canoes they found.[98] Ironically, while returning from this ambush some of the French encountered a sudden storm that left nine dead, including Le Comte, the surgeon Pagre, and la Fontaine, a sergeant. It was a huge blow to the French, but the conflict of succession it unleashed caused more disruptions. Le Fort, the major and highest ranking officer, immediately took over the colony. In retaliation for the destruction of their settlements and deaths, a flotilla of canoes, with about 212 men, attacked the small fort, Fort du Mariage, and settlement at Grande Ance that had recently been established south of the Grand Fort. About six colonists were killed and "at least half a league of well settled land" destroyed.[99]

Informed of the death of Le Comte, Governor du Parquet sent Louis de Cacqueray de Valmenière, a prominent resident in Martinique, to replace him. The appointment and arrival of de Valmenière from Martinique in October 1654 unleashed a power struggle between the new governor and two prominent colonists, Major Le Fort and Captain Le Marquis. Le Fort, the second in command under Le Comte, believed that he rightfully should be appointed the new administrator and Captain Le Marquis the major. The two men, together with their supporters, retreated to their fortified residences at Beau Séjour following the arrival of de Valmenière in protest of his authority. To suppress the insurrection against his government, de Valmenière solicited the help of the hired soldiers who had recently taken up residence in Grenada. After a skirmish with Le Fort, Le Marquis and their followers, the two leaders were captured and imprisoned by de Valmenière. Du Parquet sent du Coudray, his judge from Martinique to conduct the trial, but Le Fort committed suicide "with poison innocently given by a negress," leaving Le Marquis alone to face trial for sedition.[100] Du Coudray subsequently condemned

Le Marquis to be hanged, but he appealed his sentence to the Council at Martinique, which decided to reduce the sentence to banishment and the confiscation of his possessions.[101] Though the episode was short-lived, it nonetheless created a major disruption in the colony and divided the loyalties of the settlers. It did succeed, however, in exposing the fragility of the colony. It also resulted in the deaths of a number of colonists, and the loss of two of its most prominent leaders, Le Fort and Le Marquis, who, since they arrived on the island, had been instrumental in suppressing the Island Carib resistance. The fissure likely established a precedence that was to be repeated a few years later.

While the internal power struggle occupied the energies of the entire colony until April 1655, the Island Caribs took the opportunity to stage a massive assault against Fort d'Esnambuc at Morne des Sauteurs. The October 1654 attack was carried out by about 1,000 Island Caribs, but was repulsed by the soldiers of fortune. Yet, the Island Caribs succeeded in forcing the retreat of the hired soldiers to the Grand Fort for the remainder of their stay in Grenada and the abandonment of the fort situated among their settlements.

For the first half of 1655 the French were relieved to be left alone by the Island Caribs who had curtailed their attacks, but in August two colonists were killed in an ambush and another two before the end of the year. The colony was at a low point by September when the surviving eighteen of the original sixty-four hired soldiers from Brazil left the colony after being somewhat successful in reducing the Island Carib threat, but about 72 percent of them had been killed in attacks by the Island Caribs. Governor du Parquet sent only six men as replacements, all he could spare because Martinique was also experiencing renewed attacks by the Island Caribs.

Despite the constant attacks and guerilla war against the colonists, the French colony at Grenada survived and had grown from one to three settlements or quartiers; the French added the third settlement at Grande Ance. The attacks, however, had a devastating effect on the overall progress of the colony, not least in the declining population, many of whom were killed in ambushes. Governor du Parquet continued to replenish the ranks of the colonists, sending about ninety people from Martinique and the abandoned colony of St. Lucia between March and October 1656. Yet, the situation remained precarious as Dutertre, visiting that year, states that for each grouping of about six houses, "there is a small fort of frame and a two-story dwelling... where the inhabitants of the six huts go to sleep at night to prevent them from incursions and surprises by the Savages."[102]

Unbeknownst to the Island Caribs Governor du Parquet signed a contract in October 1656 to sell Grenada to the Comte de Sérillac, but they still continued their attacks against the colonists. The French, tired of the attacks, resolved that the best way to eliminate the Amerindian threat was to take the fight to them rather than wait for their attacks or ambushes, which they had so far been unable to defend against. So in May 1657 about sixty colonists attacked two Island Carib settlements in the north of the island. The Island Caribs escaped, but their *kabays* were burned and the dwellings destroyed. The Island Caribs retaliated, but the conflict was also taking its toll on them in lives and resources. Unable to dislodge the French from Grenada the Island Caribs approached the colonists in September 1657 and sued for peace. Realizing that they did not have the resources to chase the French off the island and their own survival was now in jeopardy after so many years of bloody conflict, Captain Dubuisson led a group entreating the French who were all too eager to discuss peace. Though feigning disinterest in the peace, the French held the upper hand and insisted that all the Island Caribs of St. Vincent, Dominica and Martinique must agree otherwise they would not sanction a peace. On 21 December 1657 the Island Caribs, under Dubuisson, returned to confirm that all, Island Caribs and Galibis of the neighboring islands, were agreed on the peace, and as a token of friendship they brought "three nice [sea] turtles, a rich caret [turtle] and some lizards."[103] The French, in accepting the peace overtures, offered some trade goods and "feasted them the best we could."[104] After the celebration of peace the Island Caribs "were completely satisfied, returning with all the gladness of the world, and since they came and usually visited us with some hunt or fish, local fruits, in order to receive some gift from us. So here is a second peace with the Savages after a bloody and unpleasant four years."[105]

After seven years of colonization and the costly fight subjugating the resident Island Carib population, du Parquet, now failing in health, decided to sell the island when approached by Father Dutertre on behalf of the Comte de Sérillac.[106] According to Dutertre, concerning the colonization of Grenada, "That colony has drained the greatest part of du Parquet's wealth," and together with St. Lucia "were the two leaches that exhausted the best part of his wealth" because of the Carib-French wars and the establishment of the colonies.[107]

Though the peace held, 1658 proved to be a difficult year in the new relationship between the Island Caribs and French. It began with a quarrel between the former governor, de Valmenière, and "Chief" Dubuisson. Two slaves belonging to Dubuisson were taken by de Valmenière after they had escaped from him; de Valmenière refused to return them, claiming that they were not in his possession even though they had been seen farming his garden. The Island Caribs threatened to break the peace and take the slaves by force if they were not dealt with fairly. A second incident took place in Martinique and had far-reaching consequences. A French colonist killed Captain Nicolas and about eight Island Caribs in revenge for the killing of a group of colonists by Island Caribs. Another incident involved the capture and sale of some Island Caribs by a French colonist at Martinique. Though the Island Caribs believed these incidents were violations of the peace they had agreed to, surprisingly the peace held.

In 1659 the conflict took on a different tone and was influenced by the alliances of the Island Caribs and the various European powers. Captain Warner of Dominica, his father believed to be the former English governor of St. Christopher, seemed to owe his allegiances to the British. Though Captain Warner had expressed his friendship to the French colonists on Grenada who had given him gifts "to induce him to take care of our interests," his warriors staged an attack against the Beau Sèjour settlement in June 1659. About eight colonists were killed and their houses destroyed. Again, the Island Caribs of Grenada, who seemed to want no further confrontations with the French, sought to assure the colonists that they supported the peace. It would not be the last time that French colonists in Grenada were killed by Island Caribs, but the Grenada Island Caribs had been forced to accept the French colony and many continued to live on the island. The decade-long struggle between the Island Caribs and the French led to the latter succeeding in subjugating the Island Caribs, thus freeing them to pursue the development of Grenada as they had originally planned.

Between 1649 and 1659 at least seventy French colonists were killed by the Island Caribs, many of them in brutal attacks.[108] On average, that is almost seven colonists killed per year, representing just under ten percent of the total population arriving on the island in the first decade of its settlement.[109] Considering that diseases, overwork and accidents claimed many lives in a frontier settlement like Grenada, the deaths caused by the Island Caribs must have been an added pressure on the society; many others left the colony as well. The brutal deaths suffered at the hands of the Island Caribs served to discourage the present settlers as well as prospective colonists.[110] Within that same period the Amerindians also wrecked already settled areas, burnt houses, and destroyed gardens and crops. The colony, in the first decade, failed to grow primarily because of the conflicts with the Amerindians, though they were also preoccupied with internal strife, which would be the most consuming issue during the ownership of the Comte de Sérillac.

Illustration 1.1

Willem Blaeu's "Insulae Americanae in Oceano Septentrionali," c. 1638 map of the greater Caribbean.

Grenada and the Grenadines are identified as "Granada" and "Granadillos" respectively, with Bequia the only island in the Grenadines identified by its name.

78

Illustration 1.2

"Cynocephales" ("Dog-headed") from Lorenz Fries' *Uslegung der Mercarthen oder Carta Marina* (Strasbourg, 1525).

Depiction of Amerindians with dogs' head, seen here partaking in a cannibal feast. This view was long held in European tales of the Indies.

Illustration 1.3

Depiction of an Island Carib man and woman, from Jean-Baptiste Dutertre's *Histoire générale des Antilles, habitées par les François* (Paris, 1667-71), 2: 356.

The Island Carib man is shown with his bow and arrows, and *boutou* or war club. The Island Carib woman is carrying a basket. In the background is a papaya tree.

Illustration 1.4

Island Carib hammocks, manioc strainer (*couleuvre*) and press (*presse pour le manioc*), from Jean-Baptiste Labat's *Nouveau voyage aux isles de l'Amérique* (Paris, 1742), 2: 100.

The manioc strainer and press were used to squeeze the juice from the grated manioc or cassava before it was roasted to make cassava flour.

Illustration 1.5 Depiction of two households of Amerindians in the Caribbean and North America, from Joseph Lafitau's *Moeurs des sauvages Amériquqins...* (Paris, 1724), 2: 80.

To the top right is a partial view of a *kabay*, showing a Carib in his hammock under which is a small fire. Five women are preparing cassava bread: one grates cassava, another crushes it, a third sifts the flour through a sieve, the fourth makes cassava bread on an iron griddle, and the fifth carries wood for cooking on the fire. At the bottom are cassava and sweet potato plants. Two examples of the cassava press can be seen, one hanging from the *kabay*, and another in the foreground; used to expel the juice from the grated cassava. The other images are of the Iroquois.

Illustration 2.1

"Amerigo Vespucci leads landing craft in an attack on the natives of the island of "Ity," from Theodor de Bry's *Les Grands Voyages* (1592).

Vespucci and Alonzo de Ojeda lead their men in battle against Caribs on an unknown island in the Lesser Antilles, 1499. Many were reportedly killed and some taken hostage.

Illustration 2.2

Spanish ships (A) and Island Carib pirogues (B) meet off Grenada, c. 1614, from Nicolás de Cardona's *Descripciones geográficas e hidrográficas…, en especial del descubrimiento de la California* (1632), 28. Image possibly captures Irwin's Bay, and the St. Partick's River, not far from the present Sauteurs.

Illustration 2.3

Depiction of a "Carib attack on a settlement," from Gottfried's *Reisen.*

Published in James Rodway's *The West Indies and the Spanish Main* (London, 1896), 89.

Illustration 3.1

Depictions of Amerindians using tobacco for recreation (top) and healing (bottom). Top image from André Thevet's *Les singularitez de la France Antarctique* (Antwerp, 1558), 97; and bottom from Girolamo Benzoni's *La historia del mondo nuovo* (Venice, 1565), after 55.

Illustration 4.1

"Bouton ou massüe des Caräibes," from Jean-Baptiste Labat *Nouveau voyage aux isles de l'Amérique* (Paris, 1722), 2: 82.
The Island Carib *boutou* or war club was the primary weapon for close combat and it was often recorded as the cause of the death of French colonists. The word is still used in Grenada, meaning truncheon, stick or club used to strike someone.

5

Comte de Sérillac's Colonial Misadventures

De Sérillac was a restless sort of man who
had become imbued with the spirit of adventure.[1]

The narrative of European colonization in the Americas is filled with the misadventures of those who came in search of wealth and failed miserably in their quests. Some were over ambitious, others unprepared, and still others inspired by greed. Many had visions of grandeur, fueled by stories of those who had been successful as conquistadors, planters, privateers and pirates. The tales of the early adventurers were well known, and though a few did have stellar moments, many died before they could claim their fame or fortune. The tales of Don Antonio de Berrio and Sir Walter Raleigh and their search for the fabled El Dorado are but two well-known examples of colonial misadventures. In the case of Grenada, Jean de Faudoas, Comte de Sérillac, can only be described as one of those unfortunate men to have embarked on a colonial enterprise in the Americas, though he was rather fortunate to have only lost his financial investments and almost ten years pursuing a dream. He was also following in the footsteps of fellow countryman Philibert de Nouailly who had failed in his attempts to colonize Grenada in the mid-1640s.

In early 1655 the Comte de Sérillac approached Father Jean-Baptiste Dutertre, now living in France after sixteen years residence in the French Antilles, for "advice and assistance" on pursuing colonization in the Americas. De Sérillac "had certain plans of his own for colonizing in America for which he needed the advice and assistance of Father Dutertre."[2] The Comte de Sérillac, in his initial interaction with Dutertre used the identity of another, believing he would receive more candid information if his identity remained unknown. After discussions with de Sérillac, Dutertre concluded that his colonization plans were unrealistic and even impossible, trying his best to discourage him, but de Sérillac "had made the resolution to establish himself there [in America]."[3]

De Sérillac did not fit the typical profile of the seventeenth-century colonizer or adventurer. At the age of fifty-five years he was older than most and he had already amassed considerable wealth, and "everything seemed to be leading him in a direction of a peaceful life."[4] Colonizers like d'Esnambuc embarked upon privateering and subsequently colonization to regain lost wealth and social status; so did du Parquet and a host of others. In fact, it wasn't until 1653 when his squireship of Couteilles was made into a county and he became Comte de Sérillac, did he begin thinking about colonization and wanting to build "a fief for himself in America."[5] Latron speculates that de Sérillac "let himself be taken by the fantasy of the islands; perhaps he was fascinated by the tales of his parents or friends, one of these *cadets de famille* who had been forced, by necessity, to seek their fortunes or survival, outside of France, across the sea."[6]

After further prodding by a friend of de Sérillac's, Dutertre relented and agreed to assist de Sérillac despite his view that such an undertaking was perilous. Dutertre recalled that "In my experience I had seen the terrible difficulties that were encountered in establishing colonies in the uninhibited parts of the New World, where it was necessary to clear land, which ordinarily ruined the first entrepreneurs, or they didn't live long enough to taste the fruits of their labors."[7] As such Dutertre recommended that an island already settled would be more advantageous. In 1655 there were few islands left in the Lesser Antilles that were "unoccupied," i.e. by Europeans. There were Dominica and St. Vincent, but both were heavily populated with Amerindians, which discouraged any attempts at European settlement; Tobago was also occupied by Amerindians, but with a few Dutch settlers on and off since 1628; and du

Parquet had failed to establish a settlement on St. Lucia. In supporting the view that an already settled territory was more ideal, Dutertre suggested Grenada, it having been colonized and its "hostile" Amerindian population practically subjugated. Dutertre believed that Grenada could provide a "profit immediately from purchase and pay for the expense of buying the land and for the voyage there."[8] Purchasing Grenada at this time also presented advantages in that it was an economic burden for du Parquet who was concentrating his energies on Martinique, and its low state of development would make it relatively less costly, or so Dutertre thought.

Dutertre, having accepted to assist de Sérillac, set out on a voyage in early 1655 to locate a possible colony for the count. He arranged passage on a ship in Nantes bound for the Antilles, but it was captured, resulting in a delay of four to five months until another ship was available. Together with des Marets, de Sérillac's emissary, and his second Meline, Dutertre left Nantes on 11 July 1655, but the ship was captured by an English frigate the following day and taken to Plymouth, England. Dutertre was accused by a Huguenot pilot from Dieppe of having tried to instigate a mutiny and was interrogated at length. After some six weeks his friends were able to secure his release and he returned to France, notifying de Sérillac of his misadventure.[9] Though very discouraged because of his ordeal and personal losses, Dutertre was persuaded to make yet another attempt in the company of Jacques de Maubray who would handle the business end of the venture. So at the beginning of July 1656 the two set off for the Netherlands where they boarded a ship for the Antilles as it was a much safer route since the Dutch and British were not at war. Difficulties with bad weather forced the ship to put into port in England on two occasions, thus making the journey twelve weeks long, but they arrived safely in Martinique on 28 September 1656.

It is not clear which other islands the two visited before deciding that Grenada was the best choice, but Dutertre, in a letter to de Sérillac, admits that "we did all what you wished, we truly traveled and visited over all these islands, and we inquired with unbelievable attentions from all the most sincere, the less suspicious and the most experienced in every country where we passed over."[10] Following the conclusion that Grenada was the best choice, they approached Governor du Parquet, "and after learning he was about to decide to sell Grenada, we sailed over there [Grenada]," arriving on 14 October 1656. Two days later Dutertre and de

Maubray departed Grenada for Martinique, both convinced that it was the best choice and immediately approached du Parquet to sell. The two, after visiting the various islands

> were obliged to attach ourselves to the first bit of advice that I gave you, and de Maubray was obliged to admit that, in all America, there wasn't a deal more assured, more useful, or more hoped for, than the one we arranged; so much so that having decided between ourselves to return here [to France] without doing anything, or to bargain for Grenada.[11]

After negotiations with de Maubray, du Parquet agreed to sell Grenada and the Grenadines to the Comte de Sérillac.

The initial contract, signed by de Maubray on behalf of de Sérillac on 30 October 1656 in Martinique, was very extensive, covering many aspects of the handover and the properties de Sérillac was purchasing.[12] Some of the important points included the ceding of all rights and ownership of the islands to de Sérillac; the terms of the payment of 30,000 *écus* or 90,000 *"livre tournois"* (45,000 l.t. of which had to be paid no later than the following feast of All Saints' Day, another 30,000 l.t. one year after taking possession, and the remaining 15,000 l.t. six months after the 2nd payment); the transfer of du Parquet's title of lieutenant general of the king, should the king consent to it; the transfer of all properties belonging to du Parquet, including slaves, indentured servants (*engagés*), buildings, fortifications and munitions; and the establishment of the ownership of land already granted by du Parquet to the inhabitants and the Church.[13]

In his letter to de Sérillac written following his return to Europe in January 1657, Dutertre writes glowingly of Grenada and the many qualities that made it suitable for de Sérillac: numerous streams thus ample supply of water, plentiful supply of game and fish, a large natural harbor, an excellent fort, and the population of 300 who will be happy to welcome the new governor.[14] He explains the negotiations involved in the transaction, crediting de Maubray's skill in achieving the good terms of the sale since du Parquet had at first insisted on 100,000 l.t., and was not initially willing to accept rent, IOUs, or a lease. He assured de Sérillac that "the high cost should not surprise you, as I am allowed to assure you that if you believe the council of your friends, you will not only do a very notable business, but before three or four years, you will get in addition to the principal ten times as much as you have put."[15]

The Anonymous author disputes Dutertre's report on the visit and sale, and describes the entire transaction by de Maubray as deceptive, meant to defraud de Sérillac. De Maubray is described as a Scotsman, "knight and baron of Barabouquil," and is harshly criticized when the Anonymous author asks, "Why then always trust rather in foreign people, the more the Scot ones? Here is the misfortune of most of our persons of high rank to look for such men, rather than those of their own nation."[16] Interestingly, the Anonymous author fails to mention Father Dutertre's role in the entire affair, probably choosing not to implicate a fellow Dominican priest in what he views as fraud. The Anonymous author continues that "everybody was of the sense, even the most attached to the service and the interest of the Lord General [du Parquet], that the price was too high. They believed that the cause was "the trick of the stick," that some suppose having been pushed up to twenty thousand [l.t.], some others to ten, the most moderate to four with his lieutenant of Martinique."[17] The Anonymous author also questions the rather quick appraisal of the island carried out by de Maubray and Dutertre, the latter claiming that "we sailed over there and have visited it nearly everywhere, as well as the Grenadines..."[18] The Anonymous author contends that de Maubray "managed like those whimsical men who judge the wine according to its color, and those giddy lovers who get married unexpectedly."[19] They made trips to the Point des Salines and to sound the cul-de-sac (possibly the harbor), without enquiring seriously of anyone the advantages and disadvantages of colonizing the island.

In 1650 du Parquet had purchased three fairly large islands, namely Martinique, St. Lucia, and Grenada and the Grenadines, the latter a group of small islands and islets linking Grenada to St. Vincent in a chain, for a total of 41,500 l.t. Six years later Grenada and the Grenadines were sold for over twice that amount, though it was quite evident that du Parquet had already put resources into the island and, as he claimed, "was starting to cull the fruits that he had planted on Grenada, and that he was advised by Captain Baillardet that there was pearl fishing on a reef connected to the island [of Carriacou]."[20] Boucher described the price as exorbitant, agreeing with the Anonymous author.[21] Whether or not Grenada and the Grenadines were worth the 90,000 l.t. may be a point of debate, but de Sérillac was now the owner and part of his dream of becoming a lieutenant general of the king was a reality. So on 4 May 1657 de Sérillac was named governor of Grenada, and on 11 June 1657 he confirmed the contract in Paris in the presence of notaries and du Parquet's representative, and made the deposit of the 45,000 l.t.; the contract was ratified on 27 August 1657.

Since approaching Dutertre in early 1655 for assistance, it had taken over two-and-a-half years to finally find a suitable colony and sign a contract to take possession. The mission had been fraught with difficulties from the beginning, but they were only harbingers of what were to come for de Sérillac as he began his misadventures. Dutertre recalled that de Sérillac had "already warned me of all the horrible difficulties that he encountered in all of his enterprises, but that he didn't let this deter him from overcoming them and succeeding."[22]

After confirming the contract in June 1657 de Sérillac began the preparations to establish his colony in Grenada. His plan was to outfit three ships, two to carry the colonists and himself to Grenada, and the third, a small flyboat, to sail to the coast of Guinea, West Africa and purchase about 100 slaves.[23] The total cost of the three ships and provisioning the voyage to Grenada was 16,000 "francs." The ships were to be readied by early October 1657 since de Sérillac had to take possession by 27 December 1657 so as not to incur additional expenses associated with maintaining his indentured servants and slaves already on the island.

At the end of August de Sérillac and his contingent of about 300 men, including two of his sons, arrived at Havre de Grâce where the ships were being readied. The ships not being ready, de Sérillac and his party were forced to wait, the majority of them living on two tenders at the expense of Captain Pape, the ship's owner. De Sérillac and some colonists were housed at the port of Honfleur, a short distance away. According to Dutertre who was also making the journey, the accommodations "produced suffering more than they would have in three Atlantic crossings."[24] Dutertre continues that the colonists "ran out of money and were forced to sell some of their cloths in order to eat. They were so malnourished that half of them would have died before reaching the islands if we had continued the journey."[25] Having to pay for the accommodations of the colonists, the ship's owner finally announced that the expedition would depart and the 400-ton *St. Antoine* left port only to wreck after sailing about a league or three and a half miles. Dutertre believes that the ship's owner had no intention of leaving, having complained that he had not been paid enough and had the pilot, his son, purposefully wrecked the ship. The ship was brought back to port to be repaired, further delaying the journey by a month, at de Sérillac's expense. Dutertre insists that had de Sérillac taken his advice and used the merchants he had contacted they would not have had these difficulties.

A second attempt was made in early December 1657 when the ship left port in inclement weather. Though warned against beginning the journey in the bad weather, de Sérillac refused, seeing this as another delay he could ill afford. The storm worsened and for three days the ship was battered by it, Dutertre describing the catastrophe thus:

> I have never seen anything so pitiful, men falling on one another, cannons that weren't adequately tied down rolling about, people crying out that they were drowning…, the confusion was so terrible that one couldn't recognize a thing. Such was the horror of the night that some of the passengers confessed all of their sins.[26]

The storm left between fifteen and twenty people dead who, according to Dutertre, were thrown overboard for a quick burial. On the third day, 6 December, the ship ran aground at Portsmouth, England. The expedition was all but wrecked as "some deserted," including one of de Sérillac's sons, but he was later apprehended. De Sérillac left the survivors of the ill-fated expedition at Portsmouth while he went to London and sued the captain of the ship before the British Admiralty Court.[27] Left to fend for themselves, many of the 160 colonists left, including Dutertre who made his way back to France and abandoned his mission to Grenada.[28] It would be four more months before de Sérillac was able to regroup after feeling betrayed by his trusted associates, and send out a much smaller expedition to take possession of Grenada. De Sérillac himself decided not to make the trip and sent in his place François du Bu, along with some seventy men, to continue the journey.[29]

Before the departure of François du Bu and the others to take possession of Grenada, de Sérillac wrote four letters, one to du Parquet, a second giving authority to du Bu to represent him, and two with instructions for du Bu that outlined the plan for the colony until his arrival with additional colonists and supplies.[30] The first letter, written on 10 April 1658, was addressed to Governor du Parquet and told of his failed attempts to sail to Grenada and his current situation. Another letter, written on 15 April 1658, appointed du Bu to command the colony at Grenada; he was given the authority "to govern it during our absence and order every useful action, for the utility of our settlement there, enjoining everyone to comply with his orders as it would be to our person." In the event of du Bu's death Bonnebourg, the captain of the guards, would take command.[31] With his letters of introduction, authority and instructions, du Bu and the colonists left England on 25 April 1658. The appropriately named ship *The Hope* sailed to Barbados, from where the party would take a second ship to Martinique. On 8 June *The Hope* arrived in Barbados and after a fifteen-day stay the party proceeded to Martinique, landing there on 25 June 1658. While staying in Barbados, du Bu met with acting Governor Daniel Searle, who among other things, shared some advice with du Bu on governing a colony, counsel that he seemed to have disregarded once he arrived at Grenada.[32]

Following his arrival du Bu immediately presented his credentials to Madame du Parquet, Governor du Parquet having died in January 1658. De Sérillac had hoped that du Bu would be given permission to take his men to Grenada and assume command of the islands without taking possession, more as a forerunner party to prepare for the eventual arrival of de Sérillac. The implication of this seemingly minor detail meant that the financial obligations of the contract would not be put into effect and de Sérillac would not have to make the second payment of 30,000 l.t. upon possession, but at some later date while his lieutenant embarked on his colonization plans. Madame du Parquet would have none of it, and informed du Bu that if official possession was not taken he could not go to Grenada and establish himself there. He tried to persuade her otherwise by insisting that he did not have the authority to proceed until further word from de Sérillac. His request to remain in Martinique until further word from de Sérillac was granted by Madame du Parquet, but a number of officials advised that he should take possession as he might see his party desert him for prospects in the French Antilles. Du Bu subsequently produced the letter by de Sérillac which was accepted as giving him authority to take possession of the islands. In an official handing over ceremony in Martinique on 1 July 1658 du Bu, in the presence of Madame du Parquet, was granted command and control over Grenada and the Grenadines. Officials from Martinique accompanied du Bu to Grenada, landing there on the morning of 7 July 1658.

On 8 July 1658 the over 350 inhabitants on Grenada, including the new arrivals, gathered to witness the transfer of the colony from the du Parquet family to the Comte de Sérillac's deputy, François du Bu. As part of the ceremony, the then Governor de Valmenière tendered his resignation as per his instructions from Madame du Parquet. François Rolle de Laubière, judge at Martinique and guardian of du Parquet's sons, led those gathered to the shore where he "struck the seawater with the flat hand and returning to the church, took some holy water, crossed himself, knelt down in front of the high alter, lifted the sheet and kissed it…."[33] The contract, de Sérillac's letter authorizing du Bu to take command in his name, and the handover from Martinique were read to everyone. In front of Fort de l'Annonciation, de Valmenière ordered the inhabitants and militia "to acknowledge the said Comte de Sérillac as lord owner of the said Grenada island and the Grenadines, and governor on account of the King, and the said du Bu as his lieutenant being well empowered to take command in his nascence and to swear to the said du Bu to the said name the oath of loyalty."[34] De Valmenière handed over the keys to the fort to du Bu, officially handing over command of Grenada to de Sérillac. Du Bu took control of the inventoried properties and the leading inhabitants and officials from Martinique signed the act of possession.[35]

Though the officials at Martinique and du Bu had accepted that de Sérillac had provided written authority to allow du Bu to take possession, the Anonymous author vehemently denounced the possession as illegal.[36] He believed that since the "hold of possession" was not specifically mentioned in the letters given to du Bu, de Sérillac did not intend such to take place. He cited a passage in one of the letters that all had agreed granted authority for possession: "If something is omitted in this memoir and others, you shall eke out the missing and you shall do your best in everything, empowering you for all."[37] De Sérillac had instructed du Bu and the party to remain in Martinique if du Parquet did not allow them to go to Grenada without possession and await his arrival. The act of possession was seen as being in the interest of the du Parquet family who wanted to be rid of a burden and set the remaining payments in motion, and du Bu who wanted to take control for his own personal gain. The Anonymous author discounts the cost of remaining in Martinique as an excuse and reads into du Bu's actions sinister deeds because he is writing with knowledge of the future in which he played a pivotal role. However, it is almost certain that de Sérillac did not have a problem with immediate possession other than to not initiate the final payments.

Once the ceremonies were over du Bu had specific tasks he had to accomplish to prepare the colony for de Sérillac and establish his command as outlined in de Sérillac's letters. As the second in command he named des Merets as the major, a trusted associate of de Sérillac who had accompanied Father Dutertre on his first failed attempt to the Antilles. Du Bu divided the colony into two quartiers or administrative districts and designated the officers of each of the two militia companies. For the district of Beau Séjour he named du Tot the lieutenant, Fiacre Tané as the sergeant, and Charles Tellier as corporal. For the district of Grande Ance he named Henry Cuperoy as lieutenant, François Roussan as the sergeant, and Hector Le Frant as the corporal. It is not clear what the boundaries of the districts were and whether or not the primary settlement around the port was part of either or on its own. Du Bu appointed himself the only judge who presided over all criminal and non-criminal cases, "and wanted to be alone as judge, lawyer and prosecutor, and registrar and notary and sergeant, and party and witness."[38]

François du Bu was a nobleman from Le Mans, France, a knight and lord of Coussé. When he commanded the group of colonists to take possession of Grenada in 1658 he was about thirty-eight years of age. He was a trusted associate of de Sérillac and highly recommended by him for the position as his lieutenant general: "to all who will have the right after taking the perfect knowledge we have of the loyalty and experience as regards to the arms of Sieur du Bu."[39] Dutertre encountered him when he accompanied the failed attempts to sail to Grenada in 1657, but said nothing of him or his character. Who he was remains a mystery, but the events that unfolded in Grenada under his command and his subsequent execution at the hands of some of his fellow colonists are well documented. That account provides a very detailed picture of the governor, but because it is almost certainly written by someone who "perhaps instigated" the revolt against du Bu, it presents a number of problems.

Father Bénigne Bresson, a Dominican priest resident in Grenada between 1656 and 1659, is the believed anonymous author of the manuscript.[40] According to Roget in his introduction to the anonymous manuscript, "He [the author] has written here, in great haste, a text obviously meant to justify those who were accused of murdering du Bu, local deputy of the new lord of Grenada, who had revealed himself to be an absolute tyrant. However, he [the author] had not been satisfied with the usual plea for mercy; using older settlers, his friends, as witnesses, he gives us a rich and precise chronicle of the little known beginnings of one of the small French Caribbean islands."[41] Though the details of the island's history by Bresson are taken as accurate, his view of du Bu most probably contains some bias and should be treated delicately when used to create the picture of the events concerning the rule of du Bu.

In appointing du Bu his deputy, de Sérillac outlined his expectations of the tasks until he arrived. Du Bu's primary duty was in preparing the colony for de Sérillac and some 600 colonists he planned to bring when he was finally able to make the journey from France. Du Bu was to plant a number of crops so that the colonists would have enough food to eat upon their arrival. The Anonymous author comments on the progress or lack thereof of du Bu's task: "It would be to believe that it is on accord of this project [his own agenda] that he left fallow the land of the fort to return to their first state, after having taken away all the provisions and never having planted new ones."[42] Du Bu also had to construct dwellings for the colonists who accompanied him which were probably completed by the individuals themselves. And once the 100 slaves de Sérillac had purchased had arrived from Africa, du Bu was to put them to work; de Sérillac was unaware that the slave ship he had sent to West Africa had sunk on its way back, killing all on board.[43]

One of the first problems du Bu confronted was a situation between the former governor and the resident Island Caribs who accused de Valmenière of stealing two of their slaves. It was a delicate situation because the Island Caribs threatened to disrupt the peace that had been in effect for about a year and a half if the abducted slaves were not returned. In early 1658 the slaves had escaped from the Capesterre and were found by a party of French colonists out hunting. De Valmenière claimed the slaves for himself and put them to work on his farm. The Island Caribs, observing the slaves at work, demanded their return, but de Valmenière refused, insisting that he did not have them. He, however, decided to generously compensate the owners for their loss. The refusal of de Valmenière was such a contentious issue between himself and Father Bresson that it led to a political disruption in the colony. When du Bu took over Father Bresson was asked about the incident and suggested that de Valmenière was in the wrong and should return the slaves, believing that his dishonesty could lead to the resumption of war with the Island Caribs and not in the best interest of de Sérillac. Du Bu disagreed with Father Bresson and sided with former Governor de Valmenière, and retaliated against Father Bresson by not allowing him to say mass at the chapel. Thus began the estrangement between du Bu and Father Bresson that would eventually lead to the latter conspiring to remove du Bu from office.

The Anonymous author, writing in hindsight, describes the handing over of command of Grenada to du Bu, which he viewed as illegal, as an "unhappy day, when the intent got the better of the duty, the passion of the reason, the ambition of the justice, the perfidy of the loyalty, and the iniquity of all laws and all orders."[44] The Anonymous author claims that as soon as du Bu was installed, he began with his tricks, debauchery and illegal activities. For the next year and a half the island was plagued with political intrigue. Du Bu exercised his authority quite harshly and some colonists left for other French territories in the region, particularly Martinique.[45] He also circulated "talks of a possible conspiracy," stemming from the Island Carib-French conflict in Martinique which soon became a "convenient excuse to exile [from Grenada] anyone he didn't like."[46]

Since there is only one eyewitness account of the events that took place on the island during du Bu's time in office, it is difficult to weigh the complete accuracy of the information presented by the Anonymous author against du Bu. It would appear that within the first six months on the island, du Bu clashed with many of the inhabitants, some of whom he once had close ties. It was not too long before some of the colonists accused du Bu of having committed numerous crimes, including blasphemy, insulting the King, disloyalty towards his employer de Sérillac, tyranny over the people, and violation of the human and divine laws.[47] Of these, the worst crimes he was accused of seem to have been the making of counterfeit coinage, adultery, rape, and plotting to poison de Sérillac upon his arrival in Grenada.

It is not exactly clear when du Bu and some of the colonists clashed, but within the first six months he definitely moved against those he considered his enemies, including some of the original settlers, "gentlemen" who had accompanied him from France, and even the Dominican priest, Father Bresson.[48] A number of colonists complained about du Bu's activities and behavior, and he soon initiated actions against them. As the highest authority on the island, du Bu promulgated an act in mid-December 1658 against three of the notable colonists, two of whom had traveled with him to Grenada. The charge against the three (de Mouchet, Knight of St. Marc, de la Jussaye and Jean Blanchard) was that they were planning to have him killed at the home of du Tot, the lieutenant of the militia company at Beau Séjour. Following inquiries, du Bu banished de Mouchet because, according to the Anonymous author, "it was he who gave him the most umbrage and was more to be feared."[49] De Mouchet—who had been elevated to nobility by du Bu though he had no authority to do so—left the island on 2 January 1659. The charges against the other two gentlemen, both sons-in-law of de Mouchet, were subsequently dropped. The Anonymous author contends that accusations were no more than "a few complaints made in the liberty of their private conversations, some words said by detestation of such a damnable behavior [of du Bu]."[50] He was also angered by the charge, claiming that de Mouchet, "this generous knight, had stood firmly for the interests of de Sérillac," which was why he was persecuted by du Bu who "wanted to get rid of him so that he wouldn't be watched so closely and with such eyes and in order to cover his project he had to proceed by feint of justice."[51]

The litany of crimes du Bu was accused of characterized him as a tyrannical ruler, possibly exhibiting psychological pathology; he is practically portrayed as a madman.[52] It may have started with his adulterous behavior with the wives of his fellow colonists that created dissension among the inhabitants. Not only was he publicly having sexual liaisons with married women, he was further accused of a sexual relationship with a nine year old who was brought to him by her mother. But his sexual depravity achieved a new low when "his brutality led him one day in the country to violate by force a young girl he met on the way. This poor child went all bleeding, as she could and fully weeping towards her father."[53] The Anonymous author accused du Bu of operating adultery and prostitution in the fort of the King. Father Bresson seemed to come in for some of the harshest treatment because he confronted du Bu about his actions, beginning with the du Bu's support for de Valmenière against the Island Caribs.

The situation with the Island Caribs on Grenada seemed to have remained calm, but conflicts on Martinique reverberated throughout the region in mid-1659. The murder of Captain Nicholas and a number of Island Caribs on Martinique spilled over in Grenada when "Indian" Warner, leading a force of Island Caribs from Dominica, attacked settlers in the Beau Sèjour area. The colonists had entertained "Indian" Warner, showering him with gifts and respect "as to maintain the peace… [and] induce him to take care of our interests… Nevertheless, traitor as he was," Warner gave orders to his men to attack Grenada.[54] The Anonymous author seemed to reserve most of his anger for du Bu because he charged that he was aware of the impending attack by "Indian" Warner and did nothing to stop it. He goes on to accuse him of collusion with "Indian" Warner because he refused the colonists' many pleas for assistance, resulting in the deaths of eight colonists, destruction of the Beau Sèjour settlement, and the escape of the enemy. When du Bu finally showed up at the settlement "he said that they [those who died] were not people who could be of good use for the colony, nor people from whom good services could be received."[55] The Anonymous author continues: "What a comfort, please and from that who supposed that he would go hand in hand with our enemy, treason from his point and felony in all his behavior."[56] It was even suggested that du Bu "had sold for that price [of fifty pounds] the booty of this quarter which stately got used and blossomed more than all others of the island."[57]

Though du Bu's "brutal manners" forced many settlers to leave, a small group, evidently with strong support among the colonists, took matters into their own hands. As the Anonymous author notes, "Let us see now the fall [of 1659], which is not exempt of misfortune, although it was an action of justice, the most heroic and courageous among all those they happened in the islands. As Sieur du Bu went on with his hateful way of life, the justice of God followed him step by step and suddenly pounced on his criminal head, like the lightening on the top of a rock."[58] It is not clear when the colonists began planning the revolt against du Bu and who actually instigated it, but "Many of his colony who were deeply recommended to him by the Sieur Comte de Cerillat as his own children are dead by refusal of some assistance which could be given only by himself; others did nothing else than languish a long time on account of his cruelty; and others are gone as they could no more endure without some humanness."[59]

Yet, it is evident that Father Bresson played an organizing role in the conspiracy and was very aware of the intricate details of the plot; he often used "we" when speaking of the perpetrators. Though many of the colonists who had had conflicts with du Bu had left the island or were forced to leave, quite a few remained who had serious grievances against him. Among those who remained were Jean Blanchard, de la Jussaye and Dominique de la Bedade who must have played a prominent role in the conspiracy as two of them were later charged as ringleaders in the plot against du Bu. They surely had much to gain in getting rid of du Bu. The Anonymous author does not identify any by name who were instrumental in the plot, but the ones who had been wronged by du Bu seemed to be many. The continuing deterioration in the administration of the colony seemed to have brought together the colonist against du Bu. The Anonymous author does describe them in rather heroic terms:

> The most courageous of them considering the disorders in the past, riveting his eyes on the present ones, and forecasting those which would no doubt come, if they soon would not oppose to this havoc, preventing them by a constant liberality, having compassion on so many inhabitants who unceasingly grumbled of their hearts in the bitterness, and were afflicted at their wretchedness which at each time grow more unbearable, gives secretly notice to the boldest who decide between them to catch him and banish him from Grenada as a despicable blasphemer, a perfidious against the King and his landlord, a public concubinary, a tyrant of the people, the plague of the island and the shame of nature.[60]

The Anonymous author describes the leader of the plot as "this gallant being [who] secured as many men he needed for the execution of such a courageous project...." The plan was simple. On the morning of Sunday 28 October 1659, "Those of the project then came early in the morning to the fort under the pretext to attend the mass, so covering their approach with the mantle of piety, also with a heart full of piety, as it is justice."[61] The mass began with du Bu in attendance, though the Anonymous author claims that "he was warned by one of his good girlfriends, but he was convinced that nobody would ever put their hands on him."[62] The usual ringing of the church bell during the offering of the sacraments would be the signal to seize the fort which was accomplished "without any noise nor opposition."[63]

They would then fire a cannon shot to let all know that they had succeeded and to be prepared for the final undertaking. The firing of the cannon caused du Bu to leave the church to ascertain the cause. While the others remained in the church to receive the sacraments, he ventured out alone and was ordered by four sentries to halt. He pulled a gun and fired, but missed as the sentries pounced on him and disarmed him. As per the plan he "was seized by the strongest of them previously put as sentries, and from here put in chains, then they would seize his trunks and papers, examine in a process what profit he made, and sentence would be drawn up about the grievances of which he would be charged and convicted."[64] The anonymous manuscript abruptly ends and the author leaves it to the imagination the conclusion of the events.

To complete the story it is necessary to turn to other sources for the details. Dutertre, however, has very little to say except, "I do not know how [du Bu] conducted himself there, nor of the crimes of which he was accused, but the inhabitants served a warrant on him and he was taken by force of arms."[65] According to Jean-Baptiste Labat, the court established by the colonists to try du Bu comprised "humble folk, so to speak the rabble of the island," among whom only one man, referred to as Archangeli, could write. Dominique de la Bedade, who had performed the office of clerk since March 1649, signed the document "Mark of M. de la Brie, council for the court."[66] It would appear that the person who prosecuted the case was a blacksmith, who, instead of a signature, sealed the court's decision with the stamp of a horseshoe. Labat definitely seemed to be very critical of the leaders of the revolt against du Bu, almost deploring their act of defiance against the established authority, despite their greviences.

The plan of the colonists may have been to banish du Bu following a trial. The plotters wanted to make sure that a sense of justice prevailed in du Bu's conviction as opposed to the supposed injustice he presided over. The colonists probably realized that banishing du Bu could present problems for the colony in that he might return, or get revenge on his accusers. Gathering evidence from du Bu's belongings, a formal trial was convened, following which, it was decided that du Bu should be executed for his many and serious crimes. Maybe his crimes were judged too many and too heinous to allow him to go free. According to Labat, du Bu was condemned to be hanged, but he pleaded that as a gentleman he should be beheaded. He was instead shot since the executioner was not adept at beheading.[67]

The French Crown, on learning of the civil unrest, reportedly sent a military ship with a police chief and troops to restore order, and established a commission of enquiry to punish those guilty of du Bu's execution. Following the investigation the police chief decided against punishing most of those involved after realizing that they were "only poor wretches." He did, however, banish the clerk and notary,

Dominique de la Bedade, from the island because of his very public role in the trial and execution of du Bu.[68] Labat continues the tale of Archangeli, a name he may have received for his leading role in the revolt. According to Labat, de la Belade ended up on the island of Marie Galante where he lived until the British invaded the island in 1692. Supposedly, he revealed to the British where the French governor was hiding, but the British nonetheless hanged him and his two children outside the church because of his treachery. Labat seems to relish the result, insisting that it was the secret wish of God and implied that he had finally paid for his crime.[69]

Meanwhile, the Comte de Sérillac was determined in his efforts to realize his dream of colonial greatness in the Americas. After his two failed attempts in 1657, he made another attempt on 14 April 1658. Together with twenty others, de Sérillac left Dieppe and made what probably seemed to be the innumerable attempt to reach Grenada. On 27 April their ship was attacked by a Portuguese frigate and forced to surrender and taken to St. Sebastian, arriving there on 21 May. De Sérillac was released "as the peace was promulgated," arriving in Bayonne on 1 June. He must have been beside himself, but the Anonymous author describes him as a man of strong character:

> As if God had permitted it just to give him the opportunity to triumph with more glory over the bad fortune; he asserted that he shall hire another more brighter and more magnificent crew and promised for himself thanks be to God a success all the more complete so as the previous ones were so unfortunate. What a nice vision this strong courage which rises up over all those events that ruined so badly all his hopes.[70]

Dutertre was incorrect in stating that "Monsieur de Sérillac went there in 1658 after having again undergone inconceivable misfortunes of which I am insufficiently [acquainted] and I would rather say nothing more for fear that I would be mistaken."[71] Thus, had de Sérillac been successful on this attempt he might have been able to alter the disastrous path on which the island was headed, but his luck failed him again, as well as that of du Bu.

The journey that finally brought de Sérillac to Grenada for the first time was uneventful, reaching the island in December 1660; over three years since purchasing the islands. Traveling with the Comte de Sérillac were two of his sons and "his gentleman's gentleman, d'Esturais."[72] It was over a year since the execution of du Bu and it is unclear what the status of the colony was when de Sérillac arrived. One of his first actions was the establishment of the "Chambre criminelle de la Grenade" to try a number of individuals for "the crime of felony, sedition, revolt and rebellion" against the King and his authority.[73] Two colonists, Jean Blanchard and Dominique de la Bedade, who figured prominently in the events as described in the Anonymous manuscript, were tried and found guilty of the "crimes of felonies, mutinies, revolts and rebellions while in the service of the King and against his authority, attempt against his person, [and] disturbing the peace."[74] Both were apparently condemned to death, but there is no evidence that they were at the trial which convicted them. Labat indicates that de la Belade was banished from Grenada by a French official probably in 1659, and Jean Blanchard was listed on the 1680 Marie Galante census, so he too must have left Grenada around the same time.

The Comte de Sérillac remained in Grenada until August 1662 probably trying to see what he could salvage, but the political and social climate only became worse. De Sérillac had invested thousands of *livres* into a colony Dutertre had assured him would be able to produce a return within four years, but his affairs had gone badly since making the arrangements to buy the island in 1656 and had received little returns to date. Within the first four years of the colony there was no progress made and de Sérillac only experienced losses. On 29 July 1662 he dictated his last will and testament to the new notary and clerk of the court of Grenada, Pierre de l'Isle, and sailed for France shortly afterwards.[75] He left his two sons behind, appointing Jean III as lieutenant general and d'Esturais as his deputy. Probably to recover some of his debts and his authority over the remaining colonists, his sons exerted a iron grip on the colony to the detriment of the island's political and social stability, if there was any left.

The colony of Grenada had gone from bad to worse, both economically and politically. With the departure of many of the colonists, agriculture suffered, and the struggling colony floundered. De Sérillac had many plans for his new colony, one of which was the importation of slaves from Africa to expand the cultivation of the island. Like many of his other plans, that too failed, but it was probably one of the earliest attempts to import slaves through a French merchant. Interestingly, de

Sérillac had not followed through with the final payments owed to the du Parquet estate as per the 1657 agreement. It is possible that he was unable to make the final payments because of the difficulties he had had with establishing the colony; his attempts to reach Grenada in 1657 and 1658 had proved costly. According to the agreement the final payment should have been completed no later than January 1660. Not receiving the payments the du Parquet estate sued de Sérillac, but in 1661 lawyers for both parties came to "an amicable settlement" over the remaining payments owed to the du Parquet family.

After fifteen years of colonization Grenada had made little progress. Its population, totaling about 350 in 1657, had dwindled to about 150, with most of the prominent planters having left in disgust for Martinique and Marie Galante during the political upheaval between 1658 and 1659 and the subsequent governorship of de Sérillac and his sons.[76] Dutertre adds that had not Prouville de Tracy and the Compagnie des Indies occidentales françaises (French West India Company) given the colonists assurances "they would certainly have deserted [the island by 1664]."[77]

Eventually, the French Crown, desiring to pursue empire building, decided it needed colonies. In 1664 Jean-Baptiste Colbert, in an attempt to take away the trade of the French West Indies from the Dutch, established the Compagnie des Indies occidentales françaises that was to administer all French territories in the Americas. To accomplish this, the government forced the private proprietors to sell their colonies to the company, and de Sérillac was ordered to give up Grenada and the Grenadines.

6

A Tenuously Held Colony

Some believed Grenada could be transformed into a base to attack the Dutch at Curaçao, [but] Governor-General Phélypeaux viewed it as fit only for indigo.[1]

After fifteen turbulent years of proprietary rule Grenada remained a tenuously held French outpost. Its distance from the other French colonies in the Caribbean isolated it to the periphery of an economic, military and social center located over 150 nautical miles north at Guadeloupe and St. Christopher, and particularly Martinique, its administrative center.[2] With a population of roughly 150 colonists in 1664, scattered among a few settlements along the western coast, the colony struggled desperately to survive. The colonists were described as miserable, and those who chose to stay were on the verge of starvation, forced to survive on hunting and fishing. Proprietary rule had failed to provide the resources and leadership necessary to alter this frontier settlement, leaving it little changed from when the French first arrived in 1649.[3] The Island Caribs in the neighboring islands of St. Vincent and Dominica, who had posed a serious threat to the French from the beginning, continued to resist the French colonial expansion despite the subjugation of the resident Amerindian population. It was within this downward economic, political and social spiral that the Compagnie des

Indes occidentales françaises (French West India Company) stepped in to reorganize the administration of the French islands in the Caribbean under a Crown-sanctioned charter company.

Compagnie des Indes Occidentales Françaises

It was obvious to many, including the French Crown, that France was the owner of Caribbean colonies in name only since they benefited little from commerce with them. It was the Dutch, long established in the region, who controlled the trade of the French Antilles. One estimate was that the Dutch "employed 200 ships and 6,000 seamen" with revenues amounting to "two million *livres* of sugar and one million of cotton, tobacco and indigo, all of which they took to France."[4] One observer warned that "if one continues to abandon this commerce to the Dutch, these colonies, which have cost the lives of so many Frenchmen to establish, will, to the disgrace of the nation, be lost forever."[5] Between 1660 and 1663 a number of reports were published supporting colonial trade and how French commerce might establish itself in the region.

By the early 1660s a plan to establish a company to take control of French colonies in the region was taking shape. The primary objective was to displace the Dutch who controled the regional trade. Since the mid-1600s when the bankrupt Compagnie des Iles de l'Amérique sold off its assets to their respective governors, the Crown and French merchants had reaped little in profits or revenues from trade. The prevailing French economic view of the time was that colonies should be for the benefit of the mother country, primarily through taxes and trade, which was minimal between France and its American colonies. Another important reason for the proposed takeover was the deteriorating economic and political conditions in the French islands under proprietary rule; Grenada was a perfect example of this failure. Colonists, particularly planters, complained of the harsh and exploitative rule of the colonies' owners. These conditions coincided with the ascendancy of Louis XIV as the king of France and an emerging French nationalism, with a strong desire to rebuild, or rather create a French colonial empire in the Americas.

The Compagnie des Indes occidentales françaises was a stock company, with investors including the French king, government officials and other influential citizens; Chief Minister Jean-Baptiste Colbert was the primary policy maker. It embarked on achieving the impossible, wrenching the commerce of its colonies from the Dutch, which it was not in a position to do, financially or otherwise. Yet, by establishing the monopolistic company, the French embarked wholeheartedly along this path. Before the king had signed the documents creating the company in May 1664, Colbert had organized an expedition under the command of Alexandre Prouville de Tracy to sail to the islands and impose company rule. The company took over physical ownership of all French territories in the Americas, with exclusive rights to trade with those colonies as well as a monopoly on the almost non-existent French slave trade. Its objective was to secure French territories in the Americas, consolidate the administration of these disparate territories, and displace foreign traders in the French Caribbean, particularly the Dutch.[6] Colbert hoped that the transfer of the French Antilles "into the hands of a strong company, which would be able to equip a number of vessels in order to colonize and furnish them with all the merchandise of which they had need," extending French trade and thereby commercial benefits to France.[7] In effect, this would help France to establish the base for a colonial empire.

In June 1664 de Tracy arrived in Martinique to establish company rule in the Americas. For the next few months he was occupied with the many problems he encountered in Martinique, Guadeloupe, and the other French islands in the northern *Iles du Vent* (Windward Islands). Far removed from these islands and of little economic importance at the time, Grenada did not receive immediate attention even though its situation was dreadful after years of ineffectual rule. Reports reached de Tracy that the colonists at Grenada were discouraged with their current situation and many were prepared to abandon the island for Martinique or Guadeloupe. To persuade the colonists to remain in Grenada, he sent assurances that he would travel there by the first of October 1664. The date having passed, the "abandoned and miserable" colonists

> composed a request which contained their complaints against [de Sérillac] and his sons, the details of which were so lengthy and odious; and it suffices to say that de Tracy was so touched, nearly to tears, that he put aside all of his other affairs, however pressing, in order to go there and rectify things.[8]

Leaving Martinique, de Tracy finally arrived at Grenada on 22 November 1664 to establish the rule of the company.[9] With him were a dozen soldiers, and between 60 and 80 residents of Martinique and Guadeloupe who had agreed to relocate to Grenada in an attempt to help replenish the small population.[10]

When de Tracy arrived he found the colony "in a strange misery, abandoned by any aid from Europe because of the actions of the governor and oppressed at home by the actions of those who only gained their fortune by the exploitation of the inhabitants whose numbers had been reduced from 500 to 150 since the arrival of de Sérillac."[11] The dire situation in Grenada was illustrated by the two Capuchin fathers who "had been reduced to surviving on wild game."[12] At a ceremony on 24 November 1664, similar to those of the islands already under the rule of the Compagnie des Indies occidentales, de Tracy was received by the residents of Grenada, and four days later he accepted their pledge of loyalty to the company. De Tracy, angered over the colonists' state of distress, decreed that they be paid 80,000 *livres* by de Sérillac, which he calculated was owed to them; there is no evidence that anyone subsequently received compensation.[13] On 28 November de Tracy installed Vincent as the governor of Grenada.

Following the legal establishment of the Compagnie des Indes occidentales, the respective proprietors of the islands were informed that ownership of the islands would be transferred to the company and they were obliged to sell immediately. According to Mims, "For the West India islands sums were to be paid to the several proprietors which would represent the original purchase price plus a certain amount for improvements and increased value, to be determined by commissioners appointed by the king."[14]

The Comte de Sérillac, when informed of the decision to take over his colony, refused to negotiate with the company.[15] It is reported that Madame de Sérillac, among others, sent a protest to the French parliament "beseeching that august body not to register the charter; but in the end they were forced to yield."[16] It was a year before de Sérillac finally agreed to relinquish Grenada and the Grenadines for 100,000 *livres tournois* (l.t.) per the contract signed with the Compagnie des Indies occidentales on 27 August 1665.[17] The contract stipulated that the Comte de Sérillac will receive 20,000 l.t. immediately, 40,000 l.t. in six months, and the remaining 40,000 l.t. six months later. For this sum he was expected to transfer to the Compagnie des Indies occidentals:

The manorial seat and property of the islands of Grenada and the Grenadines with the forts, dwellings, weapons, ammunition, nègres and négresses [i.e. Black slaves], cattle, and generally all that belong to the known lord seller of Grenada and the Grenadines, same as the fruits which could be on the grounds without anything being excluded, retain nor to reserve, if not the movables and merchandises belonging to the lord seller.[18]

Despite the contract, the de Sérillac family did not receive final payment until 21 January 1672. The commissioners must have thought Grenada little improved from the 90,000 l.t. de Sérillac had paid for the islands eight years earlier, especially since some of the proprietors of the other French islands received substantial profits. It also did not take into account the considerable investment de Sérillac had already spent in his failed attempts to occupy and develop the island.

Fledgling Outpost

Governor Vincent, described by Dutertre as "a gentleman of honor and rare merit, esteemed by all who knew him," had served as the commander of the Regiment d'Orléans, one of four regiments that accompanied de Tracy to take control of French territories in the Americas.[19] Following the installation of Vincent, de Tracy went to the small palisade fort and "threw out [Governor Jean] de Sérillac, Jr. and forced him to live alone in a particular house where he stayed for two months before de Tracy sent him and Maubry back to France."[20] Governor Vincent, together with a sergeant and twelve soldiers went about establishing company rule on the island following the departure of de Tracy on 30 November 1664. Before he departed de Tracy approved an ordinance forbidding the "practice of the so called reformed religion" as he had been informed that "heretics assembled in a certain house to practice their religion."[21]

In his short visit to Grenada de Tracy was captivated by the island and its potential. In communication with Colbert he spoke glowingly of the prospects of the island, despite the ruin caused by de Sérillac during his tenure. De Tracy believed that Grenada was "a hidden treasure in which one is safe from hurricanes; the land is so rich, fish and game abound, and the armadillos are common for six months of the year; that this island could furnish all that is necessary for the life of the inhabitants."[22] Though Colbert did not immediately act upon de Tracy's recommendation, the island was to receive some attention by the chief minister in the 1670s. As far as the 1660s were concerned, however, Grenada continued to struggle despite Governor Vincent's attempts to bring about positive change.

In early 1665 Vincent received a commission as governor of Grenada from the Compagnie des Indes occidentales for three years. According to Dutertre, Vincent did not want to accept it until he had received the approval of the king, which he subsequently did. Vincent immediately initiated changes, one of the first was to allow the colonists to freely hunt and fish for consumption and for market; these activities had been forbidden by de Sérillac. The colonists continued to produce crops for transport to Martinique, including tobacco, ginger, indigo, and possibly cotton. They were joined by the approximately 60 to 80 colonists who had arrived with de Tracy and were given land, "of which the greatest part was communal land."[23] With little or no additional resources, the colonists set about the task of building a colonial economy which had eluded the island's owners for almost two decades.

The conduct of Vincent seemed to have motivated the colonists who, according to Dutertre, "began to recover a little under the wise guidance of Vincent."[24] The euphoria of the establishment of the Compagnie des Indies occidentales and the appointment of Governor Vincent soon dissipated as the realities of French neglect and official monopolistic policies took hold. On 30 September 1664, even before the company had taken control of Grenada, a law (arret) was issued by Colbert forbidding the respective colonies from trading with Dutch ships, and "the trade with the Dutch began to stop... and the inhabitants to suffer."[25] Grenada, being so far removed from the other French colonies, had always relied on trade with the Dutch or any others who would stop at the island. Since foreign trade was made illegal Grenada could only rely on whatever trade came from Martinique. The policies of excluding all foreign trade, despite the fact that the French could not replace the Dutch, led to severe food shortages in the colonies. The Compagnie des Indies occidentales clearly deserved the blame for the situation as it was unable to supply all of the colonies with needed resources. Confronted with widespread revolts in the larger colonies, it "concentrated its activities on Martinique, Guadeloupe and Cayenne, neglecting all of the others or sending them so few provisions that they languished."[26] Within a short period Grenada returned to its previous economic state and it was nearly abandoned by the Company, having only the supplies brought on a single bark of one of the inhabitants, which also carried their goods to the other islands. Several other barks also brought supplies, but these were so meager and so far apart that many of the colonists who had come over with de Tracy left and would talk no more of returning to Grenada and all of the best hopes of de Tracy were ruined and the progress of this island slowed; waiting for more favorable times than we had at the present.[27]

One of the many problems Governor Vincent had to confront was possible attacks by the Amerindians. Dutertre charges that "the savages, who had reestablished themselves on the island following de Sérillac's arrival, saw that the French were nearly abandoned and thought to take advantage of their weakness by making war on them."[28] The Amerindians on Grenada had informed Governor Vincent that "[it was] the savages of Paria, [Trinidad who] planned to make war on him."[29] Vincent, suspicious of those who brought the news, took this as a threat of impending attack and immediately placed the settlers on alert. He insisted that no one was to go out of doors without arms and should travel in groups in order to better defend themselves. He also halted all trade with the Amerindians which seemed to have sent a message that the French were serious about the threats. Vincent's actions caused the Amerindians to seek council with the French because "they feared for their own safety."[30] The French insisted that they had no intentions of attacking the Amerindians, but they would retaliate forcefully if attacked, and they had no way of telling a friendly Amerindian from an unfriendly one. The French reactions to the threat were enough to dispel the rumors of war and there was no more talk of conflict between the groups during Vincent's term as governor.

In the midst of "confusion and uncertainty in the 1660s" France, because of a 1662 treaty that obliged it to come to the assistance of the Dutch in the event of war against England, entered the Second Dutch War (1665-1667) in January 1666. The English were hoping to end the Dutch dominance of trade in the East and West Indies. Though most of the fighting took place in Europe, it was the first major colonial conflict that spilled over into the Caribbean, despite attempts by the French and the British in the region to avoid war. The governor of Martinique, de Clodoré, sent notice to Governor Vincent soon after receiving word in March 1666 that France had declared war against England and instructed him to prepare as best he could to defend the island. Vincent was probably already aware of the war since the English had captured Tobago from the Dutch in January 1666, bringing the war awfully close. The French, however, capitalized on their strength in the region and in April 1666 attacked the English on St. Christopher who were between their colony on either side of the island. It was captured in a few days, despite heavy fighting. The French also captured Antigua in November and Montserrat in May, but lost Cayenne to the English in September 1667.

Grenada's role in the war was minimal considering its insignificance and far distance from the major conflicts in the Lesser Antilles. Though the English had captured Tobago, 94 miles southeast of Grenada, they made no attempt to attack Grenada even after the French had declared war against them. Grenada was the "weakest of all the islands inhabited by the French," and "Governor Vincent considered discretion the better part of valor, for he had only 60 men capable of bearing arms, and he ordered a general retreat into the mountain fastnesses of Grenada."[31] With all of the French forces concentrated in the northern Lesser Antilles, Grenada was at least three days sail away, so assistance would be long in coming. Probably its best defense was its destitution, and the English would not waste time or resources to attack it; there were no sugar plantations to sack or slaves of any consequence to claim as booty.

The French capture of English colonies in the Leeward Islands, however, must have encouraged their compatriots at Grenada. Despite their limited ability to defend the island, they decided in late August 1666 to stage an attack against the small English garrison occupying Fort James at Plymouth, Tobago. According to Dutertre, Governor Vincent "sent an officer... with twenty-five brave volunteers; well armed and supplied with plenty of ammunition and two drums" in the bark *Gilles Gaspert.*[32] Dutertre continues that the party arrived at Courland Bay without being discovered, and sent the officer and fifteen men towards the fort. Just short of the fort, the French came upon fifteen British soldiers guarding a plantation and surprised and killed the sentry, but the other fourteen escaped and sounded the alarm. The next morning, the French demanded the immediate surrender of the British, pretending that the large French force at their disposal was in a hurry and did not want to waste time fighting for such a small prize. The drummer, also carrying his rifle on his shoulder, approached the fort with a flag of truce. He was met by the fort's commander who requested to see the French force, and the drummer led him to a hill where he saw the dozen or so armed French.

Realizing he was tricked, he attempted to defend himself with his sword, but was immediately disarmed by the armed drummer and made prisoner. The British commander was led back to the fort which surrendered on seeing the French approaching. The French returned to Grenada with the fifty British soldiers as prisoners of war, along with captured cannon and other booty. Governor Vincent later sent a small garrison that retained control of Tobago until March 1667 at which time they set fire to the fort before abandoning the island.[33]

Following negotiations to end the war, the Treaty of Breda was concluded in July 1667, with negligible changes in the Caribbean as the status quo ante bellum was restored. Grenada, though playing a minor role in the conflict, entered into the negotiations when the French inhabitants at St. Christopher proposed that instead of returning the British part of the island to them, the British could accept Grenada in exchange.[34] It is not difficult to see why the colonists at St. Christopher would have wanted to exchange a fledging outpost like Grenada for control of the entire colony of St. Christopher which was far ahead in its development; it had quite a number of established sugar plantations and built infrastructure. It was reported that Governor Willoughby of Barbados considered the exchange "no ill bargain," but it does not appear that the proposal was a serious suggestion "for the French ambassador who was sent to London to work out the details of the treaty obtained no concessions on this point, and the treaty stood as written."[35] As the return of the English part of St. Christopher dragged on for years due to the complications of compensation to the French, even Colbert believed that "he might be able to persuade the English government to relinquish its claims in exchange for some other island or for a sum of money."[36] Grenada was not identified at that time, but it probably was what Colbert had in mind since it was the least developed of the colonies. This episode illustrates the general view of Grenada's wretched economic state in the 1660s, a mere outpost that French colonists in the region campaigned to exchange for more valuable real estate. The proposal was quite telling!

Mapping Grenada

French participation in the Second Dutch War revealed how unprepared the colonies were for their defense. To aid the colonists in the defense of the islands King Louis XIV sent out a large fleet in September 1666, which was instrumental in capturing Antigua and Montserrat, and defending St. Christopher and Martinique. One of the officers in the expedition was François Blondel, an engineer, "who was charged with the construction of whatever fortifications he might deem necessary"[37] because "the king wished to have at least one good fort on each island—a fort capable to protect the French fleet, repel an enemy, and keep the colonists in subjection."[38] Sometime in 1667 Blondel visited Grenada for the sole purpose of assessing the island's defenses and designing a fort capable of defending the main settlement. To date, the island had relied on the palisaded Fort de l'Annonciation that was constructed in 1649 and enhanced over the years; there were also earthen batteries, including three in the area of the Carénage (Illustration 6.5). It may have been adequate for the small settlement in its defense against attacks by the Amerindians, but it was deficient for the expanding colony and the looming colonial conflicts.

Blondel chose the crest of a small peninsula or promontory about 100 feet above sea level, overlooking the entrance to the harbor, for the location of the fort. It commanded the approaches to the primary settlement and the bay, despite the fact that it was dominated by higher ground to the north and east, which Jean-Baptiste Labat criticized when he visited decades later. According to Dutertre, the fort was to comprise

> A pincer of some 30 fathoms in length, flanked by 20 foot tall bastions on either side of the mountain, which face to the northwest where access is easiest. The bases of the bastion end at the edge of the rock escarpments; in the middle of the curtain is a six foot wide door in front of which is a protective demi-lune seven fathoms long which is defended by the shoulders of the bastions.[39]

Blondel designed the small fort to be constructed from "earth and fascines," but Governor Vincent, "having learned that such construction doesn't last long in the islands, ordered that it be built of stone such that the port is perfectly defended."[40] Thus Fort Royal was constructed between 1668 and 1669, Grenada seeing its first major infrastractural improvement since its settlement. Though a fort did not guarantee stability it did put the colonists at ease and made them feel more secure, especially as the fort was manned by a handful of French troops.

When Blondel designed the small fort in 1667 he referred to it as

Fort Royal, so he may have been responsible for naming it as well. The name was not new, for one of the primary forts in Martinique at the time was called Fort Royal and Blondel had worked on improving its defenses. The similar layout of Fort Royal, Martinique and Fort Royal, Grenada may have been what led Blondel to name the new Grenada fort after the one at Martinique. The similarities are quite striking: both are located within large bays, both are situated on promontories extending into the bay, both had a Carénage or shallow inlet for careening ships to the east, and both would develop towns to the west.[41] Thus Blondel laid the foundations of the future Ville du Fort Royal that would spring up literally directly under the guns of Fort Royal.

Before Blondel departed Grenada he produced a number of plans of the island, two of which have been credited to him: *L'Isle de la Grenade* (Illustration 6.1) which most definitely represents the first detailed map of Grenada, and *Le Port Louis de l'isle de la Grenade*.[42] A third image, with two separate plans, the *Veue du Fort Royal, Bourg, Etang et du Port Louis de l'isle de La Grenade* (which is a copy of *Le Port Louis de l'isle de la Grenade*) and *Plan du Fort Royal de La Grenade, 1667* in the catalog of the Bibliothèque Nationale de France, is not credited to Blondel, but is most assuredly his work (Illustration 6.2). Blondel's general map of Grenada is a relief map and shows the many coastal place names that identified French and Amerindian settlements.[43] It clearly shows that by 1667 the French had already established settlements along the west coast or the Basseterre, but the Amerindians occupied the north and east or Capesterre. It is rather intriguing that Blondel's map shows Grenada upside down, an anomaly that would be repeated on many French maps of Grenada for decades.[44] In fact, Blondel records Grenada's location as "Latitude S[outh] 12 D[egrees]," though his compass correctly indicates north oriented to the bottom of the image. The plan of the fort and port for the first time records the name of the primary settlement and port as Port Louis, after the reigning French King Louis XIV. It is possible that the settlement had only recently received the name since the king had assumed full power in 1661 when he achieved his majority and the island was taken over by the Compagnie des Indes occidentales françaises in 1664. Again, the plan of Port Louis is quite revealing in that it shows the location of the new fort to be constructed, Fort Royal, three existing batteries, the settlement of houses on the sandbar, the palisade fort, and a small church.[45]

The First Census

It is not clear when Governor Vincent left his position, but he definitely served out his original three-year appointment which ended in late 1667 and was still on the island as the governor in 1668; he must have been reappointed. Vincent served as governor during a difficult period and his leadership brought some stability to the colony, but its economic and social situation were little improved because the island remained a backwater of the French *Iles du Vent*, and received little attention from Martinique or France. During Vincent's tenure the island witnessed one major improvement, a small fort built of stone that could technically defend the largest settlement, and thus the island.

There is some confusion as to the appointment of the new governor, Louis de Canchy, Sieur de Lerole. Canchy, a cousin of Alexandre Prouville de Tracy, arrived in New France in 1665 as part of the Regiment Carignan-Salières that was sent from France to suppress the Mohawk Indians who were attacking French settlements there.[46] In mid-1666 he was captured by the Mohawks while out hunting and held prisoner for a month; a cousin was killed in the attack. It appears that Canchy arrived in Grenada as early as July 1668, and by October 1669 was in command of the "garrison."[47] With Vincent out of the island Canchy was given the command at least by the end of 1669.

Canchy's claim to fame was his relationship to de Tracy and his capture and release by the Mohawks. His experience was very limited, but he arrived at an opportune moment when the French crown seemed to have redoubled its efforts to bring about positive changes in the *Iles du Vent*. The brief war against the British had almost brought the Compagnie des Indies occidentales françaises to bankruptcy, while it was obligated to defend the islands and continue supplying merchandise and transporting produce to France. Its meager resources were stretched to the limit, and many believed that at the close of the war it would soon collapse and the islands restored to their previous owners.[48] Colbert, however, had no intention of dissolving the company just yet. In an effort to preserve the company, its directors decided to allow private French traders to freely trade in the colonies beginning in September 1668.[49] The company had been unable to supply the colonies, creating the fear that the Dutch might return or rather, not leave. It was hoped that private French traders would do a better job than the Compagnie des

Indies occidentales françaises and actually displace the Dutch traders in the region.

The directors of the company also instituted a number of changes, one of the most important being the appointment of a governor-general for the French Caribbean, Jean-Charles de Baas. In so doing, the governors of the individual islands were now under the command of de Baas, who had been given specific tasks to accomplish, including the "maintenance of law and order, encouragement to early marriages, promotion of clearing new lands and increased production."[50] A number of policy changes sought to make the French Antilles more secure, with the construction of new fortifications as in Grenada, and productive, especially in respect to commerce with France. Another of these policy changes was the taking of "a complete census..., classified according to localities, race, sex–this for the benefit of Colbert" for the individual territories, including Grenada.[51]

The census of October 1669 listed a population of 506, comprising 284 whites of which 55 were *engagés* (indentured servants), and 222 slaves (Table 6.1, Appendix 1).[52] It is one of two nominal censuses, but the first official census, and records the heads of households by name, the number of family members, and ownership of *engagés*, slaves and livestock. It is the most complete household census identified to date and representative of the period prior to 1713 because of only slight changes in the population during that period, especially for the white population relative to the slave population.[53] For these reasons a detailed analysis follows to illustrate the social and economic make-up of the population of the island pre-1713.

By 1669 the French settlements on Grenada had occupied roughly a third of the island, though settlements were limited to coastal areas because of the ease of access and the ever present threat of Island Carib attacks. This region, which the French called the Basse-Terre, was bordered by the Caribbean Sea on the west and south, and mountains to the east which separated the French from the Amerindians who technically occupied over two-thirds of the island, called the Capesterre. The boundary separating the two groups was arbitrary since both went back and forth for hunting and trading, though the natural topography of hills may have served as an observable demarcation.

The French-occupied region was divided into four administrative districts. The Quartier du Fort "began at the springs up to the Sainte-Jean's River," and was the original and primary settlement, containing the recently constructed Fort Royal (Illustration 6.2). It possessed a relatively safe, deep-water harbor and a place where ships could be careened. To its north was the second oldest settlement, the Quartier du Beauséjour, which "began at the Saint-Jean's River up to the Beauséjour River." Further north still was the Quartier des Palmistes that "began at the Beauséjour River," and bordered the settlements of the Island Caribs, possibly as far north as Grosse Pointe; there were at least two known Amerindian settlements north at Grand Pauvre and Duquesne. The fourth settlement, the Quartier de la Grande Ance, which "began at the salt works up to the springs," was located in the southwest of the island and bordered the Quartier du Fort.

The 1669 census is quite detailed, especially for the seventeenth-century period. Tables 6.1 and 6.2 (Appendix I) present the various classifications of the population–gender, race, free and enslaved–and the family structure, respectively. The most obvious conclusions are (i) the white population comprised the majority (56%), slight though, which was unusual for most of the islands in the region where African slaves constituted the majority, but common for some of the newly settled colonies; (ii) as would be expected for the period and a new colony, adult males, inclusive of slaves and white servants, constituted a slight majority (54.8%); (iii) the Quartier du Fort, the administrative district and central port, made up almost half of the population (46%), while the Quartier des Palmistes, the most remote settlement, contained the least (11%); (iv) white children (12%) and white women (14%) were each less than 15 percent as might be expected for an infant colony; and (v) married couples accounted for 68 percent of the population, but 60 percent of those were childless, illustrating older couples, high infant mortality, or recently married.[54] The latter seems more likely in light of the policy to increase the population by encouraging young persons (girls 14-15 and boys 18-19 years) to marry earlier.[55]

Though the Quartier des Palmistes appeared the largest settlement geographically, it contained fewer inhabitants (11%), slaves (11%), engagés (7%) and no livestock most probably due to its recent settlement, close proximity to the Island Caribs, and mountainous terrain.[56] The Quartier de la Grande Ance, located in the southwest, was relatively flat and drier than the rest of the island which may account for the large number of livestock there (43%) since the dry scrubland was agreeable to its production.[57] Its climate and geography, agreeable to the cultivation of cotton and indigo, may also account for the relatively large number of slaves (23%) and *engagés* (18%). Its most valuable asset was the salt works. Though the Quartier du Beau Séjour contained 27 percent of property owners, they owned only 22 percent of *engagés*, just under 10 percent of slaves, and six percent of the livestock. This district, with 36 percent of households, had the highest white population (37%) and the highest white male population (37%). The demographics of this quarter suggest that the majority of the settlers were small freeholders, cultivating a few acres of land, with approximately half owning a slave or the services of an *engagé*. Seventy-five percent of households were married, with 46 percent having from one to four children; children constituted 25 percent of the quarter's population, with more kids than elsewhere.

The relationship between social titles and wealth is quite evident from the data. Titles were identified from the household heads as "Le Sr," (Le Sieur: esquire, a title of respect reserved for French gentlemen); "Le Commandeur du Sr," and "Le R. P."; the latter a religious title "Révérend Père," the former was political as the individual was an official of the Compagnie des Indies occidentales françaises at St. Christopher. Of the ten individuals with titles, nine resided in the Quartier du Fort and some were possibly employed by the Compagnie des Indies occidentales françaises. They constituted 14 percent of property owners and owned 25 percent of the *engagés*, 31 percent of the slaves, and 12 percent of the livestock. Of the 56 property owners a small number stood out because of their large possessions, and therefore greater wealth. Of the heads of household, nine of them had appeared on earlier censuses of Martinique, illustrating the direct connections between the two islands.

The 1669 census was instigated by Colbert who showed a growing interest in Grenada because of its proximity to South America. In June 1669 Colbert wrote to Governor-General de Baas that he should "Always hold the inhabitants in the exercise of the arms, and take care to populate the island of Grenada as much as it will be possible for you."[58] Again, in September, Colbert mentions the population, imploring de Baas "also that you endeavor to populate Grenada."[59] Following the 1669 census, de Baas wrote to Colbert about the difficulty of increasing Grenada's population:

The isle of Grenada, Monseigneur, is very difficult to populate.... The isle can increase its inhabitants only by a small number, and this small number can come only from the antipathy of some private individuals of St. Christopher, and of Guadeloupe, who almost died from the last hurricane. It have five or six of them there who asked permission to go to Grenada, because they will not be subjected any more to the accidents of this tempest, I allowed them to go there and to transport same of their pieces of furniture, and that the Governors complained that I desolate their Islands, nevertheless I will send there those who ask.[60]

The peopling of Grenada continued to be a problem for the French authorities, but Colbert continued to push to see the island develop and capitalize on its proximity to the Spanish in South America.

Though the majority of planters in Grenada cultivated indigo and cotton, there is circumstantial evidence that sugar production was in its infancy by 1669. Information on the 1669 census suggests that one of the settlers, Aaron Franco, was "holding a contract" with the Compagnie des Indes occidentales.[61] Identified on the census as "Jewish,"[62] Franco owned the services of three servants, eleven slaves and was a wealthy planter in comparison to the other freeholders; he also owned oxen, cows and horses. Franco was probably one of the Jews who had settled in the French Antilles following their expulsion from Brazil by the Portuguese along with the Dutch in 1654, and had contributed both capital and expertise to the establishment of sugar production in Martinique and Guadeloupe.[63]

On the 1664 Martinique census, Aaron Franco is listed as a resident there so he must have arrived in Grenada between 1664 and 1669.[64] Was he one of the people who had accompanied de Tracy to Grenada in 1664, or like a number of residents from Martinique and Guadeloupe, took up residence there following the establishment of company rule.[65] Franco was given a six-month contract by the Compagnie des Indes occidentales to establish sugar manufacturing in Grenada, and may also have came directly from Martinique to carry out this agreement. Grenada was the only French colony that had yet to embark on sugar production and the company was hoping that it could finally initiate its production there.[66] The 1660s saw a growing emphasis on sugar production in the French Caribbean, and to encourage it the French crown created a number of incentives, including a prohibitive tariff on foreign sugar imports, and granting a three-year exemption from the head tax (on slaves) for newly established estates, and two years for estates which switched from other crops to sugar.[67] Though no evidence exists as to whether these incentives directly affected the plan to establish sugar manufacture in Grenada, it could have played a part.

It was a common practice by French stock companies to give contracts to individuals to establish industries in the islands. The failure of private capital to establish sugar production in Grenada was clear to the new company and it therefore tried to create incentives towards that end. Such was the case in Guadeloupe in 1638 when the Compagnie des Isles de l'Amérique granted a contract to Turque to establish sugar production on that island.[68] There is no further mention of Turque, but in 1639 Trézel, a Dutch merchant of Rouen, was given a contract to establish a sugar mill in Martinique.[69] The specifics of Franco's contract with the Compagnie des Indies occidentales are not known. It appears that Franco may not have made the expected progress in the agreed six months and his contract was ended in October 1669. The ten remaining slaves were handed over to one Merman to assist the masons completing the construction of Fort Royal.[70] Though Franco owned three *engagés*, eleven slaves, seven oxen, ten cows and four horses which were listed under his own name, he was also recorded as "holding a contract with the company" with thirteen "Black males" (i.e. slaves), six oxen and four cows. The latter would have been the barest minimum of resources with which to begin a sugar plantation, i.e. possessing a mill, powered by animals, to grind the sugar cane. Based on the 1669 census, only one other planter had the resources to produce sugar. Jean Ferés lived in the Quartier du Fort with his wife and owned the services of seven *engagés*, 27 slaves, four oxen, nine cows, 15 calves and eight horses. De Chambré of St. Christopher owned a habitation in Grenada and 40 slaves, but no livestock.

In his 1675 publication, *Le parfait négociant*, Savary recorded that the island of Grenada produced sugar, the first known reference to the island's sugar production.[71] If the island was producing sugar of any consequence in 1675, the industry must have been several years old. Though the quantity was probably very small relative to the other French colonies, it seems likely based on the above analysis that at least two planters had begun sugar production after 1669. The success of their efforts is not known, but sugar production most likely got its start from these early attempts.

Dutch and Island Carib Attacks on Grenada

The resurgence of the Dutch at Tobago and the Dutch-Franco War brought unusual attention to the southern Lesser Antilles. The Dutch had occupied Tobago off and on since 1628, oftentimes sharing the island with settlers under the Duke of Courland who had established a claim in 1637. It was the closest island to Grenada that was occupied by other Europeans. Tobago, unlike Grenada, was able to establish sugar plantations and had a population of 1,500 colonists, 7,000 slaves and over one hundred plantations by 1660. In January 1666, however, the Dutch were forced to surrender it to the British, with much of the settlements destroyed thereafter. As discussed above, a small force from French Grenada then captured the meagerly defended British garrison in August 1666, abandoning the island in March 1667 after burning the fort. The Dutch returned in 1667 and rebuilt settlements only to have it captured by the British in December 1672. With the Peace of Westminster in 1674, the island was given to the Dutch who returned in 1676 and reestablished themselves. Prior to the 1670s the French at Grenada benefitted from the Dutch at Tobago, trading for slaves and goods with them, but the colonial conflicts in the 1670s brought the fear of direct attack by the Dutch or indirectly through their Island Carib associates.

The outbreak of war caused much concern in the region once again. The Franco-Dutch War (1672-78) saw different combatants, with the English and French against the Dutch. With the Dutch situated only 95 miles southwest of Grenada at Tobago, they were seen as an immediate threat to the poorly defended colony. As early as February 1672 Governor-General de Baas wrote of the specific threat of the Dutch at Tobago against Grenada and proposed defensive measures to protect the island from attack.[72] One of those measures was the appointment in February 1674 of the Marquis d'Amblimont, to take charge of the defenses of Grenada. A naval captain, he took up his post, but soon ran into problems with Governor de Canchy over who should be subordinate to whom. Canchy seemed to have perceived d'Amblimont's appointment as a threat to his authority since, as the governor, he was supposed to be the principal military leader. While these officials, charged with protecting of the island, were engaged in quarrels, Island Caribs from St. Vincent staged an attack against the colonists in Grenada in June 1674, killing fourteen inhabitants. The surprise attack brought renewed attention to Governor de Canchy's leadership.

The Island Caribs at Dominica and especially St. Vincent remained a threat to the French at Grenada, constantly harassing the colonists, but there hadn't been a death of a colonist in over a decade. The 1660 peace treaty that made Dominica and St. Vincent exclusive to the Island Caribs may have contributed to the detente, but both the French and British still had their sights on occupying those two islands. Though the French colony at Grenada had continued to feel threatened by the Island Caribs, the violent attacks of the 1650s had lessened by the 1660s, and were perpetrated only by non-resident Island Caribs. The situation changed quite suddenly in June 1674 when a group of Island Caribs, fleeing St. Vincent for the continent, stopped at Grenada and attacked the French, leaving fourteen colonists dead. Among those killed were the island's judge and several slaves. The incident began when a French ship arrived on St. Vincent to retrieve Jesuit missionaries who had decided to abandon their fruitless mission among the Island Caribs, but its crew had "somehow insulted some Caribs, who then promptly murdered the crew."[73] As Prichard notes, the deaths of the colonists resulted from "a sudden, sharp deterioration in relation with the Carib Indians of St. Vincent, who with their arrows and wooden clubs, were wrecking more havoc than the Dutch."[74]

The Island Carib attack took the colonists by surprise and only caused them to live in fear of these unpredictable attacks. Governor-General de Baas, commenting on the raid there, believed "that such assaults paralyzed the settlers with fright."[75] In the middle of war with the Dutch, the French feared that an all-out war with the Island Caribs of St. Vincent was imminent. De Baas saw the incident as a failure of the leaders at Grenada to engage the Island Carib chiefs to make sure incidents like this never occurred; he later dismissed the governor. He was forced to send three companies of soldiers and a ship to reinforce Grenada during the winter until the promised relief squadron under d'Estrées arrived.[76]

The French lacked the resources to retaliate against the Island Caribs, and repeated requests to Colbert for assistance to crush them were met with appeals to find a peaceful solution. Governor-General de Blénac saw such an opportunity in February 1678 with the arrival of Admiral d'Estrées' fleet. With such a large force behind him, he was able to "force peace on two Vincentian chiefs, Pierre Moignac and Ionana. They agreed not to inhabit Grenada or even go there without permission of the colony's governor. They pledged, also, to fight for the French in all future wars. Finally, the chiefs promised to inform Caribs on Trinidad and on the mainland of this agreement and to try and gain their consent."[77] Boucher concludes that "this peace initially breathed life into the struggling Grenada settlement," but it was only temporary.[78] By August 1679 the French were complaining of the many Island Carib breaches of the treaty and were discussing plans for the destruction of the Island Caribs on both Dominica and St. Vincent. In discussing the current situation, they concluded that "Grenada would inevitably have to be abandoned, if at the nearest opportunity we were not to strongly repress their insolence, since they did not even spare the children, whom they ripped out of the bellies of their mothers."[79] When the plan was sent to Paris for approval and resources to carry it out, the response was that they were "to contain these peoples and prevent them from creating any obstacles to commerce and to the security of my subjects, without going to war against them."[80]

Governor Canchy's tenure as Grenada's governor had been problematic for a number of years. It was not the first time that he had ended up on the wrong side of his superiors. In 1670 he had allowed a Dutch ship to trade slaves, and as a result his leadership was called into question. The governors of the colonies had always been lenient with regard to illegal trade, especially because it kept the planters happy and oftentimes brought them illicit gains. Some of the inhabitants also complained that they were treated unjustly by Canchy. The relationship between Canchy and company officials deteriorated, and in March 1671 he returned to France. In late 1671 he was back in Grenada with an official appointment as governor due to the continued absence of Vincent.[81]

Canchy's return to Grenada was not welcomed by the majority of the inhabitants, and his superiors reported on the "bad effects produced" by his continued presence. His youth was cited as one of the possible causes of his rash behavior. In 1673 the situation took a turn for the worse when Canchy accused La Blennerie, the captain of the island's militia and a long time resident who was popular among the inhabitants, of "wanting to drive a popular uprising to replace him and take over the government of the island."[82] Not too long after he got into another conflict with François Bituat de Bléor, a ship's captain, over the seizure of an English ship illegally trading at Grenada. In 1674 he was again caught allowing a Dutch trader to sell slaves illegally in Grenada. With his superiors having grown tired of his conflict-ridden leadership and unpopularity among the colonists, Canchy was replaced in mid-1674.

The end of 1674 brought many changes to Grenada and the French Caribbean. Most noticeable was the dismissal of the governor and the appointment of his replacement Pierre de Sainte-Marthe de Lalande who was appointed by the summer of that year though his official appointment was dated May 1675.[83] The problems of the Compagnie des Indies occidentales françaises became quite evident soon after its establishment in 1664, yet it wasn't until December 1674 that it was dissolved, with the French colonies in the region becoming royal colonies under the direct rule of the Crown. Grenada, during its previous 25-years occupation by the French, can best be characterized as a frontier colony, but more truthfully an outpost. Its continued existence as such was in question as it battled internal political conflicts and external attacks by the Amerindians whose lands it occupied. It was barely able to retain a sustainable population in the face of these conflicts, and its economy remained rudimentary. Though its location in the southern Caribbean excited those who desired entry into the lucrative trade with the Spanish, the island remained unexploited and underdeveloped after two and a half decades of French occupation.

Grenada's new status as a royal colony did little to enhance its deplorable economic, social and political state. As a matter of fact, 1675 proved to be quite challenging. The appointment of Pierre de Sainte-Marthe de la Lande, a 26-year old as the governor, seemed to reinforce the view of the island's unimportance within the French Caribbean. There is no evidence that the new governor had held any official position in his two-year residence in Martinique. He was the most inexperienced of any of the previous governors, despite the fact that he had enlisted in the French military as a cadet at the age of fourteen years like many of the boys of his status. His major qualification may have been the fact that he was the son of Chevalier de Sainte-Marthe, the respected governor of

Martinique. He may have also come to the notice of Governor-General de Baas after distinguishing himself in July 1674 when the Dutch, under de Ruyter, attacked Martinique. Governor de Sainte-Marthe was instrumental in repulsing the Dutch and his son may have played a noticeable supporting role in that battle.

The new governor arrived in Grenada by October 1674 and soon realized the pressing challenges he faced in trying to administer an island possession that had been neglected for many years. He immediately carried out an inspection of the island's defenses and was appalled by what he found: The fort was in a piteous state, needing urgent repairs; The garrison of 13 soldiers was underpaid, having to resort to fishing to supplement their diet; six of them had died of "poverty and misery," and there was no medicine or doctor to attend to them. There was no ammunition in the stores and the arms were in a bad state. There was no oil or candles, forcing the soldiers to have to collect wood for lighting.[84] It became clear to the governor that Grenada, far as it was from the other French colonies, lacked the resources to defend itself from even the most benign of enemies, privateers and Island Caribs. Sainte-Marthe sent his list of needed supplies to Governor-General de Baas, but it was too late to stop the impending attack.

Only two months after he arrived to take command of Grenada, the island was attacked by privateers. In early December 1674, Jan Erasmus Reining, a Dutch privateer known to the French as Rasmus, pillaged a number of villages and carried off as many as 60 slaves from four plantations on Grenada.[85] It is believed that Frenchmen on his crew who had lived on the island informed Reining of the island's weak defenses and inability to respond to sudden attacks on coastal habitations. The frigate *La Friponne* that was assigned to protect the island was nowhere to be found, the privateers completing their pillage without opposition. Captain de Grosbois of *La Friponne* was later accused of disobeying orders when he abandoned the island to pursue his own commercial interests at Martinique.[86] It was a huge blow to the island's economy, already suffering from a shortage of slaves, losing as many as thirty percent of its slave population. Thus began Governor de Sainte-Marthe's administration of Grenada, but it was to get worse before things would begin to improve.

It was rumored that Reining, after pillaging Grenada in December 1674, had sent word notifying the governor that he would return shortly "to install himself as master of the entire territory."[87] Governor de Sainte-Marthe and his superiors may have taken the threat seriously and Grenada received some supplies and reinforcements when Governor-General de Baas sent barrels of gunpowder and a company of 50 men "from the Navy under the command of de la Tour."[88] De la Tour's orders were to dispatch the troops in the parts of the island where the Island Caribs had been causing problems.

If Reining did in fact threaten to return he did not fail to disappoint when on the morning of 28 March 1675, a "vessel and a frigate of 80 tons armed with eight cannons" landed just before dawn at Grand Mâle Baye (presently Grand Mal), about a quarter of a mile from Fort Royal.[89] Reining, together with Jurriaen Aernouts, a well-known Dutch privateer, and about 100 men, returned to take control of the island they had earlier pillaged and knew was poorly defended. Unknown to the privateers was the presence of the *Emerillion* which had arrived that morning for an unrelated issue and was moored under Fort Royal, as well as the 50-man force under de la Tour. "Using two inhabitants [from Carriacou] as their guide," the privateers dispatched 24 men to attack the fort, with another 80 men bringing up the rear. Some began battering the doors of the fort while others tried to scale the walls of the fort with ladders. Heard by the guards, the alarm was sounded within the fort after Governor de Sainte-Marthe ordered the firing of cannons to alert the inhabitants.

It soon became clear to those in the fort and the surrounding area that the island's fortification was under attack and being besieged by Dutch privateers who attacked with "grenades and fire pots." The presence of the *Emerillion* and its captain, de la Clocheterie, unknown to the attackers, provided the French with a secret weapon. Captain de la Clocheterie happened upon the Dutch ships, capturing their frigate while its five-man crew escaped with the brigantine, leaving the attackers no means to leave the island. The capture of one ship and departure of the second only strengthened the privateers in their goal to capture the fort, realizing their dire predicament. The orchestrated attack by the large band of privateers with muskets, grenades and fire pots overwhelmed the small number of guards within the fort, but they put up a spirited defense. Governor de Sainte-Marthe, in particular, "arrives to knock down the ladders; he kills two of the attackers with his own hand and wounds several of them. But he receives to the head and the arm the glares of grenades, then two rifle shots, under his armpit... the other towards his

129

backbone."[90] During the four-hour long battle, two French soldiers were killed and two wounded out of the nine who defended the fort. Badly wounded, the governor was forced to request quarter from the enemy, which they granted. The doors to the fort were opened and the privateers took control, replacing the French flag with that of the Dutch (Illustration 6.3). Luckily for the governor, a surgeon who was exiled in Grenada attended his wounds.

The Dutch found themselves in a precarious position even though they had gained control of the small fort and had the wounded governor as a hostage. The fighting had exhausted much of their ammunition and there were little provisions left in the fort, leaving them besieged by the French force which had by this time assembled for a counter attack to retake the fort. The French rejected the offer by the Dutch to leave should their ship return. The privateers' only option was to surrender, and "thirty-four hours after entering the fort, they had to leave" after capitulating. So on 29 March Reining and Aernouts, together with 72 men, embarked on the *Emerillion* bound for Martinique where "the two chiefs were locked up in the fortress at Sainte-Pierre, their men employed at Fort Royal to serve as masons and to assist with the works in progress."[91] Another ten privateers, Frenchmen, were later transported to Martinique, their fates unknown. In June 1675 Reining and Aernouts, together with six companions, managed to escape in a dugout canoe "by drugging the guards with wine." Pritchard questions whether "the French probably allowed the Dutch to escape in return for surrendering on Grenada a few months earlier, a reasonable quid pro quo."[92] The trouble for Reining and Aernouts did not end there as they were captured by the Spanish at Venezuela on their way to Curaçao, but escaped the following year to rejoin the Dutch and met the French in the battle for Tobago in 1676.

With the return of the Dutch to Tobago in 1676, the French at Grenada expressed fears that an attack against them was imminent. They especially did not like the relationship between the Dutch and the Island Caribs as the former "soon made peace with the [Island] Caribs and supplied them with guns to attack exposed French habitants at Grenada."[93] The French were all too aware of the damage the Island Caribs could inflict as they had often used them against the Dutch, but they also had the fresh memory of the attack two years earlier that left twelve people dead. The year 1676 also brought a large Dutch squadron under Jacob Binckes to the region that captured Cayenne, Marie Galante and St. Martin, transporting "confiscated slaves, beasts of burden, and even a few willing French planters to strengthen Dutch Tobago."[94] The French realized that they had to retaliate if they were to halt the Dutch once and for all, and following the arrival in early 1677 of the long awaited fleet under Admiral Comte d'Estrées the conflict came to a head. The subsequent French attack on Tobago in February 1677 left both sides bloodied, but the Dutch retained Tobago. Admiral Jean d'Estrées, his force badly damaged, stopped at Grenada after claiming "victory" over the Dutch.

The French sent out a second larger fleet under d'Estrées, which sailed directly for Tobago. In December 1677 the French destroyed Dutch forces, including Binckes, and "From that time on, the Dutch never again presented a serious threat to the French islands."[95] It is interesting to note that Reining, who had attempted to capture Grenada in 1675, took part in the defense of Tobago with the Dutch, but escaped to Curaçao following their defeat. The French attempt to attack Curaçao in May 1678 proved disastrous when the French fleet failed to find the target and much of the fleet was wrecked in shallow waters. To aid the many injured soldiers and sailors, d'Estrées had a temporary hospital set up on Grenada before he returned to France. The Treaty of Nymwegen, signed on 10 August 1678, brought to an end the Dutch wars and their dominance of trade in the region. Tobago, a Dutch colony, was ceded to France. The French failure to take Curaçao dealt a blow to their plans for Grenada to replace the Dutch slave trade to the Spanish, and interest by Colbert in Grenada's proximity to the Spanish soon waned.

Glimmer of Hope

Despite the various plans and attempts to improve its overall economic condition, Grenada entered the last two decades of the seventeenth century in a very low state of development. At the heart of its problems were the scarcity of resources which had to be shared between the competing colonies, and its isolation from the center of French colonizing activities. Grenada was in the second tier of island hierarchy, ranking at the bottom of the colonial totem pole, and lagging far behind the other French possessions in almost every respect. It was seen as too small, too far away, and offered too little in return relative to the larger and longer established colonies of Martinique, Guadeloupe and St. Christopher, and the vastly attractive St. Domingue. No wonder that a popular expression of the period illustrated Grenada's place in the French Antilles: "The nobility inhabited St. Christopher, the middleclass at Guadaloupe, the soldiers at Martinique, freebooters at St. Domingue, and peasants at Grenada."[96]

The next three decades beginning in 1680, however, proved to be far more encouraging, not withstanding two prolonged colonial conflicts that left the region unstable and increased Grenada's insecurity. The inability of French colonial officials to enforce trade restrictions in this volatile environment led to an increase in Grenada's illegal trade, particularly in slaves. The decades of war freed it from its direct dependence on Martinique and allowed it to benefit from the availability of illegal resources offered by other European nations. A more profound consequence of the wars was a southern shift with the loss of St. Christopher in 1713, the abandonment of St. Croix and St. Barthélemy, and the growth in trade with the Spanish Main that developed prior to and as a result of the French *asiento*. Grenada's slowly increasing slave population fueled the expansion of its nascent sugar industry and helped boost the growth of its primary economic activity, indigo production. These changes led to Grenada experiencing marked improvements in its overall economy as it moved from a marginal to a stable colony.

When naval captain Nicolas de Gabaret, the chevalier de Saint-Sorin, arrived in 1681 to replace Chambly as governor, he found a backward colony struggling to survive. One of the most serious problems he confronted was the devastating attacks on the island's isolated settlements by privateers. The small and scattered population was vulnerable to these attacks because they were unpredictable and thus hard to defend against. As data from the 1683 census showed, the 150 men capable of bearing arms were scattered along the island's coasts and were inadequate to properly defend isolated homesteads. The 1675 attempt to capture Grenada by the Dutch privateers demonstrated that it lacked adequate defenses. The French were aware of the deficiencies and had made some improvements in both infrastructure and manpower. Yet the island's small, scattered and isolated settlements exasperated its ability to defend many of the colonists, especially those who settled at some distance from

Fort Royal. Though there were no ongoing conflicts for most of the 1680s, Grenada proved quite susceptible to these attacks. Governor de Gabaret had expressed his reservations concerning the island's defenses in 1684, but the absence of open conflicts in the region put all at ease until a number of serious attacks threatened the colony's existence.

The first serious attack came on 25 April 1685 when a "Spanish half-galley, carrying an international crew of eighty men, anchored on the uninhabited [eastern] coast of the Capesterre, seized a boat that was preparing to go fishing, and the four inhabitants and a Negro [i.e. slave]. Some of the men of the crew came ashore, was shown the way to a sugar plantation, plundered it, and took 20 slaves there."[97] The Island Caribs, aware of the attack, informed Governor de Gabaret, who immediately sounded the alarm and sent six soldiers and some militia, but the Spanish had already re-embarked and departed with their booty. In July 1686, the Spanish captured two French brigantines, and "adding sting to insult, forced the crew to sail to Grenada and there aid in stripping its inhabitants [of slaves]."[98] Governor de Gabaret reported that the pillaging of slaves was a menace to the island.[99]

A second attack by the Spanish on 21 May 1687 was quite severe. With a half-galley and a large dugout, they "approached in the middle of the night with the first dwellings, far away from the fort by four miles while the inhabitants slept. After having plundered eleven houses, the Spanish took along three whole families, a black male [i.e. slave], six black females [slaves], a female savage [i.e. Carib Indian], 16 black children, and three convicts [i.e. *engagés*]."[100] By the time Governor de Gabaret was made aware of the attack and sent assistance, they had departed. It was alleged that the privateers had come from Carraque [Caracas or Carriacou], and among them were French who apparently had lived on the island and were able to guide them to where the inhabitants lived. It is reported that the captives were sold "like slaves in Margarita," and several escaped, with one managing to return to Grenada the following year.

In December 1688 two Spanish men-of-war from the Bay of Biscay again ravaged the coast of Grenada.[101] To better provide a quicker response a detachment of 20 soldiers under a lieutenant was stationed at Pointe des Palmiste, halfway along the western coast where some of the attacks had taken place.[102]

After being informed of these attacks, the king in 1689 requested Governor-General de Blénac "to take special care of the defense of

Grenada against the Spanish."[103] These attacks continued during the wars in the 1690s and early 1700s as happened in July 1692 when privateers from Jamaica made a descent.[104] These raids "ravaged the coasts of our colonies more than once. Martinique as well had been visited by them, but in Guadeloupe and Grenada especially, the inhabitants had had to suffer from their descents in the remote districts."[105]

Louis XIV's ambitions were at the heart of many of Europe's conflicts in the late seventeenth and early eighteenth centuries. Between 1666 and 1713 there were four major military conflicts in the Caribbean, all stemming from European wars involving France, England, the United Provinces (Holland) and Spain; each conflict witnessed shifting alliances. Few territories changed hands permanently, each treaty returning them to the status quo ante bellum. The purpose for the conflicts in the Caribbean, according to Watts, "were not to expand into new territory, bearing in mind the limitations of the available capital, but rather to damage and destroy the existing property and plantations of rivals, gaining some short-term advantage in European markets... for the sale of their sugar crop."[106] Wars were also responsible for the disruption of trade, so vital to the economic existence of the colonies, since they depended on the home countries for merchandise, including food and vessels to transport their perishable produce. Sometimes, privateering activities against each other were more widespread than actual fighting.

Grenada, because of its marginal economic state throughout the seventeenth century, played a negligible role in the many conflicts because "the inevitable focus of warfare at this time, therefore, was directed towards those islands which had already undergone, or were about to undergo, development into sugar cane agriculture."[107] This meant that the major battles were fought in the area of the Leeward Islands, especially the island of St. Christopher which was jointly occupied by the English and French, and the French islands of Martinique and Guadeloupe.

After a short reprieve, conflict resumed in the late 1680s as European countries found themselves engaged in another war, the Nine Years War, which began in December 1688. French aggression against its neighbors led to a united force against it, as the United Provinces, Spain, England, and others formed the Grand Alliance to resist Louis XIV's army. Once the conflict spread to the Caribbean in early 1689 the French went on the offensive by capturing the valuable trading island of St. Eustatius from the Dutch in April 1689, and the British portion of St. Christopher in August that same year. The British replied with the capture of French St. Barthélemy in December 1689, the destruction of Marie Galante in January 1690, the recapture of their territory on St. Christopher in June, and St. Eustatius (for their ally the Dutch) in July. British attempts to capture or destroy Guadeloupe in 1690 and Martinique in 1693 failed. Though there were these larger battles and the fear of territorial attacks and capture, it was the predominance of privateering that dominated this conflict.

Grenada, isolated and defenseless, was probably in little danger of an all out attack by the British or Dutch. The island's low economic state was its best defense because it offered little prize to anyone who dared to attack. An assault on Grenada, with the intention of occupying it, would be a total waste of resources, knowing that at the conclusion of the war it would probably be restored to the French. Yet, privateering raids could be highly profitable as was evident in the raids on Grenada in the 1680s, and at least one raid by privateers from Jamaica in 1692. Though these raids continued during the war, it would appear that Grenada, despite its weak defenses, was not overwhelmed by privateers. It may have also helped that the French were heavily represented among the privateers and inflicted heavy losses on the Dutch.

Consumed with its war in Europe, the French left the islands to their own defenses. The smaller islands were especially vulnerable as was evident with the pillaging of Marie Galante by the British. Grenada's location away from the immediate center of the conflicts may have been another benefit, but isolation also meant that any request for assistance from Martinique would be long in coming. Fearing for these smaller territories, or maybe needing the inhabitants to help defend Martinique, Governor-General de Blénac in 1696 proposed that both Grenada and Marie Galante should be abandoned and their populations transported to Martinique.[108] Fortunately for Grenada this proposal was not implemented, and though the inhabitants may have been apprehensive about possible attacks or raids, they weathered the war with little adverse effects; Marie Galante, however, was temporarily abandoned.

Trade and the Spanish Main

The French had always viewed penetration of Spanish America as a particularly beneficial undertaking, and had invested a great deal of time, if not money, to gain access. Like his predecessor Colbert, Minister Pontchartrain was "preoccupied with penetration of Spanish America and sought to check Anglo-Dutch competition by seizing their wealth and creating a colony similar to Curaçao somewhere close to the American mainland."[109] Grenada had been previously mentioned as the possible competitor to Curaçao, but the French had so far failed to destroy the Dutch trading port. Once again Grenada's potential surfaced, and once again nothing came of it. The French used their resources to attack the Spanish, gaining tremendously from the capture of Cartagena in May 1697. In September the Treaty of Ryswick ended the Nine Years War and the status quo in the Caribbean was restored.

Though the French had proposed plans to exploit Grenada's geographical advantage since their occupation in 1649, nothing materialized due to the lack of financial investments. When de Tracy visited Grenada in 1664 to establish the Compagnie des Indies occidentales françaises, he "attentively considered the advantages of this good island" and wrote to Colbert who became interested.[110] As Prichard writes, "In 1669, Colbert encouraged new efforts to settle the island with the vague idea of establishing a base for contraband trade with Spanish America."[111] Colbert knew that to exploit Grenada he had to encourage development on the island, one of the most important issues was its population. In September 1669, in a letter to Governor-General de Baas, he addressed the issue of increasing Grenada's population: "In addition, he would like you to undertake the task of populating Grenada as it is the nearest island to the mainland of America [i.e. South America], and may provide the best development potential."[112] It was not an easy task considering all of the French islands were having difficulty recruiting French citizens, and African slaves were in short supply and very expensive. De Baas' reply was that Grenada was just too difficult to populate, especially when he allowed residents from the other colonies to go to Grenada, the governors of those islands complained that he was depopulating their islands.

Despite the difficulties, "Colbert's chief interest in these years was the development of Grenada, an island assumed to be most appropriate either to launch an attack on the Spanish empire or as an entrepôt for its economic penetration. Time and again the minister returned to his pet project."[113] According to Newton, Colbert wanted to develop Grenada "into a second Curaçao, with slave-pens for the maturing of the Negroes to be sold to the Spaniards, and warehouses for the storage of cargoes of French manufactures."[114] Before Colbert could achieve that goal he had to find a way to destroy the Dutch control of the slave trade, which is why he pursued war against them in the Antilles. In the early 1670s "he encouraged de Baas to conduct a proxy war against the Dutch entrepôts at St. Eustatius and Curaçao by assisting the Caribs of St. Vincent, currently hostile to them."[115] He also advised the intendant of the islands, Pélisser, "to consider the advisability of having the West India Company send 2000 slaves to the Spanish Main, 'for these Spaniards never refuse to buy slaves and always pay the Dutch at Curaçao very dear for them.'"[116] Yet by 1682, with the absence of official trade with the Spanish Main, Colbert concluded that "Trade even with the Spaniards is to be prohibited, for His Majesty is of the opinion that no Spanish vessels are likely to come from the Spanish Main."[117] Newton concludes that "Grenada proved unsuitable owing to difficulties of navigation between it and the Spanish Main, and the prices of the French goods were so much higher than for those sold by the Dutch that the colonists would not look at them."[118] The more likely reason for Grenada's failure as a slave depot was the failure of the Compagnie des Indes occidentales to adequately supply slaves and merchandise to the islands, particularly because it lacked the necessary capital and ships to supply the French Antilles. It would not be the last time, however, that Grenada would be linked with Spanish America.

In 1675 a plan for Grenada's development was proposed by Auné de Chambré as part of a larger prospectus.[119] It was at least the second plan since Governor de Canchy had submitted his proposal to the Compagnie des Indes occidentales in November 1670.[120] Canchy's plan was basically to establish commercial trade with the Spanish by sending ships from Grenada with French merchandise to the coast of South America that would be exchanged for livestock, especially horses, mules and cows. Canchy had hoped to use his relations with the Galibis, especially the son of a resident Galibis Chief Baba, to assist the French.[121] Canchy never received the merchandise he requested and his plan came to nothing.

Chambré arrived in the Caribbean in February 1665 to manage the affairs of the Compagnie des Indies occidentales françaises, with the title of agent general or intedant. He was instrumental in consolidating the administration of the colonies for the Compagnie des Indies occidentales and most likely visited Grenada as its representative. Like de Tracy, he seemed to have been taken with the potential of Grenada and designed a plan for its development. In 1669 he was replaced by the new position of intendant, but remained in the region in a private capacity.

Chambré proposed a detailed prospectus "For the establishment of a strong colony at Grenada, from where one can embark on the Continent."[122] Like many before him, he saw Grenada's proximity to South America as an advantage the French should exploit. He outlined the island's attractions: "land is fertile, good for growing sugar cane, cassava, [sweet] potatoes, yams, tobacco, cocoa to make chocolate, ginger, indigo, silk, legumes, etc."[123] He continues with Grenada's geographical advantages, particularly the harbor and its ability to hold numerous ships, and its location outside where hurricanes wrecked havoc. In order to make this project successful, Chambré proposed an increase in the population, expanded agriculture by clearing forests and making available slaves and indentured servants, construct a fort of stone, place the colony under good leadership, exempt exports and imports from taxes, procure at least two ships to facilitate the island's trade, and provide two or three priests of the Society of Jesus (Jesuits) to administer to the colonists. Chambré provides detailed lists of the needed resources to achieve his goals: number of skilled workers, number of slaves, cost of the construction of the fort, ammunition, number of soldiers, the required food and cost, animals, and various other supplies. He proposed the immediate establishment of "five or six [sugar] factories… that will be in little time in flourishing state." Needed were 203 Frenchmen, among who should be 60 lumberjacks, 60 laborers, 75 skilled workmen, 20 experienced slave drivers from the other islands, and 600 slaves. For the slaves, he proposed sending one or two frigates to Guinea, which could also trade for "elephant tusks and gold dust"; all did not have to arrive the first year. The garrison of the fort should comprise 50 men total, including 38 soldiers and 11 officers who should also be prepared to do "light work to feed themselves." Chambré believed that investing these resources would first establish the colony as a stable base from which to engage the Spanish, though he did not propose what that relationship would entail.

It is not clear what the cost of this venture would be, but it was a major plan to transform the fortunes of this struggling French outpost. On the 1669 census, Chambré was listed as a "head of household," owning 40 slaves; he was the largest slave owner. Chambré, believing strongly in the potential of Grenada, did personally invest in property and slaves in Grenada, but no large scale investments like what he proposed were undertaken by the French due to the lack of finances throughout the region. Thus the island continued to languish because it could not compete with the other French territories, particularly Martinique, Guadeloupe, and increasingly St. Domingue, for scarce resources.

Though the French settlers in the larger islands had recommended in 1713 to surrender Grenada for the British-occupied portion of St. Christopher or the neutral islands close to Martinique, the French authorities disagreed. The importance of Grenada was strategic. Though Grenada did not develop as the slave and merchandise entrepôt as planned, it did aid the French in their trade with the Spanish and connected the French trade from French Guiana to Martinique.

Grenada's participation in the trade with the Spanish seems to have finally taken root in the 1680s, especially with the involvement of Governor de Gabaret. Like many other endeavors in the colonies, this one developed because of the personal input of the colonists themselves. It is not clear when the governor became involved with the trade, but "by 1683, illicit trade involved major planters on the islands. Producers like..., Nicolas de Gabaret... are mentioned in complaints."[124] By 1688, after serving eight years as governor, Gabaret had established a trade between Grenada and the Spanish Main. There are no official reports because he seemed to have remained undetected, but there were rumors of his involvement. When Father de La Mousse visited in 1688, he reported that "It is said that Governor [Gabaret]..., acquired a considerable benefit by means of two small boats which belong to him and which he sends out to the mainland [of South America], that is distant from this island only 28 or 30 leagues, where he makes a small business, particularly by the trade in slaves, because these [Indian] nations, like everywhere else, make war with each other and sell the slaves that they take from their enemies, that Europeans buy."[125] It seemed rather unusual when Governor-General Blénac granted permission to the colonists at Grenada to engage the "Sauvages of the Spanish mainland [of South America]" in this outlawed trade in June 1691, but it was probably the influence of de Gabaret, the then governor of Martinique, who may have advocated for this course of action.[126]

When Governor de Bouloc arrived in Grenada in 1701 he immediately began looking at how the island could develop. His foray into trade (i.e. illegal trade in slaves with his old associates in St. Thomas), got him into trouble with the colonists and the authorities when he was unable to fulfill his obligations to his customers and refused to return their money. In 1702, with the French gaining the *asiento* or contract to supply slaves to the Spanish, Grenada's location finally assumed its potential. A number of commentators like Raynal places Grenada's post-1714 economic jumpstart to the expansion of trade between Martinique and the Spanish Main, but it is in the 1690s and during the period of the *asiento* that the foundations of this lucrative trade was established.[127] It didn't take long before Governor de Bouloc came up with his own plan to capitalize on this increasing trade, and as early as August 1704 he proposed the establishment of Grenada as an entrepôt for the Assiento Company.[128] Slave ships coming from the Guinea coast could then stop at Grenada to refresh before setting off to the Spanish Main to sell their slaves. Grenada at that time, however, did not have the infrastructure to accommodate what de Bouloc was proposing. The island needed warehouses for slaves and supplies, and to augment its defenses since it would be housing valuable merchandise.

As part of his plan Governor de Bouloc requested that the island's fortifications be upgraded. De Caylus, the engineer-general for the French islands, visited in March 1705 and concluded that Grenada's defenses were too weak to establish an entrepôt of the Asiento Company. He developed a plan which involved the expansion and enhancement of the small fort, with larger bastions facing north to protect from higher ground, more quarters for officers and soldiers, and a parade ground (Illustration 6.6).[129] Though it would be at least five years before the new fort was completed, Governor de Bouloc had found the means to establish the base that would eventually lead to the island's economic growth during the decades of peace after the 1713 Treaty of Utrecht. Governor de Bouloc also found support for his plan among officials in France who were very interested in making inroads into the Spanish American trade. Other aspects of de Bouloc's plan, his advocacy for using Grenada as the staging point for a settlement on the Spanish Main and from which to stage an attack on the Dutch at Curaçao, connected with similar ideas. Resources for these ventures, however, never materialized, and like many before them they just languished.

Only five years later, Louis XIV's ambition was again the cause of the start of the next war in 1702. Yet it was the assumption of Louis' grandson, Philip, to the Spanish throne that saw other European powers align to form another grand alliance against Philip, who was also in line for the French throne. The War of Spanish Succession would see the unlikely allies of Spain and France against England, the United Provinces, Portugal, the Duchy of Savoy and the Holy Roman Empire. As usual, it would spill over into the Caribbean, pitting the English and French against each other again.

Grenada's continued low economic state excluded it from much of the violent conflicts in the northern Lesser Antilles, except one or two raids. Indeed, the war proved a boon for the island as the French relentlessly pursued legal (*asiento*) and illegal trade with Spanish America. As Pritchard observes, "The war encouraged market forces to flourish as never before.... It may be that more trading than fighting occurred during the middle years of the war in the Americas."[130] Grenada was no longer isolated because it was located directly enroute to and from ports on the Spanish Main.

As the war engulfed some of the islands in the northern Lesser Antilles, Grenada's Governor de Bouloc saw an opportunity. In 1707 when St. Croix was captured by the British he proposed that the inhabitants be transported to Grenada, and extended his offer to the French at St. Christopher when they were booted out by the English in 1708. Unfortunately for Grenada, the deportees went either to Martinique or St. Domingue. Grenada still had a bad reputation within the French Antilles as a place of banishment rather than opportunity, and could not compete with either of those two destinations. At the negotiations for the Treaty of Utrecht in 1713, "French island officials advised Versailles to abandon all claims to islands like Tobago and Grenada in order to secure clear title to the islands adjacent to Martinique (Dominica and St. Lucia)," but the French government ignored this suggestion.[131] Grenada's location proved to be its saving grace.

Despite the progress Grenada had made during the years of war, its overall slow development reinforced its poor reputation among the inhabitants and officials of the *Iles du Vent*. When the French were threatened with the loss of St. Christopher on at least three occasions, they were willing to sacrifice Grenada without a thought because it was seen more as a burden than an asset. To populate St. Domingue, its governor suggested that colonies like Grenada should be abandoned, and when defense became an issue during conflicts abandonment was seen as a solution. Yet French occupation continued despite its detractors primarily because of its location on the periphery of the Spanish Main and the possible role it could play in trade with the Spanish colonies.

In November 1712 Governor-General Phélypeaux made an official visit to Grenada to review its development. His report left no doubt that he had little regard for the island and its potential. As part of his report, he provided an analysis of the islands fully or partially occupied by the French and which should be retained to the benefit of the French.[132] He suggested that Tobago, French since the 1678 Treaty of Nymwegen, should be exchanged with the British for clear access to the neutral islands of Dominica and St. Lucia which were of strategic importance to the valuable colonies of Martinique and Guadeloupe. St. Vincent, due to its large Island Carib and Black Carib populations, should never be occupied and would be of little value to the French. He concluded that "Grenada is not worth being kept," and it was "fit only for indigo," claiming defense costs would be too high and concluded the island was indefensible."[133]

The Treaty of Utrecht in 1713, however, brought about some profound changes in the Caribbean region, the most important being a prolonged peace that spanned three decades. That peace, or rather the absence of open hostilities among the colonial powers, in turn facilitated extensive economic growth within both the French and British colonial economies in the region. At the heart of that growth was the expansion of sugar manufacturing. To a lesser extent, the almost unhindered participation in trade, merchandise and slave trades between Europe, her Caribbean colonies, North America and Africa, facilitated that expansion.

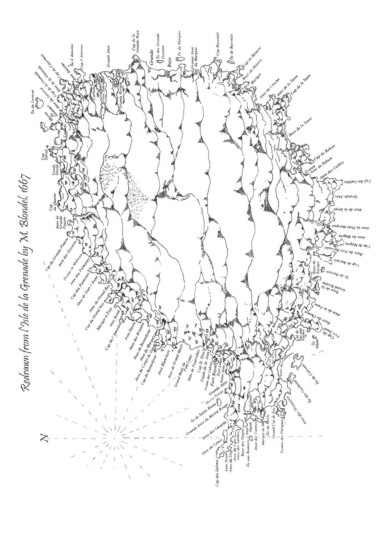

Redrawn from l'Isle de la Grenade by M. Blondel, 1667

Illustration 6.1

Map of Grenada drawn from François Blondel's "L'Isle de la Grenade, 1667" (GE D-8808, BnF) which showed Grenada upside down.

The majority of the coastal place names recorded here remained in 1762, and many survive today in their original form or as translations.

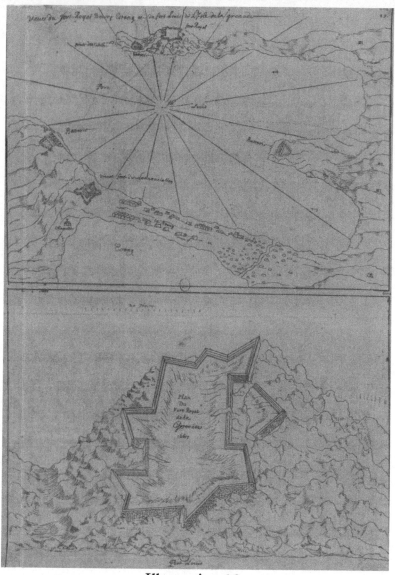

Illustration 6.2

François Blondel's "Veue du Fort Royal, bourg, estang et du fort Louis de l'isle de La Grenade" (top), and "Plan du fort royal de La Grenade, 1667" (bottom). The images show Port Louis on the strip of land on which the initial settlement was built, including the palisade Fort de l'Annonciation, a chapel, and houses scattered along the sandbar; plan of Fort Royal (BnF, MFILM P-184789).

Illustration 6.3

"Pirates land on shore and attack fortifications and a dwelling" from Dionysius van der Sterre's *Zeer aanmerkelijke reysen gedaan door Jan Erasmus Reining, meest in de West-Indien* (Amsterdam, 1691), 36.

The image, taken from the biography of Jan Erasmus Reining, may be a representation of Reining's unsuccessful attack on Grenada on 28 April 1675.

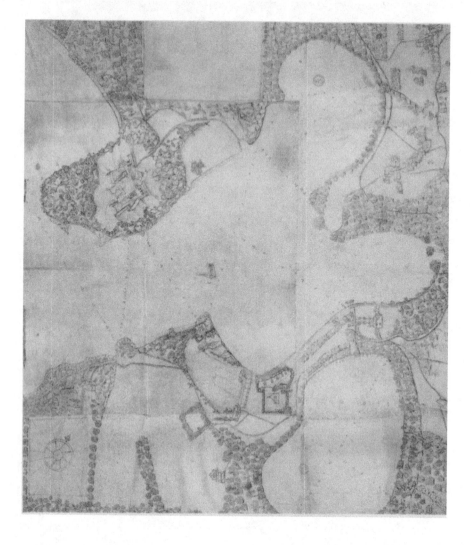

Illustration 6.4

"Port-Louis dans l'isle de la Grenade," c. 1670s (CAOM, DFC Antilles éstrangères, n° 278).

The initial French settlement, with the palisade Fort de l'Annonciation, chapel, and houses scattered along the sandbar; Fort Royal across the bay; two batteries at Pointe des Cabrits under Fort Royal and a second on Morne des Pandus, directly across from the fort. The settlement enclosed the "Étang" or lake on the other side of the sandbar.

146

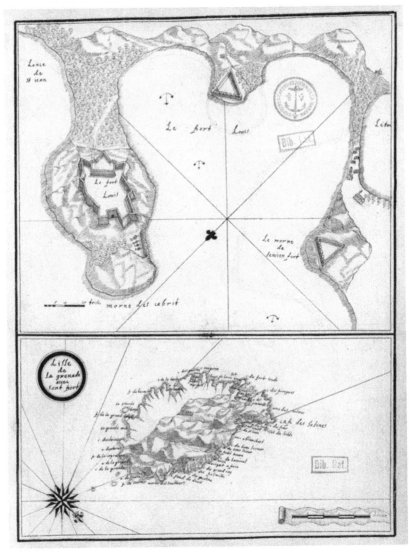

Illustration 6.5

"L'Isle de la Grenade avec sont fort" (Grenada with its fort), c. 1680s. BnF, Départment des cartes et plans, GE SH 18 PF 142 DIV 1 P 2.

Notice the inverted position of Grenada. This inaccuracy dated to François Blondel's 1667 map of Grenada and was repeated on Guillaume De L'Isle's 1717 map of the French Antilles. It was not corrected until 1747 by Philippe Buache. See Labat, *Nouveau Voyages…*, 3: 283 for a discussion of the error.

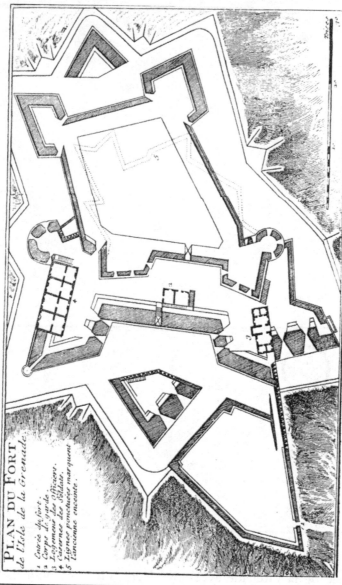

Illustration 6.6

Jean-Baptiste de Caylus' "Plan du Fort de l'isle de la Grenade," c. 1705, from Jean-Baptiste Labat's *Nouveau voyage aux isles de l'Amérique* (Paris, 1742), 6: after 214.

Key: **1**. Entrance to the fort, **2**. Guardhouse, **3**. Officers' quarters, **4**. Soldiers' barracks, **5**. Outline of the old fort designed by Blondel and built in 1668-69.

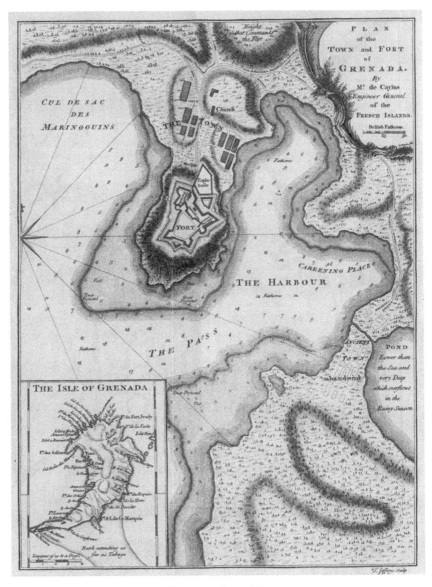

Illustration 6.7

Jean-Baptiste de Caylus' (engineer general of the French islands) "Plan of the Town and Fort of Grenada," c. 1705, from Thomas Jefferys' *The Natural and Civil History of the French Dominions in North and South America*, Pt.2: after 156. (London, 1760).

De Caylus designed the enhanced fort and laid out the small town on a grid. Notice the incorrect orientation of the island in the inset.

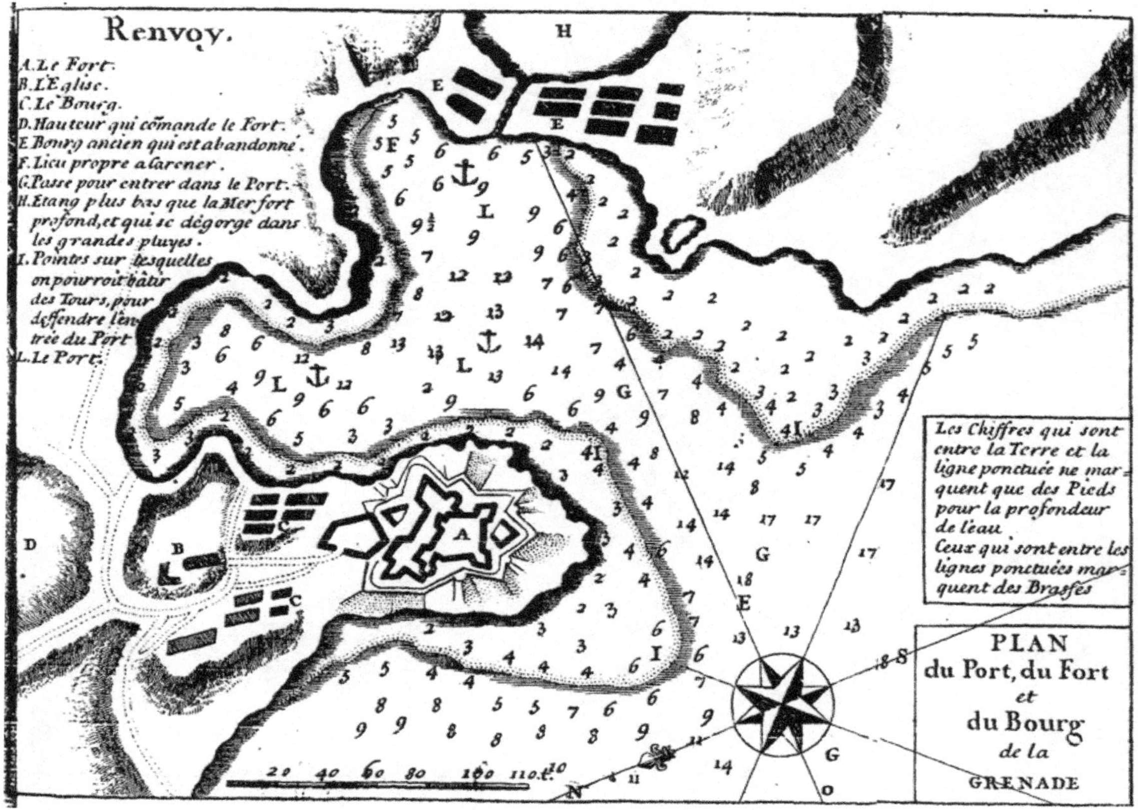

Figure 6.8
"Plan du Port, du Fort et Bourg de la Grenade," c. 1705, from Jean-Baptiste Labat's *Nouveau voyage aux isles de l'Amérique* (Paris, 1722), 4: 420.

Key: **A**. Fort; **B**. Church; **C**. Town; **D**. Heights commanding fort; **E**. Abandoned town; **F**. Careening place; **G**. Port entrance; **H**. Pond lower than the sea, which overflows in heavy rains; **I**. Points on which can be built towers, for defending entry to the port; **L**. Port.

7

Peopling Grenada's Slave Society

"The island of Grenada, Monsignor, is very difficult to populate."[1]

G renada remained a frontier settlement for the first six decades of French occupation, never achieving a total annual population beyond two thousand people, both enslaved and free. Though all concerned recognized that increasing its population was instrumental in advancing its stability and productivity, Grenada failed to attract Europeans and compete in purchasing appreciable numbers of African slaves. It was, however, not unique as peopling the French colonies proved an almost insurmountable problem, despite efforts to encourage indentured immigration.[2] There was serious competition between the colonies for French migrants and slaves, with the most significant colonies of Martinique, St. Christopher, Guadeloupe and later St. Domingue receiving the majority, while the others had to settle for the little that remained. Unlike the British who transported hundreds of thousands of their nationals across the Atlantic to their colonies in the

Caribbean and North America, the French managed only tens of thousands.[3] Though a number of national issues were the cause for the differences in the propensity to migrate among French and British nationals, the lack of labor remained a major problem for the French colonies and was at the heart of their measured development and adoption of large-scale sugar production in the seventeenth century. For Grenada, increasing the population remained a primary concern for both the colonists, governors and the French administration for much of the seventeenth and even the beginning of the eighteenth century until African slaves began to arrive in appreciable numbers.

Seemingly preoccupied with peopling the colonies, census data were constantly requested by colonial authorities. As such, there is a fair amount of population statistics available for Grenada, especially after the 1680s (see Appendix 3). The Grenada censuses date from 1669, and though most were numerical, they provided important social and economic data demanded by the home government. Despite the fact that Grenada's population was small, only two (1669 and 1696) were nominal censuses, providing names of the heads of household, number of family members, and property ownership. These censuses were carried out chiefly "to know if there has been an increase [in the population] since the last [census]."[4] As Boucher notes, the fascinating amount of information available from these censuses is a "mixed blessing" in that the data have to be viewed within the context of why it was collected in the first place.[5] Census data, especially from this early period, are notoriously inaccurate and stem from logistical problems, deliberate attempts to mislead by informants or government officials, omissions, and miscalculations. Their frequency, who collected the information, and for what purposes, influenced the quality of the data.

The primary motive for censuses was the payment of taxes, and as a result there were many reasons for providing inaccurate information. The most obvious is undercounting, especially of slaves, though the state provided incentives to census takers by ceding a portion of sales from fraudulent underreporting. Though the accuracy of Grenada's censuses might be questioned, the frequency of them does lend some credibility to the overall numbers. Despite evident discrepancies, the data clearly demonstrate trends and illustrate a number of interesting characteristics about the Grenadian population, and ultimately, the development of this semi-isolated, struggling French colony. Between 1669 and 1761 at least twenty complete censuses were carried out, but the type of information enumerated varied. The analysis of this data, viewed together with the available narrative, provide a detailed picture of Grenada's demography under the French, and offers insights into the roles of the different groups and how each affected the island's change in status from an outpost to a stable slave colony.

The Amerindian Population

Amerindians, comprising the Island Caribs and Galibis, were settled on Grenada when the French invaded and established themselves. Despite an initial friendly relationship that depended heavily on trade, the Amerindians soon resisted the French expansion and their inherent political domination. In the violent clashes in the 1650s at least a few hundred of them were killed, greatly reducing their larger numbers over the French in the two decades or so after 1649. By the time Grenada became a crown colony in 1674, the Amerindian population had ceased to be a threat. The French colonists and their African slaves soon outnumbered and overwhelmed them, pushing the majority to the periphery of the emerging plantation society. Though conflicts surfaced intermittently, the Amerindians were ultimately forced to accept the permanent French colony and their dominance of the island.

There is no data on the Amerindian population resident on Grenada at the time of the French occupation, but by the 1660s they probably numbered between 300 and 500. While some subsequently took refuge on the continent or on the last remaining Amerindian-occupied islands of St. Vincent and Dominica, a fairly conspicuous group remained in Grenada. They continued to occupy a few of their villages primarily in the east and north of the island, and maintained a quasi-independent existence from the French as they freely traded and communicated with them. As the French colony expanded, there gradually emerged two distinct Amerindian populations as some began living among the French, slowly abandoning their aboriginal lifestyle.

Data on this latter group were recorded on censuses between 1678 and 1735 under the vague terms "*Sauvages*" and "*Caraïbes libre*" (Table 7.2). The data are not consistent from year to year and probably do not provide the most accurate count of the actual numbers of Amerindians who resided within the French colony, and their role remains speculative because of the limited information. Amerindian servants were not unheard of in the French Antilles and those in Grenada probably served as such. On the 1678 household rolls for the *Compagnie Colonelle*, for example, seven *Caraïbes* are listed by name in various households (under the term "*Sauvages*")[6] beneath the slaves ("*Nègreses*"), suggesting they were part of the household's labor force. In 1688 the census listed a population of twenty-two "*Caraïbes libre*," which implies a free status, but according to Father Jean de la Mousse who visited for three months that year, there were "Indian slaves" in Grenada.[7] It is possible that those identified as *Sauvages* or *Caraïbes* on this and later censuses were employed by the French "as personal servants and food provisioners,"[8] or maybe there were others, not native to the island, who were neither free nor bonded. These Amerindians included females, males and children, who probably moved into the colony voluntarily, or were incorporated as the colony expanded into their areas. What is not evident from the data is whether some of these children were the result of sexual laisons between Amerindian females and French males, which was not unheard of at the time. The annual numbers of Amerindians within the colony remained below twenty until the French had spread across the island and occupied the Capesterre, which had been the domain of the Island Caribs.

A second, larger group of Amerindians continued to occupy their traditional villages beyond the boundaries of the French colony. As many as eight to ten *cabets* were present in 1649 when the French arrived. In 1688 Father Mousse estimated that "two or three Kabeys of the Carib Indians, who are free, masters of themselves and separated from the French,"[9] lived in the northern and eastern part of the island. Two or three *cabets* were probably around 200 to 500 people. When Labat visited Grenada at the turn of the seventeenth century he made reference to a small group of Island Caribs that he encountered squatting on the Dominicans' property at Grand Pauvre (presently the Victoria area). He expressed disbelief when informed "that there were many others, which were tolerated in the Capesterre for some trivial advantage the colony gets out of them."[10] Labat did not mention the "trival advantage," but the French often traded with the Island Caribs and may have used that to influence relations with Amerindian groups in South America; or maybe it was the fact that the Island Caribs captured and returned runaway slaves to the French. Labat believed that allowing them to live among the French was foolhardy because he feared that they would revolt against them and renew "their former massacres, if ever we want to move them from the places they now occupy? They are in a better position to resist us than they were before: our colony is weaker, and they might receive very great assistance from the fugitive Negroes, who have settled down with the savages of the island of St. Vincent, and who, multiplying rapidly, will one day be compelled to seek other lands in order to live."[11]

Five years later there was an incident that may have been provoked by the pressures alluded to by Labat. In August 1705 Olivier, an Island Carib, attacked a Frenchman named Catinat, stabbing him several times with the bayonet he had taken from him; he also killed a slave when he attacked another French family.[12] It is not clear as to the cause of Olivier's anger towards the French, but it seems that a French colonist had accused him of stealing a pig, and Olivier accused a French colonist of kidnapping a female relative of his. In that same period two other French colonists and a slave were killed by the Island Caribs over land disputes, much as Labat had predicted. Living in close proximity to each other created pressures that resulted in violent confrontations. Some colonists, terrified by the killings, threatened to leave if the authorities did not put a stop to the attacks. It was, however, the last recorded violent incident between the Island Caribs and French colonists in Grenada. By the 1730s the remaining hundred or so Amerindians quietly integrated into the growing free non-white population and their distinctiveness gradually disappeared from the island. It had taken the French less than a century to totally absorb or rather eliminate most of the Amerindians who had resisted them for decades. Despite their eventual disappearance from Grenada, the Amerindians have left an enduring legacy of resistance to European colonization, with their decades-long and inspiring struggles against the French.[13]

The Slave Population

Like much of the history of the French in Grenada, the story of slavery has received very little attention, with the picture being very sketchy or nonexistent at all. The few available statistics on the slave population for a number of specific years and even less on the lives of the enslaved population for over a century of French occupation is rather disappointing. For a population that have had such an enormous impact on the development of plantation society in Grenada, very little has been uncovered to date. Though this research sheds some light on the slave population, much of what is presented here about the slave trade and slavery have been gleaned from censuses and other records, particularly statistical data. The data examined speak of slavery in abstract terms of how many, providing little details of who the slaves were and how they lived out their difficult lives on a daily basis. The history of specific episodes, like the struggles to escape slavery, is better documented because of its importance to French planters and government officials due to the negative impact on the slave society and economy. The story of *marronage* can be told more fully and enhances the narrative of slavery from those who tried desperately to escape it. Though a partial picture emerges where little have existed before, a great deal remains to be written.

Traites Négrières

In the French Antilles in the mid-1600s slaves were expensive and in very short supply, with only a dozen or two trickling into Grenada in the years under Governor du Parquet, whose colonizing efforts were concentrated on his valuable colony of Martinique. The Comte de Sérillac, upon purchasing the island from du Parquet, decided that importing slaves directly from Africa would be more advantageous despite the fact that the French slave trade (*traites négrières*) was practically nonexistent. As part of outfitting his expedition to Grenada in late 1657, he engaged Dieppe merchants the Hamel brothers and Théodoric Dubour who sent the ship *La Fortune*, captained by Dubois, to sail to the Guinea coast and return with 100 captive Africans; ironically, the ship sank on its way back, killing all on board.[14] It would be decades before a slave ship would arrive in Grenada directly from Africa. During the decade and a half under proprietary rule French indentured servants surpassed African slaves in the colony, but that changed dramatically thereafter.

The Compagnie des Indes occidentales françaises, after its takeover of the island in 1664, supported the desire of planters to increase the numbers of African slaves, yet it proved quite difficult supplying a frontier colony like Grenada. French policies of restricting foreign trade and its own inability to adequately supply its colonies meant the relegation of secondary colonies like Grenada. Unable to depend on the insignificant French slave trade, the colonists turned to the other available markets, especially the Dutch out of Curaçao and St. Eustatius. In April 1669 at least 25 slaves from the Dutch ship *S. Franciscus* were sold in Grenada.[15] In 1670 the Dutch ship *Vredenburg* was captured by the French after illegally unloading as many as 95 slaves.[16] When Dutch merchant Drik Jansen, trading under a passport authorized by the Compagnie des Indes occidentales françaises, arrived in January 1670 with 200 slaves aboard the *Reine Ester*, Grenadian planters eagerly seized the opportunity.[17] With Governor de Canchy's approval, the slaves were landed, however, the French authorities at Martinique sent a ship post haste and seized the slaver and took it to Martinique pending resolution of the case. It is not clear if Jansen ever received payment for the slaves, but he eventually got his ship back.[18] In 1674 Barke, a Dutch trader, sold 80 slaves in Grenada, and again the authorities in Martinique objected and took action against those involved.[19] Despite all the restrictions and difficulties, the colonists at Grenada had amassed over 200 slaves by 1669, the majority illegally bought from foreign traders.

When these foreign markets were absent or completely restricted, planters were forced "to purchase slaves from slaveholders in other French possessions," particularly Martinique.[20] Grenadian planters complained about the high cost of these slaves, as well as the fact that the slaves from the French islands were considered "rejects" or "undesirables."[21] A case in point occurred in 1691 when a ship, operating under the French slave-trading Senegal Company, arrived at Martinique with 150 captives, but the ill health of much of the Africans resulted in a bitter dispute and accusations of attempting to sell them under false pretenses. Rejected by Martinique planters, the captives were divided between Guadeloupe and Grenada, its planters in desperate need of slaves.[22]

These meager supplies of slaves were still not enough for the planters, a small number of who were embarking on sugar production and demanding more slave labor. Munford claims that "by war's end the Blacks in Grenada,... had been worked to death without replacement, and planters in these islands... were abandoning plantations as inoperable."[23] The situation had become very desperate by the 1690s, forcing the authorities to take drastic measures. Few slaves had been landed in the 1680s and the raids carried out by Spanish privateers were effectively depleting the already small slave population. One such raid in 1685 purloined 20 slaves, and another in 1687 abducted 27 slaves and free-coloureds.[24]

Governor de Gemosat, arriving in Grenada in 1690, "admitted that white settlers were helpless without Blacks. He would be satisfied were the Senegal Company to manage to send his island even a mere dozen slaves a year."[25] Since the Senegal Company failed to supply Grenada, drastic measures had to be taken. In 1691, despite a 1683 ordinance forbidding the French from trading in slaves with the Island Caribs, Intendant Dumaitz allowed "a unique slave trade [to spring] up temporarily on Grenada between the French and Carib Indians, who brought slaves from South America."[26] The Island Caribs had a history of abducting slaves from the Spanish, and Dumaitz, following a visit to Grenada in 1688, realized that radical measures were needed to augment the slave population in Grenada otherwise planters might begin abandoning the already deserted colony. In another attempt to supply slaves to the islands, the Sovereign Council of Martinique recorded an ordinance of the King on 7 January 1692, ordering that slaves taken in battle as booty would be distributed to colonists, including those at Grenada. The distribution, however, left Grenada colonists at the bottom and it is doubtful if they received any of this booty.[27] By 1707 things had become so desperate that an expedition under slave trader Montaudouin proved unproductive due to high prices and difficulties with the Senegal Company. Pontchartrain, secretary of the Navy, promised Montaudouin to acquire permission from the Senegal Company "to send his vessel the *Gaillarde* to Martinique, to convey 60 Negroes to Grenada, and 100 in Guadeloupe, which were short of them."[28] As late as 1714 Montaudouin and others were still requesting permission from the Senegal Company to be allowed to transport slaves to underserved colonies like Guadeloupe, Grenada and Guiana.[29]

Concerning all trade, and in particular the slave trade and the distribution of slaves in the French Antilles, Grenada was lowest priority. The usual practice was for ships to unload their cargoes at Martinique and then factors would resell slaves to the other islands, with the buyer having limited choices; it was a seller's market. Grenada's distance from the legal slave markets meant that the choice of slaves available to its planters were limited because it was relatively far away as compared to Guadeloupe or Marie Galante. By the time Grenada planters became aware of newly arrived slaves all the healthy ones would have been bought by the planters living closer.

Between 1670 and 1761 a number of slave ships did stop off at Grenada, oftentimes for refreshments, on their way to other destinations. In 1709 the *Mignon, Coventry* and *Le Duc de Bretagne*, with over one thousand slaves between them, bypassed "Grenada without unloading any of their cargoes, on route to more capacious and profitable markets at Martinique or St. Domingue."[30] It can be argued that Grenada was not a lucrative slave market at the time, lacking the financial resources and did not produce enough to make it worthwhile for slavers to stop there. In retaliation for this slight, however, officials at Grenada took advantage of some of these slavers stopping for refreshments. In February 1711 *Le Jason* found it necessary to stop to refresh before continuing its journey to sell its slaves in Spanish America, but was forced to exchange a few of its slaves for needed supplies. At least two of these ships, *Le César* in 1709 and *L'Impudent* in 1714, did "sell" a few of their slaves before sailing on to Martinique and St. Domingue.

Between 1718 and 1723 a total of nine slave ships of the Senegal Company stopped at Grenada to refresh before continuing on to the French colony of Louisiana in North America. That onward journey was three weeks to three months away, and the opportunity to refresh and recover could mean the difference between profits or losses (i.e. life and death). Yet stopping to refresh was a risk for any captain in that he could be forced to sell a portion of his choice slaves or all of his cargo. So most of these ships had instructions to avoid the French islands altogether, particularly Martinique and St. Domingue, because the officials there might force the captains to sell their cargoes under false pretenses.[31] Some were given instructions that if they were forced to refresh, avoid all of the French colonies "except at the island of Grenada," remaining there for as little time as possible.[32] Grenada, however, was no pushover as expected because its officials often demanded the sale or exchange of slaves before any refreshments could be had. This was the case of *L'Afriquain* and *Le Duc du Maine* in 1721 when it was reported that de Pradines, the king's lieutenant, "forced them to exchange their best blacks for those who were old or sick. Otherwise he refused to sell them food."[33] The captain of *Le Duc du Maine* reported that he "exchanged ten good blacks for blacks who were habitual maroons, old, or sick."[34] Though other ships like *Le Courrier de Bourbon* in 1723, and *La Mutine* in 1725 complied with the demands, others resisted as was the case with the captain of *La Néréide* in 1721 who "refused to trade his slaves for supplies, making do with what he had."[35]

The first recorded French slave ship to actually stop at Grenada to sell slaves was *Le César* in 1709, which sold "a part" of its 210 slaves before going on to Martinique to sell the remainder.[36] In the next half-century a total of ten slave ships would put in at Grenada and sell part or all of their cargo of slaves to Grenada planters (Table 7.3). The expanding island's economy, especially the growth in sugar production, made the emerging Grenada slave market a profitable one. Among the slave ships were two British slavers that were captured, the *Judith* in 1758 with 259 slaves sold in Grenada, and the *Sally* in 1761 with 150 slaves.[37] Eltis, et al, based on the recorded data, concluded that Grenada received a total of 2,242 slaves between 1661 and 1760, which accounted for 0.2 percent of French slaves disembarked.[38] When the British captured Grenada in 1762, however, there were at least 15,000 slaves in the islands, showing that the majority of slaves entered illegally or through the factor market at St. Pierre, Martinique, not from direct imports.

The official import numbers only account for a small fraction of the slaves the island received during French rule, especially if death rates are taken into consideration, abduction of slaves by privateers, and *marronage*. It is quite evident that illegal and unrecorded trade accounted for the larger portion of the slave imports into Grenada. This is partly illustrated by actions in the early 1700s when the island's governor attempted to supply the planters with slaves from St. Thomas.

Governor de Bouloc, having been the king's lieutenant at Port-du-Paix, St. Domingue, was willing to be a bit more adventurous. His former boss was Governor du Casse, who "promoted African slave imports by all means possible, sanctioning illegal commerce with the Dutch of St. Thomas."[39] As a result, Governor du Bouloc had arranged to have slaves transported from St. Thomas to Grenada planters who advanced him money and commodities for the slaves. Unfortunately for the planters, he was unable to fulfill his promises, and refused to refund those who did not receive the number of slaves requested. Thus a few of the planters, upset at being defrauded by the governor, took the matter to the authorities in Martinique. Reporting the complaints to Paris, the intendant was quick to relay the rumors of illegal trade, informing them that "I have learned from various sources... that M. de Bouloc, Governor of Grenada, has established a trade in Negroes and other merchandise with St. Thomas...."[40] The governor received a reprimand.

The majority of slaves that entered Grenada legally during the French period did so on small ships and schooners from Martinique, or illegally from the Dutch and British colonies. Only a handful of French slave ships arrived in Grenada directly from Africa, and so the historical view of planters and others going onboard slavers anchored on the Carenage or other ports to purchase slaves newly arrived from Africa was a rare occurrence.[41] In fact, the norm was the arrival of coasting vessels from Martinique with small numbers of slaves for sale from warehouses by either merchants from Grenada or Martinique. According to Eltis, et al., some 70,000 slaves were re-exported from Martinique prior to 1750, and some of those would have been sold to Grenada.[42]

By the 1750s when Grenada had achieved an increased level of economic development, with over 80 *sucreries* (sugar factories) it does not seem to have had difficulty attracting slave ships to its shores. It is not clear from the evidence if its demand for slaves was met, but the incoming British would immediately see the need for some 10,000 slaves to increase the island's productivity and utilize its uncultivated lands.[43] By 1770, eight years after the British takeover and their purchase of many French plantations, the slave population had grown to just over 30,000, double the population. The majority were supplied by the British, accounting for a total of 157 slave ships between 1763 and 1770.[44]

Esclavage

The arrival of captive Africans to Grenada dates to at least the mid-1500s, brought by Island Caribs who captured them from the Spanish and Portuguese on the South American mainland. The Africans were kept as slaves to work their gardens, as was the case with captured Europeans. This practice was continued into the 1600s, with the French colonists capturing or stealing at least six slaves from the Island Caribs in 1657 and 1658.[45] The French settlers from Martinique brought slaves to Grenada, probably as early as 1649 or 1650. The earliest reference, however, dates to 1654 when Major Le Fort, with the aid of his female slave Barbe, committed suicide with poison she brought to him in jail.[46] In 1656 Dutertre listed "twelve adult slaves and several younger ones" as belonging to Governor du Parquet, and in 1658 six males, six females and a slave child were handed over to de Sérillac following his purchase of the island.[47] In 1658 two slaves belonging to the Island Caribs were held by the French governor of Grenada and the already tentative peace was almost broken because he refused to return them to the Island Caribs. He was willing to risk war with the Island Caribs over the slaves because they were so valuable to him.[48]

The first census in 1669 recorded a total of 222 slaves (*esclaves*), just under half of the total population, but by 1690 the slaves numbered just over 50 percent, and dominated the population thereafter (Tables 7.1 and 7.4). The growth in the slave numbers was far greater than the whites and accounted for much of the population growth thereafter. During the decades of war between 1688 and 1713 the slave population increased eightfold, however, it did not increase enough to facilitate the expansion into sugar-cane cultivation and thereby transform the island's economy. Though indigo factories had gradually increased to over 86, maybe even as many as 100 by 1713, sugar plantations numbered less than ten. The number of slaves needed to produce indigo was far less than that for sugar production which owed its establishment and development to slave labor. According to Watts, "no development at all took place until slave populations had reached ratio-levels of between 3-4 to 1, or even 10 to 1, over their white masters."[49] In Grenada these ratios were not reached until between 1715 and 1718 when the ratio topped 3 to 1, and it was not until 1755 that it reached 10 to 1 (Table 7.5).

The slave population between 1669 and 1713 was not so dissimilar to the white population in a number of characteristics. As Table 7.4 shows, men accounted for on average close to half of the slave population while women recorded between 22 and 30 percent. What is quite evident is the disproportion between men and women in the general population, but it was much more acute among the slave than the white population (Table 7.6). The percentage of slave children grew from 14 to around 25 percent of the slave population, the cause of which, either natural increase or fresh imports, cannot be gleaned from the data (Table 7.6). But one possibility was that the growth was due to the purchase of slave children because they may have been more readily available than desired adults. Because of the scarcity of slaves it was possible that natural births were

162

encouraged, but the health and survival of slaves in the seventeenth and early eighteenth centuries did not support this. The numbers are relatively small so neither natural increase nor imports can be ruled out, but the ratio of men to women and the health conditions of slaves in the era, especially in frontier colonies, make natural increase highly unlikely.

By the end of the seventeenth century the slave population in Grenada had surpassed the white population, even though its availability was limited by the economic conditions on the island and restrictive French colonial trade policies. Beginning in the 1690s, but especially after the end of war in 1713, the situation changed dramatically and the slave population grew quickly and in leaps and bounds (Tables 7.1 and 7.4). As Table 7.4 clearly illustrates, the slave population showed continuous and large increases between 1718 and 1761. As a percent of the total population their numbers increased from 80 percent in 1718 to 88 percent in 1762, climaxing at 85 to 90 percent between 1741 and 1763. The male to female ratio was above 1.5 to one for most of the period, recording a high of 1.84 in 1725 and a low of 1.34 in 1755 (Table 7.7). Though the infant population grew, it most likely was due primarily to imports and not natural increase. Without sufficient data on slave imports for the period of French colonization, it is difficult to determine the direct origin of the slaves and their numbers. For the eighteenth-century period it is commonly accepted that imports accounted largely for the growth in the slave population because it was believed more economical to import rather than reproduce, for a number of reasons. Prominent among these were (1) the unequal ratio between males and females (Table 7.7), (2) the poor health of the slaves, many of whom died within three years of arrival, (3) the poor health and nutrition of the female slaves who could not support pregnancies (Table 7.6), and (4) if the females were successful in producing offspring their survival was doubtful for a variety of reasons, including infanticide and disease. Therefore, natural increase was most probably a small component of the growth in the slave population post-1700, if at all. The disabled and aged slave population averaged around seven percent, accounting for between five and six hundred slaves. Table 7.8 shows the percentage geographic distribution of the population in 1749 and 1755, with the slaves constituting, by far, the majority (over 77% and above) in every district. The density of the slave population was greatest in the districts of Sauteurs and Grand

Marquis, and the urban district of Fort Royal, though a sizeable portion of the slaves in the latter were employed as skilled and domestic labor.

Bwa Nèg Mawon[50]

Fleeing the plantation (*marronage*) proved to be the most effective and leading form of slave resistance. The desire to be free must have been harbored by every slave, but only a few took steps, often dangerous, towards that end. Slaves, for reasons ranging from inadequate food supply, overwork, and harsh treatment or punishment, ran away at the first opportunity. The African-born slaves, unused to the restrictions of captivity, must have contemplated escape, but attempts may have been few. Among the Creole slaves, field slaves, because of the harsh daily work conditions, were believed the most likely to attempt escape.

Despite the steady growth in the slave population beginning in the 1690s, there were a number of setbacks to French planters, particularly the abandoning of the plantations by the slaves. Slaves had probably escaped into the dense interior as early as the late seventeenth century, but numbers remained very small. Attempts at recapture would have proved difficult because of the dense forest and the numerous opportunities for the slave to evade recapture. Plantation owners made the distinction between the two types of absences from the plantation by slaves, *petit marronage* and *grand marronage*. *Petit marronage* was the temporary absence of slaves and was quite common and tolerated, but nonetheless punished, oftentimes severely if the offender was habitual. It was a "short-term escapade in which the slave goes AWOL, as it were, absenting himself only for a short time, remaining in the near vicinity of the plantation."[51] Usually a slave absconded alone or with his/her mate, rarely with more than a few people. She eventually returned or was apprehended and sent back to her plantation. This absence would either be to a neighboring plantation to visit a close friend or mate, or across the island to a town where they could be anonymous for a short time.

Grand marronage was altogether different. Some slaves attempted to escape the brutality of their predicament upon arrival on the plantations. To the white minority slave-holding class, marronage was the most frightening consequences of plantation slavery.[52] Maroons presented a dire threat to the slave society and represented the most successful form of resistance to a system that sought to exploit, degrade, dehumanize and ultimately destroy them. The existence of maroons was a constant indictment of the slave society and its inhumanity towards its captive African labor force. Though their numbers were small, usually less than five percent of the slave population, they instilled fear among the whites and sometimes lived up to their fearful reputation for violence. In the case of Grenada, due to its ecology and geography, there were two types of *grand marronage*–the usual fleeing to the mountainous interior, and maritime *marronage* which entailed escaping the island altogether by sea.

From the available evidence, maritime *marronage* was the first type of *grand marronage* that became a serious problem for the French colonists. Though slaves had probably been taking to the seas since the late 1600s, it was not until the early 1700s that it became significant, thus resulting in extensive record keeping.[53] In 1702 as many as 13 slaves (10 adults and three children) were reported as fleeing to the Spanish colonies to the south, particularly Margarita and the surrounding mainland. The availability of small boats that were so essential for transportation around the island and for fishing made it easy for the slaves to steal them; in some cases slaves were known to construct their own canoes in the forest. It was a great risk to get into a small boat or canoe and travel many miles on the sea not knowing where they were going before reaching land. Though some slaves may have had experience from operating a fishing boat or ferry for their masters, it was nonetheless a difficult and dangerous journey. It is not clear why the slaves would have chosen to flee the island when the interior was generally available to them, but it is possible, as Hall contends, "that in small islands where geographical factors were hostile to the formation of permanent maroon communities, *grand marronage* tended to mean maritime marronage."[54] Or maybe the conditions were not geographical at all, but political because of the presence of the Island Caribs in the Cabesterre who may have deterred the emergence of maroon communities in the initial years. The Island Caribs were known to cooperate with the French and may have agreed to return escaped slaves they found wondering the interior or assisted in capturing them for a price. In 1691 the French colonists in Grenada were given permission to trade in slaves with the Island Caribs who had historically captured them from Europeans on the mainland. The slave was therefore convinced that fleeing the island was his best opportunity for freedom.

Luckily for the escapees they received a welcome upon their arrival in Spanish territories. The Spanish authorities not only welcomed fugitive slaves from Grenada and other foreign colonies, but offered freedom and protection, thus encouraging a steady flow of runaway slaves. Spanish colonies like Margarita and on the mainland were always short of labor and therefore welcomed the fugitive slaves on condition that they swear allegiance to the Spanish king, convert to Catholicism, and were willing to bear arms against Spain's enemies. The Spanish may have also wanted to destabilize enemy colonies by encouraging slave desertions. By 1721 the French saw the situation as detrimental to the colony's continued progress and had to take drastic measures to stop the hemorrhaging of slaves when 120, possibly as many as 200, adult slaves commandeered small boats, canoes or skiffs and made their way south to the Spanish islands and the coast.[55] French authorities accused the Spanish, especially at Margarita, of harboring the runaways. According to Pritchard, "Though the island held a large concentration of slaves, it lay too close to the South American mainland to hold them. Slaves continually deserted, easily stealing small boats along the shore and making their way south. More than 10 percent of the adult slaves deserted in 1721 alone, which probably accounts for the five percent decline in population from just three years before."[56] This exodus resulted in an ordinance on 20 September 1721 forcing owners of boats and canoes to secure them to stem the outward flow of slaves.[57] In January 1722 the inhabitants also insisted that the authorities in Martinique approve a request for a special court to try and punish slaves locally as opposed to sending them to Martinique; they believed that if the slaves witnessed the harsh and immediate punishments inflicted on the maroons they might be discouraged from running away.[58] One of the few actions by Governor du Houx before his sudden death was to grant an amnesty to the maroons in June 1722, believing they would return from the bush in large numbers.[59] It is not clear if the 1722 amnesty met with any success at all, but the problem of maritime *marronage* appeared to have lessened after 1732 as records of these escapes become fewer.[60] The problem, however, did not disappear, as the British would also encounter it decades later.

As the French were working to stem the outward flow of slaves, they were confronted with the emergence of the local maroon communities which had grown to over fifty and began threatening isolated plantations in the Capesterre. French settlements, "in contrast to English settlements, [where] residents' houses were usually clustered in small villages [along the coast], so as to minimize the continued dangers of Carib attack," left the mountainous interior forested for many years after settlement.[61] These areas, beginning in the late 1600s, became the home of the few slaves who were successful in escaping enslavement and avoiding recapture for extended periods. The community, remaining small until the early 1700s, attracted little attention from the French colonists, except the occasional attack by an individual or small group, or the capture of a maroon (in 1722 the captain of *le Duc du Maine* reported that he "exchanged ten good blacks for blacks who were habitual maroons...."[62]). Their gradual growth and the simultaneous expansion of the French plantation economy, which incorporated more and more of the interior, brought about a violent confrontation between the two.

By the second decade of the eighteenth century, the maroons had grown in numbers. Isolated incidences could be tolerated if they did not threaten the entire slave society. Since at least the 1690s, colonists became perturbed by the bureaucracy involved in dealing with maroons. In June 1725 the maroon problem became acute. In describing the maroon problems in the French Antilles, Dabein noted that "all of these disturbances were nothing in comparison with the trouble the maroons caused in Grenada in 1725...."[63] A 1726 report from Grenada outlines the extent of the activities of the maroons that had taken place in the previous year.

> There are in this island of Grenada a troop of 60 Black maroons who have several chiefs, the most notable of whom being Petit-Jean, who belongs to Sieur Gillot; La Fortune, belonging to Sr. Achallé; Samba, belonging to Sr. de la Mitoniere; Jacob, belonging to Madame de Gyves; and Bernard, belonging to Sr. Roulleau.
>
> These Black maroons previously contented themselves with marauding homes during the night to steal food for their subsistence: they then stole sheep, calves, cows, and bulls; seeing that this succeeded so well for them, it got into their heads to surprise some townspeople on the heights; this, they did at the home of one named Lucas, resident of Capesterre, where they were during his absence, pillaged all that they found there, ripped the earrings from the ears of his wife; it is even believed that they violated her, but this is an act that has not yet been sufficiently proven. Finally, having removed the mask, they were, on April 5th of the preceding year [1725], at 9 o'clock in the morning, at the home of Mrs. Cassé, also of the

Capesterre, whose husband had not yet returned from a voyage to France, when, armed with rifles, pistols, and sabers, they set fire to the house, the kitchen, and the henhouse, without allowing the said young woman to take the least item that there had been in the house, and during the inferno, they fired more than thirty rifle and pistol shots; and Petit-Jean killed in the savanna all the game and wildfowl that he could; they only retired after having burnt all the buildings; and while a detachment coming in aid had almost arrived, then they left, beating a drum, without the detachment being able to catch any of them, no matter with what care they took.

They were, the 9th of the same month, at 8 o'clock in the morning, at the home of the Sr. Geffrier, also of the Capesterre, on whom they fired several rounds, by which he was wounded in the left eye, that it is believed he will lose, and also in the left arm, from between 12 and 15 other wounds, of which the second house was offended; they seized his wife, who had given birth only 18 hours before, by the hair, tied her feet together, threatened to strike the head of her newborn against a post, and forced the mother, in order to save her child, to kiss the rear end of the said Blacks; this, she felt compelled to do to save the life of her child; they also ripped out her earrings, wounded a horse with pistol shots; following this unworthy action, they went to the home of Sr. Lequinio, who was at table with the Srs. Duplessis and Fery, and fired more pistol rounds, some of which wounded the said Sr. Duplessis in the right hand while defending the door: he acquitted himself with much valor on this occasion: because, while they were nearly thirty, after being wounded by a pistol shot, and being taken bodily by another, which he almost got through without being wounded, he set them to flight, and pursued them rather far.

These are the grave facts: and one learns every day, by those who were taken, that their intention was to bring the domestic Blacks [i.e. slaves] into their party, and come to a general action, in which they would have accorded life only to an equal number of the most distinguished and beautiful white women of the island to serve them as concubines.[64]

Living in the Cabesterre, primarily in Sauteurs and Grand Marquis, the bands of maroons oftentimes raided habitations for food and sometimes female slaves. As Dabien adds, "In point of fact, the most frequent crime was the abduction of Negresses."[65]

The French were so shaken by the daring of the maroons that they termed their actions a revolt, and immediately went maroon hunting. In the next few months the hunting parties killed eleven maroons, among them Marion, a woman, leaders Petit-Jean, Jacob and Bernard, and captured another fourteen, including leaders Samba and La Fortune.[66] Those captured were sent to Martinique for trial, which was contentious for the French in Grenada. According to the above cited report:

> To such an evil one could take too violent a remedy. When these Blacks are taken, they must be put on trial, then sent to Martinique, sixty miles away; to be judged by the Council; they will arrive there when a session has just ended; they will have to wait for another, that will happen two months later. All the delays will do considerable wrong to this Island, where the Blacks are nearly ten to one more numerous than the whites; thus unless a prompt and severe example is made, the Colony will find itself at risk: it is for this reason that the sentiment of all the inhabitants would be, that for the conservation of the island, that the [Governor-]General and Intendant should obtain from his Majesty the establishment of a Council on this Island to judge these bandits as a last resort.[67]

The French at Grenada complained that they needed a local tribunal to deal with runaway slaves as opposed to sending them to Martinique to be judged by the Council and punished. The colonists felt that "the public spectacle of agonizing executions just might calm the unruly Blacks and dissuade them from continuing to 'run amok.'"[68] In June 1726 the Royal Chamber (*Chambre Royale*) was approved for the trial and punishment of slaves, with the following criteria: (1) It will be composed of five judges: king's prosecutor, clerk of the court, the judge of the island who will preside, the royal lieutenant, and notable inhabitants, preferably the gentlemen or the officers of the militia; (2) That the governor and the king's lieutenant will hold session before the judge, and have a deliberative voice, and the Chamber can only be called after having informed the governor; (3) That its jurisdiction is restricted in cases pertaining to maroons, revolt, voluntary homicide between slaves, rapes, or poisoning; crimes implicating whites have to be sanctioned by the Council at Martinique; (4) The royal attorney will send to the *procureur général* the explanations of the criminal procedures used and the judgments rendered so that he can give a summary to the Council, and remedy any abuses; and (5) That the Chamber be held only during the morning, and after mass so that all the officers must attend.[69]

The problems of the maroons were a direct result of the system of slavery, and despite the fact that the French in Grenada established a court to judge captured maroons, disturbances continued throughout the remainder of French rule. In an attempt to dissuade the slaves from fleeing into the mountains and participating in depredations against plantations local residents took matters into their own hands. When maroons were captured by hunting parties they were tried and beheaded, with their bloody heads left on spikes along the main roads as a warning to others of what awaited them.[70] Informed of these displays, the Conseil Supérieur at Martinique prohibited the colonists' despicable display of barbarity.[71]

The census of 1749 listed a maroon population of 62, only seven percent of the total slave population, but significant to warrant recording. They were located mainly in the parishes of Megrin (18) and Sauteurs (25). In 1761, the last census under the French, the maroon population had grown to 256. The threat they posed, however, is not clear since plantations had by the mid-1700s encompassed much of the island, though many remained undercultivated. They were restricted to the most isolated and mountainous parts of the island, and therefore did not encounter the French on a regular basis, their activities restricted to stealing food and other items.[72]

Blancs

The frontier colony of Grenada did not attract men with resources, they instead flocked to the more prosperous colonies of St. Christopher and Martinique, and later St. Domingue. A popular quote from the mid-1600s was quite direct when it stated that the "Nobility inhabited St. Christopher, the middleclass at Guadeloupe, the soldiers at Martinique, and the peasants at Grenada." In Grenada there were lots of poor whites who were pushed out of the fast developing islands, most forced to eke out a living in frontier colonies where they still had access to land. It was one of the primary reasons that the island took so long to adopt sugar production and why coffee and cocoa production remained important secondary crops for many years.

Policy after policy, especially in the late seventeenth century, attempted to affect an increase in the white population by natural increase through early marriages and immigration. It usually took some devastation in the other islands like natural disasters to cause people to want to immigrate as was in the case in 1689 when about "seven or so persons of St. Christopher established at Grenada."[73] In June 1707 Governor de Bouloc proposed that the entire French population at St. Croix, which had been abandoned as a result of war, could be transported to Grenada[74]; and in March 1708 he proposed that the French at St. Christopher could be sent to Grenada due to the island's capture.[75] Of course, these colonists chose to relocate to St. Domingue and Martinique instead, leaving Grenada to slowly increase its population without much help from the colonial authorities.

Between 1669 and 1713 the overall white population on Grenada increased by about 100 individuals, just short of 25 percent in the 45-year period, and an increase of under one percent per year (Table 7.9). The increase in the white population, especially natural births, was small initially, and migration of whites, mainly *engagés* (indentured servants) who served in Grenada and former *engagés* from the other islands, was also very small. Children, however, made up a significant portion of the white population, increasing from 22 percent to just over 50 percent between 1669 and 1704 (Table 7.9), which may have partly resulted from the early marriage policy. Almost all would have been by natural increase, though not specifically Grenadian births as families from other islands may have migrated to Grenada in pursuit of access to available land. The large numbers of white children illustrate higher birth and survival rates than the slave population due to somewhat better nourishment and overall health (Table 7.6). The ratio of adult males to females hovered around 1.4 to 1, leaving a relatively large number of men without an opportunity to find European wives. Thus, some engaged in relationships with enslaved women, fathering mixed-race children and creating a new dynamic within Grenadian slave society (Table 7.11).

The white minority was a varied group consisting of a few wealthy planters, a handful of small merchants, many smallholders or middling planters, a large number of poor whites eking out a meager existence, a few dozen soldiers, government officials, and a very small number of *engagés*. The free white population increased by 166 percent between 1718 and 1761 (Table 7.1). The majority of that increase was between 1718 and 1741, and had probably begun to stabilize at the latter date once the plantation society was approaching a climax under the French.[76] The adult male to female ratio was as low as one to one in 1725, but by 1755 it was 1.7 to one, having increased over the past three decades.[77]

By the 1740s the Grenadian white population was beginning to resemble the white population of the larger Caribbean though it may have differed in one respect. Throughout the British Caribbean, small and middling farmers were often pushed out by larger planters, especially after sugar cane became the primary crop. Though present in the French Caribbean to a lesser degree, the cultivation of secondary crops like coffee, which were not in direct competition with sugar for land, may have saved many of the peasant farmers in Grenada from joining the ranks of the poor and forced to migrate.

Though their numbers were small, *engagés* represented the most consistent group of white immigrants that were added to the population annually. *Engagés* entered Grenada with the first group of settlers in 1649. According to Labat, Governor du Parquet "gave land to all of those who asked for it, on condition that those who had no servants or hired people come together."[78] Dutertre reported in 1656 that du Parquet owned "twenty to twenty-five men engaged for three years, who didn't yet achieve the first," but two years later only "eleven engaged Frenchmen" were handed over to de Sérillac.[79] Some of the other planters most probably had servants. In 1658 when du Bu took control of the island his group came from France with a number of *engagés*, though de Sérillac did not seem to have invested much in indentured labor while he was preparing for his occupation of Grenada.

The *engagés* came to the French Antilles to improve their standard of living, enticed by the higher wages in the growing agricultural sector. They were under contract, salable from one master to another, for three years of service, hence the name *trente-six mois*, or the "thirty-six monthers"; Colbert later reduced the length of service to eighteen months in the hope that more Frenchmen might be enticed to go to the colonies. The majority was young men, especially in the early years; in 1658 two women servants arrived in Grenada. The life of the *engagé* was oftentimes difficult, sometimes harsh, and many died before the termination of their contracts from diseases, lack of proper and adequate nutrition, and abuse by their masters. It was reported that their treatment was "worse than slaves for the simple reason that the planters benefited from their labor for only three years compared to the lifetime, albeit short, of the slaves."[80] In 1651 two *engagés*, Le Flamand and L'Anglois, killed their master, Pierre Savari, because "they were poorly fed and often badly beaten by him."[81] Those who managed to survive indenture became

172

freeholders, farming small plots of land, eventually becoming part of the free permanent white population. A case in point was Nicolas Fremont who in 1664 was listed as an *engagé* in Martinique, but in 1669 was a freeholder in Grenada, along with his wife.[82]

Almost every governor in Grenada after 1674 pleaded with the French authorities to send even a handful of *engagés*, particularly women. In 1680 Governor de Chambly requested that sixty French, half now and thirty a year later, be sent to Grenada; he also wanted twenty "women to marry the soldiers" who were in Grenada as part of the *troupes de la marine*, with the hope of them becoming *habitants*.[83] Remarkably, the island received two dozen women as part of a shipment of 150 *filles du roi* (girls and women reqruited by the king and sent to the colonies for marriage) sent to Martinique, and by March 1681 twenty-four of them were married to men in Grenada.[84] It would be the last time that requests for female immigrants would actually be met, but the demands never stopped. In 1702 Governor de Bouloc sent an urgent plea, "We have real need of twenty or so young women (*jeunes filles*). I would undertake to get them married as soon as they arrived. But, if you please, Sir, they should be sent here direct, and not stop anywhere on the way."[85] As late as 1718 King's Lieutenant de Pardines requested that "the annual dispatch of twelve *engagés* would be the only means to develop the colony."[86]

The French authorities were much more generous when it came to disabled prisoners (*forçat invalids*) who seemed to be plentiful in the 1680s. Bégon, a former intendant of the *Iles du Vent* and now intendant of the Navy, wrote to Seignelay, secretary of state for the Navy, about sending *forçat invalids* to the islands. In reply, Seignelay approved of the idea, "Since you estimate necessary to send a good many convicts to the island of Grenada, you must convince the captain of the vessel *Concorde*, which newly arrived from the America, to transport 134 disabled persons there contained in the roll which you sent me."[87] So in 1687 Grenada was among those that received these convicts. The 1688 census listed 70 "*forçats*" or convicts, but in 1690 they were only 34 listed (in 1687 three convicts were among those abducted by Spanish privateers).[88] There were many complaints against the convict immigration scheme because the island authorities "were appalled at the aged, decrepit, and crippled lifers who proved to be utterly worthless additions to the population."[89] The deportations had nothing to do with supplying the colonies with indentured labor, being more to rid the galleys of invalids and undesirables, and perhaps even rid France of religious undesirable Huguenots.[90] In 1691 the remaining convicts demanded *"lettres de réhabilitation"* (letters of pardon that also restore the honor of the convict).[91] The scheme itself only lasted two years, 1686 and 1687, and involved over 800 deportees.

Between 1669 and 1744, the annual population estimates for *engagés* were never greater than 65, with a low of 36; in 1669 there were 55 *engagés* or *"blancs"* (Table 7.10). In 1690 there were 34 *engagés*, and from Table 7.10, it would appear that their numbers averaged averaged around 35 much of the time. As late as 1737/38 six *engagés* left France for Grenada.[92] One of the last French censuses in 1755 recorded 19 *engagés*, among the last to serve in Grenada. The British capture of Grenada in 1762 ended the practice of white indenture.

In the early period of Grenada's colonization *engagés* possibly played an important role as hired labor in the production of food crops and tobacco. Though the labor of indentured servants had become obsolete in the French Antilles by the 1670s following the increase in sugar-cane cultivation and the reliance on cheaper slave labor, the French government sanctioned by law the continuance of the practice. Its stated goal was to counter the large slave population which had exploded in the colonies and aid the creation of the militia to oppose the threat of a slave revolt. It also supplied artisans whose skills were in demand on the plantations. In the French colonies, the supply of *engagés* never kept pace with the demand, and the total number brought to Grenada probably amounted to a few hundred, definitely under one thousand, over the entire French period. Fines were even imposed on planters and merchants who failed to meet minimum imports of *engagés*, but the economics of labor in the region had already made white indentured labor redundant. Added to this was the social environment which did not create the necessary incentives for increasing the number and size of white families. Thus the white population saw its numbers decrease relative to the slaves and even the growing free non-whites. There was a concern over the growing slave population as was clearly evident with the continuation of white indentured immigration from France. The possibility of slave revolts and violence, especially after escaped slaves had begun to attack remote plantations, were uppermost in the minds of the minority white population who were at times obsessed with protecting their persons and property. Yet, the economic demands of the plantation economy necessitated the continued importation of more and more Africans to supply the expanding sugar industry and replenish the premature deaths of many slaves. Their continued social exploitation was maintained by the body of laws known as the Code Noir and if necessary, which often was the case, by force.

Affranchis

Intermediate between the ruling white minority and the majority slaves were individuals who comprised at least two social categories, but nonetheless shared a similar ambivalent legal status. As such, they could be viewed as neither free (as whites) nor slave, but according to Munford, they could be seen as communal property as slaves were individual property. The two segments of this group of free non-whites or freedmen (*affranchis*) comprised the free people of color (*gens de couleur libre*) and free blacks (*nègres libre*).[93] The former were mixed race, the result of black and white procreation. Since their emergence in the late 1600s, persons of mixed race or mulattoes (*mulâtres*)[94] remained "a paradox and a social enigma" throughout slavery.[95] By the 1680s, with their growth in numbers, French Antillean slave society began to take notice of them (Table 7.11). They were regarded as second-class citizens, subordinate to whites but above the slaves, holding a precarious intermediary position in Grenadian slave society. Some whites feared them because they were neither "white nor black," and thus they, like the maroons, represented a contradiction within the white minority-dominated plantocracy. The free blacks, though sharing a similar legal status, encountered a somewhat dissimilar reaction due to the politics of race then emerging in the region.

The history of the mixed-race population under the French is very fragmentary, with very little commentary beyond inconsistent census data. A census of the French Antilles in 1683 recorded only three "*mulâtres*" in Grenada, but in 1687 there were 31.[96] Between 1687 and 1735 censuses recorded data on the mixed-race population separately so the upward trend in the numbers are quite evident; beginning in 1741 the data grouped all non-whites together, including Amerindians (Table 7.11). Because of the way the data were compiled, they do not afford much analysis other than illustrating the growth over time and gender; the inconsistency of the data makes further analysis problematic. It definitely shows a gradual, but growing trend over the half century, with a greater growth in the adult female population as opposed to the male. However, it is probably more useful to cluster the two groups of the free non-white population as one for reasons of statistical analysis.

By 1700 the *affranchis* had grown to 52, a very small increase over the past 13 years (Table 7.11). Like the rest of the population, growth was very slow, and due to the low disparity in the ratios of white men and women did not increase dramatically until much later. The economic prosperity of the post-1714 era impacted the *affranchis* population which had grown to 107 by 1718, of which over 50 percent were *nègres libre*. In 1735 that population recorded 157, and in 1744 increased to 189. In 1749, 38 percent of *affranchis* lived in the urban parish of Fort Royal, many probably possessing skills that kept them lucratively employed (Table 9.3). The *quartiers* of Sauteurs and Goyave were the others with sizeable populations. The 1755 census revealed a startling increase in the *affranchis* population, especially in the rural *quartiers* of Grand Pauvre and L'Ance Goyave, illustrating most likely their growing involvement in small farming of secondary crops or as skilled craftsmen in either the rural centers or on plantations. However, the growth in the number of adult females and children accounted for the majority of the overall increase, which was likely due to white men freeing their slave "wives" and children. In 1761 the *affranchis* population climaxed at 574, but by 1763 when the British took over the island, it had decreased to 455, representing 3.3 percent of the total and 27 percent of the free populations.[97]

The growth in the *affranchis* population and especially the *gens de couleur libre* were a result of the social dynamics of gender and race in Grenada's developing plantation society. There was an acute shortage of white women of marriageable age and colonial authorities seemed incapable of remedying the dire situation, especially in this frontier colony. It is quite evident from the available information that white men of means often procured wives from the larger French colonies, particularly Martinique. Those without adequate means to find white mates relied on whatever the local situation presented, thus some men engaged in sexual liasons with slaves and free black or mixed-race women.

Recognition of the effects these relations could have on the social structure led the French authorities to issue prohibitions in the *Code Noir* of 1685, attempting to legislate the sexual behavior of white males to deter the increasing population of not just mixed-race children, but the freedom of their black slave mothers. As the problem of the dearth of white women was never addressed adequately, the taking of slave or mixed-race females as mates continued unabated, eventually becoming a component of the social structure that was accepted and even promoted. In the French colonies the practice of concubinage using black and mixed-race females became known as *plaçage* (from the French *placer:* "to place with") and was no longer restricted to a need for female mates. Young white males, especially those with means, engaged in these relationships even before marrying a white spouse. The arrangement, often described as left-handed marriage (*mariage de la main gauche*), was a common-law marriage with provisions for the *placée* and her children. Housed usually in the town, the man would live with her or visit if he was married and provide for the children, in some cases even sending the children to school in France. Though many *placées* and their children were shortchanged or even exploited by this arrangement, some were often allowed to take the name of the white father and thus the children were identifiable in the society.

In the case of Grenada little research has explored the relationships between white men and black and mixed-race women and the effects on the *gens de couleur libre* and *affranchis* population.[98] That such practices like *plaçage* played a role is evident, but other relationships contributed and may have played a greater part. More prominent was "marriage," both legal and common law, of white men with non-white women where the men remained with the women and children as one family. The only official document that actually supports the existence of these marriages was the 1750 Carriacou census which records as many as five families with either white men and black or mixed-race women constituting the household; three of them had mixed-race children. The other evidence is anecdotal, and can be gathered by looking at the family names and residence of the mixed-race families, and, when available, the wills of white males who provided for their mixed-race children. Some of the more prominent families included Honoré Philip and his "*nègresse libre*" wife Janette, Pierre Fédon and his "*nègresse libre*" wife Bridgette, and Espirt Fauchier, owner of Tivoli estate, who returned to France with his nine mixed-race children and their two black mothers (formerly his slaves), Nanette and Franchine.[99] Probably the most prominent white family to have offspring with black and mixed-race women were the

Cloziers, leading the Reverend Francis MacMahon, as an indictment, to describe Clozier d'Arcueil and Clozier Decoteaux as having "had a numerous progeny of coloured children"; these have resulted in mixed-race family names of Clozier, Decoteau and Chantemel.[100] In the case of *plaçage*, it is a little more difficult to determine the extent of this practice in Grenada, again only anecdotal evidence is available. The prominent Clozier family was known to have multiple families, but one member, Clozier Decouteau's only family was his mixed one.[101] Other possible families as a result of *plaçage* included Besson, Beltgens, Madey, La Touche, Roy and St. Bernard.

Reacting to the growth of the *affranchis* population in the early decades of the eighteenth century, a number of laws (like that of October 1713 which forbade manumissions without official sanction, and the application of the head tax to *affranchis* in 1724), sought to control the growth and potential of the *affranchis*. These laws were a direct consequence of the growing prosperity of *affranchis* in general, and mixed race in particular who through inheritance and entrepreneurship were gaining economic prominence as small planters and artisans.

Geographic Distribution of the Population

The geographical distribution of the population can be inferred from only two of the French censuses carried out in 1749 and 1755 (Table 7.8). By the former date, it is quite evident that within 100 years the population had spread across the island. This dispersion most probably took place in the 1720s and 1730s when both the overall population grew at an average, annual rate of 4.68 percent (between 1726-41) and sugar cane cultivation grew at a rate of 7.70 percent (between 1722-38). Based on the population distribution data from the 1669 census, the increasing population had spread north and east from the southwest. Only 16.3 percent of the population resided in the "urban" *quartier* of Fort Royal, while the bulk of the population, 83.7 percent, lived in the rural districts. In 1749 seventy percent of the population lived in newly occupied areas of the island since 1669. Just about 50 percent of the population was concentrated in two *quartiers*, Grand Marquis and Sauteurs, which contained the most productive *sucreries* (sugar factories) on the island and a large number of the coffee estates.

The slave and the total population distribution showed a direct correlation with the estates in each district, particularly *sucreries* (Tables 9.3 and 9.4). The higher the number of *sucreries* in a particular district meant the higher the percentage of both slaves and the total population. The slave population was almost evenly distributed across the island percentage wise, but larger numbers resided in the *quartiers* of Grand Marquis and Sauteurs which contained about 50 percent of both the coffee and sugar estates. The white population showed a different distribution, it was highest in the *quartiers* with the smaller overall populations. This was due to the abundance of middling and small farmers producing primarily coffee and cocoa in the *quartiers* of Gouyave and Grand Pauvre, and both crops required less slaves for cultivation and processing than sugar cane.

The data on the slave population is most complete and provide a picture of the geographic distribution of the slaves. The slave population's distribution was based on the number of estates in each district and mirrors numbers for the years 1749 and 1755 for which data exist (compare Table 7.8). For the free population there is no corresponding geographic distribution for 1763, but Table 9.5 gives an idea of the distribution of slave owners that compliment the data for 1749 and 1755. Changes in the geographic distribution of the free population were probably minimal.

8

Production in Grenada's Slave Society

*With no real incentives, continuing conflict,
and little capital, agriculture developed slowly.*[1]

Until the cultivation of sugar cane became primary after the 1730s, the island's economic base was built on a number of crops that assumed importance for specific periods of time. These various crops, though later assuming a secondary role in the economy or altogether disappearing from the landscape, were vital to the economic development of the colony, especially during the period of exploration. Tobacco gave the colony its first crop and with it came the beginning of the plantation system. It was closely followed by indigo, which for over fifty years, developed the plantation economy and laid the foundation for the expansion into sugar production. For this reason, the eventual secondary crops were primary in their impact on the developing plantation economy.

Between 1649 and 1762 Grenadian planters produced a variety of tropical export crops. Of these, coffee, cocoa, tobacco, indigo, ginger and cotton, were the most important and on which the island depended at various times and in varying degrees. Yet, by the mid-1700s sugar cane had became the primary crop and usurped the largest share of land, labor and capital, leaving the other crops a distant second. Though these crops were secondary they were important to the colony's economy, especially before sugar production dominated. Their increasing cultivation by the early 1700s showed the growing trend towards plantation agriculture and signaled the ascendance of sugar cane cultivation. And as a compliment to sugar, crops like coffee and cocoa were important to middling and small farmers because they allowed a larger segment of the population to participate in the growing economy, as well as empowering a class of small planters. This fact is valuable in charting Grenada's social and economic development under the French.

The rapid economic growth evident in Grenada in the post-1713 period was part of the larger growth experienced throughout the region, especially among the French Antilles which had so far lagged behind the British colonies since their establishment in the mid-1600s. According to Wilson, "In the period following the Utrecht settlement, these islands [in the French Antilles] enjoyed an economic development hitherto undreamed of."[2] Sheridan adds that,

> But far outpacing the British were the French West Indies. Incomplete statistics show that Martinique's sugar output increased from 115.4 in 1710 to 410.9 in 1753, Guadeloupe's from 126.6 in 1730 to 158.0 in 1767, and St. Domingue's from 138.9 in 1714, to 848.0 in 1742, and to 1,252.8 in 1767. The increase was 25 percent for the Dutch colonies, nearly 100 percent for the British colonies, and approximately 365 percent for the French colonies.[3]

The prolonged absence of hostilities among the various colonial powers resulted in the redirecting of energies and resources toward the economy, primarily the plantation.

Tobacco

Tobacco, asserts Boucher, was a "gift" of the Indians to the Europeans, which ironically accelerated the process of Island Carib decline in the region.[4] It was the crop that incited northern Europeans to settle the Lesser Antilles and became the first important staple of both the British and French colonies. The profits derived from Caribbean tobacco production between 1624 and 1635 resulted in the founding of a number of new colonies by both the French and English.[5] Though its boom period in the 1620s and 1630s was never regained, its cultivation in the islands became established and continued into the eighteenth century, despite severe competition from the North American colonies, especially Virginia, and low market prices. Even after Barbados had adopted sugar cane as its primary crop in the 1640s, the French Antilles continued to rely on tobacco and thus Grenada initiated its cultivation in 1649.

The tobacco plant (*Nicotiana tabacum*) is native to the Americas and was grown in the Caribbean by the Amerindians when Europeans arrived there in the late fifteenth century. Though utilized as a medicine and snuff in Europe thereafter, it was its adoption as a cigar, especially among the British in the late 1500s, which spurred a growing consumer demand that led to the settlement of the Lesser Antilles as tobacco plantations by northern Europeans.[6] The failed attempt to settle Grenada between April and September 1609 by a "London-Dutch syndicate" was, according to Andrews, "intended to found a tobacco producing colony."[7] That failure to establish a tobacco colony in Grenada by the British, however, may have led directly to the introduction of "Spanish" tobacco in Virginia where its cultivation transformed the struggling colony and guaranteed its subsequent survival.

Du Parquet's primary goal in the first months of settlement, according to Dutertre, was the production of subsistence crops for the sustenance of the colonists. He did not want them to plant trade goods,[8] yet the settlers embarked on tobacco cultivation about three months after landing in Grenada, possibly soon after clearing enough land in the vicinity of the initial settlement. Around October/November, just prior to the first Island Carib attack on the colony, the settlers "had already reaped a harvest of tobacco, which was found so good that a pound was worth three of that of the other islands."[9]

Tobacco was "an ideal product with which to begin a plantation"[10] because of its relative ease of production, which suited the labor and capital requirements of newly settled areas like Grenada. Once the difficult task of clearing land had been accomplished the process of tobacco production was essentially one of planting and weeding.[11] A crop native to the region, tobacco was harvestable in less than a year, and a good product could be produced by a single, reasonably skilled planter with minor help in the final processing stage.[12] Unlike indigo and sugar, tobacco required no extensive labor and capital investments in order to return an immediate profit. Land, which was free and required only clearing, was readily available.[13]

The cultivation of tobacco begins in a nursery where the seeds are sown. After about one month when the seedlings are about two inches they are transplanted to the field into "small hillocks," usually at the beginning of the rainy season. Weeding, at least once a month, is very important and is its most demanding field task. Insects and caterpillars, if allowed to persist, can have a devastating impact on the yield, even destroying the entire crop.[14] After approximately fifty days in the field the plant is topped to curtail its floral development to benefit its leaf growth until it matures in another fifty days. Topping, the process of removing the floral buds, was a very important step because it determined the quality of the leaves, both the number and size harvested. The entire tobacco plant was cut and left to wilt in the sun, beginning the curing process. Bundled together in heaps, it was sweated for 3-4 days before removal to the curing shed. There, for 8-10 or 12-15 days depending on the source, it was hung from the rafters of a shed to allow air to circulate between the leaves.[15] The final process, its most time consuming which often required additional labor was the rolling of the tobacco onto sticks (Illustration 8.1).[16]

That the crop was produced for over five decades is the only available evidence of tobacco cultivation in Grenada, and was most likely produced exclusively, especially after indigo and sugar cane cultivation began, by poor small farmers. Though the market price had fallen drastically since its heyday, it still afforded a profit to small farmers who had low labor and capital costs. There are no figures on the number of tobacco farms, area under cultivation, or production from Grenada for the over fifty years of its production there. This is due possibly to small production by peasant farmers and though important to them, relatively unimportant to the overall French Caribbean economy or even Grenada's. Hence Grenada's production became part of Martinique's if it was legally exported. That the crop was cultivated is confirmed by a number of sources beginning with the Anonymous author.[17] Savary, in his 1675 publication *Le parfait négociant*, recorded that Grenada produced "bon tabac."[18] Around 1700 Labat, on a weeklong visit, recorded that the captain of the ship he sailed on took on a cargo of agricultural produce of which tobacco was one of the crops bound for Martinique.[19]

Tobacco, because it required so little investments of labor and capital, was the crop of choice of the peasant or small white farmer. Additional labor was restricted to indentured servants and one or two slaves on the larger plantations of wealthier planters. On his small grant of land the peasant farmer cultivated tobacco and sold his produce at the market price. Because investments were minimal, he was able to make a living even though the price on the European market was relatively low in relation to some of the other crops being produced. Watts believes that the small farmers in the French Antilles continued to produce tobacco partly because of "a natural predisposition towards growing crops with which they were already familiar," but added that the acute labor shortage may have been a contribution, which was the case in Grenada.[20]

Though the price of tobacco never regained its late 1620s climax, it still enabled producers to earn a decent living in the French Antilles. It wasn't until 1674 when the French government established a marketing monopoly that Caribbean tobacco became unprofitable.[21] Production in Martinique and Guadeloupe subsequently decreased and disappeared by 1680, increasing their sugar cane and indigo cultivation. St. Domingue was slower to abandon tobacco, but the detrimental effects of the continued monopoly forced its disappearance by the mid-1680s. Its effects must have been devastating to the small farmer in Grenada who, unlike the larger planter with available resources to switch to indigo production, had no other alternative but to continue producing an almost worthless crop. Mims' description of the small planter is apt:

> The small planter was idling away his time in the sunshine with his hungry children about him. Before him was a small tobacco field. As he gazed upon it, he doubtlessly thought of the days when the large green leaf, turning to a rich yellow for the harvest time, brought its reward for the days of sweat and toil. The bitterness of defeat and disappointment and rebellious anger must have been in his soul. The curse was writ upon his brow.[22]

It is understandable then that Grenada experienced only marginal economic growth in the seventeenth century when its small farmers, who comprised the majority of free holders if the 1669 census is taken as representative for the period, were forced to continue to produce a crop with very little remuneration.[23] But some farmers, wealthy enough to afford the capital and labor investments, did discontinue tobacco cultivation and diversified into either cotton or indigo production which afforded, for a time anyway, greater economic profits. Some small farmers did switch to ginger production, its demand on the European market growing because of its use as a spice, and as medicine.

Ginger

It is possible that ginger may have been grown in Grenada since the 1650s. If not, the continuing low market price for tobacco, especially in the 1660s, may have led to the adoption of new crops like ginger (*Zingiber officinale*) that brought temporary but greater returns. The Spanish had produced ginger in the Greater Antilles for many years, but its cultivation in the Lesser Antilles would surpass previous Caribbean production.[24] Since the 1640s, following the collapse of tobacco and cotton prices due to over production, ginger was produced in the French Antilles by small farmers. To aid diversification in the presence of growing sugar cultivation Colbert thought it wise to decrease the total area under sugar cane by encouraging the cultivation of various secondary crops like ginger, cotton and indigo, even spices like pepper and nutmeg.[25]

Ginger is originally from Southeast Asia, and has a long and colorful history as one of the spices of the legendary Spice Trade between Asia and Europe. Though enjoyed as a spice in Europe "when mixed with pepper, cloves and cinnamon," it was, however, its use as a health remedy, still common today, that made it popular in the seventeenth century.[26] It reproduces vegetatively from rhizomes or underground stems which are cut into small pieces about three inches and planted in raised beds. In about six months it can be harvested. Processing includes the scraping of the pericarp or outer skin before drying in the sun. Boiling, a common method to remove the skin, discolors the ginger, leaving it hard and of lesser value than when scraped.[27] César de Rochefort records the only seventeenth-century reference to ginger's cultivation in Grenada in his *Histoire naturelle et morale des Antilles de l'Amérique*.[28] As it was a crop grown by the small farmer its production was most likely minor, perhaps insignificant, but it seemed to have persisted into the eighteenth century. As late as 1752 it was among the exports bound to France from Grenada (recording only one *quinteaux* at 40 *livres*) in a ship's cargo.[29]

Silk

The idea of producing silk in the French Antilles originated directly from France, of personal interest to Louis XIV who sanctioned its production. In 1673 Chief Minister Colbert suggested the idea to Governor-General de Baas as a way to diversify the islands' agricultural economy away from sugar cane which had become almost addictive for planters.[30] In 1682 seeds of the mulberry tree, necessary to feed the silkworms, were sent to Martinique, but they did not meet with success. The king, however, was not discouraged and in 1687 provided funds to aid the establishment of silk manufacture in the islands.[31] Grenada was among the islands that received mulberry seeds which were distributed to planters to cultivate in preparation for the silkworms. A year later, Governor de Gabaret reported to Martinique officials that the mulberry trees had failed.[32] Thus ended the island's attempt to produce silk. Martinique was more successful, sending a sample of silk to France, but by the end of the 1680s the mulberry trees throughout the colonies had died and with it the French dream of Caribbean silk.[33]

Indigo

Indigo was to Grenada what tobacco was to Barbados, the first lucrative crop that laid the foundations, both economical and social, for the "sugar revolution" of the eighteenth century. Unlike ginger, which had a restricted European market, indigo had an established market because of Europe's historical demand for tropical dyes. Yet its early use was for medicinal purposes and had a long history of American production by the Spanish, especially in Guatemala. By the mid-1600s indigo, because of its lower cost of production, had succeeded in ousting woad (*Isatis* spp.), a European dye plant, from the market and dominated it until the early 1800s.[34] The production of the French colonies, especially St. Domingue, dominated European markets in the eighteenth century.

Indigo (*Indigofero tinctoria*), a Southeast Asian plant, was introduced to the region by the Spanish in the sixteenth century.[35] It is a small shrub which, following an elaborate process, yields a blue dye from its leaves that was used to color cotton fabrics in Europe.[36] It is "best grown on thoroughly cleared savanna land"[37] and was cultivated in the south of Grenada where it found an agreeable climate and soil. Planted in the rainy

186

season, its most demanding labor requirement in the field was weeding, at least five times during the three month growing period. Weeds and caterpillars were its worse enemies and the latter could destroy a crop within hours. After growing for between six and twelve months, the appearance of flowers signals the first harvest when cuttings are taken, leaving 5-10 cm (2-4 in) of the stem to ratoon.[38] At least 4-5 cuttings are taken at 6-8 week intervals before the plant is replanted, but the quality of the dye in the leaves diminishes after each cutting.[39]

The processing of the leaves is a very intricate operation and determines the quality and therefore the value of the final dye. Bundled cuttings are packed into a large brick or stone vat (10x10x3 feet), called the *tempoire*, and immersed in water and allowed to ferment.[40] After about six to twenty hours the water-soluble dye in the leaves seeps into the water. Residue precipitation time is very important because if leaching is left too long bacteria will begin to consume the dye and leave a slimy residue.[41] A short steeping results in the purest color but less dye, while a longer steeping resulted in a lesser color but increased dye.[42] The yellow to orange pigment was then drained into a smaller vat, called the *batterie*, where a mechanical wheel or paddle, powered by slave, later animal or water power, was used to aerate the water and induced the indigo to oxidize and precipitate as a blue water insoluble solid which fell to the bottom of the tank.[43] The thick pigment, according to Dutertre, was packed into small wooden boxes, and hung to drain.[44] It was then placed on trays to dry in the sun.[45]

Though indigo cultivation did not appear on the Grenada census until 1687 it was cultivated since the late 1650s. Dutertre, in his January 1657 letter to de Sérillac describing the island of Grenada, wrote that M. Renaudin, who was left to secure de Sérillac's interests on the island, "will operate an indigo plant: [for which] he will have to put to work your slaves and the *engagés*."[46] So it is most likely that indigo cultivation was long established in Grenada before it became large scale or important enough to be recorded on censuses.

The cultivation and production of indigo required some investments of capital and labor, and therefore was not a crop for the peasant farmer working a few acres. As Batie notes, "it was not a one man affair."[47] It was the first plantation crop cultivated in Grenada which, according to Batie in evaluating the seventeenth-century industry, "may have led to economies of scale in the production of indigo" because of the "need for sizable vats."[48] Though one tank could be employed in the processing of indigo as may have been the case in the Greater Antilles, the usual was two, but some planters utilized as many as three and four, depending on the size of the plantations (Illustration 8.2).[49] The production of indigo was undertaken by fairly large planters because of the capital investment required to procure vats, fields and additional labor. Though its production in Grenada possibly dated back to the late 1650s, its widespread production seems to have begun in the 1660s, influenced no doubt by the growing slave population and the influx of wealthier planters from the other French colonies.

A number of planters recorded on the 1669 census, at least 28 percent, owned a large enough number of slaves and *engagés* and probably were producing indigo and not involved in the production of tobacco, ginger or other secondary crops.[50] Since census data did not include sizes of plantations or the slaves attached to them, no conclusions can be drawn about the productivity of indigo works or factories (*indigoteries*) in Grenada. In 1671 the colonial government gave exemptions for two years to indigo plantations in an attempt to increase production. It is not known what effect this had on production in Grenada because there are no available figures, but it is most likely that the royal edict of 1693 exempting indigo duties on the re-exportation of indigo helped spur its cultivation because *indigoteries* increased from 34 in 1690 to 58 in 1700. In 1696 there is a glimpse of one indigo planter, Jacques Ferray, who had been on the island since the 1670s. He was 39 years old, had a wife and three children, and owned 22 slaves laboring on two *indigoteries*. Between 1687 and 1722 Grenada's indigo plantations increased gradually, almost an average increase of four per year (Table 8.1). On an official visit to Grenada in 1712, Governor-General Phélypeaux viewed the island as fit only for indigo production, thus devaluing Grenada to support his view that it was of little importance to France and should be relinquished.[51]

In 1722 at its climax there were 159 *indigoteries* (indigo processing plants), but there were additional planters producing indigo and utilizing the available processing facilities.[52] There is no information on acreage under cultivation and production data to complement the data on the number of plantations, restricting estimates of labor employed in indigo production; the basic plantation data nonetheless illustrate the continuous growth in indigo cultivation/production and demonstrate a definite upward trend after 1687. It would appear that in 1722 Grenada planters reacted positively to the exemptions on capitations for new sugar factories as only a year later the number of *indigoteries* began to decrease, recording 140. They continued to decline thereafter until 1742 when indigo plantations stopped appearing on censuses, but cultivation continued. The 1761 census recorded the cultivation of indigo planted on 69 acres.[53] The immediate cause of the decline was due to the rapid expansion of sugar cane cultivation in the 1720s and its greater profitability usurped the land and labor previously allocated to indigo production[54] (Illustration 8.2). The emergence of coffee as a crop for the middling and small farmer may have also affected indigo production negatively. It is also possible that the dominance of production in St. Domingue led to the shift in Grenada. In the 1720s it was reported that indigo produced in Grenada was not as good as St. Domingue's and sold for 8-10 francs less per pound because of its inferior quality to that of the larger island.[55] Censuses thereafter did not include statistics on the number of indigo processing plants or production most likely because it had become relatively small in comparison to crops like sugar cane, cocoa and coffee. In 1739 indigo was listed as part of the produce bought at Grenada by one ship's captain (recording 25 pounds at 4 l.t. per pound). The overwhelming majority of production was concentrated in the district of Basse-Terre, but very small amounts were also cultivated in the districts of Megrin and Grand Marquis. Though under British rule, Grenada (and Carriacou) exported approximately 27,000 pounds (12, 273 kg) of indigo to England in 1762,[56] from cultivation on a number of plantations, no estate exclusively cultivated it. Most of the production in the first few years of British rule was from French plantations which already possessed the processing vats. The British may not have invested in indigo because in 1776 production remained the same. On Carriacou only three of the French plantations produced indigo. Production continued under the British until its final demise in the early 1800s.

Though the decrease in the number of *indigoteries* was mirrored by the increase in the number of sugar plantations, the increasing cultivation of the latter was directly related to the history of cultivation of the former (Illustration 8.2). The production of indigo was "like sugar manufacture, [which] involved the articulation of relatively more complicated, expensive scientific processes and technology and built up a labor force necessary for the entry into sugar production.[57] By 1741, when the number of *indigoteries* had decreased to three as the number of sugar plantations had increased to 56, the latter was well on its way to becoming the primary sector in the island's agricultural economy. Indigo was seen as a transitional or intermediate crop and paved the way for successful sugar production.

Annatto

Another dyestuff produced in Grenada was *roucou* or annatto (*Bixa orellana*). This small shrub, growing to about 5 m (6.4 ft), is native to the Caribbean. It was used by the Island Caribs to decorate their bodies and possibly as a sun and insect block, and was most likely growing in Grenada before French occupation. According to Labat, it was cultivated on savanna land and in Grenada that environment would have been the south, meaning it and indigo were planted on the same land.[58] Roucou grew from seed planted at the beginning of the rainy season and was harvested twice, at Christmas and at St. John's time.[59]

The dye was extracted from the pulp surrounding the seeds by macerating them in water for "seven to eight days until the liquid began to ferment."[60] The seeds were extracted from the dye-colored water by a sieve. The thick liquid was then boiled, causing the pigment to coagulate and the bright orange-red coloring was skimmed off as it frothed.[61] The cooled roucou, packed in 2-3 pound balls or cakes, was wrapped in clean leaves for export. It was used as a food coloring and a cloth dye.

Though the Spanish cultivated *roucou*, it was the French, according to Batie, who were the foremost producers.[62] The only reference to its cultivation in Grenada was given by Labat who recorded it as one of a number of crops transported to Martinique.[63] Production probably dates to the 1660s and continued into the early 1700s by small farmers.

Cotton

The tree cotton (*Gossypium histura*, variety marie-galante) was the plant used for cotton cultivation in the West Indies in the seventeenth and eighteenth centuries.[64] It is believed to have been 'cultivated' by the Island Caribs even before the advent of Europeans in the region. It was a perennial, drought-resistant shrub which produced a soft lint. Its production was carried out by small, but not poor farmers because it required some, if small amounts of capital and labor investments. The popularity of cotton was due to its low demand for continuous care as was the case with indigo and sugar cane. Cultivation was restricted to areas primarily in the southern part of Grenada and some of the islands of the Grenadines, where suitably dry and sunny conditions prevailed.[65] Cotton is harvested after six months and continues 3-4 times thereafter.

The first reference to cotton production in Grenada was by Labat who recorded it as one of the crops taken on board a ship to carry to Martinique around 1700.[66] Its cultivation most probably dated from the late 1600s. Between 1700 and 1762 production was small, cotton being a secondary crop, far behind sugar cane, coffee, cocoa and indigo. Figures for cotton cultivation date from 1718 when it was first recorded on censuses (Table 8.2). That year "400 *pieds de cotton*" were grown, but it was an insignificant amount in comparison to cocoa which recorded "126,010 *pieds*" (about 126 acres). Cotton showed up on lists of produce taken on board ships bound for France in 1739 (18 *quintaux* at 95 l.t.) and 1752 (7 *quintaux* at 190 l.t.). In 1761 the census recorded that cotton was grown on 89 acres. It was the primary crop in Carriacou during the French occupation, but there is no indication as to its level of production compared with that of Grenada. Based on the 1763 survey, only one plantation of 64 acres and worked by 18 slaves (belonging to Jean St. Bernard) cultivated cotton in Basse-Terre. That district was responsible for over half of the island's production, with l'Ance Gouyave producing around a third, and the other districts producing very small amounts. It is clear that many small planters, working with a few slaves on a few acres, produced a great deal of the crop. Grenada's exports of cotton to England in 1762 amounted to 46,713 pounds,[67] 166,686 pounds in 1763 and 368,032 pounds 1764.[68] Cotton became a significant crop after the British took over the islands, with a major shift to larger plantations in the Grenadines, worked by scores of slaves and owned by British, particularly Scottish planters. Alexander Campbell's cotton plantation on the island of Mustique was a good example.[69]

Cocoa[70]

The cacao tree is native to Central America and was first commercially cultivated in Martinique around 1660, thereafter spreading throughout the French Antilles.[71] It is not clear when the cultivation of cocoa in

Grenada first began, but it probably dates to the last decades of the seventeenth and most definitely by the first decade of the eighteenth century. It is often recorded that the plant entered Grenada from Martinique after 1714, but that is probably too late since recorded cultivation dates to the 1718 census and it was pretty much established by then[72] (see Table 8.2).

A small tree growing to 20-25 ft. (6-14 m), cocoa (*Theobroma cacao*) was cultivated in the Greater Antilles by the Spanish since the 1630s. It became established in Grenada in the early 1700s and a trade item by at least the end of the second decade of the 1700s. Cocoa, with rather exacting climatic and topographic requirements, finds an agreeable environment in many parts of Grenada with its high rainfall, abundant sunlight, suitable soils and hilly terrain.[73] The cocoa tree produces thousands of pink and white flowers and its subsequent fruits on the trunk and larger branches (less than fifty of the flowers develop into fruits). From November to February, and again from April to June, fruits are harvested. The 20-60 cocoa seeds or beans are surrounded by a white, mucilaginous pulp and housed in a ribbed, irregularly shaped yellow or red pod, 6-10 in. (10-32 cm) long. The seeds are then removed from the pod, placed in a wooden box (in the "sweating boucan" or shed) and covered with banana leaves for six to eight days to allow fermentation ("sweating"). This process gives the cocoa beans their distinct flavor. The beans are then dried on large trays in the sun for about seven days and stored in a boucan. Following drying the brown beans were exported to Europe where there was a growing demand for the beverage. Its claim to fame was enormous as in this 17th century description by Charles de Rochefort:

> The drink taken moderately causeth Venery, Procreation and Conception, and facilitates Delivery, preserves Health, and impinguates: It helpeth Digestion, Consumption and Cough of the Lungs, Plague of the Guts, and other Fluxes, the Green-Sickness, Jaundise, and all manner of Imflammations and Oppilations: It cleanseth the Teeth, and sweetth Breth, provoke Urine, cures Stone and Stangury, expells Poyson, and preserves from all infectious Diseases; all which vertures are attributed to it by several creditable Authors.[74]

Cocoa was not the easiest crop to cultivate, but by 1718 Grenada recorded 126,010 "*pieds de cacao*" (about 252 acres) being grown. Between 1718 and 1726 cultivation increased dramatically, recording 600,000 *pieds* (about 1,200 acres) in the latter year as middling planters pursued its production. The reason for its dramatic increase was due to the fact that only 15-20 slaves were enough to maintain 100,000 trees, so planters with a few slaves could produce a small orchard for a good return.[75] Disaster, however, struck in 1727. It is not quite clear what was the cause, but a number of islands saw their cocoa fields destroyed, Martinique's partially linked to an earthquake that year. Contemporary sources describe the cause as a "blast," which has been interpreted as either weather phenomenon like a hurricane or drought, or a fungal attack.[76] Dand adds that the criollo variety, common throughout the region, "was susceptible to all manner of diseases and drought."[77] The disaster seemed to have affected small farmers in Martinique to such an extent that quite a few left the island for better prospects, some to Grenada.

To help rejuvenate cocoa cultivation and also to spur coffee production, a royal declaration in 1730 exempted all new cocoa and coffee plantations from the head tax on slaves for two years. It seemed to have had little effect on cocoa production as census data between 1731 and 1741 show minimal cultivation probably from the trees that survived the "blast." It was not until 1745 that cultivation improved to 1718 levels, reportedly due to the introduction in the early 1740s of a new, sturdier variety of cocoa from Cayenne. In 1761 cocoa cultivation was recorded at 138,500 *pieds* (about 277 acres). Cocoa beans, though in rather small quantities, were listed as part of ship's manifests leaving Grenada in 1746 (21 *quintaux* at 60 l.t.), 1749 (88 *quintaux* at 110 l.t.), 1751 (66½ *quintaux* at 50 l.t.), and 1752 (6 *quintaux* at 60 l.t.).

It is not until the end of official French control of Grenada that data on cocoa cultivation and production become available when the British carried out a survey of the island and its plantations. The 1763 survey shows that (1) there were only four plantations exclusively growing cocoa; (2) the majority of cocoa cultivation was engaged in by planters who were also producing coffee; and (3) the hilly districts of L'Ance Goyave and Grand Pauvre were by far the primary areas of production, at around 80 percent, the former producing twice as much as the latter (Table 8.3). No conclusions can be drawn by looking at the plantations exclusively producing cocoa because there were too few and only scant information available on them. For example, François d'Imbert, in the district of Fort Royal, owned 114 acres with eight slaves producing cocoa, while the Chevalier du Suze, in l'Ance Goyave, owned 352 acres with 39 slaves.[78] There is no breakdown of the data for the twenty-four joint coffee and cocoa plantations, but it seems likely that cocoa and coffee were not intercropped, for as Clarence-Smith observes, reference to this form of cultivation was "not mentioned in treatises on coffee before the 1840s."[79] It was also rarely successful. Based on the 1763 survey, it is possible to estimate the total acreage owned by cocoa producers to be less than 1,500 acres, with 930 acres comprising the four estates exclusively producing cocoa.[80] Williams, et al., estimates that the actual area under cultivation in 1763 was 740 acres, much higher than the 1761 figure from the census.[81] In 1762 Grenada exported 75,530 pounds of cocoa to England,[82] which a year later had increased to 196,300 pounds, over 80 percent of cocoa exported from the Ceded Islands.[83] Exports for the next five to seven years were exclusively from French era cultivation and reached 305,400 pounds in 1770, probably as a result of increased investments in labor. Exports continued to increase and cocoa would become one of the primary export crops in Grenada for the next two hundred years, but under the French it lagged far behind that of coffee.[84]

Coffee

Coffee (*café*) was the last of the secondary crops to be introduced and cultivated in Grenada under the French. It was brought to Martinique around 1723 and cultivated in Grenada shortly thereafter; its cultivation was readily adopted and expanded rapidly. The romantic story of Gabriel Mathieu de Clieu is well known, and though he may have brought a plant or two to Martinique from Paris in 1723 there were most likely plants already growing in the French Caribbean, specifically St. Domingue since 1715. Cocoa cultivation suffered as a result of coffee's expansion since both competed for similar resources. By 1731 Grenada had already recorded cultivation and for the next three decades it would expand rapidly.

Coffee (*Coffea arabica*) is a small tree which grows well under shade at relatively high elevations, temperatures of 60-70°F, and 60-90 inches of rainfall. It grows to 16 feet if not pruned, a regular practice to keep as a shrub to afford easy harvesting. Trees can begin bearing fruits after 3-4 years, but optimal production begins after 6-8 years and continues for at least 20 years under good husbandry conditions.[85] It fruits 7-9 months after flowering, producing red, cherry-like berries. Coffee cultivation, Trouillot contends, "was a protracted but not particularly complicated process."[86] The beans are picked when red and "washed" before preparation for decortication. After a number of days the seeds are placed on a *glacis* or smooth platform to dry in the sun. A mill, usually drawn by mules, water, wind, or rarely slaves, broke the barks which enabled slaves to finish the process of bark removal. Coffee, like cocoa, was grown across the island, particularly in the quartiers of Basse-terre, Grand Pauvre, Megrin and Grand Marquis (Table 8.3 and Illustration 8.3).

Coffee's cultivation in Grenada was meteoric. In 1731 coffee recorded cultivation of "11,300 *pieds*."[87] Four years later cultivation recorded 951,855 *pieds* (about 952 acres), and by 1741 had doubled again (Table 8.2). In 1755 Grenadian cultivation reached 3.1 million *pieds* (about 3,100 acres), and in 1761 it reached its highest at 3.4 million *pieds* (about 3,369 acres). Its growth was phenomenal, not only in Grenada, but throughout the French Antilles by the mid-1700s. Though coffee had been grown on a large scale in the region since the mid-1720s, its production did not take off until the 1730s, primarily because "restrictions on importation of Caribbean coffee into Europe were lifted after the 1730s."[88] Beginning around the mid-1730s and into the early 1760s, coffee production in the Antilles underwent rapid growth. During this first boom period its profits were second only to that of sugar, and although a distant second, they were significant.[89] Coffee plantations (*Caféières*) assumed great importance in colonial agriculture and other crops, such as cocoa and cotton, became secondary to it as resources were redirected to its production.

A combination of factors in the international market made coffee cultivation very lucrative, beginning in the second quarter of the eighteenth century. Primary among these were the growing consumer demand for coffee as a drink in Europe due to the availability and decreasing price of sugar which was added to the drink. Many of the island's small farmers, who did not possess the large sums of capital and labor necessary for sugar production and previously engaged in the production of other secondary crops, found coffee cultivation lucrative. Coffee cultivation was most likely responsible for the increasing wealth of small farmers, rescuing them from the poverty that came from growing less highly valued secondary crops and elevating them to the status of middling planters. Coffee's adoption by the free coloreds, more evident in the later British period, may also have elevated these second class citizens to an economically and socially relevant group. According to Trouillot, "Coffee could be a small investor's choice, an underdog's stepping stone, and many in the Antilles tied their fortunes to its promise."[90] Coffee production, moreover, did not require the high labor demands of sugar cane. Once a coffee, and for that matter cacao, plantation was planted its development was assured with only limited capital and labor input. The highest labor requirement thereafter was the seasonal harvesting of the beans. *Caféières*, in addition, did not require weeding.

Like the other crops, production and export data for coffee during the French period are not available. Because it is a tree crop that takes between four and seven years before maturing and continues to produce for many more, the available data during the first few years of British rule can reveal some of its French history. The 1763 survey reveals a great deal about coffee production under the French, providing, for the first time an idea of the area under cultivation and the size of the plantations. The data show that (1) coffee was the second most important crop in terms of acreage under cultivation; (2) the total number of estates exclusively producing coffee numbered 162, with another 24 producing both coffee and cocoa, and 16 coffee and pasture; and (3) the total acreage owned by coffee planters was over 25,000 acres, with the average plantation size approximately 148 acres, ranging in size from 20 to 512 acres (Tables 8.3 and 8.4). The majority of these plantations were much underutilized, with only about 12 percent actually under coffee production. With investments under the British coffee plantations would see huge inputs of labor, and production and yields would increase tremendously in the mid-1760s and 1770s.

The 1763 survey makes no mention of the number of slaves owned by coffee planters, but the *Capitation Rolls for the Quarters...* for 1763 lists property owners and the head tax incurred for their slaves, and identifies the slave owners by the type of crop they produced. Though the data are not altogether consistent, what emerges when these two documents are merged is a clearer picture of coffee cultivation in Grenada at the end of the French period. As Table 8.5 shows, coffee planters were far greater than the 1763 survey revealed, some owning as little as one slave, but many owning between five and ten slaves. Of the 316 planters recorded as cultivating coffee, they owned over 5,500 slaves as calculated from the

Capitation Rolls for the Quarters..., amounting to as much as 40 percent of the slave population. What was interesting was that a large number of coffee planters cultivated small plots or a few acres alongside large plantations with scores of slaves, primarily in the districts of Megrin, Basse-Terre, Grand Marquis and Grand Pauvre, though every *quartier* cultivated a fair amount of coffee. Exports to England in 1762 amounted to just under 1.25 million pounds, steadly increasing to 1.33 million pounds in 1763, and 1.46 million pounds in 1764; it reached 2.4 million pounds in 1772. Despite the fact that sugar was the primary crop coffee held a strong second place, but it would gradually lose ground as British planters invested heavily in sugar plantations they bought from the French, in some cases converting coffee to sugar plantations. Additionally, following the British takeover, some French planters who cultivated coffee left the island.

Sugar cane

The census of 1687, almost twenty years after the possible establishment of the industry in Grenada, records four sugar plantations with mills (*sucreries*) operating in Grenada (Table 8.5). This rather small increase may have been due to the overproduction of sugar in the French Antilles between the 1660s and 1680s, and lack of resources for investment.[91] In 1704, seventeen years later, there were only six *sucreries* operating on the island. Here, colonial rivalries between 1688 and 1697 may have been the immediate cause of the stagnation of the industry. Though the number of mills in operation is a reasonable measure of sugar production, the fact that smaller planters who could not afford the capital to purchase a mill, were still cultivating sugar cane leaves some room open for speculation on numbers. As a matter of fact, the practice of cultivating sugar cane and paying a portion of the crop, usually half, to the owner of a mill to have one's cane milled and processed were common in the formative years of sugar production in the region.[92] Though there were risks involved in such production practices, it is possible that a number of planters practiced this. To what extent it may have been practiced in Grenada, if at all, is not known.

Grenada's sugar industry developed slowly as was the case in the entire French Antilles, yet Grenada's growth was far behind that of all the other French colonies. For all of the seventeenth century the industry was practically stagnant (Table 8.5). This was due to a number of factors, primarily unavailability of investment capital and labor, i.e. slaves. Yet other factors like colonial rivalries in the region discouraged the growth of the industry. Watts provides a general list of factors he believes inhibited sugar expansion, including

> warfare; worn-out soils; sugar gluts and declining markets; over-extension of existing capital, leading to debt; restricted labor; interference with trade routes; declining prices, and/or increasing taxation; restrictive legislation; food shortages and/or famine; absenteeism; hurricanes and other storms; and insect pests.[93]

Many of the above factors were definitely affecting the sugar industry in Grenada between the 1670s and 1713.

By the 1660s Grenadian planters had adopted aspects of the plantation system of agriculture then common throughout the region, utilizing African slaves as the primary labor force. Beginning in the 1660s, but more so after 1713, sugar cane was added to that mix, creating a social and economic dynamic that came to characterize the region. Though cash crops like tobacco, indigo and cotton were the early favorites for a number of reasons, sugar cane was the crop which transformed Grenada's colonial economy from one of malaise to one of stability. Not only was the economy transformed, but a significant part of the colonial society was reorganized around the cultivation of sugar cane (*canne à sucre*) and its processing into sugar (*sucre*). The cultivation of secondary export crops continued and was a vibrant part of the economy, but they recorded a distant second to sugar cane which engaged by far more land, labor and capital (Table 8.3). A picture of the Grenadian landscape by the mid-1700s would have illustrated the pervasiveness of sugar cane grown on large plantations, and the industrial complex—sugar mills, production houses and large storehouses—necessary for the production of sugar (Illustration 8.6).

If there was an ideal crop suited to the Caribbean environment and the plantation mode of agriculture it was most probably sugar cane. It was one of the first crops cultivated in the region as a cash crop, dating back to the early 1500s, with its cultivation and production under the Spanish in Hispaniola. The Portuguese at Pernambuco, Brazil demonstrated its economic success as well as developed the mode of production which characterized it throughout the Lesser Antilles in the seventeenth century.[94] There were a number of features which made sugar a profitable commodity for Caribbean producers: (i) increasing European demand, (ii) comparative advantage, and (iii) its variety of uses. More so than tobacco which experienced its climax in the 1620s and early 1630s, sugar revolutionized the agricultural economy in the Caribbean and made these colonial possessions valuable real estate.

Sugar cane cultivation and sugar production were not readily established in Grenada, at least in the first seventy-five years of French settlement. A number of issues contributed to the general low state of the economy in the latter half of the seventeenth century, but there were also particular characteristics of sugar manufacture which made it difficult to establish. These barriers to entry—particularly land, labor and capital—though not exclusive to the sugar industry, were nonetheless more acute relative to the other crops so far cultivated in the region.

The one characteristic that made frontier colonies like Grenada attractive was the availability of cheap land. Land grants were apportioned freely to anyone willing and able to cultivate them. According to a report from Grenada, "The number of Squares (i.e. area), which are allowed in a Grant is sometimes regulated in Proportion to the Abilities and Fortune of the Person who demands it."[95] Grenada, affected by the availability of land in the entire French Caribbean, must have experienced some increase in its population between the 1660s and 1670s, many of whom were seeking land grants. According to Munford, "land grants ceased to be available to former indentured servants between 1660 and 1670 in Martinique, Guadeloupe and St. Christopher" due to the expanding sugar industry and the increasing value of land there.[96] When Tracy arrived in Grenada in 1664 he did in fact bring with him some sixty to eighty inhabitants from Martinique and Guadeloupe and distributed land among them.[97] Yet, Grenada, though becoming attractive to dispossessed former *engagés* in search of available land, had to compete with St. Domingue, the most attractive frontier French colony in the 1660s.[98]

Though the late 1600s may have witnessed the distribution of land grants to small planters who cultivated tobacco, indigo, ginger and cotton, the early 1700s exhibited signs of change. In the first quarter of the eighteenth century Grenada was beginning to look like Martinique and Guadeloupe between 1660 and 1680 when they were on the verge of the "sugar revolution." A list of properties or homesteads (*habitations*) in 1723 appears to bear this out. Rochard, the judge, possessed five grants, each at different locations, comprising 429.5 *carrés*[99] (1,374 acres), with the plots 120, 116, 93.5, 50 and 50 *carrés*; madame de Pivay possessed 305 *carrés* (976 acres), comprising three plots of 150, 80 and 75 *carrés* at different locations; Bourneuf possessed 110 *carrés*, comprising two plots of 50 and 60 *carrés* at different locations.[100] Of the approximately 25 habitations listed, none owned under 110 *carrés* (352 acres) in total, though individual plots were as small as 20 *carrés* (64 acres). It is possible that Grenadian plantation society had already begun to reflect the growth in the size of plantations as wealthy planters purchased smaller units.

In the case of Grenada, land was readily available and cheap. As a matter of fact, land was probably very cheap relative to the other colonies in order to attract settlers, at least as late as the early 1700s when the population remained low. The immediate problem with the land was that forests covered much of the island and had to be cleared for sugar cane cultivation. A further problem in the French colonies in the early years of sugar manufacture, as late as 1722 in Martinique, was that land owners failed to cultivate large portions of their grants; this would be the case in Grenada as late as 1762. The French government responded by issuing legislation to force planters to cultivate more of their land in sugar cane within a certain number of years or forfeit their grants.[101] Based on the 1723 list of habitations, it is clear that large grants were uncultivated: Pinard possessed two grants, totaling 200 *carrés* (640 acres) at different locations, 150 *carrés* (480 acres) of which was fallow (*en friche*); of 377 *carrés* (1,206 acres) comprising four grants, Le Jeune had 105 *carrés* (336 acres) in "wood."[102] These examples may not reflect a trend since planters usually left large areas in wood for purposes of fuel, building, etc. Though some of the land would have undergone *défrichement* (forest clearing and ground breaking for tillage) for tobacco, indigo and provisions, sugar cane required large tracts of land for economical production. Clearing land, primarily tree removal, was backbreaking work, especially because tree-felling instruments were few and primitive. The other important issue then became one of labor. Land clearing demanded large inputs of labor.

The slow growth in population in the latter half of the 1600s and even into the early 1700s was detrimental to the island's early economic development. Labor of both indentured whites and enslaved Africans were in short supply in the early years of the colony. The demand for *engagés* far outstripped the supply as was the case within the entire French Caribbean. Even after African slave labor had replaced white indentured servitude, the island continued to suffer from the lack of available labor. A constant complaint of Grenadian planters was the shortage of reliable slaves, due not to their scarcity in the region but to colonial restrictions on trade with other European nations like the Dutch who could readily supply them with slaves at a reasonable price.[103] Even if labor was readily available at a reasonable cost the next issue was one of capital. The management of a profitable sugar plantation required large inputs of labor which in turn required large outlays of capital for its procurement and upkeep, and inevitably its replacement due to the high mortality among the slaves.

The unavailability of capital proved to be a major stumbling block for Grenadian planters. Like labor, capital was not easily attracted to Grenada in its early years of settlement because of the island's high risk as a frontier. There was also tremendous competition for this resource throughout the region and especially the larger islands of the French Caribbean whose sugar industries were far more developed. Sugar production demanded large investments of capital for both the labor force and its upkeep, and the equipment necessary for the manufacture of sugar. With a lack of both labor and capital for the entire second half of the 1600s, sugar cane remained a minor crop in Grenada, engaged in by few planters who possessed the necessary resources to establish it. Though other factors as well restricted its growth until the first half of the 1700s, the unavailability of large quantities of slaves and capital were primary.

In 1718 there were nine *sucreries* and over the next 44 years it would reach its climax under the French. Prior to 1718 the development of the sugar industry had been extremely slow, but between 1725 to 1762 *sucreries* increased by 64, on average almost two new *sucreries* per year. The greatest growth in sugar production took place between the 1720s and 1750s. Sugar expansion, according to Watts, was due to peace; availability of virgin land; expanding markets; adequate capital, labor, food supply and trade routes; and favorable prices and legislation.[104] Also, falling production costs allowed less wealthy planters to enter the industry.

The growth in *sucreries* was paralleled by a decrease in indigo plantations (Table 8.1). The two industries were very much related to each other in terms of labor and capital demands. Indigo cultivation and production, with its relatively high demand for capital, labor and processing skills relative to the other cash crops, created the foundations upon which sugar production expanded. As sugar production grew indigo production experienced a corresponding decline because they both competed for similar resources. Since sugar production yielded much higher profits it was not a matter of how but when indigo would be replaced by sugar. In 1740 there were no indigo plantations though the crop was still being produced on a number of plantations as a secondary cash crop.

The growth in sugar production in Grenada was facilitated by a corresponding increase in the slave population. The two became synonymous and inseparable. Successful sugar cultivation and production depended on an abundant supply of cheap slave labor. As Munford notes, "More than any other economic factor, it was the so-called 'sugar cane revolution' which made slavery indispensable in the French West Indies. Sugar transformed the islands from mixed forms of labor exploitation into a socio-economic formation dominated by slaveholding production relations. Stated bluntly, more slaves were required to raise sugar cane than tobacco or indigo."[105] There was a direct correlation between the increase in sugar cane cultivation and increased slave labor imports. As Table 7.5 clearly indicates, the increasing slave population in Grenada in the early to mid-1700s paralleled the increase in sugar plantations. As Watts states, the ratio of slaves to whites had to exceed at least 3-4 to 1, or even 10 to 1 before sugar cane cultivation became the dominant agricultural commodity.[106] This was the case with the other islands in the region.[107] In Grenada these ratios were not reached until between 1715 and 1718 when the ratio topped 3 to 1, and sugar mills showed a 50 percent increase in the same time period. It was not until the 1750s that the population ratio reached 10 to 1 and sugar mills increased by over 800 percent.

In 1723 the census listed 17 plantations. The only other available data which give some idea of the growth of the *sucrière* to that point is the list of habitations for 1723 which explicitly records at least seven *sucreries*, though most of the others were probably sugar estates as well. Since no *indigoteries* were listed as such the list is specific to *sucreries* then established on the island. The seven *sucreries* identified as such reveal some information that adds to the picture of the sugar industry in the period.

They ranged in size from 80 *carrés* (256 acres) to 300 *carrés* (960 acres), a large number divided into smaller plots of land. These were worked by between 19 to 97 slaves each, which showed that the industry was in its infancy. If the number of slaves listed for the 26 odd habitations are totaled they amount to 910 out of a total slave population of 3,106 for the same year. The percent of the slave population engaged in sugar production was about 30 percent. Indigo production, with 140 estates, would have engaged the majority of the slave labor.

By the late 1730s Grenada's *sucreries* had increased tremendously and achieved a climax by the 1750s. By the variety of sugars exported they were on par with the other colonies in the French Antilles. These types included: clayed sugar (*sucre têté*) which was a lower quality clayed sugar (so named because it was situated at the "head" of the clayed loaf); non-refined white sugar (*sucre blanc*) which was the highest quality clayed sugar and often mistaken for refined sugar; common sugar (*sucre commun*) which was a lower grade of white sugar but higher than *sucre têté*; and muscovado (*sucre brut*) which was a brown, unrefined sugar. Production figures for Grenada are nonexistent, but some export data give an idea of production for specific years (Table 8.7).[108] It is not clear whether these figures were annual totals or just random export data from ships.

That the majority of Grenadian sugar exports comprised grades of clayed sugar demonstrated that planters were taking full advantage of the higher prices offered for clayed sugar. According to Stein, "Since the late seventeenth century, clayed sugar's obvious advantages for the colonists had made it a favorite among planters and a source of anxiety for metropolitan refiners.... Planters, particularly in the highly developed Lesser Antilles colonies, did not take long to realize that it was more lucrative to produce a clayed sugar that could compete in many areas with refined sugar, than muscovado that required further treatment elsewhere."[109] It also illustrates that the industry was well developed and not just producing the cheapest grades of sugar as was the practice in the smaller islands in the British Caribbean.[110]

A survey of the island in 1762 revealed some data on the extent of the sugar industry established by the French. As Table 8.3 shows, there were 82 sugar plantations, occupying about 31,165 acres. According to Williams, based on tax returns for over half of the 82 *sucreries* in 1762, only two contained between 150-200 slaves; three between 100-150; 25 between 50-100; 12 between 25-50; and two less than 25 slaves (Table

8.6).[111] Forty-four estates utilized between 2,200 and 3,950 slaves out of a total population of over 15,000 slaves. The 82 *sucreries* had just above half of the total slave population. What this data show is that Grenadian *sucreries* were relatively small compared to their French counterparts. In 1762 Grenada exported 64,095 hundredweights (cwts), 71,640 cwts in 1763, and 65,669 cwts in 1764.[112] It appears that plantations were underutilized, supported by contemporary observations like that of Richard Tyrrel who in 1764 remarked, "the sugar plantations are very large, but the French planters have not Negroes sufficient to cultivate them, therefore, there is not near the quantity of sugar made in the island that might be made with good husbandry and a sufficient number of Negroes."[113] The incoming British would alter that situation dramatically and very quickly.

Subsistence Agriculture

When the first colonists arrived in Grenada their foremost activity, following the construction of a fort, was not the production of export crops but that of subsistence crops (*vivrières*). They arrived with sufficient food for three months and if the colony was to survive they had to achieve food self-sufficiency almost immediately. The most immediate cause of failure of a new colony was starvation, if they were also able to defend themselves against enemies. It had happened throughout the region in the early days of colonization, and experienced colonizers like du Parquet were quite aware of its consequences. To avoid examples like Guadeloupe where the first colonists experienced starvation when their food supply failed, forcing them to raid the Island Caribs' gardens and risk retaliation, du Parquet made ample provision.[114]

According to Labat, du Parquet immediately "had the land cleared that lay at the foot of the mountain, alongside the lake. There he started a large plantation, not with a view to establishing a market [crop], but to ensure there being enough food for the support of the new settlers."[115] Colonists were given plots of land to work, and they began to cultivate regional food staples, mainly food crops like manioc or cassava, sweet potato, maize, plantain and banana, all of these except the latter two were indigenous food crops then grown by the Island Caribs. The Anonymous author continues that "[o]ur first colony was living in great harmony [with the Island Caribs] ...; they furthered the discovery of the land around the fort, [and] they filled it with food and maintained it."[116] As well as their own produce, "The Savages came to visit them often, bringing them figs, bananas, good fishing and hunting" in exchange for European goods.[117]

Unlike the Spanish, the northern Europeans did not introduce many European food crops to the region. They relied on the crops that were either native to the region or were the result of successful Spanish introductions in the Greater Antilles. The French colonists in Grenada, coming from Martinique, had already been used to the cultivation of food crops, which the first colonists had learned from the Island Caribs. With that knowledge they soon established gardens modeled on those of the Island Caribs. Boucher's remark concerning tobacco as a "gift" of the Indians to the Europeans that ironically accelerated the process of Island Carib decline in the region is applicable with regard to subsistence crops and their cultivation by Europeans.[118] The colonists utilized the Indian digging stick to prepare the soil for planting and much of their methods of cultivation and processing.

Subsistence crops were produced throughout the new settlement and various vegetables were added, some from Africa. The visits of both Dutertre in 1656 and Labat around 1700 record the cultivation of subsistence crops. Dutertre recorded that "the whole place was planted with manioc, [sweet] potatoes and peas, and set with orange trees and other fruits."[119] One document from de Sérillac recorded "the wide hill [was] in potatoes and the next in peas, millet, and manioc, numerous and ninety pits," as Governor de Valminière was told to plant "provisions for feeding the Comte de Sérillac's men."[120]

Due to the ongoing conflicts with the Island Caribs the vegetable gardens of the early colonists were often destroyed and provisions had to be brought in from Martinique; the French also destroyed the Island Caribs' gardens when they retaliated against them. Not only were gardens destroyed but because of arbitary attacks the settlers were unable to cultivate their gardens at will.[121] It must have been very difficult for the early colonists and hunger was probably a constant threat. After one attack, the Anonymous author lamented, "Here they are naked, with no shelter, no bread, nothing whatsoever. Who will shelter them? who will feed them?"[122] Though hunting and fishing could have supplemented their meager diets, again, the attacks by the Island Caribs made both difficult to say the least, and oftentimes deadly.[123]

Labat recorded vegetables as one of the exports of Grenada to Martinique, the latter island suffering from a lack of provisions to feed its slaves since they were occupied with export crop production.[124] He adds, according to Governor de Bellair, that even though it was "entirely poor, Grenada was acting as foster-mother to Martinique which, itself lacking in livestock and poultry, was provided for by the smaller island."[125] It would appear, as was common with the smaller islands in the French Antilles, Grenada was exporting garden crops to the sugar islands like Martinique where the expanding cultivation of sugar cane occupied more and more land previously assigned as provision grounds. Earlier, the Grenada colonists had supplied game to the larger island. After the Treaty of Utrecht in 1713 and the growing development in the region, ships from Martinique to the Spanish Main stopped to refresh and take on supplies, among these vegetables.[126]

Though Grenada had probably achieved food self-sufficiency by the late 1600s, the sugar islands in the *Iles du Vent* were suffering from insufficient food production. This led to a number of laws to encourage and enforce measures that would increase food crop production, especially since cash crop production had become so valuable. Planters, in their quest for huge profits from exports, often neglected food production, with devastating consequences. With the growing slave population it was absolutely necessary to procure a stable source of nourishment for them. Laws, especially after the *Code Noir* in 1685, forced planters to provide slaves garden plots and time to produce some of their own food. Though most of these garden plots were on marginal lands they aided food production and staved off hunger numerous times.

The only figures for food crop production date from the late 1730s (Table 8.8). The numbers illustrate the importance of subsistence crops in the life of the colony, especially following the increase in the slave population in the post-1713 period. Cassava, long a staple food, was the primary food crop. It had been the primary food of the French colonists and became the major food of the slaves. Several characteristics of manioc—its resistance to drought, can be harvested several times from the same planting, phenomenal caloric yield (3 times that of maize), high starch content, can be harvested 9-10 months after planting, and it grows well on both acidic and alkaline soils—made it the food crop of choice.[127]

Cassava, after harvesting, was either grated to make a flour from which bread and porridge were made, or boiled fresh as a vegetable. In

1745 manioc cultivation was 4.4 million *pieds* (about 2,212 acres) and intended to feed a population of 8,747 slaves. The majority of this production was by slaves in their allotted garden plots. It appears that the reason production data were kept had to do with a 1710 law which established that for each slave 500 heaps (*fossés*) of manioc had to be produced.[128] Based on that law, production in 1749 was adequate for 7,720 slaves while the island had 8,638 slaves, and in 1755 production was adequate for only 9,750 when there were 12,608 slaves. By 1761 production had climbed to 5.5 million *pieds* (about 2,729 acres) to feed 14,308 slaves, but nutritionally adequate for only 10,916.

The next important crop was sweet potato. It was most probably produced in large quantities because it was harvestable only four months after planting. It is rich in sugar and added taste to bland manioc dishes; it was eaten boiled or roasted. In 1749 cultivation was recorded at almost four million heaps. Much of this would have been grown by the slaves in their small garden plots. In 1755 cultivation was 165.5 *carrés* (about 528 acres), and in 1761 it was 1,647 acres.

Banana, which included plantain as well, was the last of the three major food crops that made up the basic nutrition of the colony. It was reputedly liked by the slaves, and formed a major part of their diet. It was eaten more as a vegetable either boiled or roasted when green than as a ripe fruit. In 1744 production of bananas was just under a million "baskets." In 1755 its cultivation was 1.1 million *pieds* (about 1,137 acrs) and 1.2 million *pieds* (about 1,202 acres) in 1761.

Other food crops grown included: yams, pulses like pigeon peas, Guinea corn, okra, and a variety of native and introduced fruits like watermelon, papaya, guava, citrus and coconut. Some of these were African introductions, brought by slaves or ships' captains and became important additions to the slaves' diet.

Hunting and fishing were two activities that brought some variety and added taste to the diet of starchy foods so prevalent in the colony. Grenada, for much of the 1600s, was described as possessing good hunting and fishing. Dutertre, in 1656, described "[t]he hunting and fishing on this island as better than all the others; and it is an astonishing thing to see the quantity of game, tatoo [armadillo], sea turtles and all sorts of fishes. There is also an abundance of armadillos which have meat similar to pork, and another sort of animal called a manatee" or sea cow.[129] De Tracy, in 1665, commented that "the land there is so rich, fish and game abound... that this island could furnish all that is necessary for the life of the inhabitants."[130] So abundant was the game that the colonists marketed some of what they caught to Martinique. Until the mid-1700s and the widespread cultivation of cash crops throughout the island, wild game was available and important in the diets of the colonists and most probably the slaves.

The diet of the settlers in Grenada, both the white colonists and slaves, was basic. The above food crops were oftentimes supplemented with wild game or fish, and less so with imported cured meats. The latter was most probably absent from Grenada especially in the first fifty years because of the poverty of the colony. As the colony grew wealthier imported meats like salted codfish from the British American Colonies became more important but probably in only small quantities.

Livestock

Agricultural development in the Caribbean in the seventeenth and eighteenth centuries depended heavily upon livestock. The Spanish, in settling the Greater Antilles, had brought in almost every kind of livestock and many did well, especially the hog and cattle. Hides were a major export from the Greater Antilles even after agricultural crops had become primary in the Lesser Antilles. Livestock was important for a number of reasons, primarily as draught animals, transportation, and to a lesser extent food. They were always in great demand, the supply, especially from the home country, were restricted. The high demand was caused partially by a high death rate due to the tropical climate, but the need for animals on the plantations continually increased. Because of the high demand and low supply they were very costly.

The most important animals in the development of the colonies were the cattle and horse. Since neither of these animals was native to the region they had to be imported, which meant that supply was always low, especially in the 1600s.[131] Much of the early Caribbean supply came from the Cape Verde islands, Madeira and Curaçao, the latter was the trading center of the Dutch. Both horses and cattle were the primary draught animals, though the cattle seemed to have borne the heavier burden. Horses tended to be used more for transportation of man while cattle carried the heavy loads on the plantations and were used to run some of the machinary as well. Though cattle could have been used for meat it was rarely used as such unless it died, the meat not allowed to be wasted. Because neither was native to the region, their lifespan was short. Overwork and diseases were the main causes of sudden death, which was not uncommon.

Between 1669 and 1755 censuses recorded fairly consistent data on livestock production in Grenada. They were usually grouped as horned animals (*bestes á corne*), wool animals (*bestes á laine*) like sheep and goat, and cavalry animals (*bestes á cavalines*) like horse and mule (Table 8.9). In 1669, there were 89 horned cattle and 14 horses/mules. Only fifteen households, slightly over 15 percent, owned these animals, illustrating their prohibitive costs. There was no mention of any of the smaller animals most probably because their numbers were small, if present at all. The livestock population grew gradually, influenced no doubt by the growing prosperity of the island's plantations and its growing adaptation of sugar production. Of the 81 sugar plantation in 1763, at least eight of them depended on cattle because their mills were powered by them. One estimate prescribes five horses and eight cattle as the necessary draught power on a 100-acre plantation.[132]

The other livestock were mules, sheep, goats and pigs (Table 8.12). The mule population grew gradually and supplemented the draught animals because it was used for transportation of both man and produce. Watts nonetheless contends that "mules were also considered [but] they were found to be unsuited."[133] The smaller animals–pigs, sheep and goats–were used primarily as food, either locally or to trade with the larger islands. These succeeded more readily in the Caribbean after suitable varieties were found. The European pig had been common in the islands since the 1500s, having been released by the Spanish after their arrival and become wild thereafter.[134] Many islands contained wild population of pigs, but the pigs of the colonists were bred in pens. The goats were imported from the Mediterranean and the sheep from West Africa. These formed the major locally produced meat source once wild meat was exhausted. Poultry, though no data exist, were free range and supplied some local meat.

9

Plantation Society

*Left alone, sugar cultivation rapidly transformed
Grenada into a mature plantation society.*[1]

The Treaty of Utrecht in 1713 brought about some profound changes in the Caribbean region, the most significant being a prolonged peace that spanned three decades. This absence of hostilities between the colonial powers facilitated extensive economic activity within both the French and British colonial economies in the region. Central to that growth was the expansion of sugar manufacturing, which became established throughout the region in that period and earned it the name "king sugar." Accompanying that expansion was the extensive participation in trade, merchandise and slave trades between Europe, Africa, its Caribbean colonies and North America.

Though some French officials in the region, during the last peace negotiations, had again recommended the exchange of the struggling colony at Grenada for the strategic "neutral" islands around Martinique, i.e. Dominica and St. Lucia, Grenada remained under French control. It would, despite all indications to the contrary, subsequently develop into a viable economic entity within the *Iles du Vent*. Its economic development, however, was never assured, considering that for the past seven decades it had experienced only minimal growth and was more akin to an outpost than a colony. Between 1714 and 1762, however, the island underwent extensive demographic and economic changes that had profound implications. It saw improved infrastructure, like the establishment of hamlets and a town (*bourg*) as its administrative center; the spread of religion to the overall population with the establishment of parishes and the erection of chapels; the establishment of the Slave Code (*Code Noir*) to manage the growing slave population; and political and defensive enhancements. All of these made the colony more independent and secure, laying the foundations for a prosperous plantation economy within the French Caribbean colonial realm, with the distinctive social stratification that maintained the minority whites at the top, free non-whites somewhere in between, and the majority blacks enslaved at the bottom.

According to the Abbe Raynal, in reference to Grenada in the decades immediately following the peace,

> The face of things was totally changed towards the year 1714; and this alteration was affected by Martinico. That island was then laying the foundation of a splendor that was to astonish all nations. It sent immense productions to France, and received valuable commodities in return, which were most of them sent to the Spanish coasts. Its ships touched at Grenada on their way, to take in refreshments. The trading privateers, who undertook this navigation, taught the people of that island the value of their soil, which only required cultivation. The execution of every project is facilitated by commerce. Some traders furnished the inhabitants [of Grenada] with slaves and utensils to erect sugar plantations. An open account was established between the two colonies.[2]

Based on Raynal, Grenada's post-Utrecht development has been historically viewed as being initiated by the peace of that year, but the foundations were certainly laid in the waning decade of the 1600s and the short-lived French *asiento* that brought more French trade to the southern Caribbean. Though it was not until the 1730s that widespread economic and social changes became evident, the second decade of the 1700s was the transition period when the island's economy stopped being stagnant and gradually embarked on one of steady economic growth.

Like Martinique and the other French colonies, Grenada experienced rapid expansion in the post-1713 period, and as Sheridan points out, it was due to the "relaxation of trade-restrictions, lower taxes, government support for the African trade, sober and industrious colonists, humane treatment of slaves, and the availability of fertile and uncultivated lands."[3] Yet the direct influence on Grenada's economy was Martinique. As Raynal suggests, the trade between Martinique and the Spanish Main, and the investments in both slaves and the necessary hardware allowed the establishment of large, profitable sugar plantations in Grenada. Some of the large proprietors who invested in sugar plantations came to Grenada from Martinique, young men who were scions of established families there. Others were merchants, like Élie Faure de Fayolle, a merchant at St. Pierre, Martinique who traded with Grenada and owned over one thousand acres in Basse-Terre which he invested in with his son-in-law the Chevalier d'Ars to create a successful sugar plantation. Others were established families like Lejeune, Rochard, Clozier, Babanneau, Roume de St. Laurent, Delpech and Madey who gradually amassed the resources to invest in large sugar plantations. As Labat had pointed out, Martinique was also benefiting from its relationship with Grenada in a number of ways, especially the truck trade, i.e. locally produced foodstuffs. Grenada's geographic location finally proved an asset as many had predicted it could, but not in the way most had envisioned.

Plantation society in Grenada by the mid-1700s had achieved the region-wide characteristics for which it was noted. One of these features was its exploitation of the land and African slave labor for the benefit of the white minority. In that regard, a number of writers viewed the resulting societies as temporary or transitory, unlike the North American colonies where settlement was a primary objective. As Ragatz notes in this indictment of the Caribbean colonial ventures, "No considerable body of persons inspired by motives higher than a desire to extract the greatest possible amount of wealth from them in the shortest possible time ever reached the smiling shores of the Caribbean colonies."[4] As a result, there was little initial interest placed on social development unless it directly impacted the economy. Yet there were differences between and within the various colonial societies which impacted the type of development pursued. As Ragatz qualified in the case of the French in comparing them to the British, "the French Caribbean held but slight attraction for others than persons of average means, contemplating actual settlement."[5] As a result, with the possible exception of St. Domingue, "A sound social

212

organization developed in the French West Indies. Homes were established there, local ties grew strong, insular pride and feeling appeared."[6] Thus was the case with Grenada under the French as evident by the *grand blancs* who took up residence there on their plantations, but more so among the ordinary planters with their families. It was probably what caused many French to remain in Grenada under British rule.

Grenadian colonial society by the late 1600s had already begun to exhibit the general social and economic characteristics prevailing in the established colonial societies in the region. A major characteristic of these societies was its social stratification based on race, social status and wealth. These were held in place by an economic system centered on multiple plantation units producing various crops, primarily sugar cane, and utilizing imported African slave labor. Compliance within this oppressive system was maintained by a minority white planter class which was dominated by the wealthy property owners (*grand blancs*) and supported, oftentimes reluctantly, by larger, yet relatively small (in regard to the total population), middling and poor-white classes (*petit blancs*). Movement, i.e. social mobility, within the minority white groups was possible, yet as the colony became more developed, that advancement leveled off as the wealthy planters bought out many of the unsuccessful or marginal middling and small planters. Yet, the cultivation of profitable secondary crops like coffee on land unsuitable for sugar cane aided the retention of vibrant groups of small and middling farmers.

The lack of demographic growth was a major stumbling block to economic expansion prior to the early 1700s. Economic growth in the post-Utrecht period hinged upon the corresponding demographic growth in the overall population. Though every segment of the Grenadian population exhibited growth in the post-1713 period, it was the slave population that exhibited considerable increases (Table 7.1). These demographic changes were due directly to the increased emphasis on sugar production and its demand for cheap abundant labor, together with increasing coffee production and its demand for small numbers of slaves, but by many planters. Unlike the other French and British colonies in the region, there was no stark contrast in the growth between the black and white populations in the first three decades of the 1700s because the need for planters, merchants, skilled craftsmen, overseers, soldiers, government officials and the like contributed to the growth in the white population. Until 1735 they both experienced comparable rates of increases, but thereafter the white population exhibited relative decreases while the slave population continued to grow due to the changing characteristics of the plantation economy, with its expansion of the sugar industry. This overall growth in the total population, and especially the slave population, created the basis for the economic growth that brought a level of prosperity in the second quarter of the eighteenth century and established the plantation economy in Grenada by the mid-1700s.

The Plantation

Slave society in the Caribbean developed its unique form of the village, the plantation. For the majority of the people living in Grenada, the plantation was the center of their world, each its own self-contained village, especially for its slaves. As development spread across the island, the large plantations, particularly those producing sugar, formed pockets of economic and social activity. Slaves on neighboring plantations, however, interacted with each other and often congregated on market days or holiday celebrations. That was generally the prevailing form of agricultural production in Grenada during slavery–large sugar plantations, scores or hundreds of slaves, yet the existence of profitable secondary crops like coffee also accounted for a sizeable portion of the economy and therefore an alternate mode of production.

Sugar plantations accounted for approximately 30 percent of conceded lands and as much as 55 percent of slaves. Yet a large number of slaves, 40 percent, laboured on smaller coffee, cocoa and cotton plantations, and around five percent were not attached to estates, but lived in towns and performed primarily non-agricultural work. It should be kept in mind that the development of sugar production in Grenada was gradual, almost paralleled by the growth of coffee. Illustration 9.1 shows a graph of the range of slave ownership based on the type of production at the end of French occupation in 1763.[7] As would be expected, sugar plantations were smaller in number and occupied the higher ranges of slave ownership because of their demand for large numbers of slaves to carry out the multiple functions associated with sugar production. Coffee, cocoa and cotton plantations, in much greater quantity, almost spanned the entire range and showed a greater diversity of labor regimes, climaxing at the mid-level range. The graph clearly shows the larger participation of smaller planters in coffee, cocoa and cotton production, illustrating the lower investments necessary for entry into the economy. The "Other" category captured slaves engaged in an assortment of activities, including domestic servitude, in the service of local merchants, or as fishermen or skilled laborers; some were probably rented out by their owners.

The size, type and extent of the operations of the owners meant that the slaves experienced varied lifestyles. Sugar plantations occupied extensive fields of crops and were the most consistent in their labor regime since successful production required adherence to a prescribed process. As sugar plantations were influenced by their masters to a great extent, the lives of the slaves could potentially be different from one plantation to another despite the similar nature of the work environment. Yet, there were a number of features that were predictable based on the size of the plantation, i.e. the number of slaves, and the social environment. The large number of slaves living together in the slave yard or village created a dynamic that facilitated extensive social interactions that led to a sense of community among the slaves. The layout of a large sugar plantation could also lead to a weaker relationship between the slaves and the master/overseer (Illustration 8.6). The locations of sugar plantations along the coastal areas may also have influenced the lifestyle of the slaves because it was warmer, drier, and closer to the sea, which may have provided other opportunities.

Coffee and cocoa plantations did not compete with sugar plantations for land because these tree crops occupied the steeper slopes and hilly regions of the island. It was the expansion of coffee and cocoa that opened up the interior of the island. These more isolated plantations experienced a cooler climate that created its own dynamic. Coffee and cocoa production were secondary to sugar, but not too far behind in terms of the overall number of acres and slaves; the number of these planters was far greater. The size of coffee plantations varied considerably, ranging from a few acres worked by the planter family and one or two slaves to hundreds of acres worked by scores of slaves. Absentee ownership was minimal, if at all, and the proprietor and his family most often lived in close proximity to the slaves. Most of these plantations were quite modest, with the handful of slaves living a more isolated lifestyle, thus creating a different structure that influenced social interactions between the slaves and the master. Slaves working on tree

215

crop plantations had more downtime, but they could be hired out to sugar plantations during peak schedules, or occupied with the production of secondary crops and provisions for sale to other plantations in Grenada or Martinique.

For all new slaves arriving in Grenada, the process of acculturation was probably similar despite their subsequent placement. If they were newly imported slave, it was the first opportunity since capture in Africa that they could begin to understand the upheavals of the past months or year. For the plantation, this was the time to allow the slave to begin the process of acculturation to the slave environment that was now his life. "Seasoning" has been described as the destruction of the slaves' identity, making them more malleable to their new environment of forced servitude. A new and foreign identity was forced upon the slave as every aspect of their former self was challenged, beginning with a new name and language; many slaves, however, retained their original or African names among themselves. Some planters believed that the slave should be rested and not sent to work immediately, but spent the first weeks recovering from their torturous journey. For some, this included "Eight to ten days of baths taken morning and evening in the sea do them much good. One or two bleedings and some purgations and above all, good food, puts them in condition to serve their masters."[8] Others, however, put their new slaves to work in the fields almost immediately.

The new slaves were taken in by the others already established on the plantation, taking up residence in crudely-constructed huts.

> The houses of the Negroes are sometimes constructed of masonry, but more usually of wood covered by a cob of rough earth prepared with cow dung. A row of rafters raised over these sorts of walls and brandished across the length of the room forming a ridgepole makes up the roof which is covered with cane leaves, reeds or palm leaves. These shacks have only a ground floor, 20 to 25 feet long by 14 to 15 feet across, divided by screens of reeds into two or three small and very dark rooms which receive light only from the door and sometimes from a little window opened in one of the gables.[9]

It was the job of the established slaves to introduce the new ones to the routines of the plantation and the rules and punishments that governed their everyday lives. The life of the slave on the plantation centered around the many fields of crops and the slave yard where they spent their free time. Le Romain continues that the furniture found in these shacks was rather meager in keeping with its simplicity: "Two or three planks raised on four stakes pushed into the ground and covered by a mat form their bed. A barrel broken into on one end to hold bananas and root [crops], some large pots for water, a bench or two, a bad table, a chest, and several calabashes and large gourds in which they stow their provisions make up all the gear of the household."[10]

Though the *Code Noir* guaranteed the slave basic nutrition, many plantation owners did the least required, often leaving the slave to secure his own sustenance. Each slave was given a piece of marginal land on which to establish a garden where fruits, roots, tubers and other vegetables were grown. Some would also raise chickens, even pigs, which were sold at weekly markets. There were times when bad weather led to the destruction of the slaves' gardens (e.g. the floods of 1724 and the hurricane in 1731), leaving them hungry if the master did not provide alternate food. It was a precarious existence for the slaves.

The primary meal of the slave consisted of boiled roots and tubers, and various dishes made from cassava flour, including boiled cassava, cassava bread and porridge. The plantation usually provided weekly rations of cassava flour or whole cassava which the slave processed into flour. They made various drinks from the many available seasonal fruits, roots and barks, and were treated to rum on special occasions or holidays. These were supplemented by the occasional fish, crabs, frogs, large lizards like iguana, agoutis, cane rats and armadillos, especially when the recommended rations of imported salt beef or salted cod were not provided by the plantation.

The primary reason for the slave labor regime was agricultural production on the plantations. As such, it consumed the short existence of the slaves. Depending on the types of crops produced on the plantation—sugar, coffee, cacao, indigo, provisions—slaves received instructions in the various tasks necessary to lead to successful production of these crops. The majority of slaves were involved with the everyday tasks like clearing fields, planting, weeding, harvesting and processing. Male slaves had more varied tasks than women, most of whom were employed as field slaves planting, weeding and harvesting crops. Some male slaves, due to the shortage of free skilled laborers, learned necessary skilled jobs to become refiners, coopers, carpenters and blacksmiths. Slaves were up before daybreak to begin the work in the fields. At mid-morning they would break for breakfast before returning to the field. At the height of the sun they would break for lunch and take a long break before returning to the fields until after sunset. They were forced to work into the night if necessary, especially on sugar plantations (during the processing of the sugar cane). A very small number of slaves worked as domestic helpers in the master or overseer's house, a position that could be advantageous, but at times proved detrimental.

The majority of the white population were homesteaders (*habitants*), making their living cultivating various crops on their habitations. Most properties, whether cultivated in sugar cane, coffee or cocoa, were managed by their owners and his family, with few absentee planters during the entire French period. A small number of absente planters however, did emerge by the 1750s, especially among the very wealthy sugar planters. The white planters can be divided into prosperous (*grand blancs*) and small (*petit blancs*) planters based on the type of production they engaged in. The *grand blancs*, with their wealth and access to resources, engaged in sugar production, but many had large coffee plantations as well. Actually, they made up a sizeable proportion of the coffee/cocoa planters. Among the *grand blancs* were a handful of noble families, some arriving ennobled while others achieved that status in the islands. Many of the large sugar planters had long established roots in Grenada, some dating to the early decades of the 1700s. Among these families were Lejeune, De Flavigny and De Gannes. *Petit blancs* were engaged almost entirely in secondary crops, even if they possessed large enough concessions of land for sugar production. Some *petit blancs* were also employed by large estates as managers or engaged in towns as craftsmen or other skilled work.

Natural Disasters

Many destructive forces operated in the Caribbean in the early colonial period, including wars, privateering and natural disasters, the latter the most destructive by far. Natural disasters like earthquakes and hurricanes struck quite unexpectedly and with such force that the entire infrastructure of an island, as well as many lives, could be destroyed in a matter of hours. There were many examples of widespread damage from earthquakes in Port Royal, Jamaica (1692) and Martinique (1727,) and hurricanes that struck Martinique (1680) and Guadeloupe (1720s). Grenada, located in the southern Caribbean, was speared much of the destruction that these natural disasters often wrought. Its location was always viewed as an advantage since it was considered free from the annual hurricanes that ravaged the other islands between June and November.

During this period only two instances of severe weather were recorded in Grenada, one of which was most definitely caused by a hurricane. Reporting in 1727, colonial authorities suggested that current economic difficulties, food shortages and the "difficulties encountered with cocoa cultivation" in Grenada were as a result of floods in 1724.[11] It is not clear if the flooding was the result of a storm or hurricane as there is no record of any severe weather in the area in 1724, nor were there reports of immediate destruction. The impact of the flooding on cocoa cultivation is evident from production figures for 1723 when there were 241,450 *pieds* (about 483 acres) of cocoa, decreasing to 140,014 *pieds* (about 280 acres) in 1725, but recovering to 600,000 *pieds* (about 1,200 acres) in 1726; there was no data for 1724.[12] There was no mention of other crops, but there was a decrease in cotton cultivation in the same period as cocoa. The dramatic decrease in *indigoteries* from 140 in 1723 to 76 in 1725, was not, however, linked to the floods as its decline was due to the corresponding increase in sugar plantations. Food shortages were remedied by imports from the other colonies in the French Antilles.

The most severe storm to visit Grenada during this period was on 25 August 1731. It was the same hurricane that struck Barbados, leaving that island in "So great a calamity that there is scarce a person throughout the whole island but who has received a considerable loss by this dreadful storm."[13] Though there were no reports of lives lost in the storm on Grenada, the hurricane's effect led to what colonial authorities described as a "disaster," leaving the island "threatened by food shortages."[14] It was reported that "almost all the sugar mills, purifying houses and other buildings on the plantations were ruined," and the loss of as many as five, maybe all nine, coasting vessels that serviced Grenada.[15] The church and the few government buildings were also reported as suffering some damage.

The destruction of provision grounds resulted in the shortage of food for both free and enslaved. What made the situation even worse was the existing severe shortage of imported foods, particularly salted beef and flour, which had caused an increase in food prices in the region as well. It was reported that all Martinique's stocks had been exhausted, and the "dryness and the caterpillars" had affected the cultivation of cassava in Guadeloupe. The colonial government was forced to purchase foodstuffs from foreign colonies in the region to provide for the people of Grenada in this dire situation. Food shortages could become life threatening as in the case of Guadeloupe when "colonists kept themselves armed as starving slaves, who were dying at a rate of 20 a day in March of 1723, and ate anything they could find."[16]

Diseases and Cures

Another threat to the colony was diseases. Grenada's warm climate, a diverse population, poor sanitation, inadequate nutrition and questionable medical practices created a cesspool of diseases and an overwhelmingly unhealthy place for all. This diseased environment played a crucial, though detrimental role in shaping the development, or rather lack of development of Grenada for many years. The initial colonists located their settlement on a sandbar bordering a lake of brackish water, itself surrounded by marshes that were breeding grounds for mosquitoes and would prove deadly. According to Labat, "Fevers very persistent, and seriously incommoded the settlers." He goes on to add that the "new colony would have grown considerable if the parts of the land that were cleared, instead of purifying the air, had not brought on fever which, without being mortal, was extremely inconvenient by reason of its length. It was this that lowered the reputation of the island for a very long time."[17] With the death of settlers from these diseases, the island earned the unenviable and uninviting designation "the grave of the West Indies." It proved to be the reason for the abandonment of the first settlement to higher ground as soon as the Amerindian threat was eliminated.

There are, however, no references to epidemics of any kind during the French period, and Grenada may have been unusual in not having its share of the many diseases that ravaged populations in the region. Despite the bad reputation, the island was lucky to have been spared a visit by the deadly yellow fever as de Caylus, writing in 1705 of the advantages of Grenada, reported that "it has not yet been affected with the dreadful results of yellow fever (*maladie de Siam*)."[18]

That many diseases were endemic, maybe even epidemic, and proved fatal to some inhabitants did not produce much discussion, because they were quite common throughout the region. So it is difficult to know what specific diseases were common, how many became ill, how many died, what treatments were employed, or who were more affected. During the French colonization of Grenada, there are only a few references to diseases and their effects. There was no hospital for many years, and the few "doctors" or "surgeons" who operated were probably not trained in medicine at all.

In the absence of data from this period, it is however, informative to provide a description of the island's diseased environment from a later period that shed light on what the French were most likely confronted with in the mid-1700s. Colin Chisholm, a British medical doctor writing in the 1790s, provides a description of diseases in Grenada that were probably not much different during the French period; one would like to think, as the evidence assumes, that in the latter time period medical conditions had improved, but probably not much.

> Were we to exclude the effects of the miasma of the marshy districts, and those proceeding from the irregular temperature of the air, we should find that, in common years, there is by no means much sickness; and that in general it is only in those places where marshes are abundant, as in Marquis, Sauteur[s], and a few detached spots in other parts of the coast, diseases *mali moris* prevail. There indeed, one year with another, fully an eighteenth part of the inhabitants annually perish; but in other districts, where these dreadful causes of disease do not exist, the mortality is not more than one in 37 or 38.
>
> The endemic diseases are either bilious, putrid, or inflammatory, as the seasons are hot and wet, or dry and cool. Thus, in the summer and autumnal months, or that portion of the year which includes the rainy and warm seasons, remittent fevers, dysenteries, flight colics, cholera morbus, phrenetic complaints, or what the French call *Coup de Soleil*, occasioned by the intense solar heat, ulcers of the legs, particularly those of the herpetic kind, are the most prevalent disorders. And in the marshy districts at this time of the year, obstinate and irregular intermittents, generally depending on glandular

obstruction and visceral inflammation, remittents of the worst kind, and hepatic dysenteries, are very common, frequently epidemic, and too often fatal. During the winter and spring, when northerly winds blow, and occasion an uncommon and disagreeable chillness; but when the atmosphere is generally less moist than at any other time of the year, pleurisies, often attended with fevers, ophthalmias, inflammatory anginas, erysipelas frequently preceded by fever, chronic rheumatism, and Guinea-worm, are the most common epidemics. At all seasons, hepatic inflammation is very frequent; and when anomalous, always epidemic. Worms also are common throughout the year, and frequently give rise to very extraordinary symptoms. The yellow fever (properly so called) sometimes appear; but observes no particular season. Ruptures, ringworms, elephantiasis, or the glandular disease of Dr. Hendy, hydrocephalus, yaws, putrid or ulcerous sore throats, mortification of the fingers and toes, chronic aphthae leprosy, and tetanus, may be ranked among the sporadic endemics of this country, and are certainly not the least tremendous of them; but fortunately they are either confined to the negro race, or rarely occur. The species of tetanus peculiar to infants, and hence called *Trismus Nascentium*, is an endemic of this island, and always a fatal one: it prevails only in the marshy and moist parts of the island, and takes place any time before the ninth day after birth; after which period it has never been known to happen. It does not appear to arise from a retention of the meconium; for however carefully infants have been evacuated, the disease has in no instance been thereby prevented. From its prevalence in moist, cold, or marshy situations, we may with more propriety attribute it to cold and impure air. This dreadful malady admits of no cure....

The island is frequently visited by the small pox, sometimes of the confluent or malignant kind. It has in almost every instance been introduced from the coast of Africa, in the slave-ships; on board of which it frequently breaks out, and commits dreadful ravages on the passage to the West Indies;... The chicken-pox is common almost every year; and as it appears without any evident introduction, it may be considered as more an endemic than a foreign disease. It is always mild, and requires no other treatment than a laxative at the turn, or when the postules dry.

The measles and [w]hooping cough seldom appear here; for in the course of ten years I recollect only two instances of the former, and one of the latter: they were of a very bad kind, and proved fatal to many children."[19]

Based on Chisholm's assessment it is quite evident that even though eight decades separated his writing from the early French colonists, marsh miasma was at the heart of what they both believed caused some of the deadly fevers. In 1714 Governor de Maupeou wrote to the authorities in Martinique that he was engaged in the "draining of the marshes which harm the healthiness of the island."[20] It was one of the few things they could do to destroy what they believed was the origin of the fevers. Over time most of the colonists and slaves would become seasoned and be able to weather many of the diseases. Newcomers, however, were always vulnerable.

The dreadful nature of tropical diseases was made more deadly by the fact that nutrition for most, and especially the slaves, was pretty abysmal. The issue of the slaves' poor nutrition was raised by one of the Capuchin priests in 1705 when he suggested that "slave owners should feed their slaves meat, presumably because slaves' meatless diet was contributing to their malnutrition and starvation."[21] For his advocacy of the slaves' diet the governor reported him to the secretary of the Navy and even suggested replacing the Capuchins with the Jesuits who he believed would probably not challenge the status quo; the Capuchins did not own plantations and thus large numbers of slaves.

Another factor was that everyone lived in unsanitary conditions that also made the disease environment more severe, especially making it easy for commutable diseases to spread rapidly. The inappropriate and illegal disposal of "night soil" contributed to the spread of diseases by polluting the drinking water. The poor quality of housing, especially the slaves', only exasperated an already dire situation of course. Compounding the slaves' problem was overwork.

Like many other facets of their lives, slaves were left to secure much of their own health. Many plantations contracted with a "doctor" or "surgeon" who could be called upon to attend slaves as needed, but that care was often ineffective as was much of the medical care at the time. For the majority of the sick, the plantation provided a sick house which was usually staffed by a slave who acted as a nurse (*infirmière*), oftentimes an elderly female with knowledge of herbs and the experience of delivering babies.

In such a precarious environment it would be prudent to make available as many of the existing resources to fight diseases as was possible, despite the rudimentary nature of medical science in the French Antilles at the time. In 1700 the island was still without an appointed royal surgeon and it would be many years before the island received a permanent medical professional in 1714. When Governor de Lépinay took ill in 1720 soon after arriving on the island he was sent off to Martinique for treatment because the authorities believed he would receive much better care there; he, however, died soon thereafter.[22]

As early as 1700 de la Hogue, the royal lieutenant acting as the governor, sent a letter signed by a number of prominent colonists to the authorities in Martinique requesting the building of a hospital, among other institutional establishments.[23] The island had been half a century into its colonization and lacked the basic means to protect its citizens, though there were people practicing "medicine" and others catering to the sick. Yet, considering that Fort Royal, Martinique did not have a hospital to date, there was no way Grenada would even be considered for such facilities. It would be another three decades before persistent requests for a hospital were approved. By the early 1730s Grenada had grown tremendously and the view of it as a useless French outpost was quickly disappearing. Yet nothing happened rapidly despite the recognition that the island was in urgent need of a hospital not only to treat its own growing population, but also its soldiers and the many sailors who were arriving on its shores. Grenada had seen the expansion of new parishes and priests in the 1720s, but still lacked many institutions and infrastructure long since established in the other French colonies.

Beginning in 1730 the government in Grenada stepped up its pressure on Martinique for funding and approval of an hospital. Governor Larnage's request of June 1734 seemed to have been taken seriously and set the final processes in motion. In 1738 the government in Martinique forwarded the request for funding to Paris, which was duly approved. It was agreed that the local government would procure the site for the hospital and with funding purchase a plantation to provide for the upkeep of the religious order that would run the facilities and operating funds. All hospitals in the region to date were run by religious orders and the Brothers of Charity (*Religieux de la Charite de St. Jean de Dieu*) were approached to run the planned Grenada facility. In July 1738 a contract of acquisition was signed by the Brothers of Charity to administer the hospital, and in August the Rivière Saint-Jean sugar plantation, located not too far from the proposed hospital site, was purchased from Lequoy de Mongiraud, under the direction of Houel, the engineer. In June 1740 Houël produced a design of the hospital building, with extensive housing for the slaves who would be the primary caretakers for the sick.

Following the construction of the hospital on a small hill overlooking the Grand Bay in Basse-Terre and considered healthy, two members of the Brothers of Charity arrived in Grenada in March 1742 to administer the facility.[24]

Between 1742 and 1760 the Brothers of Charity ran the hospital, but there were a number of issues that seemed to follow Father Damien Pillon, who was in charge. In 1749 Father Damien was called to Martinique to answer charges that he had appropriated hospital funds (a sum of 34,000 *livres* made from the sugar estate meant for the upkeep of the Hospital) for himself and his religious order. Father Damien was also accused of caring more for the sugar plantation than the hospital and its patients. He was immediately replaced by Father Prudence under whose management the hospital seemed to have progressed well. Following Father Prudence's death in May 1758, he was replaced by Father John Damascene, who was forced to return to Martinique due to ill health. Probably having no one to replace Father Damascene, Father Damien returned, but died in 1760. He was replaced by Father Thierry who also died that same year. According to Devas, with no one to replace him the colonial government took over the administration of the hospital, and appointed Joseph Maillard, a surgeon, as administrator.

Following the British capture of the island in 1762 three French inhabitants were appointed by the board of trustees to run the hospital. Towards the end of the year the board replaced Maillard with William Bryant, a British surgeon and purveyor of Hospitals of the Southern Caribbees Government. The ownership of the St. John River plantation, however, became one of the controversial issues between the French and British, with the Brothers of Charity of Martinique laying personal claim, while the British governor regarded it as the property of the hospital.

Crimes and Punishments

Colonial slave society engendered a fair amount of brutality that found expression across the spectrum of lives on the island. There were always laws and a rudimentary judicial system meant to limit the excesses, but because of the independent nature of plantations brutality was an everyday part of the slaves' lives. Masters and overseers often acted against the slaves in harsh and even brutal ways to coerce or punish minor misdeeds; more serious crimes elicited the most severe punishments, including whipping and maiming. For poor whites, and especially indentured servants, life proved difficult as they had to deal with the inequalities of the system, which though it recognized their white skin often punished their poverty. It was a harsh environment.

The judiciary, like other colonial institutions in Grenada, developed very gradually as a result of the island's economic and demographic progress. As the situation changed there was a need to alter the existing system to accommodate the growth in the population, especially that of the slaves and the rise in runaway slaves (*marrons*). Justice under the proprietary lords between 1649 and 1664 appeared quite arbitrary as it was the prerogative of the island's owners. Under Governor du Parquet they was a notary to process administrative issues, but there was no judge as one had to be brought in from Martinique in the 1654 trial of Le Fort and Le Marquis for treason.[25]

Under the proprietorship of the Comte de Sérillac, especially under his lieutenant François du Bu as stated in Chapter 5, there was an apparent absence of justice as du Bu had, according to the Anonymous author, "appointed no one as officer; himself alone was enough for everyone, as he said and wanted to be alone as judge and lawyer, and prosecutor and registrar, and notary and sergeant, and part and witness."[26] The situation quickly deteriorated and many of the colonists accused du Bu of numerous abuses of power, and in the absence of a fair judicial system on the island they took matters into their own hands. After a year of his supposed abuses many of the colonists conspired and abducted the governor, staged a trial, convicted him, and had him shot. Arriving on the island two years later, the Comte de Sérillac set up a court that tried, in absentia, those suspected of leading the revolt against du Bu. It is these few attempts that sum up the state of justice under proprietary rule.

The establishment of the Compagnie des Indies occidentales françaises (French West India Company) in 1664 saw the imposition of official justice, though it too often struggled against the interests of the company and its officials. There isn't much evidence on the course of justice during this period, but it does appear that the island at least had an appointed judge who attended to the immediate needs of the inhabitants.

The situation changed dramatically once the island became a crown colony in 1674, with the complete application of royal justice, which for the first time, meant the adaption of the Custom of Paris and a common civil procedure and criminal law.[27] This was implemented by a judge with responsibility for civil and criminal jurisdiction; he was subsequently assisted by a royal prosecutor or attorney (*procureur du roi*), a recorder or clerk, bailiffs and notaries; and still later a deputy judge (*lieutenant de juge*). These various officials were responsible to the intendant in Martinique, being his delegates in Grenada, with duties relating to law and order, including policing, crimes and disputes. Though what operated on the ground varied, the Crown insisted that judicial matters were handled by the intendant and his staff, following the processes and procedures set down, prohibiting the governor or other military officials from implementing arbitrary justice. The colonists also had recourse to appeal a local ruling to the Sovereign Council in Martinique since Grenada was never granted one, despite many requests for a local Council.

In the early years there was much disagreement between the governors and the local judges over the administration of justice. It is not clear what issues caused Governor Gabaret to complain to his superiors in Martinique in May 1687, but he felt that justice in the island was badly administered.[28] Officials in Martinique must have agreed with him because the judge was dismissed the following year.[29] Complaints continued for the next two decades over the state of the judiciary in the island. It was not until the 1720s that the judiciary seems to have settled into the regular functioning within the colony's institutions.

The details of the day to day workings of the judiciary in Grenada are not known, but the judge and his staff would have had to deal with the usual criminal activities, primary among them being thievery, sexual misconduct and altercations resulting from disputes among colonists. There were a few high profile cases of murder: in 1692 de Lugaret, captain in the militia, was assassinated; in 1726 soldier Jolibois committed a murder; and in 1757 Jean Pierre Julien, a *habitant* from Martinique was murdered in Grenada. In 1740 an altercation between Duchesne and Savary resulted in the latter's death. As part of his punishment Duchesne was made to pay compensation to Savary's wife and children in the amount of 12,000 l.t.; the widow was demanding 30,000 l.t.[30]

Probably the most prosecuted and prominent crime was involvement in illegal commerce. Most of those engaged in illegal trade were either prominent colonists or government officials, sometimes even governors. In 1670 Governor de Canchy gave permission to a Dutch captain to trade in slaves; four years later he was again caught allowing the practice and reprimanded. His dismissal in 1674 may have had to do with personal involvement in the illegal trade in slaves.[31] At least three other governors were accused, including Governor de Bellair in 1697 who vehemently protested his innocence, Governor de Bouloc in 1705 who was caught red handed, and acting Governor d'Arquian in 1712. Other government officials included royal attorneys Allou in 1704 and Clozier in 1717; Engineer Binoist was found guilty in 1725, but like most officials got off with reprimands. François Claverie, a prominent planter, was found guilty of illegally purchasing 40 slaves in 1724, as was Allair in 1726.

Though the basic system was put into place early, the judiciary lacked resources despite complaints from the island's governors. In 1712 the governor-general, on a visit to Grenada, complained that as a result of "the island being devoid of hangman and prisons, crimes there remain unpunished."[32] Thus Governor de Maupeou in 1714 requested funds for the construction of a trial chamber, prison and hiring an executioner to carry out sentences, but none were forthcoming. The revolt of the maroons in the 1720s brought the demands for judicial enhancements, but it took almost three decades before the island actually saw the funds for the construction of a courthouse (*palais de justice*) and a prison, which were constructed in the shadow of Fort Royal by the mid-1740s; the fort was used to incarcerate prisoners prior to this.[33]

There were always two strands of the judiciary operating in the island, one for the colonists and the other for the slaves. Despite the preponderance of laws to protect both colonists and slaves, there was always an element of arbitrariness about their enforcement, especially for slaves and poor whites. The Black or Slave Code (*Code Noir*), established in 1685, was meant to govern the daily lives of the slaves. It was formulated by the French colonial government under King Louis XIV as a code of conduct in dealing with the institution of slavery that was then expanding in the French colonies. Its primary goal was to organize a body of rules, laws and punishments that defined the legal status of the slave and regulated his treatment; its implicit goal was to prevent abuses that many believed would lead to "the dreaded slave revolt." The *Code Noir* was basically a codification of many existing practices already functioning in the French Antilles, with minor enhancements. In framing these laws, it recognized the primary role of the slaves as property. As property the slave could be bought and sold, but the sale of families with young children was discouraged. The Code stipulated that the slave had to be fed specific rations for adequate nutrition and provided an allotment of clothing annually. The work hours were specified between sun rise and sun set, and elderly and invalid slaves were to be cared for. It outlined the social and legal relationship between slaves and masters: children born to slaves and whites were automatically enslaved if the mother was a slave. Among its most important provisions were that slaves be baptized and given religious instruction, and the right of marriage.

Punishment for infractions and crimes was an important component of the Code. It stipulated the punishments that owners could inflict—branding, whipping, clipping of the ear, removal of limbs—for every possible crime, but they could not take the life of a slave as punishment. Yet owners did kill their slaves as was the case with François-Camille de Francesqui, a former captain aide-major in the militia, who was found guilty of cruelty to his slaves by causing the deaths of six of them by severe punishments in October 1757.[34] The local judge sentenced him to six months in prison and a 10,000 *livres* fine, but upon appeal to the Sovereign Council at Martinique his jail term was cancelled, leaving only the fine and prohibition from owning slaves. The execution of slaves was left to the state which often had slaves put to death, especially in the case of maroons who were suspected of committing crimes; owners were legally compensated from the general coffers for the slaves in such cases. The colonists had petitioned Martinique for more authority to punish slaves locally so that witnessing these punishments might deter others, but it wasn't until 1726 that permission to establish a Royal Chamber (*Chambre Royale*) was granted. Though the *Code Noir* has been seen by some as a relatively more humane body of laws dealing with the institution of slavery in the Caribbean they were primarily not adhered to by the proprietors and overseers, or policed by the government. As was quite apparent, "its provisions were likely honored in the breach rather than in the observance."[35]

Religion and the Catholic Church

Religion, specifically Roman Catholicism, was a handmaiden of French colonialism in the Caribbean from the start. Attempts to convert the Amerindians failed miserably, and in some cases proved deadly for the few missionaries who were absolutely rejected by the indigenous peoples in the region. As French colonialism established itself, the early missionaries played an important role in politics as well, oftentimes neglecting their spiritual duties. Their learned background also gave them a unique role as observers and recorders of events, many providing narratives of early French colonial activities that remain the primary sources available today. As the French became more established the clergy often found itself in opposition to the government as it fought to secure more and more resources for its members and their activities. The various denominations were often at odds with each other, and these struggles created adverse effects in the society. Religion, however, played an important role since the settlement of Grenada in 1649, and after 1685 and the promulgation of the *Code Noir*, religion took on new emphasis in the lives of the enslaved.

In 1649 when Governor du Parquet readied his party to depart Martinique for his colonization of Grenada, he took with him his personal priest to sanctify the undertaking because he was unable to find a priest to take up the mission there. During the early period priests were in short supply and those who were present often balked at going to frontier settlements like Grenada. However, André Desmares, a secular priest, provided for the spiritual needs of the colonists between 1651 and 1656, when, after many requests by du Parquet to the Dominicans for a priest for Grenada, Father Bénigne Bresson was sent to the island in 1656 (Table 9.1). And it was with Bresson's arrival that du Parquet in June 1656 allotted a concession of land in Grand Pauvre for the establishment of a parish and convent. Father Dutertre had hoped to reinforce the Dominicans in Grenada when he assisted the Comte de Sérillac in purchasing the island in 1656. In fact, de Sérillac offered the Dominicans the mission at Grenada and signed a contract with them; he also named Dutertre "superior and apostolic prefect" of the island on 17 September 1657, but while the ship was waiting to depart France for Grenada de Sérillac was persuaded to engage some Capuchins who offered as many priests as he needed for his colony.[36] Dutertre decided to not continue to Grenada following the failed attempt in December 1657, with Father Bresson the only Dominican on the island. The first Capuchin priest arrived in July 1658 with du Bu and the other colonists, and Father Bresson departed in 1659. Thus the Capuchins took over the Grenada mission in the absence of other priests, and became the only order there for the next six decades.

Father Labat, a Dominican, would later claim that the Dominicans had been administering the mission until 1677 when the governor asked them to leave.[37] Devas adds that the governor, "tiring of the white-robed sons of St. Dominic (there were evidently several of them), packed them all off to Martinique, whence they had come, and called in the bearded Franciscan Capuchins in their stead."[38] Labat did not provide the reason why the sudden change by the governor, but the episode is questionable considering that there were no Dominicans on the island at that time. Labat's reference may be to a rejection by the governor-general of the Dominicans' historical claim to the Grenada mission rather than any physical expulsion. In fact, in 1665, following the takeover of the island from de Sérillac, Governor-General de Baas identified that the island was administered by "deux Pères Capucins," and one or two Capuchins were usually present on Grenada for the rest of the 1600s, so Labat's claim is quite misleading. It was the Dominicans who had abandoned Grenada since 1659!

To illustrate the ill treatment the Dominicans received at the hands of the government, Labat provides the example of Father Godfrey Loyer who was asked to leave the island.[39] The episode took place in 1692-93 when the Capuchins, "decimated by plague," were forced to leave the island with no one to replace them.[40] Devas, like Labat, implies that the so-called expulsion of 1677 and that of Father Godfrey are one and the same. Devas explains that, "Their Superior, seizing the opportunity, quickly dispatched Father Godfrey Loyer to Grenada that he might take possession again of Grand Pauvre. After all, the Fathers surely had a right to live on the estate which belonged to them, even if the members of another religious Order were looking after the spiritual welfare of the rest of the island. But no; Comte de Blénac, governor-general of the islands… gave orders to Father Loyer to quit as soon as the Capuchins were again able to send fathers to Grenada."[41] The Dominicans, seizing the opportunity occasioned by the sickness of the Capuchins, decided to usurp them by sending Father Godfrey, who had recently arrived in Martinique, to Grenada in December 1692. It is not clear how Father Godfrey ended up in the situation, but he claims that "The savage Caribs, tied and stripped me, and, without the assistance of one of them who was Christian, I would have been slaughtered."[42] It is possible that he had attempted to convert the Island Caribs. In March 1693 Father Godfrey left Grenada to go to Martinique to procure wine for mass because

Governor de Gemosat had asked him to keep it "très digne religieux." On the boat to Martinique he attended to an ill sailor with yellow fever, thus contracting the disease, forcing him to remain on Martinique for over a month while recuperating. Meanwhile, two Capuchins resumed at Grenada, so he was obliged to leave upon his return since the governor-general had insisted that once the Capuchins returned he could not stay.

The Compagnie des Indies occidentales françaises took over Grenada in 1664, including the administration of religion (priests, churches and salaries). Providing Grenada with clergy to minister to the colonists and slaves proved as difficult for the government as peopling the colony in general since the competition for religious personnel always favored the more established islands. Along with the other colonies, Grenada witnessed the establishment of its first official parish, St. Jacques, at its primary settlement of Fort Royal, with the two Capuchins who had been on the island for at least five years. Thus the island officially became solely the mission of the Capuchins. But it was a continuous struggle to keep this one parish staffed. In 1679, one of the two Capuchins, Father Daniel died, and Governor-General de Blénac proposed that Father Épiphane replace him. Reluctantly, Father Épiphane followed orders and went to Grenada, but after a few months he left the island for St. Vincent to evangelize among the Island Caribs, which is what he had originally wanted to do.[43] The lack of priests to minister to the colonists led governors to complain to the authorities in Martinique about the meager spiritual care afforded to the population. Others saw this as contributing to the moral decay of the colony. Even when there was only a single priest in the colony, the governors complained that the services they rendered was inadequate and their conduct unbecoming. In 1691 Governor Gemosat had Father Paulin expelled because of his unacceptable behavior.

In late 1688 Father Jean de la Mousse, on his way to Martinique from Cayenne, stopped at Grenada for three weeks as the ship he was on waited to collect produce. At the time of his visit only Father Victor was on the island. He expressed joy at being able to say mass in the church as opposed to on the vessel he traveled on because it "was too small and which rolled too much." Father Jean described his encounter thus:

> I was obliged to preach at Grenada, which I did the day of All Saints' day, naked head because they did not have a doctor's cap there in all the island; the Capuchins who have care of

spiritual needs not making use of it. I even thought of preaching without surplice, that of the father capuchin, made for his dress, not being found clean with the mien, and I employed more time to put it at my use than I had not made to prepare my sermon. While I was in Grenada, I confessed a great number of people, it is not that the R. P. Capuchin is not a good honest man, to which one has confidence, but change and freedom are great charms with people not obliged to open their conscience with only one man.[44]

Father Jean failed to describe the church building where he said mass in 1688, but it was most likely as Father Dutertre had described an earlier church as made of sticks and thatch like other buildings "after the style of the country." The French had erected chapels in Grenada since the 1650s, but these were temporary constructions. It appears that a sturdy structure was not built until 1690, which "was begun and finished the same year as much by sums advanced by the King as by the inhabitants."[45] This church was consecrated on 10 September 1690, and according to the deed "we all signed it on coming out from the mass about noon of the same day, that each and all, and all our descendants in times to come may be able to give credence to it, and know the time and the day when the blessing of this church was performed."[46] Among those acknowledged were Governor de Gabaret who had rallied for more priests on the island, and Cassé, officer of the militia and churchwarden. It is interesting to note that a year later Governor Gemosat complained to Martinique that the Capuchins should be ordered "to carry out clerical functions and celebrate daily service in the church of the parish destined for the subject, and not in particular houses."[47] When Labat visited a decade later he had very little to say about the church except that "It is not large, nor beautiful, nor well built, nor clean."[48] It would be a few years after Labat's visit that a more permanent structure would be built on the same site where he had said mass. It is not clear when the new church was built, but in 1704 the two Capuchin priests on the island requested that a church and presbytery be built, which Governor de Bouloc supported.[49] The St. Jacque Church, built soon after in the parish of St. Jacques and St. Philippe, catered to the growing colony, and was the largest church on the island during the French period; a presbytery was also built on the site.

After over six decades of colonization the French had only established one parish in the main administrative center of Fort Royal to cater to a total population that had grown to just under 3,000 by 1715. That the *Code Noir* called for the baptism of the slaves (their population at 2,400 and scattered across the island), meant that religious instruction probably did not reach them by the two priests assigned to the island. For Governor de Maupeou it was not the number of priests, but their work ethic. In 1713, he placed the blame squarely on the two Capuchins "who perform none of the functions of their ministry. Since I have been on the island, I have not seen [them] teach catechism. I can assure you that more than three-quarter of the Negroes are not baptized."[50]

The next two decades, however, witnessed the creation of five new parishes across the island (Table 9.1). Though the development of the island had acted as the impetus for the creation of parishes and towns, it appears that by 1721 Royal Lieutenant de Pradines, who found himself acting as governor on many occasions during this period, facilitated the process by designating lands for towns and churches across the island; there was also a push by other denominations to establish missions in Grenada. In 1722 a number of principal inhabitants, recommending that he be appointed the next governor, praised his many contributions, including "expanding religion."[51]

The request to establish a second parish on the island dates to at least 1713, yet it wasn't until 1718 that it was finally approved.[52] The Quartier des Sauteurs was located in the north, and over the last two decades had seen the increase of its French settlers who gradually displaced the Island Carib population and eliminated their threat. By 1718 Sauteurs was a small hamlet and its inhabitants requested that it be created a parish, committing to pay for two years the allowance of the priest at 500 l.t. each year.[53] The Capuchins, already established at the Ville du Fort Royal, were appointed to serve the parish of Notre Dame du Bon Secours in the Quartier des Sauteurs.

The Dominicans had always seen Grenada as their spiritual territory, especially since they were the first missionaries, and had property on the island. According to Labat, his visit to Grenada around 1700 had been to assess the Grand Pauvre property because "it was necessary to work to put our place in Grenada to value; we made plans, and without the war of 1702 which happened, it would have been carried out, and I would again have been charged with this chore."[54] The Dominicans had been advocating for access to their grant since 1712, and were finally allowed to return to Grenada in 1722, reclaiming their property at Grand Pauvre.

They had requested to return to establish a number of habitations, including two *sucreries*, hence the designation of St. Rose in Grand Pauvre as a non-parish church. It wasn't until 1726 that St. Rose became a parish with a parish priest; the habitants were responsible for constructing a church and presbytery while the Domaine d'occident paid the salary of 540 l.t. provided it was served by a Dominican.[55]

A third parish, Notre Dame de l'Assomption, was created in the Quartier du Grand Marquis in 1722 and served by the Capuchins. In 1726 a new parish at Petit Marquis, Mégrin was created and given to the Jesuits, who were new to the island, under the same conditions as Grand Pauvre. It wasn't until 1730 that a priest was installed, but the chapel was destroyed by a storm in 1731. It was rebuilt in 1733, but abandoned in 1736 for the new site and parish of St. Jean-Baptiste at L'Ance Père, Mégrin. In 1733 the Dominicans made the natural extension north, creating the small parish of St. Pierre at Goyave. In March 1742 some of the prominent residents of the Quartier du Conférence requested that a parish, to be called Rivière d'Antoine, be created because of the great distance of three miles to the parish of Marquis; it was not created.[56] A parish in Carriacou was not created during the initial French occupation.

Religion and slavery went hand in hand in Grenada without much protest. Though the Capuchins stood out from the various religious orders by not owning plantations, individual priests did own slaves. Priests and governors often had conflicts, but few concerned slavery. In 1705, however, Governor de Bouloc, in a letter to Secretary of the Navy Pontchartrain, complained about the Capuchins in Grenada and was ready to replace them with the Jesuits because they "were preaching that slave owners should feed their slaves meat, presumably because the slaves' meatless diet was contributing to their malnutrition and starvation."[57]

The stipulation that all slaves in French colonies be baptized in the Catholic religion was part of the larger enforcement of Catholicism as the only religious practice sanctioned in the French Antilles, and dates to the establishment of the French in the region. It was institutionalized with the promulgation of the *Code Noir* in 1685, which placed the Catholic faith as central to the lives of the colonists, and that of the slaves as well. Article II of the *Code Noir* stipulated that "All the slaves who will be in our Islands will be baptized and instructed in the Catholic, Apostolic, and Roman religion. We charge the planters who will buy newly arrived *nègres* to inform the Governor and Intendant of the said islands within a week at the latest or face a discretionary fine, these [officials] will give the necessary orders to have them instructed and baptized within an appropriate time."[58] Like with most colonial laws, edicts, etc., it remained the conditions on the ground that determined if and when a law would be implemented and to what extent.

The development of religion for the overall population in Grenada was very slow. Though Capuchin priests were established in the island since the 1650s, the order found it very difficult to survive. Until around 1720, there was at most two, but oftentimes only one priest on the island at a given time, sometimes none at all. As such, the existence of religion among the slave population was lacking even though the population was initially small and grew only gradually. The scattered nature of plantations would have also made it difficult for the one or two priests to travel around the island administering to the needs of hundreds, and later thousands of slaves. In 1713 Governor de Maupeou questioned whether a quarter of the almost 2,400 slaves were baptized per the *Code Noir*.[59]

Little evidence exists to show the extent of acceptance of Catholicism among the slaves in Grenada under the French, but some sort of foundation was built that enabled the religion to be the primary one among their descendants; the same goes for the French Creole language despite the fact that the majority of slaves after 1763 were owned by British planters. That the slaves were baptized upon arrival in the island could be expected because both the church and planters supported it on the grounds that baptism would aide in suppressing the slaves' African culture and make them more accommodating to the new environment. The other rites enforced by the *Code Noir* were not well supported because they did not serve the planters' cause. Marriage, though promoted by the church, was discouraged by the planters because it interfered with the autonomy of the plantation if the slave wanted to marry someone outside of their plantation.

It was often reported that the slave was open to Christianity, but the reasons for each may have been different. For many it allowed them a degree of acceptance by both the church and authorities. The similarities between Catholicism and African cosmologies made the acceptance of the former easier, and in many cases allowed the slaves to secretly continue with some form of their own worship. With so few clergy to administer to the growing slave population, many developed new ways of observing African worship, especially of ancestors, and continuing practices based on their beliefs. Left to their own, the slave continued many of their cultural practices under the guise of Catholicism. Yet, the entrenchment of the rudiments of Catholicism among the slaves during the initial French period led to its later wider acceptance among the overall slave population during the British period.

Celebrations and Festivities

Despite the harshness and brutality of Grenada's slave society, there were opportunities for celebrations for both the slaves and free population. Only a few descriptions, however, are known of the celebratory activities slaves often engaged in. Whatever free time the slave was allowed was predominantly spent in their gardens growing food, taking care of their families, participating in the weekly market day, and a few sanctioned ceremonies like weddings, funerals and official holidays (primarily religious festivals). The ability of the slaves to actually celebrate these holidays depended on the liberties granted by their masters and overseers; while some believed that the slaves should be given opportunities to celebrate others were quite restrictive in their freetime. Also, the type of plantation, whether sugar or coffee, determined the social environment. While on a large sugar plantation slaves could get together easily to celebrate, the small numbers on a coffee or cocoa plantation meant that they would have had to visit others to engage in social activities.

Market days were festive occasions for slaves who regularly gathered to sell or exchange some of what they produced in their garden plots. These were usually held on Sundays because the planters did not want to disrupt the work schedule of the plantation despite the prohibition that it should be observed as a day of worship for all, including the slaves; market usually began after church services. Some very industrious slaves were able to save enough money to purchase their freedom, while many used the proceeds to buy things like clothes, in order to, as one commentator put it, "dress themselves neatly and to maintain their families well."[60] It would appear that the social activity of meeting and interacting with other slaves was a large part of market day. It was also a time to arrange and advertise upcoming events. Market days have been described as "cultural centres... of the first order.... They must have been

237

centres at which new items of material culture were distributed and popularised. They must have also been centres of religious activity and dance and song.... Many a friendship and family tie traced itself back to the joys and vagaries of the marketplace."[61]

One of the social activities that slaves were often recorded as participating in was dances. These were rather extravagant affairs that involved a great deal of planning and expense on everyone's part. Slaves from many plantations would show up for these dances. It may or may not have centered on a particular event like a wedding, but could have been apart of the religious calendar like Christmas or pre-Lenten celebrations. Everyone was expected to "pay for their share," which included the food for the meal and drinks, and the cost of the musicians. Slaves would dress in their finest outfit, many attempting to emulate the look of their masters in both dress and mannerisms. As the festivities began, the master of ceremonies welcomed the participants and each entrance was a display of greetings that commentators often found quite excessive. After the meal, the slaves would begin the part they "passionately loved," the dancing. One commentator described a celebration thus:

> They treat themselves from time to time on holidays. Their big feasts, principally weddings, are numerous. All those who wish are admitted as long as they bring something to pay for their share. These tumultuous meals, which the overseers survey to prevent unruliness, are always followed by dances which the negroes passionately love. Those of each nation assemble and dance in the style of their country to the cadenced beat of a kind of drum, accompanied by loud chants, by the rhythmic clapping of hands and also by a kind of four-string guitar which they call a banza. The dance that the creoles like best and which, because of this, is frequently performed, even among the naturalized Nations, was the calenda.[62]

The calenda or kalenda was a common name applied to various slave dances throughout the region and may have changed over time. Labat's 1722 description is echoed by a mid-1700s description common throughout the French Caribbean:

> The dancers are arranged in two lines, the one before the other, the men to one side, the women to the other. Those are the ones who dance, and the spectators make a circle around the dancers and drums. The most skilled sings a song that he composes on the spot, on such a subject as he judges

appropriate, and the refrain, which is sung by all the spectators, is accompanied by a great beating of hands. As regards the dancers, they hold up their arms a little like those who dance while playing castanets. They jump, they spin, they approach to within three feet of each other, they leap back on the beat, until the sound of the drum tells them to join and they strike their thighs, some beating against the others, that is, the men's against the women's. To see this, it seems that they beat their bellies together, while it is however only their thighs that support the blows. They back away immediately, pirouetting, to recommence the same movement with completely lascivious gestures, as often as the drum gives them the signal, which it does several times in succession. From time to time they interlace their arms and make two or three turns while always striking their thighs together, and they kiss one another.[63]

It is quite possible that Carriacou's Big Drum dance, or African nation dance as was practiced in Grenada got their start in this period. Slaves from various ethnic groups celebrated by demonstrating their particular dances and thus created nation dances that became associated with their specific groups. As time passed these unique dances came the identify individuals with a specific African tribe and resulted in the creation of ethnic identies that were passed on from generation to generation and as are still evident in Carriacou today.[64]

The survival of many elements of African cultures in Grenada suggests that slaves may have also participated in other activities that were not sanctioned by the master or overseer. These would most likely have taken place at night and in secret so as to avoid detection and punishment. These activities could have been of a religious nature or any celebration involving African rites and rituals prohibited by the church or the authorities. One of the most feared and forbidden African cultural practice was witchcraft, which the church and other authorities campaigned against. Slaves caught practicing witchcraft or obeah were severely punished, sometimes banished or even executed because of its potential to cause the deaths of slaves and even whites due primarily to poisons. Though it is often reported that African drumming was forbidden that may not have been the case during the French period. Certain activities where drumming was involved may have been banned.

For the whites, social activities either centered around the family or the towns. Weddings and baptisms, especially among the *grand blanc* families, were large festive occasions. Other religious holidays like

Christmas and Lent led to fêtes that became annual celebrations among every segment of the free population. Though the various groups celebrated among themselves, all found a way to enjoy these holidays. For many of the *petit blancs*, taverns and the like provided regular entertainment and places to celebrate.

One of the more popular celebrations was the pre-Lenten festival common in French Catholic countries, which gradually took on particular Caribbean characteristics. It was a favorite among the wealthy planters who staged masquerade balls, one of their popular costumes the *nèg jardan* (derived from the French *nègre*: "negro," and *jardin*: "garden," with reference to field slaves) because they dressed as their field slaves: straw hat, knee-long pant and bright colored shirt. Like the slaves who imitated their masters, the whites, in keeping with the celebration of the flesh, gave up their high positions for those of the slave for one night.

Colonial Conflicts and Defense

The defense of the island was a constant preoccupation of colonial administrators because in times of war, readiness could mean the difference between victory and defeat. Defense of the island, especially its fortifications, probably received the most attention when communications between the local administrators and the authorities in Martinique are examined. That, however, does not mean that the endless communication translated into actual physical defense. In 1712 Governor-General Phélypeaux went so far as to claim that the costs of defending Grenada would be far too high, concluding the island was indefensible and thus should be relinquised by the French.[65] Grenada's rather low economic and social state for all of the seventeenth century worked as the perfect defense since no one would waste resources to attack if there was little booty to be had. In the late 1600s the island witnessed many attacks from privateers and found it difficult to effectively respond because of its scattered population and limited resources. Its best defense proved to be the growth of its population and the expansion of its militia forces across the island that could respond immediately to these attacks.

The establishment of the militia began as a means to provide protection and defense to colonists against Amerindians whose lands they had invaded, and enemy colonial powers who were either attempting to conquer new lands or destroy enemy territories. Over time the militia developed into an important colonial institution that served both the colonists and the colonial government as it filled a number of functions within the colonial administrative structure. As a trained body of adult males bearing arms, it provided for the defense of personal property, and, in a few cases, of the colony itself since the French government provided an inadequate body of troops to defend the island. The militia was responsible for putting down internal conflicts or protest, whether from free or enslaved persons or groups. In that capacity, it served as a police force maintaining law and order, and its creation was often viewed as necessary to defend against the large slave population should they attempt to revolt or escape. Though they may not have had to deal with outright slave revolts, the militia was kept busy pursuing and capturing runaway slaves (*marrons*). In carrying out disciplinary measures, militia leaders were the first judicial officers in the colonies, especially in Grenada which did not receive a judge initially. When a judge was finally appointed c. 1685, it took a while to wean militia leaders from disciplining colonists. The militia served as an agent through which the government communicated edicts, ordinances, etc. to the colonists, collected census and other data, garnered reports, and executed its orders. It also acted as the medium between the colonists and the local administration, especially in dealing with the judiciary. As the militia came to represent a specific parish or district, it also became the defacto local administration, with responsibility for the construction and maintenance of roads, byways and sanitation; the road surveyor (*voyer*) subsequently took over these duties by the mid-1700s.

The militia, unlike French troops, was not uniformed and did not receive remunerations.[66] Membership was mandatory for all healthy white males between the ages of 16 and 60 years and resident in the colony, but males as young as 12 years and capable of bearing arms were often called upon in times of need. As the apprehensions over the threat of revolt increased due to the ballooning slave population, the colonial government was forced to conscript all free able bodied males to augment the small number of white males capable of bearing arms. Thus by 1718, free coloureds and blacks were expected to serve in the militia; white male indentured servants were also obliged to serve. Free non-whites could not, however, attain any of the coveted officer positions which were opened only to white males and oftentimes went to the wealthiest planters and minor noblemen. Since Grenada was not a colony in its own right, but a dependent of Martinique, it lacked many of the colonial institutions present in the region. As such, the leadership positions in the militia came to represent one of the few access points to a status bearing job available in the island. For the wealthy ambitious planters, it provided a boost to their power and brought privileges as well.

The structure of the militia did not change much over time, but certain things were implemented to enhance its effectiveness. One major change was the regularization of the structure of the militia and the number of regiments allotted each colony throughout the region in 1705. Grenada was allowed one regiment of militia, within which it formed companies, both infantry and cavalry. Each company was accorded a captain (*capitaine de milice*), one lieutenant and one ensign. A number of other positions were added over the years, including that of major (1716), aide-major (c. 1728), and honorary positions (*reformé*) that carried privileges for retired officers. All officers were appointed by the governor-general in Martinique and promotions followed rank from ensign, lieutenant, captain, aide-major, and major (see Appendix I). Though the officers were not paid they received exemptions from the head tax on slaves based on their positions.

The captain of the militia held a very important and powerful position. Due to his interactions with the colonists, he was often well regarded among them. Captains could become so powerful that they were highly regarded than the governor, as was the case in 1674 when Governor de Canchy accused Captain La Blennerie of wanting to stage a popular uprising against his government.[67] The captain was responsible for the training and management of his company of between 50 to 100 men. Captains' primary responsibility was making sure that members attended the weekly mandatory military practice each Sunday at the parade ground (*place d'armes*), usually held in an open area. The absence of members was a real problem and many had to be disciplined for missing practice. The captains were also responsible for judging minor contestations, manage the building and care of chapels, and administering the appropriation of slave labor for public works projects (*corvée*) like work on the fortifications, or the clearing or constructing new roads.

One of these militia captains (*capitaine de milice*) was Louis Lejeune. The son of a prominent family on the island, Lejeune grew up in Grenada after his father arrived in 1672 from St. Martin. His family was instrumental in the settlement of the Quartier des Sauteurs and the displacement of the Island Carib population there. The family was one of the wealthiest, owning a number of habitations, including *sucreries*. Louis Lejeune owned four habitations and 83 slaves in 1723. He was also chosen as the churchwarden when the *habitants* decided to create a parish in Sauteurs. He became the captain of the militia, which he commanded during the War of Jenkin's Ears (1744-48) and was awarded the cross of St. Louis in 1749. Two other brothers held positions in the Sauteurs militia. With their wealth and power they applied for letters of nobility, but these were not granted.

As the population increased, especially in slaves, and the island's economic status grew, the militia played a more prominent role. Beginning in 1674 with two companies, it grew to three infantry and one cavalry by 1713, with a total of about 170 members. Economic expansion engulfed the entire island by the 1730s, with districts demarcated and administered by the militia. By 1741 each of the six districts had its own militia infantry company, and there were also three cavalry companies, with about 500 men; the island of Carriacou did not establish a militia company until 1757. By 1755 the militia was almost 600 strong, consisting of 507 whites and 85 free coloureds and blacks, commanded by 55 officers, manning the various coastal batteries across the island and managing the six districts (Table 9.2).

Local governors continuously petitioned the government to improve the fortifications in the island to be able to respond to recurring privateer attacks, especially to defend the town. Plans to improve Fort Royal had been drawn up since 1678 when d'Estrees, stopping at Grenada following his victory over the Dutch at Tobago, had one of his engineers draw new plans. Governor Gemosat, an engineer in his own right, also designed plans for improvements.[68] It wouldn't be until the early 1700s that Grenada received any attention in this arena when Governor de Bouloc petitioned the government to make Grenada a port for the lucrative *asiento* which the French had recently won to supply the Spanish Caribbean slaves. Since Grenada's fortifications were deemed inadequate to defend an *asiento* port it needed to be improved. In March 1705 Jean-Baptiste de Caylus, chief engineer for the French Antilles, was sent to Grenada to design whatever upgrades to the island's fortification were needed that would give Grenada the capabilities to defend the roadstead, port and town. Caylus was not happy with what he had to work with, describing the construction of the old Fort Royal as "confused and badly configured."[69] Nonetheless, Caylus designed the upgrades, incorporating the previous structure. The new fortifications was much larger, with two huge bastions facing north to compensate for the higher ground commanding it and extended quarters for both officers and soldiers; though there were quarters for the governor in the new fort, governors since 1708 had accommodations in the town (Illustration 10.3). Caylus had estimated that the new design would take about two years, with the *habitants* contributing their slaves for the labor (*covée*) to construct the new works; additional slaves had to be hired to get the construction completed on time. Nonetheless, de Caylus retired after two years, thus it was engineer Nicolas Binoist de Reteuil who was left to carry out the plans and would have the greatest impact on Fort Royal because he subsequently moved to Grenada and worked on it for the next 30 years.[70]

Work on the new fortifications began almost immediately, but progressed slowly. In September 1707 Governor de Bouloc complained that the absence of engineer Binoist delayed the work on the fort because he was required to work on other building projects in various islands. The fact that the region was in a state of war may have affected the construction since other colonies demanded and got more attention than Grenada. Despite Governor de Bouloc's advocacy and promotion to make Grenada an *asiento* port, progress proved too slow to those ends. By 1710 the upgraded Fort Royal was completed, but France lost the lucrative *asiento* to the British as a result of the Treaty of Utrecht in 1713. Over the next five decades Fort Royal would see small upgrades like the installation of a large cistern in 1736, many of these designed by Binoist.

Defending the coasts from privateers had been a persistent problem for Grenada for many years. It lacked both the military resources and population to make a determined stance. It would be many years before coastal batteries would be constructed, but cannons were often mounted on vulnerable hillsides and lookouts across the island. By 1740 there were three coastal batteries, but island officials had planned another eleven to cover the most vulnerable spots, including Gouyave, Grand Pauvre, Sauteurs, Duquesne, Levera, Megrin and Fort Jeudy. By 1755 there were sixteen coastal batteries manned by the island's militia and troops.

French troops, and later the *troupes de la marine*, were responsible for manning the forts and coastal batteries in Grenada. The first permanent French troops entered Grenada in 1664 under de Tracy to take control of the island for the Compagnie des Indies occidental française. When the island became a French colony in 1674 at least nine soldiers were stationed at Fort Royal, a number of them having died from illnesses and lack of resources. Their small numbers were unable to repel the attack of the Dutch privateers in 1675, but led to the presence of additional troops in Grenada. As a result an extra company under de La Tour remained in Grenada between 1675 and 1678, and the governor-general agreed to increase the garrison to 16 men, including officers.

It wasn't until 1683 that the distribution of the *troupes de la marine* was regulated, with Grenada receiving one company comprising 50 men. The ten companies of *troupes de la marine* stationed throughout the region were rotated through the islands. The government in Martinique and local officials encouraged soldiers to become residents, often petitioning to have marriageable women sent to Grenada so they could marry and settle down in the island and thereby increase the population. It would appear that only a few decided to settle, as was the case with Captain Lugerat in 1688 who requested a position in the local militia and a concession of land to establish himself.

Though the 50 soldiers were probably not enough, or seasoned to really defend the colony, they did make the colonists feel more secure. Many of them, however, succumbed to diseases and were unfit for service much of the time. During the war in the 1690s the situation looked so bleak that the governor-general recommended that Grenada and Marie Galante be abandoned and the colonists sent to Martinique to help protect that island because he did not have the resources to defend the smaller islands. On a trip to Grenada in 1712 the governor-general felt that Grenada was indefensible and therefore of little value to the French. As the island's economy grew in the 1730s and 1740s, and war again broke out in the region, the governor petitioned the authorities in Martinique to provide Grenada with a second company. Recognizing the importance of the island, Grenada received a second 50-man company of soldiers that was transferred from Marie Galante in 1747.

The second quarter of the eighteenth century had brought prosperity to Grenada with the expansion of sugar, coffee and the increase in the slave population. This was facilitated by peace in the region between 1714 and

1739. The next two decades saw two major colonial conflicts, the latter of which resulted in the capture of Grenada by the British. In 1739 the War of Jenkin's Ear broke out between England and Spain. In 1744 the conflict expanded into the War of Austrian Succession which saw France enter on the side of the Spanish. What this war meant for Grenada was a contraction in its growing plantation economy. According to Raynal, "Grenada was clearing its debts gradually by its rich produce; and the balance was on the point of being closed, when the war in 1744 interrupted the communication between the two islands [of Martinique and Grenada], and at the same time stopped the progress of the most important culture of the New World."[71]

What impacted Grenada's economy the most was the disruption of trade. French trade throughout the region was, according to Pares, "severely hampered." Pares continues that "the service of distributing the convoys to the smaller ports and islands, and bringing the homeward trade to the rendezvous, was even worse performed. [Governor-General de] Caylus argued that the ships which came out with these convoys could only protect the trade between Martinique and France, and that the coasting trade needed a force permanently stationed in the colonies."[72] The resurgence of war in the region destroyed the coasting trade and left Grenada stranded. According to Pares, "the English took nearly all the coasting craft of the Windward Islands; out of fifteen which ordinarily plied between Martinique and Grenada only one was left at the end of the first year of war."[73] Grenada, like Guadeloupe and the other French colonies, survived on illegal trade with the Dutch because "they had then no other communication with the outside world."[74] In 1748 the war came to an end with the Treaty of Aix-la-Chapelle. For the next eight years Grenada resumed its trade with Martinique and France, and continued to experience growth in its plantation economy, particularly sugar production which "was then pushed with an eagerness proportioned to their importance."[75]

Illustration 8.1

Slaves prepare tobacco
for export, from Jean-
Baptiste Labat's
*Nouveau voyage aux isles
de l'Amérique* (Paris,
1742), 4: 496.

Key
1. Slave shredding
tobacco.
2. Slave twisting
tobacco.
3. Slave rolling
tobacco.
4. Tobacco drying.

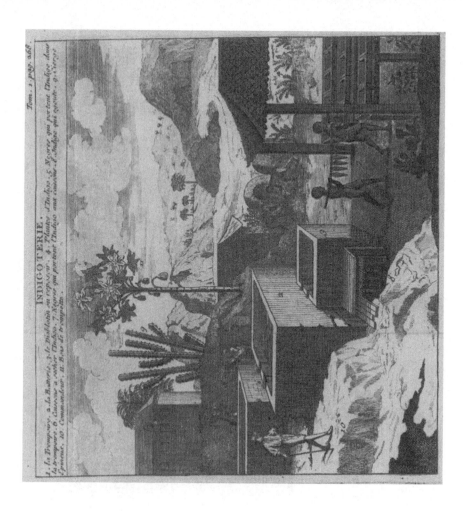

Illustration 8.2

Indigoterie or indigo factory, from Jean-Baptiste Labat's *Nouveau voyage aux isles de l'Amérique* (Paris, 1742), 1: 268.

Key

1. *Trempoire* vat; **2**. *Batterie* vat; **3**. *Reposoir* vat;

4. Indigo plants; **5**. Slaves carrying indigo to the *trempoire*; **6**. Boxes of drying indigo; **7**. Slaves carrying indigo to the boxes;

8. Indigo drain; **9**. Cactus; **10**. Overseer; **11**. Angel's trumpet plant.

248

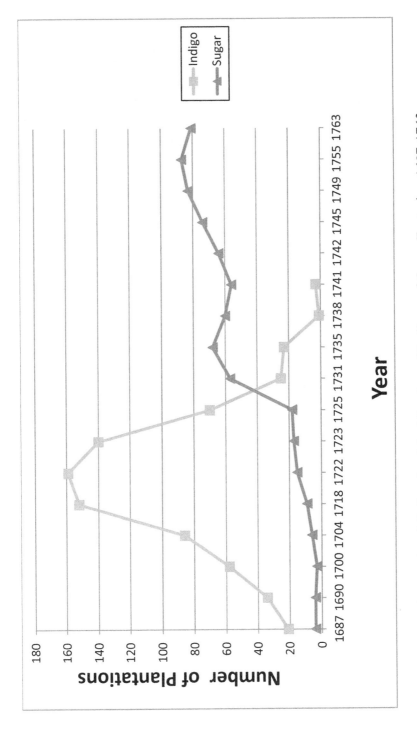

Illustration 8.3 Graph of the Number of Indigo and Sugar Factories, 1687–1763

Illustration 8.4

Cocoa tree with pods, from Jean-Baptiste Labat's *Nouveau voyage aux isles de l'Amérique* (Paris, 1742), 6: following 372.

Illustration 8.5

Sucrerie, or sugar factory, from Jean-Baptiste Dutertre's *Histoire generale des Antilles habitées par les François* (Paris, 1667-71), 2: following 122.

Key: **1.** Mill; **2.** Furnace/boilers; **3.** Sugar pots; **4.** Vinegar factory; **5.** Sugarcane plants; **6.** Coconut tree; **7.** Palm tree; **8.** Wild coffee; **9.** Taro; **10.** Slave houses; **11.** Banana tree.

251

Illustration 8.6

View of sugar plantation, French West Indies, from Denis Diderot's *Encyclopédie, ou, Dictionnaire Raisonné des Sciences, des Arts et des Metiers . . . Recueil de Planches, sur les Sciences.* (Paris, 1762), 1: plate I.

<u>Key</u>: **1**. Great house **2**. Slave houses; **3**. Pasture; **4**. Hedge; **5**. Cane fields; **6**. Water mill; **7**. Boiling house; **8**. Aqueduct; **9**. Mill discharge; **10**. Bagasse house; **11-12**. Curing houses; **13**. Vegetable gardens; **14**. Hills.

252

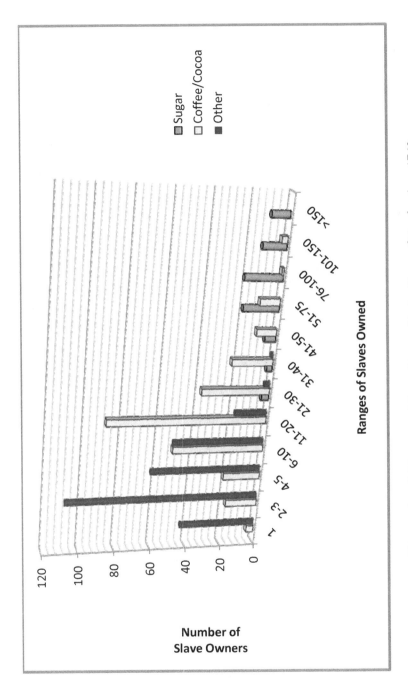

Illustration 9.1 Ranges of Slave Ownership by Type of Production, 1763.

Illustration 9.2

Slaves preparing manioc/cassava, from Jean-Baptiste Labat's *Nouveau voyage aux isles de l'Amérique* (Paris, 1742), 1: 397.

Slaves process manioc into cassava flour by scraping, grating, pressing to express the juice from the grated roots, sifting, and roasting on a griddle to make cassava cakes, a staple of their diet.

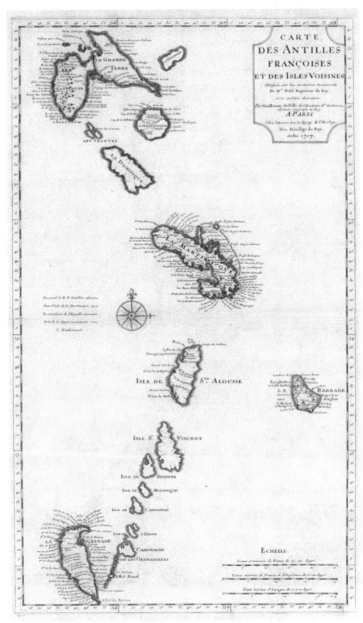

Illustration 9.3

Guillaume De L'Isle's "Carte des Antilles françoises et les isles voisines" 1717, from *Atlas nouveau...* (Paris, 1717). See Labat, *Nouveau voyages aux iles de l'Amérique* (Paris, 1742), 3: 283 for a discussion on the incorrect orientation of Grenada.

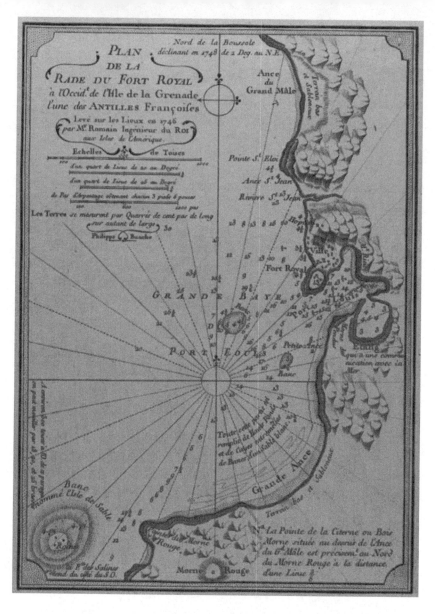

Illustration 9.4

Jean-Baptiste-Pierre Le Romain's (chief engineer in Grenada and the French Antilles, and author of articles for Diderot's *Encyclopédie*) "Plan de la Rade du Fort Royal" 1746.

Ville du Fort Royal and Port Louis, with surrounding coastal areas.

256

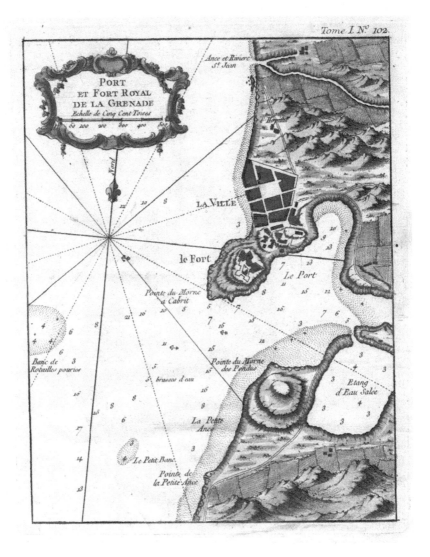

Illustration 9.5

Jacques Nicolas Bellin's "Port et Fort Royal de la Grenade," 1758, from *Le Petit Atlas Maritime Recueil de cartes et Plans des Quatre Parties du Monde* (Paris, 1764), I: no. 102.

The "Port and Fort Royal of Grenada," shows the small town (*La Ville*) with the *place d'armes*, Fort Royal (*le Fort*), the hospital (*l'Hopital*), the port (*le Port*), cultivated fields and roads.

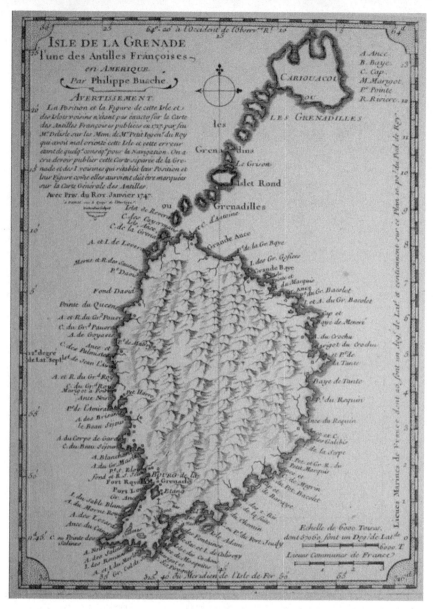

Figure 9.6

Philippe Buache's "Isle de la Grenade" (Paris, 1747), correcting the orientation of Grenada on De L'Isle's 1717 map of the French Antilles.

It was the first map to show Grenada in its upright position.

10

An Ending and a Beginning

"You and I have seen at Grenada the impossibility
of English and French ever assimilating together."[1]

The peace brought by the Treaty of Aix-la-Chapelle in 1748 did not last too long as conflict erupted in 1754 between the British and French in North America over the expansion of the British colonies there. Two years later the conflict took on a global presence as wars broke out across the world between France and England and their allies. The declaration of war in 1756 placed the colonies on immediate alert. As usual, the French colonies were left to defend themselves, with little assistance coming from France, which was concentrating its efforts and resources in the European theater.

On the eve of war the aging and ill Governor de Poincy was allowed to gracefully take his leave and hand over leadership of Grenada to a younger and abler successor. Despite de Poincy's earlier characterization of his deputy as "mediocre" and recommended that he should be replaced, Pierre-Claude-Antoine-François de Prulay de Bonvoust d'Aulnay was appointed governor in November 1757 to replace him. The son-in-law of former Governor de Pradines, de Bonvoust had resided in Grenada since 1735 when he was made a major in the militia and quickly rose to king's lieutenant. Following the death of Governor de Pradines in 1747 Bonvoust requested to be made his replacement, competing with de Poincy for the position, but lost. He had earlier served in Martinique, but the appointment of his father-in-law as the governor of Grenada led to him being named major. He soon became established on the island, owning a large sugar plantation in the Basse-Terre.

Like the other French colonies in the Caribbean, Grenada prepared as best it could with its limited resources. Unlike the previous wars when the possibility of attack seemed negligible due the island's low economic state, its status had changed. The island boasted over eighty sugar plantations and about 15,000 slaves so it made a rather attractive prize. As early as 1739, Governor de Pardines had petitioned for an additional company of *troupes de la marine* to enhance the defenses of this small, isolated French colony. The request was finally granted in 1747 with the removal of a company from Marie Galante since Grenada was viewed as being more isolated and therefore more vulnerable to attack and capture. The approximately 120 soldiers were spread between the primary fortifications at Fort Royal, a battery just beneath it at Pointe des Cabrites, three redoubts at Observatory, the Villa and Morne des Pendus, entrenchments at Morne de l'Hôpital, Richemont and Paddock, other defensive positions at Morne Molière and Morne Latoniere, and the thirteen coastal batteries across the island (Illustration 10.1).[2] Augmenting the soldiers were ten companies of the militia, seven infantry and three cavalry, comprising between 600 and 700 men capable of bearing arms; the island of Carriacou had one infantry militia company with 150 men and a number of coastal batteries.

The Seven Years War and the Loss of Grenada

Thus was the state of Grenada's defenses as war broke out in the Caribbean in January 1759 when a large British squadron under Commodore John Moore attacked Martinique, the primary French colony in the *Iles du Vent* (Windward Islands). The attack on Fort Royal, Martinique proved unsuccessful as the French defenses were formidable so the British decided to attack Guadeloupe after abandoning an attempt on Saint-Pierre, Martinique. The main town of Basse-Terre, Guadeloupe was soon captured by the British after its bombardment and burning, but it took over three months before the French finally surrendered the island to the British on the first of May. A large French force under de Bompar arrived too late to rescue Guadeloupe, thus giving the British its first major victory in the Caribbean.

The British capture of Guadeloupe altered the political dynamics in the region, especially among the *Iles du Vent*. The French became very anxious about the fate of the smaller islands, particularly Grenada, Marie Galante, St. Vincent, Dominica and St. Lucia, the latter three so-called neutral islands but surreptitiously occupied by the French for decades. If Guadeloupe, so well fortified, could be taken then these smaller islands stood little chance against the British. To help allay some of the fears, de Bompar's fleet stopped at Grenada in June 1759 on its way to St. Domingue. Beginning in February 1761, and continuing throughout the year, Grenada became a staging area for ships, troops and supplies going to Martinique from France. It appears that the loss of Guadeloupe elevated Grenada to new importance, placing it second to Martinique. It's location in the southern Caribbean also played a part as the French utilized its strategic position. Though Grenada received some needed military supplies, all of the troops and military hardware went to defend the more important colony at Martinique.

By June 1761 the French feared that the concentration of British forces in the region would result in the capture of the smaller islands, believing that the British would attack these islands before an attempt on Martinique. This proved correct, as the British hoped to capture both Dominica and St. Lucia, thus having the advantage of possessing the islands north and south of Martinique. British forces arrived off Dominica on 6 June, and "though the inhabitants made a plucky attempt at resistance, it was seized by a coup de main" the following day.[3] The British did not attempt to capture St. Lucia and satisfied with Dominica's strategic harbor overlooking its neighbor Martinique.

Though there were attempts to end the war, the failure of the parties to reach an agreement led to a large British fleet under Admiral Rodney arriving in Barbados in November 1761. Joined by Major General Monckton from Canada and other British forces in the region, they prepared for the long anticipated assault on Martinique. With the British swarming in the region, there was little communication between the colonies, and each was left to fend for itself. Governor de Bonvoust busied the colony with preparations for a spirited defense. Like Labat decades before, he recognized that Fort Royal was vulnerable because it was commanded by higher ground, hence Labat's suggestion that defensive works be built on the Morne de l'Hôpital. Preparing for the impending British attack, the French enhanced the defenses of the Ville du Fort Royal by fortifying "a very strong and advantageous post commanding the fort [Royal]."[4] Though there were entrenchments on the Morne de l'Hôpital, the reference by Walsh was most likely the entrenchments on the future site of Fort Matthew, Morne Molière and Morne Latoniere.

On 8 January 1762 a large British force under Admiral George Rodney and Major General Monckton appeared off St. Pierre, Martinique prepared for the capture of the richest French colony in the *Iles du Vent* and the headquarters of its government. After a siege of three weeks and the capture of Fort Royal, the French were forced to surrender. Around the beginning of February, however, before the surrender, the British, confident of success at Martinique, ordered Commodore Robert Swanton with seven sail of the line, two bomb-ketches and three frigates to go to Grenada and demand its surrender.[5] Upon his arrival at Grenada he summoned Governor de Bonvoust as ordered, but the governor refused to surrender. It appeared that Governor de Bonvoust believed that he could defend the island, or at least make a spirited defense. According to Dessalles,

> Bonvoust, contained in the port with 120 troops and a handful of privateers, had intended to put up a defence, but in Grenada, as was the case in Martinique, and to a greater extent in the latter, we have to be aware of the isolation of this island, and that the inhabitants were beginning to tire of the constant state of alert in which they had found themselves since the beginning of the war.
> Bonvoust, however, appeals to their courage; he endeavoured to reawaken their ancient Creole energy, this patriotic sentiments of the settlers so highly prized by their brothers. Sadly, the response was a cry which had been heard many times: France has abandoned us![6]

Undeterred by the French rebuff, Commodore Swanton used his squadron to blockade the island, but there was some apprehension, especially by Rodney, about the French squadron under Rear Admiral Comte de Blénac which was sighted in the region. The surrender of Martinique led to British reinforcements being dispatched to Grenada, with Brigadier General Huntington Walsh arriving on 3 March with the 5th Brigade and a light-infantry corps under Lieutenant Colonel George Scott. With the larger British force assembled, a second attempt was made to get the governor to surrender, with Scott, that same day, arriving "on shore, to summon the Governor, with the troops and inhabitants, to surrender, and accept the favourable terms you were pleased to offer them...."[7] The French governor again declined. "The inhabitants, however, perceiving their destruction inevitable if they held out, and assured that they would not obtain such favorable terms at any future time as at the present, they signed a capitulation on [the night of] the 4th [March]."[8] Governor de Bonvoust, together with the 120 soldiers and some privateers, were determined to defend the island until Walsh landed early the next morning "with the grenadiers, light infantry, and the 27th Regiment, and got possession of a favourable post. The Governor, finding himself abandoned by the inhabitants, and the communication with the country and every supply cut off, submitted without firing a gun."[9] Thus on 5 March, Governor de Bonvoust officially surrendered Grenada and the Grenadines to the British, despite his desire to put up a fight. British engineers later concluded that with "the situation of the fort, and the intrenched hills above it, the enemy might have defended it a long time, although they whole force consisted chiefly in inhabitants and freebooters. There were but a very small number of soldiers."[10]

According to Monckton, Grenada received "the same terms of capitulation... as the citadel of Fort Royal [Martinique], and this island had."[11] The generous terms of capitulation for Martinique were actually proposed by the French governor and Monckton and Rodney agreed to most of them.[12] The Grenada capitulation was similar to that granted to Martinique, outlining the departure of French troops and officials from Grenada, the rights of the inhabitants to freely practice their religion, the surrender of military facilities and stores, the surrender of government archives and papers, and the seizure of illegitimate ships, i.e. privateers.[13]

Go to France!

The French awoke to a new dawn on the morning of 5 March 1762. After 113 years of struggling and finally succeeding in making Grenada a thriving colony in its own right, the stark reality was that it was now in the hands of the British. The "honorable surrender" terms which the French had received as a result of not firing a single shot only underscored their defeat. The signing of the Treaty of Paris that would determine their status was still almost a year away, but there was probably little hope that the French in Grenada could retain the island. Some of the French, particularly members of the nobility and *grand blancs*, did not wait for the signing of a treaty, but made immediate plans to leave. They quickly returned to France since all of the French colonies in the *Iles du Vent* were under British rule. Among the first to depart was Jules Alexandre Deslondes de Lancelot, a wealthy French Grenadian sugar planter, who had the Duchesse d'Aiguillon intercede on his behalf, returning to Europe on a British ship. Many others would leave the island for the other French colonies in the region rather than live under the British once the status of Grenada was finally settled, thus initiating the first large-scale exodus of the French from Grenada. The majority of the French, however, desired to maintain the livelihoods they had built over the years and, chose to remain, though their reality was drastically changed.

French government officials, among them Governor de Bonvoust, and military personnel were required to leave the island per the terms of the capitulation, and the British military, under the command of Lieutenant Colonel George Scott, took over the administration of Grenada. It was a rather peaceful handover since there had been no fighting, and it most definitely created goodwill on the part of the British. Though the French may have been expecting the worst from their captors, the British military government chose not to impose British institutions, instead continuing the practice of French laws and customs (as much as possible) until the outcome of the peace was known. Between the capitulation and the signing of the peace a sort of calm existed as the French tried to go about their usual business, and the British made every effort to relay fears since the ultimate goal was "reconciling the French inhabitants to an English Government."[14]

The British colonial government moved quickly to consolidate its power by taking appraisal of the islands. Within the first year they carried out a number of assessments that provided a picture of the economy and demographics. One of the most important issues that had to be settled immediately was land ownership, which could prove very contentious. Aware that most of the land had already been granted by the French (though much of it remained uncultivated), Scott's goal was to ascertain which lands were legally granted and which remained unconceeded and could be subsequently sold to British subjects. Jean-Baptiste Pinel, a French resident who had served as royal surveyor and road inspector, was engaged to carry out the survey. The result of Pinel's survey was a detailed map of Grenada, divided into its districts and showing numbered plots, rivers and streams, primary roads, towns, ports, coastal place names and topography (Illustration 10.2). It was the most detailed map of Grenada to date and showed the extent of French development of the island. Accompanying the map was a description of the island's districts (*quartiers*), and a list of names of proprietors by *quartiers* corresponding to the numbered plots at the time of cession, the types of plantations—sugar, coffee, cocoa and cotton—and their acreage. These two documents provide a detailed picture of the French at the time of their surrender.

The other important assessment was that of the population. Though it was not a complete census, the British compiled demographic data, especially for tax purposes; they also wanted a headcount of the French inhabitants (or potential new subjects). Analyses of a number of these documents provide an indication of the makeup of that population at the end of the French occupation and its geographic distribution.[15] The British counted a free population of 1,680, comprising 1,225 whites and 455 free non-whites.[16] Based on the last French census in 1761 there was a dramatic decrease in the free population by 30 percent or 468. The white population decreased by approximately 350 (29 and 21 percent of the white and free populations respectively), most likely a result of the obligatory departure of French officials and their families and soldiers due to the British capture, and planters who chose to leave immediately. The free non-white population lost about 120 (26 and 20 percent of the non-white and free populations respectively). It is not clear why they had such a large decrease other than not wanting to live under British rule for fear of the compromise of their legal status, but some of the free coloureds may have been linked to whites who departed. A case in point was Esprit Fauchier, co-owner of the Tivoli sugar plantation, who left Grenada for his hometown of Brignoles, France after the British capture along with two female "slaves" Nanette and Franchine and their nine mixed-race children. Yet the majority of the French, primarily the small coffee, cocoa and cotton planters whose departure would have proved disadvantageous to them, decided to remain in the British colony, though many secretly longed for the day when the island might be returned to French rule.

In January 1763 Scott reported to London that the slave population stood at 13,846, which included 589 (387 males/202 females) slaves on Carriacou (Table A). There is, however, a significant error with this figure since the collection of data was not consistent across all districts, specifically in Grand Marquis where the under 14 year-old slaves or children were not recorded at all. Grand Marquis was the largest district and recorded the highest adult slave population at 28 percent in 1763; in 1755 it recorded 29 percent of the slave population. Extrapolating from this, it is clear that the under 14 year-olds in Grand Marquis were at least 1,500 slaves in 1763; in 1755 it was 1,429. Therefore, a more credible number for the total slave population would be approximately 15,346, an increase of just over seven percent since 1761. The geographic distribution of the slave population was quite similar to previous censuses, still influenced by the distribution and type of plantations. Despite the growth in the slave population under the French, the incoming British bemoaned its small size and believed that in order to make the colony prosperous at least 10,000 more slaves were needed. This would lead to the explosion in the slave population over the next three decades while the British brought thousands of slaves from Africa.

The Peace of Paris

The French witnessed the capture of all of their possessions in the *Iles du Vent* by March 1762 and the majority of French, with nowhere to go, waited anxiously for the conclusions of the peace negotiations. Between the British capture of the island and the signing of the Peace of Paris, a number of French residents departed Grenada for other French colonies and France, especially once it was clear which colonies would be returned to France. Those who returned to France were *grand blancs*, leaving their estates in the care of managers, or altogether selling off their properties. Others packed up and left for Martinique, but a large number also went to St. Lucia which would witness the influx of dispossessed French from all the ceded colonies. St. Lucia, far less developed than Grenada, offered available concessions and a new start to those who were willing and capable.

Having suffered defeats and huge losses throughout the region, the French were finally ready to sign a peace deal, but not willing to surrender all of their territories that were captured. The British, though with a huge advantage, also wanted peace because of its large war debts. That France would fight to regain the valuable sugar colonies of Martinique and Guadeloupe over Grenada was a reality the French in Grenada had to accept. As negotiations dragged on, the most popular debate was whether Great Britain should keep Canada or Guadeloupe, with various interests, including the colonists in North America, weighing in on the issue.[17] The return of Martinique to the French was never in doubt because the British knew the French would not sign a peace without its return.

In the end, the peace negotiations produced some unexpected results. Along with Martinique and Guadeloupe, the French demanded that St. Lucia, a "neutral island" just south of Martinique that they had occupied for decades, be officially transferred to them. Though Grenada was far more developed than St. Lucia, the latter's demand, based more on its location than economy, proved of greater immediate importance to the French who offered up Grenada in return. In the end, Grenada was the only officially settled French sugar colony in the Caribbean which changed hands per the Treaty of Paris on 10 February 1763. Though it was not on the same economic level as the well-established colonies of Martinique and Guadeloupe, it was nonetheless a prize the British were content with, having realized that the French would not accept the peace treaty if they did not retain Martinique and Guadeloupe.[18] Ragatz, however, describes the peace settlement as "unnatural and peculiarly disadvantageous," contending that it was "the London West India interest's opposition to any considerable extension of control over tropical America since this would seriously impair the value of existing monopoly rights" that produced that result.[19] But, Grenada still proved important to the negotiations:

> [Prime Minister, Lord] Bute was in a dilemma [over the negotiations for the Treaty of Paris]. He probably believed, like [former Prime Minister, the Duke of] Newcastle, that we should get no peace if we asked France to yield us a settled colony; yet he knew he must ask for something. He hit upon a happy compromise; *we should content ourselves with Grenada* and all the Neutral Islands, and the whole continent of North America as far as the left bank of the Mississippi. This was a very cleaver proposal; it combined the greatest possible gain for England with the smallest loss for France.[20]

Though Grenada may have been a small loss for France considering that it retained Martinique and Guadeloupe, the British were quite aware of its present economic status and potential, especially in relation to the other ceded islands.[21] From all indications Grenada was a promising plantation colony, already possessed of over 300 plantations, the majority of them over 100 acres and worked by over 15,000 slaves. Before the ink on the treaty had dried the British produced two memorials advocating the exploitation of their new colonies, particularly Grenada.[22]

For the French in Grenada, the Peace of Paris confirmed their most dire predicament when Grenada was ceded to the British. According to Article IX of the Treaty, "The Most Christian King cedes and guaranties to his Britannick Majesty, in full right, the islands of Grenada, and the Grenadines, with the same stipulations in favor of the inhabitants of this colony, inserted in the IVth article for those of Canada," which read:

> His Britannick Majesty, on his side, agrees to grant the liberty of the Catholick religion to the inhabitants of [Grenada]: he will, in consequence, give the most precise and most effectual orders, that his new Roman Catholic subjects may profess the worship of their religion according to the rites of the Romish church, as far as the laws of Great Britain permit. His Britannick Majesty farther agrees, that the French inhabitants, or others who had been subjects of the Most Christian King in [Grenada], may retire with all safety and freedom wherever they shall think proper, and may sell their estates, provided it be to the subjects of his Britannick Majesty, and bring away their effects as well as their persons, without being restrained in their emigration, under any pretence whatsoever, except that of debts or of criminal prosecutions: The term limited for this emigration shall be fixed to the space of eighteen months, to be computed from the day of the exchange of the ratification of the present treaty.[23]

The French and British had been bitter enemies for centuries, and the defeat of the French throughout the region was a huge blow to their national identity. In all the wars the two had fought in the past century, the Seven Years War proved to be a total rout of the French in the region. Unlike previous wars where the victor sought the removal of the captured and replaced them with its own subjects, this was going to be different. The French had the choice of remaining in the colony they had established, only now they would be British subjects under British laws and administration. It was a similar policy followed in all of the captured

French colonies, including Canada, with its overwhelming French population.

The provisions of the Treaty of Paris made clear that the British desired to retain as many of the French inhabitants in Grenada as possible. The British Crown believed that the French population, particularly the whites, would be an asset in guaranteeing both the external and internal security of the island, especially during the transition period when the number of British inhabitants would be small. The departure of the French population, their slaves and the dismantling of the plantations, as was customary practice, would have been devastating to the colony and a setback even if the British would have been able to replace them over time. The British also desired to take over a functioning colony, like Grenada, from where it could easily administer the other, less-developed colonies. Gonzalez suggests that the British also believed that "retaining the large French population in Grenada would keep them from migrating to enemy colonies [i.e. French colonies], thereby strengthening their numbers."[24] So despite the inherent disadvantages in adopting a relatively large foreign and historically unfriendly population, there were many immediate advantages that appealed to the British colonial government. The British also believed, or naively wished, that its supposedly superior and inherent benevolent form of government would endear itself to the French and gradually convert them, both religiously and socially, into true British subjects.

New Subjects

In the immediate period following the capture of the island, the British military government under Lieutenant-Governor George Scott did not institute any adverse policies towards the French population, and followed the directives from the colonial office in London to do all that was necessary to retain as many French as possible. This was a policy pursued by the British in many of its captured territories from the Seven Years War. Also, the small number of British arriving in the territory did not as yet challenge the rights and freedoms of the French populations though they did make their presence felt. The British declared all lands in Grenada "Crown" property, but would lease properties back to their French owners for 40 years after they swore allegiance to the English king, thus becoming new subjects.[25] Those who found these conditions too severe quickly sold out, packed up and departed Grenada, with the incoming British all too eager to purchase their properties.

As soon as the Treaty of Paris became effective on 10 February 1763 the calm that had settled in after the capture of the island suddenly disappeared. French land owners desiring to sell their proprieties had eighteen months to do so stipulated in the Treaty of Paris, and the fears and mistrust that had seemed absent immediately surfaced. The survey of the island by Pinel had been done to determine the existing land tenure and preempt any uncertainty, but there were still a number of ownership issues which had not been resolved and surfaced as soon as the French tried selling their properties. These mainly concerned French property owners who considered it an illegal confiscation of property by Lieutenant-Governor Scott's inhibiting their sale and removal of belongings from Grenada. It would appear that those who wished to liquidate their properties were cautious of the 18-month deadline (that ended on 10 September 1764), and though the British government was willing to consider extensions on an individual basis they were against a blanket extension.

One of the more contentious cases involved the Dominicans in Martinique who encountered resistance from Scott when they tried to sell their 510 acres sugar plantation at Grand Pauvre to Roger Smith and others for 500,000 *livres*. Scott had suspended all sales of property by religious orders on the grounds that he was unclear as to whether they had the right to sell since he needed to confirm if those properties belonged to the religious orders' or the Catholic Church in Grenada which was now under the British. When Father Vidal disobeyed Scott's order and attempted to complete the transaction with Smith, Scott "sent him to the Fort and allotted to him the apartment belonging to the Governor, where he continued 14 or 15 days without any violence to his person or restraint upon his actions.... And immediately upon his declaring himself sensible of having acted inadvisedly in disregarding my orders, he was restored to his liberties."[26] In December 1764 the French protested Scott's actions to the Secretary of State in London who immediately instructed Scott to allow the sale to proceed.

Another case concerned the Brothers of Charity in Martinique, who had administered the French colony hospital between 1742 and 1760. Despite the fact that they had no authority over the hospital or its administration since 1760, they nonetheless laid claim to it in what Lieutenant-Governor Scott angrily referred to as attempting "a much higher game," and in fact had orchestrated "either a real or a sham sale of it."[27] In August 1765 Father Cleophas arrived in Grenada with a power of attorney to claim the property and carry out its sale. Scott immediately denied his claim, but undaunted, Cleophas attempted to demand the slaves then working at the hospital as belonging to his order. It would appear that he was successful in spiriting away a few of them when he departed, and upon his return to Martinique convinced a slave to go to Grenada and illegally abscond with the others. Unfortunately for the slave the plan was discovered and he was arrested, tried and executed, despite his protestations that he was just a slave following his master's orders.[28]

The St. John's River plantation or Hospital estate, used for the support of the hospital, was "sold" by the Brothers to John White, which Scott referred to as a sham, especially since its transfer had not been registered by the governor at Grenada. The transaction had taken place in Martinique between White, referred to as a businessman, and the Brothers of Charity. Scott was quite critical of "the whole conduct of these Fathers, even during their administration but more particularly since that period, appears to have been one continued scene of Villany, Falsehood, Deceit and Avarice."[29] Evan as late as 1770 John White petitioned the Privy Council for the restoration of the Hospital estate that had been taken from him despite what he believed as his legal purchase of it from the Brothers; his petition was nonetheless declined.

When other cases arrived in London, the secretary of state, exasperated, insisted that being new subjects the French inhabitants had recourse to the local courts to resolve their disagreements in Grenada as opposed to going through the French government interceding on their behalf to the British in London.

The capture of Grenada by the British in 1762 resulted in the first of a number of waves of French emigration that would continue for the next three decades and ultimately lead to a significant decrease in French cultural influence. Between 1762 and 1765 a large group of French Grenadians departed after selling off their properties and either returned to France or moved to other French colonies in the region, especially St. Lucia and Martinique. They had no desire to live with the British or under their rule, and so availed themselves of the rights of the Peace to sell their plantations to the incoming English and depart. Among this initial group of emigrants were some of the wealthiest and influential residents of the islands, some who could trace their ancestry back to the frontier days of Grenada. Yet a number of prominent families chose to remain, and though some of them would leave in the wake of continued British discriminations against them, a few remained to champion their rights as new British subjects.

As the islands witnessed the first large-scale depopulation with the departure of many French, this also saw the arrival of a diverse group of British subjects. The British began arriving in Grenada soon after the capture of the islands in March 1762. The first settlers came from the neighboring British colonies, including North America, and probably comprised those of lesser means seeking opportunities like their compatriots who had flocked to Canada in 1760 from the American colonies, or those from the British Leeward Islands and Barbados to Guadeloupe in 1759 and Martinique in 1762. Many were artisans, craftsmen and small merchants seeking to gain early access to underserved markets. In the immediate wake of cession, however, the concern of the incoming British citizens was the purchase of plantations from the departing French. By the time the Treaty had been signed in 1763, the British population had grown to a few hundred, joined by more prosperous merchants, wealthy planters from the Leeward Islands and Britain, and investors from London and other British cities eager to invest in what they believed were lucrative properties.

The new arrivals included English and Irish, but the Scots were heavily represented, especially among the professional and propertied classes. They were all seeking new opportunities. Among these were planters like Alexander Campbell, John Aitchison and Patrick Maxwell from Antigua, Henry Fisher and Gedney Clark from Barbados, and Ninian Home and Robert Young from Scotland. It is clear that the British, dominated by the Scots, were interested in the larger properties, particularly sugar plantations; some who purchased large coffee plantations quickly turned them into sugar production. By 1766 the British had purchased about 38 sugar plantations, approximately 45 percent of the sugar properties on the island, and some 40 coffee and cotton estates.[30]

The high demand for these properties by British investors drove up prices and overvalued them, thus creating conditions that would result in financial difficulties later on. Though the majority of transactions were completed without difficulty, a fair number led to disagreements concerning land sales and nonpayment of contracts between French land owners and British investors and would be a major issue clogging the respective courts for decades. The prominent Louis Lejeune sold his properties in 1764 to Andrew Irwin for 350,000 *livres* and left Grenada, but brought suit against him for none payment of the agreed upon sum; the Privy Council ruled in Irwin's favor in November 1768. Another case involved the prominent de Flavigny family of Grand Marquis (St. Andrew). In 1763 François de Flavigny sold properties amounting to 1,800,000 *livres* to the English, accepting bills of exchanges in London. He sent a letter protesting the lack of payment and wanted to return to the island, but Scott denied his request to return to settle his affairs. Another major issue concerned British financial investments in French plantations that many French subsequently regarded with suspicion, and proved contentious in the next two decades.

These issues, coupled with the diverse population mix and historical cultural differences, created ethnic divisions that would have devastating consequences for the society. The next three decades witnessed infighting between the French and British as the majority French fought for political and civil rights while the British continued to institute their dominance. During the War of American Independence, Grenada was captured by the French in July 1779. Upon its return in 1783 the British retaliated for their supposed harsh treatment under the French. Though many French departed the island in the wake of these new discriminations, some remained, especially the free coloureds. In the revolutionary upheavals of the 1790s, the French in Grenada, under the leadership of the free coloureds, revolted against the British. With the assistance of a large number of the slaves, they were able to control much of the island for fifteen months before the British recaptured the island and killed, executed or banished most of the leaders. Fédon's Rebellion would result in the end of French political dominance in Grenada after 117 years of French rule.

11

... and the Grenadines

The Grenadines form a chain of innumerable and barren spots good for little.[1]

The French colony of Grenada comprised the island of Grenada and the Grenadines, an archipelago spreading over an area of 68 miles (110 km) between Grenada and St. Vincent, with numerous small islands, islets, rocks and cays. They were among the last territories in the Caribbean to be settled by Europeans primarily because they were small, lacked "surface water and springs," and "their difficulty of access, owing to their shallow bays, treacherous coral-laden foreshores, and narrow channels studded with rocks and reefs."[2] A 1664 map of the eastern Caribbean identified the island of Bequia with the comment "Sans eau donce," ("Without fresh water") which actually applied to all the Grenadines.[3] By 1762, however, Carriacou, the largest, was officially settled by the French and had colonial institutions in place. The majority of the larger islets–Bequia, Union, Canouan, Mayreau, Ronde, Petite Martinique and Moustiques–also possessed varying numbers of farming and/or fishing families who had settled there via St. Vincent and Grenada (Illustration 11.1). The history of that colonization, which began after the third decade of the eighteenth century and climaxed in the mid-1700s, remains largely unknown. The reasons for this are (1) the haphazard nature and minor importance of these settlements, (2) the paucity of original documents pertaining to them, and (3) the absence of serious attempts to research that history. There is, however, available information that can shed some light on the French colonization of the Grenadines.

Of the Grenadine islands that were settled under the French, a clearer picture emerges of Carriacou's development as opposed to that of any of the others. As Adams admits, "The prominent French historians, Rochefort, Dutertre, Labat, and Raynal wrote detailed accounts on most French and British West Indian possessions in the early colonial period but, with the exception of Carriacou, they virtually ignored the Grenadines."[4] That Carriacou is almost twice the size of Bequia and closer to Grenada may have influenced its early development, and thus importance. For example, a census of Carriacou was carried out in 1750, but no data for any of the others have surfaced.[5] It is also possible that Carriacou's subsequent development under the British, particularly Scots, gave it more prominence than the others. Like Carriacou, however, there were a few references to Bequia during the French period, and together with post-French documents like John Byres' 1776 map of the island and its property owners, a picture does emerge. For the islands of the Grenadines, therefore, colonization under the French is evident not only from the few French documents, but also from the transition from French to British rule which required evidence of property ownership for tax and disposal purposes. Among these documents are land and property transactions that recorded the transfer of ownership from the French to the incoming British, thus providing evidence of French ownership at the end of their colonization.[6]

The Grenadines, also known as *Bekos* to its indigenous population, have been historically associated with Grenada since at least the 1520s as "Los Granadillos," or simply Granadillos.[7] The name, believed given by the Spanish, implied a close association with Grenada (or Granada) as the chain appears to originate at the north of Grenada and ends just south of St. Vincent.[8] They have been better known since the seventeenth century by their Dutch appellation, Grenadines, which dates to the early 1600s.[9] Together, the many small islands, islets, rocks and cays comprise an area of 34 square miles (88 km²), with about twenty-four of them habitable, and a handful of those large enough to independently support permanent settlements. Historically, only three of these were recorded by their individual names in the early literature: Bequia, Canouan and Carriacou, three of the four largest islands.[10]

In 1650 when Governor du Parquet of Martinique purchased a number of islands from the Compagnie des Isles de l'Amérique, the Grenadines were part of the package and became forever linked with Grenada because of their geographic proximity; they couldn't have been associated with St. Vincent because that island was completely occupied by the Island Caribs.[11] It wasn't until Father Dutertre sailed by in 1656 that a bit more information on the tiny islands was provided. Dutertre states that "There is to the north of this island [of Grenada] ten or twelve small islets, which are named the Grenadines, not including Bequia, which M. de Poincy contests with M. Duparquet, who claims a number of the Grenadines."[12] He later adds that "Among the Grenadines, also, are five or six small islands, the largest of which are only a league or two at most: some of them have no trees, but are covered with shrubs resembling our sea-rushes."[13] Fifty years later Labat sailed through the Grenadines and had little to say, except that "We saw quite a number of these islets which are called the Grenadines: we went pretty close to them, but did not anchor nor even put into land, because we had nothing special to do there."[14]

The Comte de Sérillac, on Dutertre's recommendation, purchased Grenada and the Grenadines from du Parquet in 1656, with the price of the islands influenced by the belief "that there was pearl fishing on a reef connected to the island of Carriacou" at what became known as the Cul de Sac du Grand Carenage or Tyrrel Bay (Illustration 11.4).[15] Neither du Parquet nor the Comte de Sérillac pursued any settlements in the Grenadines, concentrating all of their limited resources on the much larger island of Grenada. This would be the case for the next few decades as the French crown also concentrated its efforts elsewhere. Not much was recorded because there was no immediate interest, excepting security, in the small, dry and isolated archipelago.

Carriacou, by far the largest of the Grenadines, is located 23 miles (37 km) north of Grenada and has an area of 13 square miles (34 km²), measuring seven miles (11.3 km) by three miles (4.8 km) at its extremes. The word Carriacou is the anglicized spelling of the Island Carib name for the island Kairiouacou, which Dutertre recorded as Kayryoüacou in 1656. It has been widely recorded that the word means "land of reefs," or "surrounded by reefs,"[16] but Thierry L'Etang suggests that the word might be from two Amerindian words *kairi* (island) and *ouacoucoua* (*ramier:* woodpigeon), thus Kairiouacou may be translated as "île-ramier" or "île-aux-ramiers": "island of pigeons."[17] This was reflected in the French place name Baye des Ramiers and Quartier des Ramiers in the northwest as recorded on the 1750 census (Table 11.4 and Illustration 11.5). The island has an indented coastline and a rugged interior that rises in the north and south, connected by a broken ridge that reaches over 700 feet (227 m) at opposite ends.

Though Carriacou is the largest of the Grenadines, it is Bequia, the second largest, that has had a longer historical presence because it took on the abroriginal name of the small islands. Bequia appeared on maps of the region as early as 1608 and more often and consistently than the others; Carriacou did not appear on a map of the region until 1717. Bequia's prominence possibly stemmed from its proximity to St. Vincent and its large and feared Island Carib population. It was also widely reported that the emergence of the Black Caribs on St. Vincent was partly the result of the survival of Africans from the supposed shipwreck of one or more slave ships on Bequia in the early 1600s and their subsequent liaisons with Island Carib women on the larger island.

Bequia is located about 55 miles to the north of Grenada, but only nine miles (14.5 km) to the south of St. Vincent. It should be noted that despite the fact that Carriacou is almost twice the size of Bequia (7.3 square miles/18 km²), up until the 1890s it was widely repeated that the latter was the largest island in the Grenadines when in fact it is the second largest. Labat had recorded that incorrect fact circa 1700 when he sailed through the Grenadines on his way from Grenada. The word Bequia is the anglicized spelling of the aboriginal name for the island *Békia*, which has been popularly reported as meaning "island of clouds." Its highest point is Mt. Pleasant on the east at 700 feet (264 m).

It appears from the limited evidence that aboriginal occupation of the Grenadines was sparse during the era of European colonization in the region, and without permanent populations on any of them. What seems clear is that the Island Caribs in Grenada and St. Vincent used the smaller islands as temporary shelters or staging sites on voyages to and from the mainland, as well as for foraging for fruits, fishing and tending small gardens of vegetables that could be utilized in emergencies or in times of need. In his 1666 account, Rocheforte recorded that "some Caribbeans [Amerindians] of St. Vincent's sometimes go thither to Bequia a fishing, or to dress small gardens thy have up and down there for their diversion."[18] Adams adds that "Based on the fragmentary data, it appears that the Grenadines did not support a significant aboriginal population, and the islands were mere appendages to more important settlements in Grenada and St. Vincent. The absence of surface water and springs in the Grenadines may have been the key factor in restricting Carib occupation of Union Island and other Grenadines."[19]

Carriacou was supposedly first mentioned by Hernando Colón as Cairoaco in his *Historia* as part of a list of islands in the Caribbean, though that most probably was a reference to the larger island of Curaçao.[20] According to Roukema, the Grenadines were represented on Juan de La Cosa's 1500 world map as Los Agujas (The Needles), with Diamond Islet and Isle de Ronde as Los Hermanos (The Brothers).[21] It wasn't until Father Dutertre visited the area in 1656, however, that a description of Carriacou emerged. Taken by the island of Carriacou, he gave it a quick look over on his way from Grenada to Martinique, and exclaims that "The most beautiful of all the little isles [of the Grenadines] is Kayryöuacou, where I stopped long enough to note its peculiarities. It is a very beautiful and good isle, capable of supporting a colony: it is about eight or nine leagues in circumference."[22] He goes on to describe what most definitely the French later called La Baye du Grand Carénage:

> On a line of land to the north (sic) it has a very beautiful bay, almost semicircular, and on the northern end of this bay there is a great rock which protects one of the most beautiful harbors that I have seen in the islands. Fairly close to the harbor is a pond of *chomache* water, that is to say, half salt, which cannot come from anything else than a river or a spring of fresh water that loses itself in the salt water close to the sea-shore. The color of this water is as red as blood, and even the crabs there take on this color; but the bottom of the pond is white sand covered with red slime, which makes me believe that this water passes over some deposit of ochre.[23]

Continuing his observations, Dutertre suggested that the dark soil was probably very fertile, and together with "all sorts of game in abundance," buttressed his earlier view that the small island was capable of supporting a colony. He ends his description with a long discussion of "a kind of pheasant, which had a confused sort of call, louder and more tiresome than that of several fowls together, that have just laid."[24]

For many years after the French occupation of Grenada, the settlers used the islands of the Grenadines for food gathering, primarily catching sea turtles along their extensive coastlines during the breeding season. Rochefort adds that "the inhabitants of Grenada have good fishing and hunting in and about three little islands, called the Grenadines, lying northeast of it," possibly Islet Ronde, Carriacou and Union, the three larger and closest islands to Grenada.[25] Adams adds that "Turtles, being abundant, of large size, and easy to catch, became an important staple for slaves, poor settlers, and seamen in the French and British West Indies in the early colonial period"[26] (Illustration 11.2). In 1688 one report recorded that "the inhabitants of Grenada subsisted on catching turtles [especially the green turtle or 'tortue franche' (Chelonia mydas)] and caret [or hawksbill (Eretmochelys imbricata)] in the Grenadines."[27] A number of eighteenth century writers commented on the place of the turtle fisheries in the Grenadines, with Campbell adding "that the French fishermen were active in the Grenadines," and Raynal observing that the first settlers in Carriacou were turtle fishermen.[28] The captured turtles were sold as turtle meat in either Martinique or Grenada where it probably was a significant addition to the protein-starved diet of the islanders. The shells, especially those of the caret, were exported to France and used in the manufacture of veneers and toilet articles.[29] Records show that Grenada was exporting caret to France in 1682, recording "1000 de caret," a quarter of the total from the French Antilles for that year.[30] Turtle shell exports continued into the 1750s.

Despite their extensive use for fishing, Carriacou and Bequia, like many of the Grenadines, derived their notoriety as a result of their isolation and many hidden bays that were frequented by pirates and smugglers. In 1675 two Frenchmen, who were probably turtle fishing on Carriacou, were "taken" by Jan Erasmus Reining and his privateers, using them as guides for their attack on Grenada in March of that year.[31] It was reported that "On June 29, 1710, the captain corsair Philippe Plessis, passed on the island of Carriacou, arrived just in time to seize two English corsairs who prepared to repeat the exploits of Erasmus and Arnoutsen."[32] In December 1717, the French slave ship La Concorde, with over 400 slaves on board, was captured by the infamous pirate Blackbeard.[33] The ship was on its way to Martinique through the Grenadines. It was taken to the island of Bequia where the slaves and crew were deposited on shore as the pirates converted La Concorde for use as a pirate ship, rechristening it the Queen Anne.[34]

It would appear that Carriacou's first appearance on a map of the region was in 1717 on Guillaume De Lisle's *Antilles Françoises et les Iles Voisines* as Cariouacou.[35] In October 1719, the secretary of the Navy refused the request of Cornette, a well-connected gentleman of Fort Royal, Martinique, to be given a concession as proprietor of Bequia.[36] Cornette's involvement in the 1717 revolt in Martinique) and his participation in illegal trade, probably played a part in the decision. In September 1720 the well known pirate Bartholomew "Black Bart" Roberts was observed using Carriacou to careen his ship:

> They staid not long here, tho' they had immediate occasion for cleaning their sloop, but did not think this a proper place, and herein they judg'd right; for the touching at this Island, had like to have been their destruction, because they having resolved to go away to the Granada Islands, for the aforesaid purpose, by some accident it came to be known to the French colony, who sending word to the Governor of Martinico, he equipped and manned two small sloops to go in quest of them. The pyrates saild directly for the Granadilloes [Grenadines], and hall'd into a lagoon, at Corvocoo [Carriacou], where they cleaned with unusual dispatch, staying but a little above a week, by which expedition they missed of the Martinico sloops, only a few hours; Roberts sailing over night, that the French arrived the next morning. This was a fortunate escape, especially considering, that it was not from any fears of their being discovered, that they made so much haste from the island; but, as they had the impudence themselves to own, for the want of wine and women.[37]

Sailing from Grenada to Martinique through the Grenadines a few weeks later, Governor-General de Feuquières and Indendant Bénard, remarked on the French failed attempt to intercept the pirates: "M. de Cassavo's departure from Martinique was a bit precipitated, the warning given us two days before was that of a pirate careening in the isle of Carriacou, which is between that of St. Vincent and Grenada."[38] French officials at Martinique made many attempts to curtail the use by pirates and smugglers, but they did not have the resources to patrol all of the tiny islands of the Grenadines. It does appear that they were successful in curtailing the activities of the British from Barbados who often visited the larger islands of the Grenadines to "cut great quantities of mill-timber, which was a great conveniency. But for many years past the French have not only prevented this, as injurious to their propriety, but by stationing guard-ships upon the coast, made prize, in time of full peace, of all

English vessels they found at anchor there, or even of such as appeared in sight of them; which was a very great detriment to our navigation."[39]

The location of the Grenadines, the proximity of the large Black Carib population on St. Vincent, the inability of the French government to adequately patrol the small and scattered islands, and the arid landscapes discouraged settlements there, especially when larger islands like Grenada barely had sufficient colonists to populate and protect them. By the early 1700s, however, some began to see possible advantages. It would appear that some of the French from Martinique, Guadeloupe and most likely St. Vincent had taken up residence there for nefarious purposes. In 1721 the governor-general and intendant issued an ordinance "that all the French who were established without permission in the islands of Dominica, St. Lucia, St. Vincent and the Grenadines to return as soon as possible to the French islands."[40] The islands of Dominica, St. Lucia and St. Vincent were designated neutral islands and were supposed to be off limits to Europeans, but the French government had surreptitiously encouraged colonists to go live there to keep out the British. It seems that the French government, however, was concerned about the illegal trade taking place there. Reporting in April 1731, the authorities felt "It will be useful to send a ship to go tour in Grenada, St. Vincent and the Grenadines where numerous inhabitants of Martinique left on the pretext of cutting wood or going fishing for turtle; these islands act especially as dens to the smugglers and to the deserters."[41] As late as 1737 it was reported that schooners go to Carriacou to smuggle goods, identifying one there on 26 June with five slaves and horses waiting to trade illegally.[42]

There is very little detailed information available on the French occupation of the Grenadines, but there is ample evidence that Bequia, and particularly Carriacou were settled by the French by the mid-1700s. The French were very familiar with these two islands as a result of their fishing and constant travels between Grenada and St. Pierre, Martinique transporting produce for export to France; there was also an active trade between Martinique and the Spanish Main. Sailing along the leeward coasts of the Grenadines, these laden vessels, encountering bad weather, sought the relatively safe anchorages of La Baye de Grande Ance and La Baye du Grand Carenage, Carriacou, and La Baye du Nord, Bequia.[43] Adams emphasizes that "the windward coasts of these islands as well as the other Grenadines remained inaccessible to all but the smallest vessels."[44] Thus these two islands presented advantages to the French who decided to embark on establishing settlements there because of the availability of good harbors. When Governor-General Bompar visited in 1752 he specifically referred to these various bays and their advantages. Le Blond, however, adds some doubt about Bequia when he states that "Carriacou and Union [Island] were the primary inhabited islands," but there is no mention at all of the latter as a settled territory in any communications before 1762.[45]

It is not clear at all when the French embarked on a permanent settlement on Carriacou. Around the 1730s Carriacou's potential to support a colony may have received renewed interest. What is clear, however, is that the annual, seasonal fishing expeditions developed into farming communities by the early to mid-1740s. Though this is supported by Raynal, one of the few contemporary commentators on the island's settlement, his other comments present a number of problems. According to Raynal, writing in the mid-1770s,

> Carriacou, the only one of the Grenadines which the French have occupied, was first frequented by turtle fishermen; who, in the leisure afforded them by so easy an occupation, employed themselves in clearing the ground. In process of time, their small number was increased by the accession of some of the inhabitants of Guadeloupe, who, finding that their plantations were destroyed by a particular sort of ants, removed to Carriacou. This island flourished from the liberty enjoyed there. The inhabitants collected about 1,200 slaves, by whose labor they made themselves a revenue of 20,000 *livres*, i.e. £4,000 a year in cotton.[46]

Firstly, Carriacou was not the only island in the Grenadines occupied by the French, though it most likely was the first. Secondly, the reference to the destruction of plantations by ants is probably that caused by the infamous sugar ants in the late 1760s and 1770s, primarily affecting the islands of Barbados, Martinique and Grenada. If this is what Raynal was referring to it would suggest that the additional settlers from Guadeloupe arrived in Grenada during the initial British occupation or the brief French reoccupation between 1779 and 1783. It begs the question, then, why would ruined sugar planters migrate to Carriacou? Lastly, the reference to the 1,200 slaves definitely suggest a post-1763 timeframe since Carriacou possessed just under 600 slaves at cession, reaching over

3,000 by 1772. Raynal's scenario on the initial impetus for settlement communities fits with the historical evidence, though the Guadeloupe connection remains problematic. The production of lime for building and sugar processing also played a primary role in the settlement of the Grenadines as the workers planted subsistence crops for temporary use while they worked, but gradually establishing permanent camps that became settlements.

The early to mid-1740s settlement date for Carriacou is further supported by the growth that was taking place on the larger island of Grenada, which had achieved a level of economic and demographic development by then. As sugar took prominence on the larger island by engulfing smaller indigo and cotton plantations, small planters and those in search of new concessions were forced to look to these virgin, yet marginal territories in the Grenadines. Familiar with the Grenadines as a result of seasonal fishing trips, marginal fishermen, who may have been forced to contend with decreasing resources due to overfishing, settled down and established small coastal farming communities. Some may have continued to fish while cultivating their cotton farms, most aided by one or two slaves. They were joined by smugglers, disgruntled settlers and poor peasant farmers displaced from the other French islands seeking access to land and distance from colonial authorities.

There is evidence that many of the tiny islands had French settlers on them by 1762 who were occupied in various economic activities, though the extent of these remain in question. A number of eighteenth-century writers, however, suggest that Bequia was most likely not settled by the French prior to cession despite most of the island's land being conceded. Writing in 1760, Thomas Jefferys concludes that "it does not appear from the accounts before us, that the Europeans ever formed any regular plantations upon this island [Bequia], or on any of the Grenadines."[47] Raynal, writing in 1776, also suggests that Bequia was among the majority of the Grenadines not settled, with Carriacou being the only one.[48] The most convincing evidence comes from Sir William Young, who purchased two large properties on Bequia from French owners. In 1764 he comments that Bequia "remains entirely unsettled and in wood."[49] It does appear that though Bequia had a number of settlers living there, they may not have established any plantations of consequence.

The story of Bequia, however, begins with its larger neighbor St. Vincent. Situated only nine miles southwest of St. Vincent, Bequia is believed to have been settled by French colonists from the larger island. By the last two decades of the 1600s, a population of Black Caribs, believed to be "the product of Carib procreation with African female slaves brought to St. Vincent as fugitives from other islands (especially Barbados), as captives of Carib raids, and as survivors of shipwrecked European slavers," emerged as a threat to the original Island (Yellow) Caribs.[50] Reportedly, the slave ship or ships wrecked on or near the island of Bequia where the survivors went ashore. Fearing defeat by the Black Caribs, the Yellow Caribs signed a treaty with the French in 1719 "who ceded all of their rights to the king.... The weakened natives accepted a de facto protectorate status in return for France's 'powerful protection' against the Black Caribs, 'our usurping neighbors.'"[51] The resultant French attack against the Black Caribs, failed, but the treaty led to the gradual settlement of French colonists from Martinique and Guadeloupe. These colonists, who Adams describes as "outcasts, adventurers, and individuals seeking relief from taxes, laws and government," set up small settlements that spilled over into the Grenadines as the populations in Martinique, Guadeloupe and Grenada grew.[52] Thus, sometime in the 1740s, and definitely by 1752, French settlers had established permanent settlements on Bequia that were sanctioned by the colonial authorities in Martinique.

Though cotton subsequently became the crop of choice with the widespread settlement of the Grenadines by the British in the 1760s, its cultivation may have been minimal or nonexistent on many of the small islands and islets that had been occupied under the French. Le Blond, who lived in Grenada and traveled in the Grenadines in the 1760s, suggests that,

> Before the peace of 1763, the Grenadine islands were used frequently only to make some very good lime everywhere where the proximity of firewood, and coral reefs permitted its manufacture. We preserved the name where limestone was commonly made in the country. Some clearings were planted in provisions, furnishing the subsistence of whites and blacks [i.e. slaves] occupied in this job. Schooners came to load this lime in barrels, which were transported to all the islands.[53]

Examples of some places where lime was produced are evident in place names throughout the Grenadines: Lime Kiln Bay on Ronde Island; L'Ance du Four or Lime Kiln Bay on Carriacou; and Lime Kiln Bay on Mustique. There are also ruins of a lime kiln on Saline Island, a small island off Carriacou's south coast that was used for traditional salt production, hence its name; it was owned by the Marquis Delisle who was known to be involved in the production of white lime in the Grenadines. Other evidence exists like a 1778 report on the security of the Grenadines that recorded a number of observations on lime production on islands owned by the Delisle family. On Mayreau, S. V. Morse reported that "All the wood has been cut down for the purpose of burning lime," and on the Isle des Prunes "there was formerly considerable quantity of wood, and a great deal of white coral of which Monsieur de L'Isle... has made large quantities of lime."[54] On Isle de Large he reported that "a considerable quantity of lime has been made her for which there is an abundance of the best materials." Le Blond also suggests that the manufacture of lime on these islands led to the French establishing permanent settlements after clearing forests to use as firewood for the lime kilns and planting provisions for their temporary subsistence.

In the official correspondence concerning Grenada, there are a few references to numbers of men bearing arms on Carriacou, but the most valuable document is the 1750 population census. It provides a very detailed picture of the French colonists, their slaves, and their occupation of Carriacou at that point in time.[55] It is further proof that Carriacou was most likely the first and most important Grenadine settlement at the time.

In late 1749 Governor de Poincy of Grenada requested the commander of Carriacou, Lieutenant de La Bourgerie du Sablon, to carry out a count of the population.[56] Not only is it the only French census of Carriacou, but any of the islands of the Grenadines found to date. It records the population by *quartiers*, of which there were nine (Illustration 11.4). Within each *quartier* the census records the residents by households, of which there were thirty-three (Table 11.1). The census is quite detailed, often listing the names and ages of the residents and their relationship to the head of each household. Though there are a number of discrepancies, the census provides interesting information on the African origin of some of the slaves, and sexual relations between white men and black women, among other things.

The census, for the above reasons, adds to the foregoing analysis of the larger island of Grenada and reveals valuable information not available from the Grenada census data. The census does not reveal any details of the island's demographic history from its settlement to 1750.

What it provides is a picture of the island's population at a point in time during its early development. As such, it can be analyzed on a number of levels to produce geographic and racial distribution, age composition and fertility, age distribution, and sex ratios of the population of Carriacou (Tables 11.1 to 11.4).

As was pointed out with the Grenada censuses, various errors and discrepancies are present in the 1750 census as well. The most obvious is the miscalculation of the total population as "202" when in fact "199" people were actually recorded.[57] There are a number of other discrepancies like the eighteen slaves belonging to the Marquis Delisle for whom no specific data are recorded, and some confusion concerning the designation of children. The census is presented in two parts, a household by household list per *quartier*, and a "recapitulation" which categorizes the population by race, gender and age groups under heads of households (Table 11.1). Since both parts are not alike in every respect, certain pieces of data can cause confusion.[58]

The total population in 1750 of 199 is a fairly large population for the small island, especially since they mainly occupied the coastal zones and was probably ten years or less into its occupation. There were at least 33 households, though there is some confusion as to the exact number of households at Le Grand Carenage. The population was distributed across the island, but they were generally concentrated by households and not isolated from each other due to the ease of sea travel (Illustration 11.4). The northeastern *quartier* of La Baye á l'Eau (presently Windward or Watering Bay) contained almost 30 percent of the population, the largest concentration, with eleven households and 58 people (Table 11.1). Following was La Grande Ance (presently Hillsborough Bay) on the west with just under 19 percent, seven households and 37 people, and Le Grand Carenage (presently Harvey Vale) with 13 percent, four households and 27 people in the south (Table 11.1). The concentration of over 40 percent of the population in the north and east may have been due to the protection offered by the bank barrier reefs that could make entry into Baye à l'Eau, Baye des Juifs and Grande Baye dangerous to the uninitiated (Illustration 11.4). It is interesting to note that the three primary settlements possessed the best anchorages on the island and would become the main settlements on Carriacou. The settlements were along the coast as was common with early European settlements in the region, the interior still covered with forests. Both the white and non-white populations were fairly well distributed, though at least two settlements had no slaves or free blacks at all.

Interestingly, there is an equal number of whites and slaves, with a small number of free non-whites making up the balance. The 92 slaves comprised 29 men, 25 women and 20 children, with another 18 of unrecorded gender, most probably predominantly male. Though the sex ratio for the slaves is much better than white males, the age of the slaves may affect the reality. As would be expected, the fertility of the female slave was much less given the conditions compared to that of white females. A quite interesting piece of information from the census is that the tribal/ethnic affiliation was included after the names of at least 21 slaves, among them Angelique *Ibo*, L'Eveillé *Congo*, Jerome *Mondong*, Michel *Bambara*, and Marie Anne *Arrada*.[59] The 92 whites comprised 44 men, 15 women and 33 children. Of the 38 men ten were married, with a significant disparity in ages between the husband and wife; six women were ten or more years younger than their husbands. There were a number of single white men living with other single men, a common practice for unmarried white males at the time (*martelage*). Some of the slaves may also have been serving in a sexual capacity. At least four white men cohabitated with mixed race or black women, some acknowledging their free mixed-race offspring. The mixed-race or "Mulatto" population was the least represented as would be expected for new settlements, comprising 15 total: one man, two women and 12 children.

The analysis of the census data also reveals a few surprising details. Though the mean number of slaves per household is 2.2, closer analysis uncovers a more sobering picture. As Brinkley points out in her analysis, there was "not even one slave per [white] person" once age and health were factored in.[60] So there were 38 white men between the ages of 15 and 50 with a workforce of 30 slaves. What this reveals is that the white planters on Carriacou in 1750 were relatively poor and most households had one or two slaves who may or may not have had the ability to assist with production. Most of these planters were producing on a very small scale and may have been new to the island, eking out an existence.

In March 1752 Governor-General Bompar visited a number of the islands under his charge to see for himself the state of his government. Traveling from Martinique to Grenada via the Grenadines, Bompar adds that from what he had been told, only four of the small islands merit any consideration–Canouan, Union, Bequia and Carriacou, with the latter two the largest, and that each possessed a large bay that could accommodate ships.[61] He briefly stopped at Bequia and Carriacou. On Bequia he commented,

> I descended at Bequia on 24 March to visit the bay [most likely Baye du Nord/ Admiralty Bay], and received some information from the habitants who are established there; there are of the number of five or six families with several blacks [i.e. slaves].
> The soil appears good, and fit for all the foodstuffs that grow in the island, and everywhere to the subsistence. It will be able to maintain 100 men bearing arms; the bay is easily defended against pirates by means of one battery. The anchorage of this bay is always good, except during wintering.[62]

Bompar's comments on Bequia are quite interesting, especially his use of the future tense when he speculates that the island "will be able to maintain 100 men bearing arms." It suggests that the population was nowhere near that and much smaller than that of Carriacou at the time.

Governor-General Bompar sailed south past the islands of Canouan, Mayreau and Union and made no mention of settlers there, possibly because there were none that Bompar was aware of. When he reached Carriacou, he was impressed by what he saw.

> The island of Carriacou, where I also descended, is the most notable of the Grenadines; it has a good roadstead with a port [Grand Ance Baye], where very large ships can enter, and to be secure in all persons and at all times. The soil of the island is good and deep, the food and living fine; the air is very good. There is actually 80 men bearing arms; it [the island] deserves to be put in a state of defense, in order to prevent the enemies to not take possession in times of war thus cutting off Grenada's communication with the other islands.[63]

The 80 men bearing arms indicate that the population increased considerably because only white and free non-white men (between 15 and 60 years) could serve in the militia. Thus it appears that Carriacou had grown in the short span of two years, with its free male population almost doubling.

Following his stop at Carriacou Governor-General Bompar recommended that Carriacou establish a militia company to defend the island, especially during war when communication with Grenada could be interrupted. So in 1753 Governor de Poincy carried out the recommendation by creating a militia company, comprising over 100 men. One of the island's new residents, a nobleman from France via Martinique named Joseph Marie Coutochieu de Saint-Hilaire was named the captain. He retained that post until 1762 when the British captured the island; he would later hold the same position when the French retook the island in 1779.[64] There is no evidence that a company of the militia was established on Bequia.

Four years later Carriacou received some needed attention with the start of the Seven Years War. The frigate *Zéphyr* stopped there on 27 September 1756 on its way to Martinique to drop off 200 pounds of powder so the inhabitants could defend the island from the British privateers who were already causing problems in the Grenadines.[65] Within three years the number of men capable of bearing arms had increased to 150, which was quite significant. There is no other mention of Carriacou during the Seven Years War. Like many of the small islands it must have suffered from privateer attacks, yet not to cause extensive damages. On Bequia in September 1756, however, two English corsairs pillaged and destroyed a small establishment of two or three habitations.[66] Carriacou's newly established militia and coastal batteries, equipped with canons and mortars, were probably adequate enough to defend the scattered settlements across the island. There is also evidence that there was one redoubt at Bretèche in the southeast, one at Grande Ance in the west, and possibly one at Point Rapide in the north. However, they were not enough to defend against the large British naval squadron that arrived in Grenada on 4 March 1762 and forced the French to surrender, thus Carriacou, as part of Grenada and the Grenadines, also surrendered to the British without firing a shot.

Following its capture of the Grenadines from the French, the British government set in motion plans to consolidate its power by carrying out surveys to ascertain which lands were legally owned by the French residents and the rest sold to the incoming British subjects. The government believed that there was a "commercial Advantage to be derived to this Kingdom from the speedy and effectual Settlement of you Majesty's Islands of Grenada, the Grenadines, Dominica, St. Vincent, and Tobago."[67] The Grenadines, however, were not a high priority because of the small and scattered territories, as well as the fact that much of the lands were already claimed, thus there was no commercial advantage for the British government. This was quite evident in the case of Carriacou and may have been so for most of the Grenadines; the French claimed and cultivated cotton or produced lime on Bequia, Cannouan, Isle des Prunes, La Frigate, Mayreau, Mustique, Petite Martinique, Ronde, Saline, the Tobago Cays and Union islands.

Bequia was the only island in the Grenadines that was surveyed in this period because of its larger land area and availability of unconceded lands that could be available to incoming British planters; about 16 percent of the island based on the survey. In 1776 John Byres completed the survey and produced a map of the island, showing the then owners of "allotments of land claimed as private property under concessions made by different Governors of the French Windward Islands," which amounted to 84 percent of the island though not all the claims were validated at the time of the survey[68] (Illustration 11.5). It would appear that much of the claimed concessions were uncultivated as suggested by Sir Robert Young who described the island in 1764 as "entirely unsettled and in wood."[69] A contemporary Spanish map of Bequia presents evidence that there was some cultivation taking place on Bequia, with slave houses, and even a mill represented on the map (Illustration 11.6).

There is no record of land ownership and types of crops grown, or a map of the island (until the 1784 survey by Walter Fenner when the island was re-occupied by the British).[70] Nonetheless, a picture of the island at the end of the French administration is available in the form of a list of all the payees of property taxes in January 1763. All of those listed have French names so the list most definitely represented an almost complete inventory of the French property owners, i.e. of slaves and animals, on the island at that date.

The 72 French tax payers owned a total of 589 slaves, paying taxes on 387, with the other 202 under the age of 14 years and therefore exempt from the capitation tax.[71] As Table 9.5 shows, the planters on Carriacou did not own large numbers of slaves: 35 percent of proprietors owned less than three slaves each, 56 percent less than five slaves, 73 percent less than 10 slaves, 93 percent less than 20 slaves, and only 8.5 percent owned between 21 and 40 slaves. It is impossible to say how many of these slave owners possessed land and engaged in agricultural production; some most definitely were involved in other activities like fisheries or white lime production. A planter, with the labor of one or two slaves, could subsist on a small piece of land producing cotton or provisions. The rolls did not indicate the type of production engaged in, but most of these proprietors produced cotton, and a few larger planters produced indigo as well. Sir William Young, writing in 1764, confirms that Carriacou cultivated and "produces good cotton."[72] Approximately 15 planters were engaged in sheep production along with their crops, with one planter, the Marquis Delisle at Bretèche, owning 300 sheep. Of the 72 slave owners two were listed as free black women (*négresse libre*) who probably inherited their properties from their late white "husbands."

Analysis of the available data reveals the role played by a few individuals who had their base in Carriacou, but also owned proprieties across the Grenadines and engaged in various economic activities. These proprietors were rather unique in terms of the large areas they owned, including entire islets. One of these planters was the Marquis Delisle who first showed up on the 1750 Carriacou census as the owner of 18 slaves at Bretèche in the southeast.[73] By 1762 Delisle owned extensive properties scattered throughout the Grenadines, including a cotton and sheep plantation on Carriacou; lime and salt on Isle Salines, lime and cotton on Mayreau, Isle des Prunes, La Frigate and the Tobago Cays. He owned 40 slaves, which were distributed across his Grenadine holdings. Another proprietor of note was Louis Augier who owned a cotton plantation on Carriacou, co-owned a considerable plantation on Bequia with Jean-Baptiste Pierre Chevally, and lands on Union. Together with Antoine Regard, who also owned an estate on Carriacou, he was credited with establishing cotton cultivation on Union Island. Joseph de St. Hilaire, property owner on Carriacou and captain of the militia company, owned a plantation on Bequia; he would subsequently own Mayreau.[74]

Raynal suggests that cotton cultivation began on Carriacou and spread to the rest of the Grenadines.[75] Though confirming the primary role of Carriacou in the settlement and development of the Grenadines, he credits the British with the transmission, not the French who were responsible for the establishment of cotton in the Grenadines; the British contributed tremendously to its expansion throughout the sub-region and would make it a major crop in the Ceded Islands in the 1770s.

As the French were guaranteed religious and legal protections should they desire to remain under British rule, many, especially the small planters, decided to stay on in their proprieties in the Grenadines. Those who did not wish to remain had 18 months from January 1763 in which to dispose of their properties to interested British buyers; the purchase of extensive properties by Sir Robert Young on Bequia and Carriacou is a case of the latter. Like Grenada, Carriacou was well settled by the French, with much of the island already conceded. As discussed above, the only information on property ownership on Carriacou can be deduced from the 1763 *Capitation Rolls*... that listed taxed holdings, i.e. slaves and animals. It would appear that there were over 50 proprietors settled on Carriacou at the end of the French period, the majority small farmers who cultivated cotton.

Establishment of the British in the Grenadines

The island of Carriacou, like Grenada, witnessed an influx of British investors who readily purchased the plantations of French proprietors that departed the island for other French territories. In the next decade the island experienced dramatic changes as the French proprietors decreased and the British, particularly the Scots, owned large cotton plantations that they consolidated and a few even embarked on sugar production. The shift is evidenced by the presence of Scottish place names alongside the original French ones across the island as seen on current maps of Carriacou. In 1772 the 55 plantation owners comprised 30 French, 27 of them resident, who owned 2,359 acres (1,842 acres cultivated) and 970 slaves, while the 25 British, 11 resident, owned 4,493 acres (3,557 acres cultivated) and 1,788 slaves.[76] Four years later a census of the plantations showed that there were now 52 plantations with 3,153 slaves producing cotton, sugar, coffee and indigo. Twenty-two British proprietors owned 4,755 acres and 2,022 slaves, while the 30 French owned 2,172 acres and 1,131 slaves. Cotton production stood at 772,762 pounds and sugar at 133,495 pounds.[77]

The outbreak of war in the 1770s created the usual apprehensions in the islands as security for the scattered and vulnerable tiny islands of the Grenadines surfaced. With communications limited as a result, the small contingent of soldiers and militia prepared as best they could and waited. Following the capture of Grenada and the naval battle which saw the retreat of the British, Comte d'Estaing sent Pierre André de Suffren St. Tropez, with two vessels and two frigates, to secure the surrender of the various islands in the Grenadines. On the evening of 14 July, Carriacou was occupied following an attempt by the British garrison to repel the

French; Union island was taken soon after without any resistance, and the other islands followed. It was reported that "In both cases, operations are led without any depredation being exercised by the conquerors. This behaviour, far from rather common prepayment in kind to all belligerents in this epoch."[78] There is little mention of Carriacou and the rest of the Grenadines during the brief French occupation, with the British proprietors experiencing similar difficulties as those on Grenada.

One consequence of the war and capture of Grenada and the Grenadines by the French was the desire to reorganize the administration of the Grenadines to better provide for the defense of these small, scattered islands. The outbreak of war led Valentine Morris, governor of St. Vincent, to suggest to the colonial authorities as early as July 1776 that "the islands of Becquia, Balaso, Canouan, Mustique, etc. (the first almost adjoining to St. Vincent) [be annexed] to that Government."[79] Morris continued to advocate for his position during the initial peace negotiations when in 1782 he suggested "that should the island of Grenada be left to the French, and that of St. Vincent to the English, it will be absolutely requisite to have the island of Bequia, as also the other smaller islands between Union Island and St. Vincent, to belong to St. Vincent, and to be ceded with that to the English, and not be deemed appendages of Grenada, although recently held as such by Lord Macartney's commission. This was an error made when two separate commissions were made out for Grenada and St. Lucia (sic), although this was inconvenient even when the two islands belonged to the same crown."[80] His reasoning was purely from a security standpoint.

Though Grenada and the Grenadines were returned to the British following the peace the government did follow through with Morris' suggestion that the Grenadines be split between Grenada and St. Vincent to allow for more efficient administration. Thus, in 1783 when Governor Matthew was appointed "Governor-in-Chief in and over our Island of Grenada, and the Islands commonly called the Grenadines to the southward of the Island of Carriacou, and including that Island and lying between the same, and the Island of Grenada," the boundary was established. Similar instructions accompanied the appointment of Edmund Lincoln as "Governor-in-Chief in and over the islands of St. Vincent and Bequia, and such of the said Islands, called the Grenadines, as lie to the northward of Carriacou, in America." The partition, however, did not officially take effect until 1791, with St. Vincent taking over complete administration of the islands north of Carriacou. Though the evidence has not been found, it is commonly held that the boundary actually runs through Gun Point, the northern extreme of Carriacou, thus making that area the property of St. Vincent.

Following the Treaty of Paris the British regained ownership of Grenada and the Grenadines and took control at the beginning of 1784. One of their first actions was to carry out a survey of Carriacou, none having been done during their initial occupation. The survey was carried out by Walter Fenner who produced the first detailed map of the island and provided a great deal of information: the size and ownership of plantations, the island's defenses and the road network (Illustration 11.4). The survey revealed that at least three large French planters had by then sold off their properties and left the island, but the small and medium French planters had remained. And though the island had taken on a British flavor, with the majority of proprietors and residents British (of Scottish extraction), it retained a conspicuous French influence.[81] The southwest of the island was particularly French as it retained many of its original small French proprietors. Today, the area around L'Esterre is noted for its retention of its French heritage and probably exhibits the most French influences in Carriacou today. Most of the French proprietors noted on Fenner's map were still on the island in 1790 when a census of proprietors was carried out, illustrating that the French exodus had ended by the mid-1780s for Carriacou, though some went to Trinidad in the 1790s.[82]

The political upheavals of the 1790s seemed to have had little effect in the Grenada Grenadines. News of Fédon's Rebellion and what was going on in Grenada would have filtered down to the slaves in Carriacou, but there were no reports of disturbances or threat of disquiet, leading the 1897 *Grenada Hanbook and Directory* to conclude "that the slaves in Carriacou were uncommonly faithful and well-behaved during the rebellion, and this, too, although there was no garrison there, and they outnumbered their masters by at least forty to one."[83] Joachim Philipe, a member of one of the prominent free-coloured French families on Carriacou, did play a primary role in the rebellion as one of Julien Fédon's captains. Having escaped from Grenada after the rebellion in 1796, he was able to elude capture for seven years, hiding on his family's property on Petite Martinique where he was taken by bounty hunters in early 1803. He was subsequently executed for his role in the rebellion.

Today, the name Grenadines is not as closely associated with Grenada, which was known as Grenada and the Grenadines for centuries, but rather St. Vincent and the Grenadines. This change was a direct result of the partitioning of the Grenadines, and gradually St. Vincent began to be referred to as St. Vincent and the Grenadines, which by the early 1900s was in widespread usage as is now its actual name. Though Grenada is still occasional referred to as Grenada and the Grenadines, its official name is Grenada, Carriacou and Petite Martinique, highlighting its inhabited and largest constituents.[84] Though the majority of the Grenadines have little historical associations with Grenada and its early influence on them, there is a cultural link that persists between all of the islands of the Grenadines. And though always politically linked to Grenada, Carriacou and Petite Martinique exhibit a unique social environment that has more in common with many of the Grenadines.

12

Legacy of the Island Caribs

"What is to happen to the poor Carib?
Is he to go and live in the sea with the fish?"[1]

The Island Caribs on Grenada encountered Europeans as early as 1499, by which time the invaders had already formed preconceived notions of them as soulless savages, more akin to beast than human.[2] European narratives of the period are filled with images of marauding, bloodthirsty cannibals whose only desire was to consume them. Ironically, it was the Island Caribs and their culture that were consumed by the onslaught of an aggressive European civilization, despite fervent efforts to defend their way of life against foreign invasion and domination. Within ten years of the French landing on Grenada in 1649, the resident Amerindian populations were subjugated. Though they had successfully fought off the Spanish for well over a century and dispatched most of the 200 British colonists in 1609, the prolonged bloody conflicts with the French decimated their population. Centuries on, little is known of them on Grenada. There were probably a few hundred, maybe a thousand, resident when the French arrived. Of those, scores, possibly hundreds, died during the bloody confrontations with the French.[3] Some most probably escaped to the continent, while others joined the growing refugee populations on the last remaining Island Carib islands of Dominica and St. Vincent. But scores remained on Grenada and lived alongside the French, absorbed into the free non-white population and ultimately disappearing as a distinct group.

Yet, they are not forgotten. The memory of the Island Caribs lives on when Grenadians use words like ajoupa, boutou, mabouya, mauby, morocoy and titiri, which have become part of the islands' idiom (through French Creole). Added to this are their methods of subsistence agriculture and crops that have been incorporated into local practices. The Island Carib occupation of Grenada, however, is clouded in centuries of mythology that has overshadowed the search for a more factual picture. Unlike the islands of St. Vincent and Dominica, there was no population of Black Caribs, the offspring of African slaves and Island Caribs, in Grenada. It is possible that the small Island Carib population on Grenada did not provide a refuge for the escaped slaves. As a matter of fact, escaped African slaves were often returned to the French, or sold to them as the 1691 agreement between them illustrated. During the 1500s and in the initial years of French occupation, the Island Caribs were recorded as owning slaves which they used to farm their own gardens. So there did not develop a relationship between the Island Caribs and escaped slaves in Grenada like on St. Vincent.

The town of Sauteurs at the extreme north of the island, as the site of Leapers' Hill, has been accepted as the memorial home of the Island Caribs. A monument and an interpretation center was setup to educate visitors about the lives of the Island Caribs.[4] Other surviving Amerindian place names include Antoine, Dubuisson, Duquesne, Grand Marquis, Grand Pauvre, Galby Bay and Bacolet.

One Amerindian legacy that does not derive from the Island Caribs are the petroglyphs, popularly known as "Carib Stones." The term Carib Stones, first applied to these petroglyphs because the Island Caribs were the last Amerindian inhabitants of Grenada and the supposed artists, turned out to be a misnomer since the artists were most likely their predecessors. These aboriginal drawings or rock art found on large boulders across Grenada, covered with figures of "faces" and geometric designs, were probably used as altars for ritual ceremonies. At least five such sites can be found on Grenada with beautifully preserved petroglyphs.

Morne des Sauteurs

I leapt for the pride of that race at Sauteurs.[5]

The most enduring legacy of the Island Caribs of Grenada is one of fierce resistance to European enslavement and genocide. In the over two centuries after they unceremoniously disappeared from Grenada, the Island Caribs are, however, still remembered.[6] Though that legacy is laced with the widely accepted "man-eating myth" and other negatively ascribed characteristics, they remain a symbol for the people who inherited the region. Every Grenadian child learns of the heroic self-sacrifice of the Island Caribs on Leapers' Hill, the ultimate legacy for a people who died defending their culture against European domination.

It has been over 360 years since the massacre/suicide of approximately fifty Amerindian men at the site that became known as Caribs' Leap and Leapers' Hill (from its French original Le Morne des Sauteurs: "Hill of the Jumpers"). The events that led to this historic "leap" off the cliff at Sauteurs on the night of 30 May 1650 are shrouded in a tale of bloody conflict, 17th century European colonization, cultural survival, unrequited love, revenge, greed, deceit and genocide, and have been subjected to centuries of mythology and conflicting accounts. It is, however, remembered with reverence and holds great symbolism for Grenada and the wider Caribbean.

To date, little research has been done on the event and therefore the episode has not been scrutinized. Over the years, the mythology has surpassed the facts, hence the confusion of the multiple tellings of the tale. Two contemporary accounts of the massacre at Leapers' Hill have been identified to date, though much of what is recorded in historical texts, local mythology and travel magazines is based on the writings of Jean-Baptiste Dutertre, a French Dominican missionary who resided in the Lesser Antilles in the early years of French colonization in the region. Dutertre did not live in Grenada, and only visited the island for less than a week in October 1656, to assist the Comte de Sérillac in acquiring the islands from Governor du Parquet. The details of this event as recorded by Dutertre are in contrast to that of another Dominican missionary, Bénigne Bresson, who resided in Grenada between 1656 and 1659.[7] In his chronicle of the French colonization of Grenada in the *Histoire de l'isle de*

Grenade en Amérique, Bresson recounts a very detailed narrative of the protracted conflict between the Island Caribs and the French colonists during the first decade of the French invasion of the island. Though Bresson was not an eyewitness to the Leapers' Hill incident or some of the other events he chronicles, his version is probably more accurate than that of Dutertre's. Besson had resided on the island for four years and knew the environment intimately, but more importantly, he obtained much of the information from records kept by Dominique de la Bedade, the islands' registrar and clerk between 1649 and 1658. Dutertre's account of these early events is not absolutely inaccurate, but it does contain factual errors, and at times confusing because the events are jumbled together, especially when contrasted with Bresson's detailed chronological description.

May 1650 or June 1651?

One of the most glaring discrepancies between the two narratives is the date of the event. Almost every telling of this tale records 1651 as the year of the massacre of the Amerindians at Sauteurs because only Dutertre's account was widely accessible. Dutertre's narrative format makes it difficult to determine the exact date of the event, but he puts it sometime after February 1651. Since Bresson's work was not published until 1975, the 1651 date is pervasive, including its recording on the Caribs' Leap monument erected in 2007 and in almost every history book of Grenada and the Caribbean (Illustration 12.1).[8] Since Labat relied heavily on Dutertre's *Histoire générale des Antilles* (1667-71) in writing his *Nouveau Voyage aux isles de l'Amérique* (1722) it is understandable why he recorded the same year. The rest is history, as historians from Bryan Edwards (1793), the *Grenada Handbook and Diectory* (1897), Devas (1974), Brizan (1984) and Steele (2003), have repeated the 1651 date, despite some who wrote after the discovery and publication of Bresson's French manuscript in 1975.

Bresson provides an exact date of 30 May 1650 in contrast to Dutertre's 1651.[9] The error appears to stem from Dutertre's attempt to legitimize his friend Governor du Parquet's occupation of Grenada, which he records as June 1650 rather than the correct date of March 1649. It was a deliberate attempt to cover-up du Parquet's illegal occupation since he had not purchased Grenada until June 1650. The massacre at Sauteurs thus had to be advanced a year after the arrival, hence the incorrect date of 1651.

There are also a number of versions of Dutertre's account that date from the seventeenth century, including that of Major John Scott.

> Anno 1651: These Christian inhabitants having a good crop in the ground of tobacco and the Caareebs judging themselves abused by the trick Monsieur [du] Parquet had pass upon them in respect of the English (which came to light by the Indian first entrusted with the secret, being as he imagined afterward slighted by Monsieur [du] Parquet) fell upon the French, slew many of them, but Monsieur le Comte, like a good soldier soon put himself into a defence posture and dispatched a vessel to Monsieur Parquet, who Immediately dispatched in convenient shipping 300 good men completely armed and by them sent a full Commission and Peremptory Order (without any capitulation to fall upon the Indians, and to put all to the sword they could find in any part of the Island).
>
> In few days being arrived at the Granada, they found the Indians continuing their horrid murders upon the French their countrymen, which spurred Monsieur le Comte to action. The Indians gave them battle at the foot of the Northern Mountains near a fastness they had naturally. Tenable on three sides and the fourth access very steep where having prepared great pieces of timber and very ponderous stones which the French not knowing pursued them so far in their retreat till the Indians had opportunity to let go the timber and stones they had provided which by reason of the steepness of the hill fell upon the French with that violence that besides the many killed and wounded it put them into great disorder which advantage the Indians prosecuted to the damage of the assailants. The news of this battle was soon carried to St. Vincent, the chief seat of the Caribs who likewise gave notice to the Indians of Dominica who in ten days made Ready many peroges and embarked for St. Vincent where they embodied and soon joined with the Grenadians (The distance being not above 14 Leagues, and Windward of Grenada) where being arrived the[y] gave the French battle, and both parties showed great bravery, but the French being most West-India hunters were expert men at their arms Good marks-men, with sorely Gaules the Indians and outdid them in their own way; for the Caribs being put to flight, the French pursued them with such quickness that besides many slain in the pursuit. The French had the Caribs at great advantage, the Indians having their choice either to charge through the French, or throw themselves down a steep cliff, which abundance of them did to the amazement of the beholders.

Dutertre's description of the event is presented as a narrative of the continuous conflict between the Island Caribs and the French colonists.

> This last attempt [the killing of Sieur Imbaut] having persuaded the Sieur Le Comte to make war, he prepared to attack them in one of their cabets which was on the top of a mountain, nearly steep from either part. The Savages coming in front of him on the shore of the sea, opposed as much as they could to his landing, throwing a lot of arrows upon all who tried to jump out of the boats, and of the canoes, where some of them were wounded; but though their resisted, ours having out feet on the earth [shore], they were pushed back up to the mountain, where they were fortified; nevertheless as there was only one way which they courageously defended, having big trunks of trees roll down upon ours, they were compelled to withdraw.
>
> Shortly after that the Savages of Dominica and St. Vincent having joined those of Grenada, all together launched an attack against the Frenchmen, who having received them very courageously, after a rather intense fight where several Savages were killed, they pushed them in the woods and obliged them to withdraw on this mountain where they thought to be safe; but our Frenchmen having discovered the way up and surprised them, putting their hands upon what they found on their way.
>
> Those who escaped ran towards the precipice, where being closely pursued, after having put their hands before their eyes, jumped from this high mountain into the sea, where they badly perished, about forty in number, moreover another forty who were lain on the place...
>
> The mountain from where the Savages jumped in the sea, has been called since, the Hill of the Jumpers. The Frenchmen lost only one man in this expedition, after which they set fire to all the huts, destroyed the gardens, removed the cassava, took away all what they found in the huts of the Savages, and went back all joyfully, thinking that those who escaped would be foolhardy enough to undertake another attack.[10]

Dutertre writes that the Leapers' Hill event was precipitated by the killing of a French colonist named Imbaut, but Bresson says Imbaut was killed in 1654. It would appear that Dutertre's tale is chronologically confused, and he may have taken liberties with some of the information, or his memory failed him. Labat's account more or less echoes Dutertre's and Scott's as he relied heavily on Dutertre's version.

According to Bresson, however, the story begins with the Island

Carib Thomas, who desired the hand of Captain Duquesne's daughter in marriage. The girl's brother rejected the proposed union so Thomas, seeking to assuage his rejection, killed the brother and quickly ran away to Martinique to escape being killed. Cody sees this act as part of a larger "intra-Caraibe conflict that hinged around the occasion of one Caraibe's rejected marriage alliance with Duquesne's daughter."[11] While in Martinique, Thomas approached Governor du Parquet, who immediately questioned the reason for Thomas' visit. He responded that because of his friendship with the French, the other Island Caribs threatened his life. He further added that if du Parquet wanted to get rid of the Island Caribs on Grenada he could "deliver" them because he knew of their secret meeting place in the north of the island. Bresson added that "Sieur du Parquet decided to use the advice to advance his affairs, believing that God had sent it to him for that purpose,"[12] and he travelled to Grenada with armed men to carry out the plan. According to the Anonymous author, "since Thomas was pressing for the execution of his plan to surprise the Caribs and the Galibis…, it had to be done quickly without waiting any longer."[13]

In the afternoon of Monday, 30 May 1650 a force of sixty men, including Thomas, sailed from Fort l'Announcion in the Basse-Terre, along the west coast of the island and headed north. They were under the command of de Vertpre and Guillemin Heron, both having accompanied du Parquet from Martinique. The boat then "dropped anchor that evening near a hill called 'aux Sauteurs' for the reason that I will tell, across from the bay Duquesne, where everybody landed under the cover of darkness." The Anonymous author Bresson continues, "But before going any further they sent the Savage [Thomas] with two Frenchmen to check if the Savages were there, what they were doing, in other words: the situation, and they came back quickly as if carried by the wings of the wind, and reported that it could never be better, that they had to hurry to surround them all so no one could escape."[14]

The Island Caribs were notorious for their drinking feasts and on this night they were observed "drinking their wine and feasting, not thinking at all what might happen to them."[15] It is not at all clear how many Amerindians had gathered for the feast and the make up of the party. The group most likely comprised only men as was their customary practice. The French decided to attack the unsuspecting party in their long house (*kabay*), situated on a hill overlooking the sea, and began a bloody slaughter. As it was alreay dark, the onslaught of the French colonists, with their swords and guns, must have appeared to come from nowhere. It was probably a most chaotic ambush. Bresson describes the event as follows:

> Since they were all in the greatest gaiety, they discharged their muskets on them, this troubled their *ouicou* and suddenly changed their joy into sadness. Who moved was lying on the ground, who stayed received no better treatment, anywhere they turned there was nothing but fire and slashing sword, only one way was open to flee, but it ended on a high cliff that stopped them. What will they do? There is no quarter, they must die, and rather than by sword or by firing weapon, they jumped from the top to the bottom of the very steep hill, into the sea where they died by water while avoiding steel and fire…. However, only eight or nine were killed on the spot, all the others jumped and none escaped.[16]

Bresson did not mention the possible number of Amerindians who jumped to their deaths, but Dutertre and Labat record as many as forty Island Caribs may have plunged the hundred feet or so to their deaths. It is believed that the Amerindians, rather than offer an inglorious surrender to the French, committed an act that has left them a legacy remembered today as a symbol of resistance to European domination. The hill from which they leapt bore the French name Le Morne des Sauteurs: "Hill of the Jumpers," and was later affixed to the town that developed around the small bay. Was the name meant to remember the French victory, or to celebrate the bravery of the Island Caribs?

The French suffered no injuries at all (though Dutertre records one dead) "because when they were surprised their confusion was so great that they did not think about running to their weapons, they only thought about saving their lives by fleeing since everything was lost."[17] The French continued by destroying and setting fire to everything except what was useful to them. The Anonymous author concludes that "It is needless to ask how great was our joy for such a happy defeat of those Heathen who had given us no moment of rest: they went back to the fort where Sieur du Parquet took part in their happiness and triumphed in their glory."[18] Victorious, du Parquet returned to Martinique a week later.

The French reported that those who jumped died in a watery grave, and there is no reason to disbelieve this on the face of it. Though it was night when the attack occurred and therefore difficult to identify the outcome, the French could have either waited for daybreak before departing, or returned to survey the night's slaughter. Mythology, however, has added a fascinating story to the tale. It contends that the Island Caribs did not in fact leap to their deaths, but rather jumped off the cliff and landed somewhere on the side of the hill where they used an existing cave or caves in the face of the hill to escape from their attackers. The belief in this scenario is that it was not in the nature of the Island Caribs to commit suicide, much less mass suicide, and their escape would be in keeping with their guerrilla tactics evident throughout their struggles with the French.

Destruction of a Race

Many writers, including some historians beginning with Bryan Edwards, concluded that the French had been successful in annihilating the population of Island Caribs from Grenada in 1650. As a matter of fact, they survived into the mid-1700s in much reduced circumstances as related at the beginning of this book. Even in 1700 the population was observed by Jean-Baptiste Labat when he visited. Their population in Grenada was probably in the hundreds at the time of the massacre and only men were attending the *ouicou* at Sauteurs. Symbolically, though, the Leapers' Hill incident was the turning point in the Island Caribs' struggle against the French, and it represented their ultimate defeat.

A Traitor's Heart

Bresson offers a postscript on Thomas. It would appear that Thomas accompanied du Parquet back to Martinique and later went to Dominica to live with his parents. He subsequently joined those Amerindians fighting at Tobago, where "during a cease-fire he was given as a hostage to the [Amerindians] of Tobago who recognized that he was a troublesome and worrying spirit, they hunted him and with a shot made him pay for all his treasons and all his malice."[19] Thomas' actions were viewed as suspect even by the French, and he was seen as receiving his just rewards despite having assisted them: "We must not find it bad that [God] used him in this action." Bresson adds, "I suppose treason can be good, although traitors are worthless."[20]

One might be tempted to ask what possessed Thomas to play a role that has left him a legacy of disgrace for committing such an act of betrayal. Did the rejection of his love by Duquesne's family push him over the edge, so to speak? Did he recognize that his own life was doomed because he had committed murder and it would be avenged by Chief Duquesne's family? Did he believe that the French would reward him generously and also protect him? Looking back, it is difficult to understand why Thomas did what he did, but he joins a long list of betrayers throughout history.

What's in a Place?

There is much about this event that remains clouded in mythology, and a number of questions remain unanswered. One of the most debatable is where exactly did the event occur as no contemporary source pinpointed its location? For the past 150 years, the site behind the current St. Patrick's Roman Catholic Church, overlooking the cliff behind the cemetery and where a monument now stands, has been taken as the area from where the Amerindians leapt to their deaths. Yet, there is some evidence that raises doubt about this hallowed ground. When the Capuchin fathers decided to build chapels in Grenada, the site of Morne des Sauteurs was chosen, and in 1718 the corner stone was laid for the Notre Dame du Bon Secours chapel in the Quartier des Sauteurs. The location of that chapel, which was confiscated by the Anglicans in 1784, was on the site of the present Police Station and Court House; it was subsequently destroyed in 1795 by the insurgents during Fédon's Rebellion. The Anglicans later built their church in the vicinity of the destroyed RC Church where it stands today.

In 1841 the foundation stone of the current RC Church was laid, and completed a decade later. It is interesting to note that the name "Leapers' Hill," the English translation of the French Morne des Sauteurs, became popular in the 1840s, though it seems to date to as early as 1793, as recorded by Bryan Edwards in *The History, Civil and Commercial, of the British Colonies in the West Indies*[21]; the name "Caribs' Leap" did not appear until the 1890s.

It seems likely, however, that the lower part of the hill, behind the current Anglican Church, is the actual historical location of Leapers' Hill and not the place long celebrated as the spot from where the Island

Caribs jumped and where a monument was recently erected. The current site may have been chosen in a possible misinterpretation of the historical evidence, namely that the RC Church overlooked the site. That would have been the original RC Church in Sauteurs which dates to 1718 and was destroyed in 1796.

One other piece of evidence from Bresson states that "a fort called [Fort] d'Esnambuc, after the eldest son of His Lordship the General [du Parquet], [was] built on the hill–Morne aux Sauteurs, to serve as a vanguard post [against the Island Caribs]."[22] It is quite possible that the battery located east of the current site on the 1763 Pinel map was built on the site of Fort d'Esnambuc (Illustration 10.2). There is also speculation by some that the small hill east of the St. Patrick's River, Helvellyn, is another possibility, but there is no evidence to support this. By the 1940s, the RC Church erected prominent crucifixes in the cemetery behind the church, overlooking the precipice. It is not clear if the crosses were meant as a monument to the jumpers, but they were perceived as such by many.

An Appropriate Memorial

The Leapers' Hill site attracts visitors who are probably awed by this ultimate act of self-sacrifice, but the outcome nonetheless evokes sadness and possibly anger. It has inspired poets, film makers, singers and artists who feel compelled to retell this tragic tale in varying forms. Grenadians have been moved to pen poems,[23] and international Nobel Laureate poet Derek Walcott used this incident metaphorically in his work, as well as American poet Laurence Lieberman who wrote a book of poems titled *Carib's Leap* (sic). British film maker Steve McQueen, whose mother is Grenadian, produced the film *Caribs' Leap* (2002) which "addresses the everyday occurrences of life in Sauteurs" and the continuing presence of the past; it was filmed in Grenada. Ian Friday has produced a song titled "Caribs Leap," with evocative drumming. Grenada even commemorated the event on a postage stamp in 1975.

For centuries the solitary hill represented a natural monument to the enduring legacy of the Island Caribs who, rather than surrender or face death by the sword and musket, choose to commit mass suicide. In 2007, the La Qua Brothers Funeral Home erected a monument built of marble (Illustration 12.1). It is rather ironic that the monument, in attempting to honor the sacrifice of the Island Caribs, chose a Christian crucifix as part of the symbolism. For a people who fought against European cultural imperialism and died for their beliefs and culture, this monument is probably not the most fitting. But monuments are not generally for the dead, but the living!

So what then would be an appropriate memorial to the Island Caribs who died that dark May night 360 plus years ago? I suggest that in thinking about an appropriate way to celebrate the islands' Amerindian heritage, a number of things should be taken into consideration that would (1) Preserve the memory of this tragic and defining moment in Grenadian history, (2) Collect, investigate, research and interpret the history and culture of the Island Caribs/Amerindians of Grenada, and (3) Share that history with the rest of the world, especially with the many visitors to Grenada. To do this (1) The Government of Grenada should designate 30 May a national day of recognition for the Island Caribs/Amerindians as "Amerindian Heritage Day,"[24] (2) Use the now closed interpretation center to explore the history and culture of the Island Caribs/Amerindians (Illustration 12.2), and (3) Sponsor a national contest to design an appropriate monument to the Island Caribs at Leapers' Hill.

Illustration 10.1

John Powell's "Plan of the town of Fort Royal," from John Campbell's *Candid and Impartial Considerations on the Nature of the Sugar Trade...* (London, 1763), following 178.

It shows the French fort and batteries built to defend the town against attack by the British during the Seven Years War.

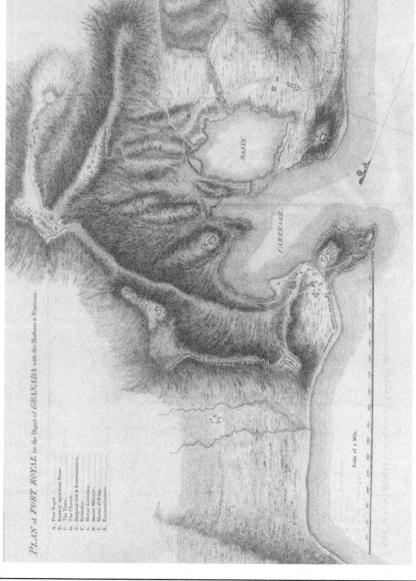

PLAN of FORT ROYAL in the Island of GRANADA with the Harbour & Environs.

A. Fort Royal.
B. Battery upon Good Point.
C. The Town.
D. The Church.
E. Hospital Hill & Entrenchments.
F. Redouts.
G. Morne Lucienne.
H. Morne Maltrin.
I. Morne of Ridge.
K. Entrenchments.

BASIN

CARENAGE

Scale of a Mile.

308

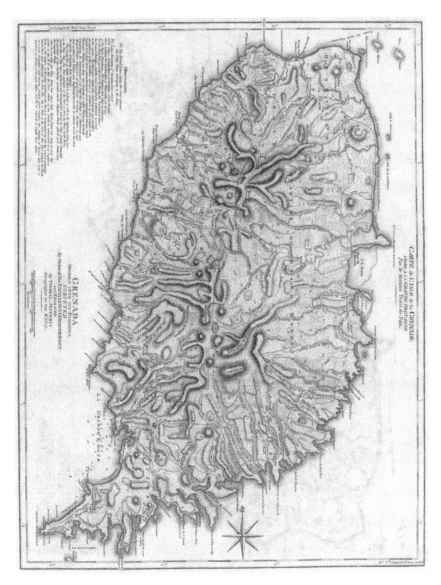

Illustration 10.2

Jean-Baptiste Pinel's "Carte de l'Isle de la Grenade" 1763, from Thomas Jefferys' *The West-India Atlas…* (London, 1775), 28.

It is the first detailed map of Grenada that shows the individual properties, roads, ports, streams, mountains, hills and French place names; many of the place names remain today.

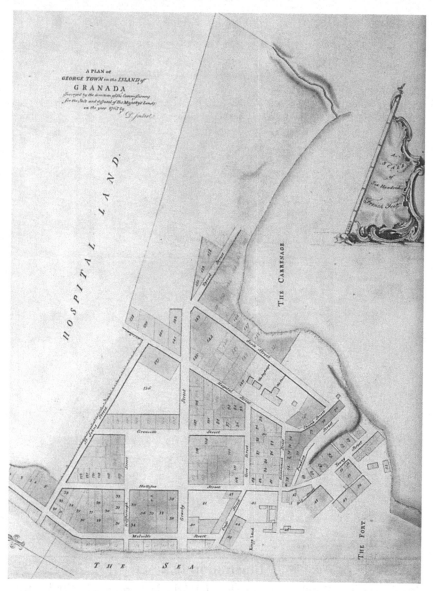

Illustration 10.3

François d'Imbert's "A Plan of George Town in the island of Grenada," 1765, showing the ownership of individual town lots. It also identifies the residence of the governor, church, presbytery, jail, fort, and the newly named streets after British personalities. The National Archives, UK. CO 700/Grenada5.

310

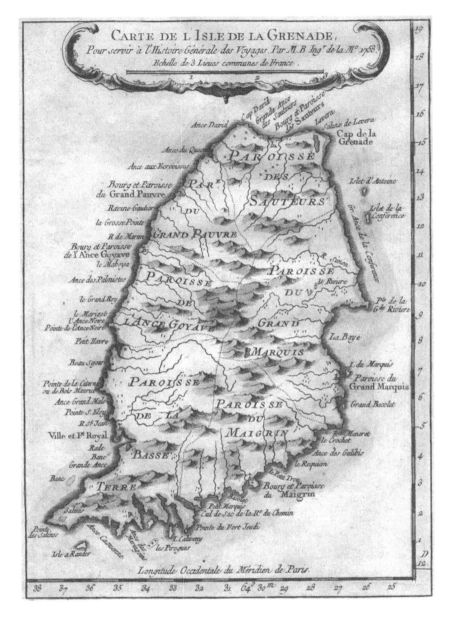

Illustration 10.4

Jacques Nicolas Bellin's "Carte de l'isle de la Grenade," 1758, from *Histoire générale des voyages* (Paris, 1758), XV: no. 14.

The most detailed map of Grenada under the French.

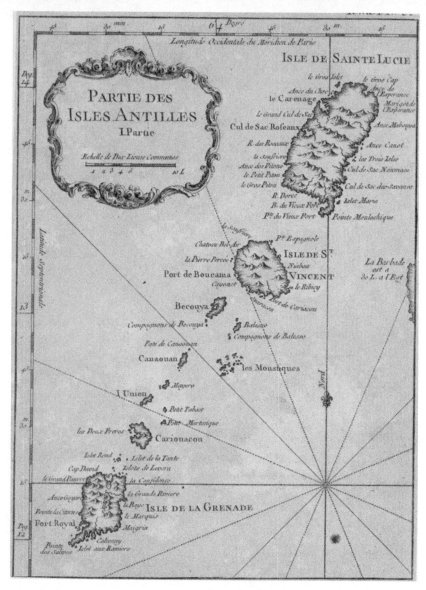

Illustration 11.1

Jacques Nicolas Bellin's "Partie des Isles Antilles," from *Le Petit Atlas Maritime* (Paris, 1764), 1: 80.

Grenada and the large islands and islets of the Grenadines are identified by name. The islands north of Carriacou would be subsequently administered by St. Vincent because of their close proximity to that island.

Illustration 11.2

Marseille Chambon's "Pesche des Tortues" (Turtle fishing), from *Le commerce de l'Amérique* (Avignon, 1764), 1, plate 4, facing 449.

The top image shows slaves in a boat fishing for turtle using a harpoon. The bottom image is of a European turning over a tortoise on the beach to slaughter. The meat was eaten and the shell exported to France. Both images taken from Dutertre.

Chaux des Isles.

Four a Chaux.

Illustration 11.3

Processing lime, from Jean-Baptiste Labat's *Nouveau voyage aux isles de l'Amérique* (Paris, 1742), 3: following 182. A slave is seen adding wood to fire the kiln (*Four a chaux*) to make white lime from coral (*chaux des isles*). Kilns were located near beaches for access to coral.

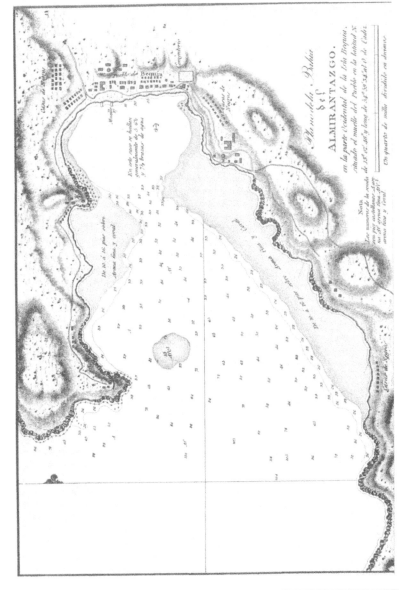

Illustration 11.4
Plano de la bahia del Almirantazgo en la parte occidental de la isla Bequia, c. 1764

Admiralty Bay, located in the western part of the island, is one of the safest anchorages in the Eastern Caribbean. The map identifies slave houses, Bequia town, cemetery, pier, a windmill, and roads or tracks through the hamlet.

Illustration 11.5

Walter Fenner's "A new and accurate Map of the island of Carriacou in the West Indies," 1784. British Library, Maps * 79457.(3.).

It was the first detailed map of Carriacou, showing individual properties, roads, fortifications, hills, reefs, offshore islands and place names.

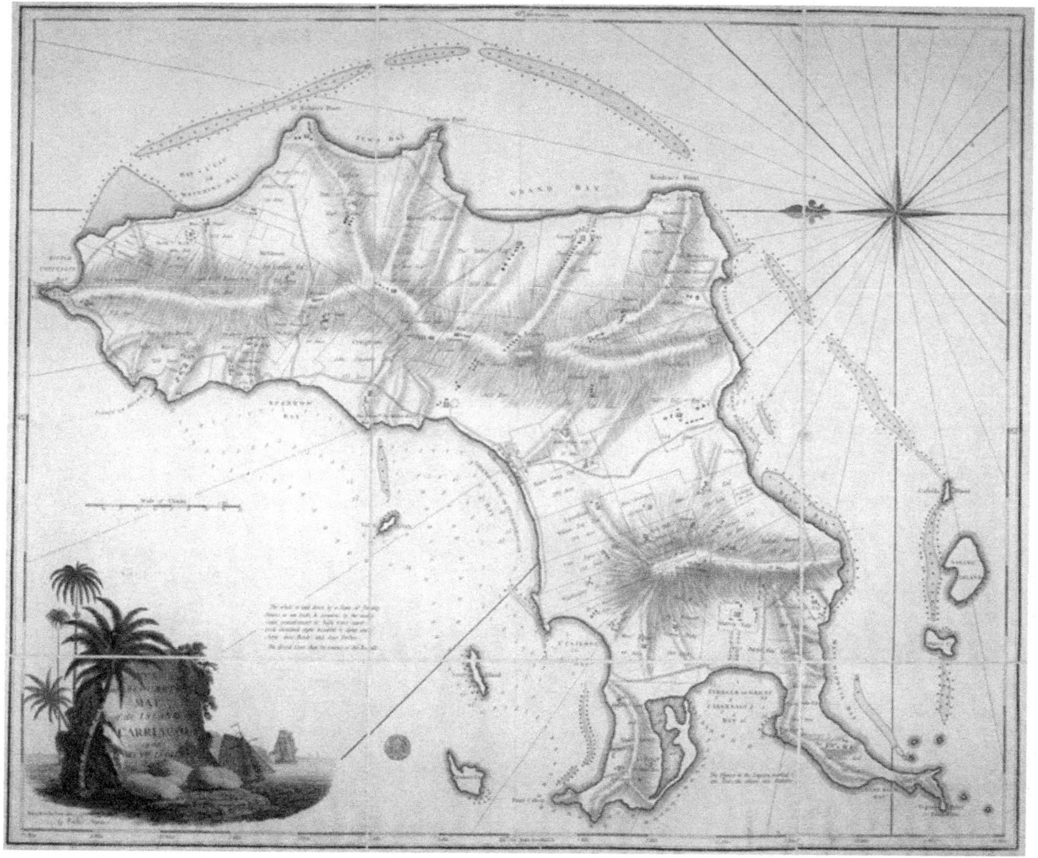

Illustration 11.6

John Byres' "Plan of the island of Bequia laid down by actual survey," London, 1776.

It was the first detailed map of Bequia, showing individual properties owned by their mainly French owners, roads and place names.

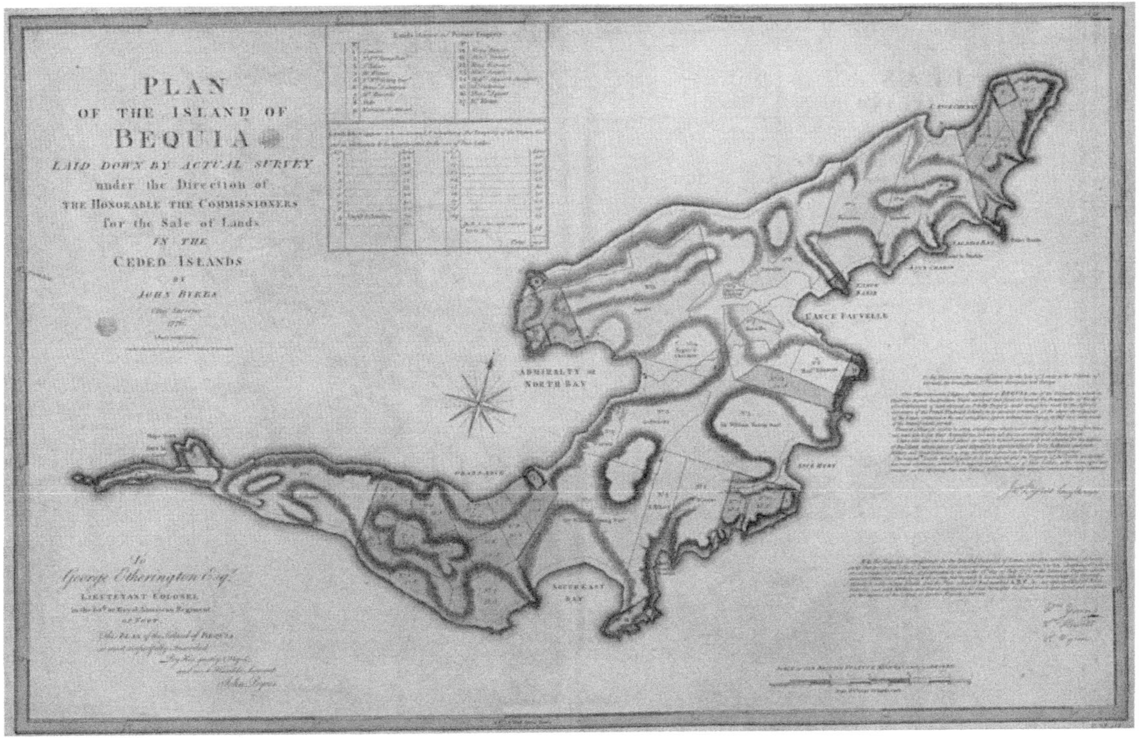

Illustration 12.1

Leapers' Hill/Caribs' Leap monument at Sauteurs, St. Patrick

It overlooks what is believed to be the site of the mass suicide of 40-50 Island Caribs on the night of 30 May 1650 when they were ambushed by armed French colonists. The date on the plaque (see insert) is incorrect, as well as the implication that it was the Island Caribs' last stand. They survived into the mid-1700s.

Illustration 12.2

Interior of the Island Carib interpretation center at Sauteurs, St. Patrick.

Artist rendition of the conflict between French colonists and Island Caribs, with the scene of the massacre in the background.

Photograph courtesy Kristopher Crown

319

Notes

Notes to the Introduction

1 J. C. Nardin, "The Old Records of Grenada," *Report of the Caribbean Archives Conference* (Mona, Jamaica: UWI, 1965), 328, commenting on the recorded history of Grenada under the French.

2 The British did not re-occupy Grenada until January 1784 when Governor Edward Mathew arrived and imposed British institutions following the departure of the French government; many of the French remained. The peace treaty was signed in September 1783.

3 Richard Sheridan, *Sugar and Slavery: An Economic History of the British West Indies* (Baltimore: The Johns Hopkins University Press, 1974), 458.

4 See for example George I. Brizan, *Grenada: Island of Conflict* (Oxford: Macmillan Caribbean, 1998); David F. Clyde, *Health in Grenada: A Social and Historical Account* (London: Vade-Mecum Press, 1985); Edward L. Cox, *Free Coloreds in the Slave Societies of St. Kitts and Grenada, 1763-1833* (Knoxville: The University of Tennessee Press, 1984); Raymund Devas, *A History of the Island of Grenada, 1498-1796* (St. George's: Carenage Press, 1974) and *Conception Island, or the Troubled Story of the Catholic Church in Grenada, BWI* (London: Sands & Co., 1932); Nicole L. Phillip, *Women in Grenadian History, 1783-1983* (Jamaica: University of the West Indies Press, 2010), and Beverley Steele, *Grenada: A History of Its People* (Oxford: Macmillan Caribbean, 2003).

5 See Ann Cody Holdren, "Raiders and Traders: Caraïbe Social and Political Networks at the Time of European Contact and Colonization in the Eastern Caribbean" (PhD dissertation, University of California, 1998) for an analysis of Island Carib historical occupation in Grenada.

6 Between 1779 and 1783 Grenada was occupied by the French, bringing to 117 the total number of years of French colonial occupation.

7 Pierre Margry, "Origines Françaises des pays d'Outre-Mer," *Revue Maritime et Colonial* 58 (1878): 283-305.

321

[8] Nellis M. Crouse, *French Pioneers in the West Indies, 1624-1664*. New York: Octagon Books, 1977.

[9] A. Latron, "Les mésaventures d'un gentilhomme colonial," *Revue Historique des Antilles*, no. 3 (June 1929): 1-14.

[10] Henri Malo, "La perte et prise de la Grenade (mars 1675)," *Feuilles d'histoire du XIIe au XXe sècle* 3, 5 (1911): 102-110.

[11] Devas, *A History of the Island of Grenada*; Brizan, *Grenada: Island of Conflict*; and Steele, *Grenada: A History of Its People*.

[12] According to Nardin, "The Old Records of Grenada," 344, Governor Leyborne reported in a letter to Secretary of State Dartmouth dated 6 January 1774 (Colonial Office, 101/17, Key, PRO), that documents of the earlier French period were incinerated in the fire of 27 December 1771 which destroyed much of the town of St. George's. There is a series of documents which are part of the *Registers of Records* in the Registrar's Office, St. George's, Grenada that specifically record some deeds of conveyance, transcripts of land grants by French governors, wills, powers of attorney, inventories after deaths, and marriage contracts. This is complimented by *Deeds of Conveyance* which date to 1764 and record the sale and mortgages of property. See Nardin for a discussion of these and other records of the French period available in Grenada.

[13] The discrepancies surrounding the exact date of the French settlement of Grenada, whether March 1649 as given by the Anonymous author (Benigne Bresson) of *Histoire de l'isle de Grenade en Amérique, 1649-165* (ed. by Jacques Petitjean Roget. Montreal: Montreal University Press, 1975), or June 1650 as given by Jean-Baptiste Dutertre in *Histoire générale des Antilles habitées par les François* (Fort-de-France: Editions des Horizons Caraïbes, 1973. 3 vols.) illustrates the lack of historical scrutiny of the island's history under the French.

[14] See *Guide des Sources de Histoire de l'Amérique Latine et des Antilles dans les Archives Françaises* (Paris: Archives Nationales, 1984).

[15] In 1941 Lowell Ragatz published a bibliographic paper on the "Early West Indian Records in the Archives Nationales" (*Inter-American Bibliographical Review* 1 (Fall 1941): 151-190), which he described as a "treasure-trove." He noted that "The Grenadan (sic) papers contain data on the island's low state in 1675; a memoir of that year on the expediency of founding a strong colony there; a report on its commerce 20 years later; details on shortages of negroes [i.e. slaves], women and indentured servants in 1702; a report on plantations in 1718; full human and livestock returns in various years as in 1719 and in 1738; detailed trade reports for 1739..." These records are at the Archives Nationales, FR ANOM COL C10A 1 à C10A 4, Île de La Grenade – Sous-série C10A (1654/1798); also FR ANOM G3 F17: Recueil de documents concernant l'île de la Grenade... xviie-xviiie; FR ANOM G3 F23: Recueil de documents concernant la Grenade... 1645-1792.

[16] See Etienne Taillemite, *Inventaire de la série colonies C8A Martinque Tome 1: Articles 1 à 55* (Paris: Imprimerie nationale, 1967); *Tome 2: Articles 56 à 121* (1971), and *Tome 3: C88B1 à 27 et index*, with the assistance of Odile Krakovitch and Michèle Bimbenet (1984), provides a comprehensive listing of records available on Grenada's French colonial past. Most of the documents indexed in these volumes can be accessed online at http://anom.archivesnationales.culture.gouv.fr/ir?c=FRANOM_00010,ead. Accessed 15 April 2012.

[17] FR ANOM G1 498: Recensements des Iles d'Amérique, 1669-1755; FR ANOM G3 F17: Recueil de documents concernant l'île de la Grenade... xviie-xviiie. See *Guide des Sources de l'Histoire de l'Amérique Latine...*, 288.

[18] Jacques de Dampierre, *Essai sur les Sources de l'Histoire des Antilles Françaises, 1492-1664* (Paris: La Société de L'École de Chartes, 1904), 146-149; and Joseph Rennard, *Essai bibliographique sur l'histoire religieuse des Antilles Françaises* (Paris: Secrétariat Général S.J., 1931).

[19] Anonymous, *Histoire de l'isle de la Grenade*, 35. See the introductory chapter in Anonymous, *Histoire de l'isle de la Grenade*, 25-35, where Petitjean Roget provides an in-depth analysis of the manuscript and its supposed author.

[20] Petitjean Roget refers to Jean-Baptiste Dutertre as the "Heroditus of the Antilles."

[21] Jean-Baptiste Labat, *Nouveau voyages aux isles de l'Amérique, contenant l'histoire naturelle de ces pays, l'origine, les moeurs, la religion & le gouvernement des habitans anciens et modernes...* 8 vols. (Paris: Theodore Le Gras, 1742).

[22] Marcel Châtillon, *Le père Labat à travers ses manuscrits* (S.I.: s.n., 1979), 35-39.

[23] Philip P. Boucher, *France and the American Tropics to 1700: Tropics of Discontent?* (Baltimore: The Johns Hopkins University Press, 2007) and *Cannibal Encounters: Europeans and Island Caribs, 1492-1763* (Baltimore: The Johns Hopkins University Press, 1992); Jean-Pierre Moreau's *Les Petites Antilles de Christophe Colomb à Richelieu*, 1493-1635 (Paris: Karthala, 1992); Stewart L. Mims, *Colbert's West India Policy* (New Haven: Octagon, 1912); Liliane Chauleau, *Dans les îles du vent: La Martinique* (Paris: L'Harmattan, 1993); Louis-Philippe May *Histoire économique de la Martinique* (Paris: Société de distribution et de culture, 1972); Gabriel Debien, *Les Esclaves aux Antilles, xvii⁹-xviii⁹ siècles* (Basse-Terre: Société d'histoire de la Guadeloupe, 1974), and "Les Engagés pour les Antilles, 1634-1715," *Revue l'histoire des colonies*, no. 1-2 (1952).

[24] *Explication du plan de l'isle de la Grenade. Fait par ordre de son excellence Monsieur George Scott, gouverneur pour sa Majesté, de la dite isle et de ses dependances, 1760* (Londres: Thomas Jefferys, [Après 1763]-1760). Accessed 15 September 2012 at http://gallica.bnf.fr/ark:/12148/btv1b55005755c. Also, Daniel Paterson, *A Topographical Description of the Island of Grenada; Surveyed by Monsieur Pinel in 1763 by Order of Government, with the Addition of English Names, Alterations of Property, and Other Improvements to the Present Time* (London, 1780). The actual survey was done in 1762 by the French surveyor Jean-Baptiste Pinel (but it was not forwarded to London until January 1763).

[25] The National Archive (TNA): Public Record Office, CO 101/1 f.18-31; EXT 1/253/2.

[26] *Registers of Records*, 1764-96, Registrar's Office, Grenada Supreme Court, St. George's, Grenada. See Endnote 12 above. These records can be accessed through the LDS Family History Centers in the US; see reference at https://familysearch.org/eng/library/fhlcatalog/printing/titledetailsprint.asp?titleno=574884.

Notes to Chapter 1: The Island Caribs of Grenada

[1] An Island Carib to Father du Montel, a French missionary who supposedly lived among the Caribs of Dominica and provided eyewitness accounts to Rochefort; quoted in John Davies, *The History of the Charriby Islands* (London, 1666; translated from Cesar de Rochefort, *Histoire naturelle et morale des iles Antilles de l'Amerique*, Rotterdam, 1665), 250.

[2] The use of the term Island Carib throughout this book will refer to the people often designated as Carib, specifically the inhabitants of the Lesser Antilles during the historical period, but can also refer to the Galibis who were part of the larger group of Amerindian inhabitants of Grenada at either contact and/or colonization. Though the designation may not express the cultural/ethnic diversity that existed at either contact and/or colonization, it broadly defines the Amerindian population in the Lesser Antilles. "Island Carib" is used throughout because of its historical acceptance and to avoid confusion, though the author recognizes the importance of "Kalinago" as a self-ascribed name for that group and its widespread acceptance, especially in the Caribbean.

[3] Boucher, *Cannibal Encounters*, 2.

[4] How Columbus understood this level of detailed information remains problematic,

considering that neither he nor any member of his crew spoke or comprehended any Amerindian languages, particularly Arawakan. This fact has been a major argument against Columbus' initial interpretations of the Island Caribs being cannibals.

[5] Peter Hulme and Neil L. Whitehead, eds., *Wild Majesty: Encounters with Caribs from Columbus to the Present Day, An Anthology* (Oxford: Clarendon, 1992), 19.

[6] Hulme and Whitehead, *Wild Majesty*, 19.

[7] Hulme and Whitehead, *Wild Majesty*, 23.

[8] Hulme and Whitehead, *Wild Majesty*, 32.

[9] Hulme and Whitehead, *Wild Majesty*, 33.

[10] Allaire, "Visions of Cannibals," 36. There is on-going debate on the origin and meaning of the word Carib; see David D. Davis and Christopher Goodwin, "Island Carib Origins: Evidence and Nonevidence," *American Antiquity* 55, 1 (1990): 37-48; and Louis Allaire, "Visions of Cannibal: Distant Islands and Distant Lands in Taino World Image," in *The Lesser Antilles in the Age of European Expansion*, ed. by Robert L. Paquette and Stanley L. Engerm (Gainesville: University Press of Florida, 1997), 33-49, for discussions of its origins and meaning.

[11] The Arawaks/Tainos on Trinidad were first labeled Caribs and thus enslaved. The Carib designation was later retracted, but the population had nonetheless suffered as a result.

[12] Populations of Black Caribs, descendants of Island Caribs and Africans, can be found in Dominica and parts of Central America.

[13] Actually, Father Raymond Breton recorded three languages spoken among the Lesser Antillean Amerindians, one by the men, one by the women and children, and a third by "warriors and other important persons on certain special occasions."

[14] Davis, et al., "Island Carib Origins," 43; Boucher, *Cannibal Encounters*, 4.

[15] Louis Allaire, "On the Historicity of Carib Migrations in the Lesser Antilles" (*American Antiquity* 45, 2 (1980): 238-245), 243.

[16] Allaire, "Visions of Cannibals," 43.

[17] Davis, et al., "Island Carib Origins," 39.

[18] Allaire, "Visions of Cannibals," 41.

[19] Allaire, "Visions of Cannibals," 41.

[20] Allaire, "Visions of Cannibals," 40.

[21] Davis, et al., "Island Carib Origins," 38.

[22] See Samuel M. Wilson, ed., *The Indigenous People of the Caribbean* (Gainesville: University Press of Florida: 1997) for an overview of the debates.

[23] See Philip P. Boucher, *France and the American Tropics to 1700: Tropics of Discontent?* (Baltimore: The Johns Hopkins University Press, 2007), 26, 28.

[24] Holdren, "Raiders and Traders," 16-22.

[25] C. J. M. R. Gullick, "Island Carib Traditions About Their Arrival in the Lesser Antilles." *Proceedings of the 8th International Congress for the Study of the Pre-Columbian Cultures of the Lesser Antilles*, ed. by Suzanne M. Lewenstein (Anthropological Research Papers, no. 22. Arizona State University, 1980): 464-472.

[26] Samuel M. Wilson, "The Cultural Mosaic of the Indigenous Caribbean," *Proceedings of the British Academy*, 81 (1993), 53.

[27] Gullick, "Island Carib Traditions," 469.

[28] Douglas R. Taylor and Berend J. Hoff. "The Linguistic Repertory of the Island Caribs in the Seventeenth Century: The Men's Language–A Carib Pidgin?" in *International Journal of American Linguistics* 46, 4 (Oct. 1980: 301-312), 301, n.1.

[29] Wilson, "The Cultural Mosaic of the Indigenous Caribbean," 53.

[30] Taylor and Hoff, "The Men's Language," 309.

[31] Davis, et al., "Island Carib Origins," 44.

³² Ripley P. Bullen, *The Archeology of Grenada, West Indies* (Gainesville: University of Florida, 1964), 56. Bullen was the first to identify the Savanne Suazey series, naming it after the site near River Sallee, St. Patrick, Grenada. He also may have exaggerated its crudeness in order to associate it with the presumed ethnic group, using phrases like "scratched" design and "finger-indented" rims, which belie the quality, and the possible continuity of the series with previous ones. See also C. Mark Donop, "Savanne Suazey Revisited," University of Florida, 2005. Accessed 15 September 2012 at http://purl.fcla.edu/fcla/etd/UFE0013281.

³³ Davis, et al., "Island Carib Origins," 40.

³⁴ Allaire, "Carib Migrations," 241.

³⁵ Holdren, "Raiders and Traders," 19.

³⁶ Holdren, "Raiders and Traders," 20. See also Arie Boomert, "Searching for Cayo in Dominica," 23ʳᵈ Congress for theInternational Association of Caribbean Archaeology, Antigua, 2009.

³⁷ Allaire, "On the Historicity of Carib Migrations," 243.

³⁸ Davis, et al., "Island Carib Origins," 42.

³⁹ Boucher, *Cannibal Encounters*, 5.

⁴⁰ Wilson, "The Cultural Mosaic of the Indigenous Caribbean," 53.

⁴¹ Davis, et al., "Island Carib Origins," 45.

⁴² Gullick, "Island Carib Traditions," 470.

⁴³ Gullick, "Island Carib Traditions," 470.

⁴⁴ Holdren, "Raiders and Traders," 24.

⁴⁵ Holdren, "Raiders and Traders," 24.

⁴⁶ Wilson, "The Cultural Mosaic of the Indigenous Caribbean," 56.

⁴⁷ Wilson, "The Cultural Mosaic of the Indigenous Caribbean," 56.

⁴⁸ Holdren, "Raiders and Traders," 35.

⁴⁹ Holdren, "Raiders and Traders," 35.

⁵⁰ The contemporary literature records a number of names of groups in Grenada: "Zamayuyu," "Kamayuyu," "Kamayuga," and "Camajugas." Holdren ("Raiders and Traders," 31) believes that the Zamayuyu "appear to be the same as the Galibi," while the Camajugas are probably a reference for the Carib." It is difficult to ascertain whether the Kamajuga were the 'Galibi,' 'Caraibe,' or another ethnic group altogether."

⁵¹ In 2005 Kalinago Chief Charles Williams protested Walt Disney's inclusion of a comical scene of cannibalism into the script of the sequel to the box-office hit *Pirates of the Caribbean*; parts of the movie were filmed in Dominica and descendants of the Kalinago were used as extras in the film.

⁵² Boucher, *Cannibal Encounters*, 15.

⁵³ See Alan Dundes, *The Blood Libel Legend: A Casebook in Anti-Semitic Folklore* (Madison: University of Wisconsin Press, 1991).

⁵⁴ Bartolomé de las Casas, *The Diario of Christopher Columbus's First Voyage to America, 1492-1493*. Translated by Oliver Dunn and James Edward Kelley (University of Oklahoma Press, 1991), 133.

⁵⁵ Willian Arens, *The Man-Eating Myth: Anthropology and Anthropophagy* (New York: Oxford University Press, 1979), 44-54.

⁵⁶ Arens, *Man-Eating Myth*, 49.

⁵⁷ See Dundes, *The Blood Libel Legend*.

⁵⁸ Boucher, *France and the American Tropics*, 32.

⁵⁹ Christopher Columbus, *The Spanish Letter of Columbus to Luis de Sant'Angel: Escribano de Racion of the Kingdom of Aragon, Dated 15 February 1493*, edited by Michael P. Kerney and Bernard Quaritch (G. Norman and Son, printers, 1893), 16.

⁶⁰ Robert A. Myers, "Island Carib Cannibalism," *New West Indian Guide/Nieuwe West-*

Indische Gids, 58, ¾ (1984): 147-184, 156.

61 Myers, "Island Carib Cannibalism," 157.

62 Myers, "Island Carib Cannibalism," 166-168.

63 British Library, Sloane MSS, 3662, folio 53.

64 Boucher, *Cannibal Encounters*, 7.

65 André Thévet quoted in Moreau, *Petites Antilles*, 118.

66 Hulme and Whitehead, *Wild Majesty*, 49.

67 Nicolás de Cardona, *Geographic and Hydrographic Descriptions of Many Northern and Southern Lands and Seas in the Indies, Specifically of the Discovery of the Kingdom of California* (Baja, California: Dawsons Book Shop, 1974), 36.

68 Cornelis C. Goslinga, *The Dutch in the Caribbean and on the Wild Coast, 1580-1680* (Gainesville: University of Florida Press, 1970), 211.

69 Moreau, *Petites Antilles*, 97.

70 Myers, "Island Carib Cannibalism," 178.

71 Boucher, *Cannibal Encounters*, 6.

72 Neil L. Whitehead, "Carib Cannibalism – The Historical Evidence," *Journal de la Société des Américanistes*, 70, 1 (1984): 69-87. For recent studies on Amerindian cannibalism see Beth Conklin, *Consuming Grief: Compassionate Cannibalism in an Amazonian Society* (Austin: University of Texas, 2001); Tim White, "Once More Cannibals," *Scientific American*, August 2001, 58-65; and Christy Turner and Jacqueline Turner, *Man Corn: Cannibalism and Violence in the Prehistoric American South West* (Salt Lake City: University of Utah, 1999).

73 Arens, *Man-Eating Myth*, 54.

74 See Whitehead, "Carib Cannibalism: The Historical Evidence," for a nuanced view.

75 Raymond Breton, *Dictionnaire français-caraïbe* (Liepzig: B. G. Teubner, 1900 [1665]), 195, provides the Island Carib name for Grenada, but not the meaning. Jean-Pierre Sainton and Raymond Boutin, in *Histoire et civilisation de la Caraïbe: Guadeloupe, Martinique, Petites Antilles...* (Paris: Maisonneuve & Larose, 2004), 75, provide a meaning of Kamahuye as "île aux la foudre": "thunderbolt island/island of thunderbolt." Antonio Vazquez de Espinosa (*Description of the Indies*. Translated by Charles Upson Clark, Washington, DC: Smithsonian Institution Press, 1968 [c. 1620]. Smithsonian Miscellaneous Collections, v. 102), adds a few references to this meaning: "There will be on those islands, and on that of Grenada, over 18,000 indians, who go naked, belong to the Carib tribe, and call themselves Camajuyas, which means thunderbolt, since they are brave and warlike." (2) "The island of Granada... is thickly peopled with Carib indians called Camajuyas, which means lightning from heaven, since they are brave" (68). See also Tierry L'Etang, "Du nom indigène des îles de l'archipel des Antilles," 7, 21 [Internet] Accessed on 15 April 2012 at http://www.manioc.org/gsdl/collect/recherch/index/assoc/HASH0177/0dab508e.dir/dunomindig.pdf.

76 Bouton quoted in Kimber, *Martinique Revisited*, 41.

77 According to Dutertre, in 1638 Governor Poincy of St. Christopher planned to settle Grenada "But the crowd of the Savages who lived there, and its distance from this of Saint-Christophe, caused him to change his mind."

78 David Henige, "On the Contact Population of Hispaniola: History as Higher Mathematics." *Hispanic American Historical Review* 58, 2 (1978): 217-237. Se also Noble Cook, *Born to Die: Diseases and New World Conquest, 1492-1650*, Cambridge: Cambridge University Press, 1998, and W. M. Denevan, ed., *The Native Populations of the Americas in 1492*. 2nd ed. University of Wisconsin Press, 1992.

79 J. H. Steward. "South American Cultures: An Interpretative Summary." In *Handbook of South American Indians*, 6: 669-672.

80 Boucher, *Cannibal Encounters*, 35, reports that the island of Dominica, which has been identified as the most populous Island Carib island in the mid-1600s, had around 5,000

due to their expulsion from the other islands.

81 See Holdren, "Raiders and Traders," for an analysis of the various archeological sites as to possible Amerindian occupation.

82 It is possible that this division is what the French colonists under Philibert de Nouailly referred to when they attempted to settle on Grenada in 1646, but found the island consumed with conflicts among the Amerindians who were located in two distinct parts of the island. See Holdren, "Raiders and Traders," for an analysis of the various archeological sites as to possible Carib or Galibi origin.

83 See Anonymous, *Histoire de l'isle de Grenade.*

84 Wilson, "The Cultural Mosaic of the Indigenous Caribbean," 50.

85 The place name Cairouane in the southwest on some old maps, however, does not appear to be associated with Captain Cairouane, but rather with sea turtles that were probably plentiful there.

86 Pierre Verin, "Carib Culture in Colonial Times," In *Proceedings of the Second International Congress for the Study of Pre-Columbian Cultures in the Lesser Antilles* (St. Ann's, Barbados: 1967), 116.

87 Charles de Rochefort quoted in Hulme and Whiteheld, *Wild Majesty*, 123.

88 The anonymous author of the 17th-century *Histoire de l'isle de Grenade*, believed to be Catholic missionary Benige Bresson who resided in Grenada between 1656-59, claimed to have written a book on the Island Caribs, but it has not surfaced to date and feared lost.

89 Though Father Breton is credited with the entire work, it may have been a collaborative effort of the French missionaries in the region at the time.

90 Boucher, *Cannibal Encounters*, 6.

91 Labat quoted in Wilson, "The Cultural Mosaic of the Indigenous Caribbean," 50.

92 Wilson, "The Cultural Mosaic of the Indigenous Caribbean," 50.

93 Wilson, "The Cultural Mosaic of the Indigenous Caribbean," 50.

94 Wilson, "The Cultural Mosaic of the Indigenous Caribbean," 50.

95 Wilson, "The Cultural Mosaic of the Indigenous Caribbean," 50.

96 Anonymous, *Histoire de l'isle de Grenade*, 55.

97 Anonymous, *Histoire de l'isle de Grenade*, 60-61.

98 There was no mention of any such breakdown in Anonymous, *Histoire de l'isle de Grenade*, but in September 1646 Philibert de Nouailly decided not to establish a settlement on Grenada because of the island had been divided into two warring factions.

99 Douglas Taylor, "Kinship and Social Structure of the Island Carib: Past and Present," *Southwestern Journal of Anthropology*, 2, no. 2 (1946: 180-212), 181.

100 Boucher, *Cannibal Encounters*, 9.

101 S. Dreyfus quoted in Wilson, *Indigenous Peoples of the Caribbean*, 51.

102 Boucher, *France and the American Tropics*, 37.

103 David Watts, *The West Indies: Patterns of Development, Culture and Environmental Change Since 1492* (Cambridge: Cambridge University Press, 1990), 70.

104 Hulme and Whitehead, *Wild Majesty*, 134.

105 Hulme and Whitehead, *Wild Majesty*, 133.

106 Hulme and Whitehead, *Wild Majesty*, 110.

107 Hulme and Whitehead, *Wild Majesty*, 149.

108 Hulme and Whitehead, *Wild Majesty*, 149.

109 Anonymous, *Histoire de l'isle de Grenade*, 55.

110 Jared M. Diamond, *Guns, Germs and Steel: The Fates of Human Societies* (W. W. Norton & Co., 1999).

Notes to Chapter 2: Prologue to Settlement

[1] Philip P. Boucher, *Cannibal Encounters: Europeans and Island Caribs, 1492-1763* (Baltimore: The Johns Hopkins University Press, 1992), 13.

[2] See Raymund P. Devas, *A History of the Island of Grenada, 1498-1796* (St. George's: Carenage Press, 1974), for a detailed discussion of the debate, 9-27 and 215-229.

[3] Bartolomé de Las Casas quoted in Devas, *A History of the Island of Grenada*, 16: "On coming out of the Bocas, he saw an island to the north, about 26 leagues [126 km] from the Bocas: he called it Assumption Island. He saw another island, and he called it Conception..." Devas, 16-18, adds that Columbus would have had to sail north at least 20 leagues [96.5 km], not directly west as Las Casas states, if in fact he saw at least the peaks of Tobago and Grenada.

[4] For an opposing view see Lucius Lee Hubbard, "Did Columbus Discover Tobago?", in *Essays Offered to Herbert Putnam by his Colleagues and Friends on his Thirtieth Anniversary as Librarian of Congress, 5 April 1929*, edited by Herbert Putnam, William W. Bishop, Andrew Keogh (Ayer Publishing, 1967), 211-223.

[5] Samuel E. Morison, in a number of his books on Christopher Columbus, such as *The Great Explorers: The European Discovery of America* (New York: Oxford University Press, 1978), 487, refers to Grenada as Asunción and Tobago as Belaforma, but in *The Caribbean as Columbus Saw It* (1964) he refers to Grenada as Concepción. Jean-Pierre Moreau, in *Les Petites Antilles de Christophe Colomb à Richelieu, 1493-1635* (Paris: Editions Karthala, 1992), 54, refers to Grenada as Asunción. Sometimes it appears as Ascensión, either as a misinterpretation of Asunción and its meaning, or after Juan de La Cosa's 1500 world map, which some have accepted as referring to Grenada, despite the fact that its location is totally off; most believe that Mayo on Cosa's map refer to Grenada. Carl Sauer, in *The Early Spanish Main* (Berkeley: University of California Press, 1966), 193, refers to the Cosa map and the "uncertain location" of the islands, but adds that "Asunción (Ascensión on the Juan de La Cosa map) was Grenada." It is interesting to note that de La Cosa accompanied Columbus on his first three voyages to the Americas and should have been aware of the possible names Columbus had already given the islands.

[6] The term Amerindian refers to the various peoples who inhabited the Caribbean islands. See Chapter I above for more on the Amerindians of the Lesser Antilles.

[7] See note 75 in Chapter 1 above for details of the origin and use of the name.

[8] The Roman Catholic Church in St. George's is known as the Cathedral of the Immaculate Conception.

[9] Edzer Roukema, "Some Remarks on the La Cosa Map," *Imogo Mundi*, 14 (1959: 38-54), 52.

[10] Exactly which island the Spanish explorers attacked remains unclear; various authors have identified the island as Grenada, St. Vincent, Dominica or Guadeloupe.

[11] Roukema, "Some Remarks on the La Cosa Map," 52.

[12] The French name "La Grenade" was derived from the Spanish name for the island "La Granada," which was possibly given it by Spanish sailors or map makers in the early 1520s, supposedly after Granada, Spain. Its present spelling Grenada, rendered by the British after 1762, is the Anglicized version of Granada.

[13] The name Taino, as opposed to Island Arawak, will be used throughout to designate the Amerindians who inhabited the Bahamas and the Greater Antilles at the time of European contact. Though the name is not self-ascribed nor reflects the diversity of the groups present in the region at that time, it is used here to allow some consistency with the historical literature. Taino is derived from the Arawakan word *nitaíno*, which referred to the nobles who included caciques, and was applied to the larger group in 1935.

14 William F. Keegan, *The People Who Discovered Columbus: The Prehistory of the Bahamas* (Gainesville: University Press of Florida, 1992), 221-223, estimates that in 1510 some 25,760 Tainos were brought to Hispanola, most of them from the Bahama Islands.

15 See Bartolomé de las Casas, *The Devastation of the Indies: A Brief Account*, translated by Herma Briffault (Baltimore: The Johns Hopkins University Press, 1974), for the Spanish treatment of the Tainos.

16 It quickly became apparent that the arbitrary distinction of unfriendly and cannibal led to the enslavement of "peaceful" Amerindian populations throughout the region despite this attempt to protect them. The case of the Arawak population on Trinidad is a perfect example.

17 Lynne Guitar, "No More Negotiations: Slavery and the Destabilization of Colonial Hispaniola's Encomienda System," *Revista/Review Interamericana* 29, 1-4 (January-December 1999), 10 (of the Internet PDF version); C. Jesse, "The Spanish Cedula of December 23, 1511, On the Subject of the Caribs," *Caribbean Quarterly*, 9, 3 (1963), 29.

18 Guitar, "No More Negotiations," 10-11; C. Jesse, "The Spanish Cedula of December 23, 1511...," 29.

19 Anonymous, *Histoire de l'isle de Grenade*, 61.

20 British Library, Sloane MSS, 3662, f° 53.

21 Moreau, *Petites Antilles*, 150. It is difficult to estimate the Amerindian population on Grenada in the era of northern European colonizing efforts in the region. Though the population may have been fairly large prior to the arrival of the Spanish, attacks and slave raids must have drastically reduced their numbers. See Chapter 1 for a discussion of Island Carib population on Grenada in the historical period.

22 Moreau, *Petites Antilles*, 166.

23 David Watts, *The West Indies: Patterns of Development, Culture and Environmental Change Since 1492* (Cambridge: Cambridge University Press, 1987), 109.

24 Antonio Vazquez de Espinosa, *Description of the Indies* (c. 1620), translated by Charles Upson Clark (Washington, DC: Smithsonian Institution Press, 1968. Smithsonian Miscellaneous Collections, v. 102), 68.

25 Vazquez de Espinosa, *Description of the Indies*, 57.

26 Vazquez de Espinosa, *Description of the Indies*, 76.

27 Don José Oviedo de Y Banos, *The Conquest and Settlement of Venezuela*. Translated by Jeannette Johnson Varner (Berkeley: University of California Press, 1987), 209-211.

28 Varner, *The Conquest and Settlement of Venezuela*, 210.

29 Varner, *The Conquest and Settlement of Venezuela*, 210.

30 Varner, *The Conquest and Settlement of Venezuela*, 210.

31 Moreau, *Petites Antilles*, 65-66, 72.

32 Moreau, *Petites Antilles*, 75-76.

33 Moreau, *Petites Antilles*, 75-76.

34 Moreau, *Petites Antilles*, 78.

35 Moreau, *Petites Antilles*, 74.

36 Nicolás de Cardona, *Geographic and Hydrographic Descriptions of Many Northern and Southern Lands and Seas in the Indies, Specifically of the Discovery of the Kingdom of California* (Baja, California: Dawsons Book Shop, 1974), 36; also Nicolás de Cardona, *Descripciones geográficas e hidrográficas..., en especial del descubrimiento de la California* (1632). Accessed 15 April 2012 at http://memory.loc.gov/cgi-bin/query/h?intldl/esbib:@field%28DOCID+@lit%28asce sp000006%29%29, 27-28.

37 Joseph A. Baromé, "Spain and Dominica, 1493-1647," *Caribbean Quarterly*, 12, 4 (1966), 35-36.

38 See Kenneth R. Andrews, *The Spanish Caribbean: Trade and Plunder, 1530-1630* (New Haven: Yale University Press, 1978) for a detailed study of the French, British and Dutch

activities in the region.

[39] See Andrews, *The Spanish Caribbean*, for the exploits of the English, French and Dutch privateers.

[40] Moreau, *Petites Antilles*, 118.

[41] Peter Hulme and Neil L. Whitehead, eds., *Wild Majesty: Encounters With Caribs From Columbus to the Present Day* (Oxford: Clarendon, 1992), 49. Jean Bontemps is described in Andrews, *The Spanish Caribbean* (p. 121-22) as a "slave-trade corsair" who in 1566 attacked Puerto de Plata, Hispaniola.

[42] Berrio had in fact usurped the plans of Francisco de Vides, who in December 1592, arrived at Margarita from Spain with a Royal commission as the governor of Cumaná, with a contract for the discovery and colonization of New Andalousie and the islands of Trinidad, Grenada and Tobago. Francisco de Vides was expected to defend the islands against French, British and Dutch interlopers, and pacify the Island Caribs on the neighboring islands like Grenada, which the Spanish believed had unknown numbers of Spanish and African captives who could populate Trinidad. See Moreau, *Petites Antilles*, 77-78.

[43] Moreau, *Petites Antilles*, 72.

[44] Don Antonio de Berrio to the King of Spain, December 2, 1594. Archivo General de Indias, 1597-1599.

[45] The only known Spanish attempt to settle Grenada is that mentioned by Froylan de Rionegro in *Relaciones de las Missiones de los Capuchines en Venezuela, 1650-1817* (Seville, 1918) 1: 83. According to the narrative, Fray Francisco de Pamplona, a Spanish Capuchin, arrived in Grenada in 1650 together with his Capuchin brothers with the intention of evangelizing the Amerindian population who he remembered as being nice to him on a previous visit. On 20 July 1649 the Capuchins had been given license by the Congregación de Propaganda Fide to establish a mission to covert the Amerindians. In 1644, the then Don Tiburcio de Redin y Cruzat, was on a ship that stopped at Grenada to refresh and was treated kindly by the Island Caribs. He had to abandon his plans because the French had already established themselves in Grenada, and Spain and France were then at war, which made his stay there problematic. See also Devas, *History of the Island*, 36-37.

[46] See J. Lorimer, "The English Contraband Tobacco Trade in Trinidad and Guyana, 1590-1617," in K. R. Andrews, N. P. Canny and P. E. H. Hairs (eds.), *The Westward Enterprise* (Liverpool, 1978) for more on the illegal tobacco trade.

Notes to Chapter 3: The British Attempt to Settle Grenada

[1] The author of the 17th-century manuscript describing the view of one of the promoters of the Grenada venture, and his reason for not embarking "on soe advantageous a designe wherein they had once Miscarried." British Library, Sloane MSS, 3662, folio 53b-49f.

[2] James Williamson, *The Caribbee Islands* (18-20), is among the first to discuss the 1609 venture as part of his larger discussion of British colonization in the region. Raymund Devas, in *The History of Grenada* some 40 years later, discusses the venture and a number of recent writers, particularly Kenneth R. Andrews, *The Spanish Caribbean: Trade and Plunder, 1530-1630* (New Haven: Yale University Press, 1978), have presented new evidence that supports the 17th-century manuscript.

[3] The unsuccessful British attempt to settle St. Lucia in 1605 was the result of a ship, meant to replenish Charles Leigh's colony in Guiana, being blown off course and landing on St. Lucia. The Island Caribs initially welcomed the crew, but of the original 67 who landed, only 16 remained when they were forced to flee the island less than a month after

their arrival. The British settlement of Bermuda in 1609 was quite accidental, the result of the wreck of two ships destined for the English colony at Jamestown, Virginia.

4 The Grenada venture occurred two years after the first successful British colony in North America at Jamestown, Virginia.

5 British Library, Sloane MSS, 3662, folio 53b-49b. Williamson, *The Caribbee Islands*, and Andrews, *The Spanish Caribbean*, accept that Major John Scott is the author of the manuscript. John Scott (1632-1704) is a rather intriguing character, and is often described as a royal historiographer, but noted for his colonizing activities in North America and his involvement in the Popish Plot. It is interesting to note that he was present in the Caribbean in 1665, particularly at Tobago and Guiana where he participated in the capture of Tobago from the Dutch in 1665. The information in the manuscript dates to that period.

6 Holdren, "Raiders and Traders," 255.

7 Williamson, *The Caribbee Islands* (18-19), notes that, "possibly [Godfrey's manuscript] exists among the manuscripts in the British Museum, as there is in the MS. Catalogue an entry under Godfrey's name without sufficient indication of the MS. to which it refers; the document, if it relates to this transaction, thus awaits an accidental revelation."

8 Following the failure of the settlement, the ships belonging to Richard Hall went on to plunder in the Spanish Caribbean and a charge of piracy was brought by the Admiralty. In the testimony given by members of the ships' crew, there was no mention of the Grenada venture that they clearly would have known about.

9 Andrews, *The Spanish Caribbean*, 241.

10 Andrews, *The Spanish Caribbean*, 242.

11 The Portuguese were the only other Europeans to establish a colony in the Americas as a result of the papal-sanctioned Treaty of Tordesillas of 1494, which granted Spain and Portugal exclusive rights of settlement and colonial exploitation of the non-Christian world, specifically the Americas, Africa and Asia.

12 Anne Pérotin-Dumon, "French, English and Dutch in the Lesser Antilles: From Privateering to Planting, c. 1550-1650," in *General History of the Caribbean Volume II. New Societies: The Caribbean in the Long 16th Century*, ed. by P. C. Emmer (UNESCO, 1999), 116.

13 Watts, *The West Indies*, 136; see also Chapter 4, 128-175, and Boucher, *Cannibal Encounters*, 31-60.

14 Arthur P. Newton, *The European Nations in the West Indies, 1493-1688* (London: A&C Black, Ltd., 1933), 149.

15 Andrews, "Caribbean Rivalry and Anglo-Spanish Peace," *History*, 59, no. 195 (1974: 1-17) 13.

16 It was supposedly coined by Sir Francis Drake in 1579. The full quote: "The Spanish shall have no peace beyond the line," a reference to the line of latitude just west of the Azores that divided the "unknown world" between the Spanish and the Portuguese by the Papal Bull of 1494. The line, since 1559, had been used as the outside limit of peace treaties signed between European powers. See Arthur Herman, *To Rule the Waves: How the British Navy Shaped the Modern World* (New York: Harper Collins, 2004), 140, and China Mieville, *Between Equal Rights: A Marxist Theory of International Law* (Haymarket Books, 2006), 180-184.

17 Spain had little interest in North America above 40 degrees.

18 See Joyce Lorimer, "The English Contraband Tobacco Trade in Trinidad and Guiana, 1590-1617," in *The Westward Enterprise: English Activities in Ireland, the Atlantic, and America, 1480-1650*, eds. K. R. Andrews, N. P. Canny and P. E. H. Hair (Detriot: Wayne State University Press, 1979).

19 Lorimer, "The English Contraband Tobacco Trade," 140.

[20] William Vaughan, *Directions for Health* (London, 1626), 81. The quote: "Tobacco, that outlandisge weede/It spends the braine, and spoiles the feede./It duls the sprite, it dims the sight,/It robs a woman of her Right."

[21] Though Sir Walter Relegh is often given credit for introducing tobacco smoking to England, he is probably more credible as the one who did more to popularize it.

[22] Pope Urban VIII issued a papal bull in 1624 threatening to excommunicate anyone using tobacco. See John Frampton, *Of the Tobacco and his Greate Vertues* (Translation of Nicholas Monardes' 1577 publication of *Joyful Newes from our Newe Founde Worlde*), New York: Alfred A. Knoph, 1925.

[23] Pérotin-Dumon, "French, English and Dutch in the Lesser Antilles," 116.

[24] Lorimer. "The English Contraband Tobacco Trade," 125-126.

[25] Andrews, *The Spanish Caribbean*, 225.

[26] King James I described tobacco smoking in his *A Counterblast to Tobacco* as "a custome lothsome to the eye, hatefull to the nose, harmefull to the braine, daungerous to the Lungs, and in the blacke stinking fume thereof, nearest resembling the horrible Stigian smoke of the pit that is bottomelesse."

[27] George-Louis Beer, *The Origins of the British Colonial System, 1578-1660* (NY: Peter Smith, 1933), 109.

[28] Beer, *The Origins of the British Colonial System*, 109-110.

[29] Beer, *The Origins of the British Colonial System*, 110.

[30] Andréas de Rojas in a letter to the Spanish Crown quoted in Andrews, *The Spanish Caribbean*, 227.

[31] See Lorimer, "The English Contraband Tobacco Trade," for details of that trade.

[32] In 1606 the Spanish Crown prohibited the cultivation of tobacco for ten years in Margarita, Cumana, New Andalusia, St. Domingo, Cuba and Puerto Rico.

[33] Andrews, *The Spanish Caribbean*, 209.

[34] Andrews, *The Spanish Caribbean*, 228.

[35] September 1609 letter to the Spanish Crown quoted in Andrews, *The Spanish Caribbean*, 228.

[36] Benjamin Wooley, *Savage Kingdom: The True Story of Jamestown, 1607, and the Settlement of America* (New York: HarperCollins, 2007), 188.

[37] Lorimer, "The English Guiana Ventures," 5, believes that attempts to settle the Guiana coast was due to the "possibility of undertaking tobacco production, to replace the Orinoco and Trinidad contraband trade." Tobacco production would also be the impetus for the settlement of St. Christopher and Barbados a decade and a half later. The contraband trade in tobacco came to an end around 1612, following concerted actions by Spanish authorities against suppliers.

[38] Pérotin-Dumon, "French, English and Dutch," 121-122.

[39] Pérotin-Dumon, "French, English and Dutch," 122.

[40] Pérotin-Dumon, "French, English and Dutch," 122.

[41] Arnold Lulls' name is spelled a number of different ways: Lull, Lulles and Lulls; sometimes Arnold is spelt with an "e" at the end. It is most commonly found as Arnold Lulls.

[42] British Library, Sloane MSS, 3662, f° 53.

[43] William Smith, *The History of the First Discovery and Settlement of Virginia* (London, 1747).

[44] Watts, *The West Indies*, 135.

[45] Virginia farmers had first grown/smoked the harsher native variety *Nicotiana rustica*, but later obtained the seeds of the coveted *Nicotiana tabacum* from Trinidad and which proved highly profitable.

[46] Lorimer. "The English Contraband Tobacco Trade," 137.

[47] John Hayward, "The Arnold Lulls Book of Jewels and the Court Jewellers of Queen

Anne of Denmark," (*Archaeologia*,108 (1986): 227-237), 229.

[48] See Hayward, "The Arnold Lulls Book of Jewels and the Court Jewellers of Queen Anne of Denmark."

[49] Andrews, "Caribbean Rivalry," 6.

[50] Lorimer, "The English Contraband Tobacco Trade," 133.

[51] Andrews, *The Spanish Caribbean*, 242.

[52] Lorimer, "The English Contraband Tobacco Trade," 138.

[53] Lorimer, "The English Contraband Tobacco Trade," 133, 138.

[54] Lorimer, "The English Contraband Tobacco Trade," 135.

[55] According to Williamson, *The Caribbee Islands*, 12, it was exactly these reasons that caused Thomas Warner "to reject Tobago and Grenada: they were too close to the Spaniards of Trinidad, and there was far too much Carib traffic passing by them on the route from the mainland to the large islands. Later projects were to appreciate that fact to their cost."

[56] Watts, *The West Indies*, 136; and Boucher, *Cannibal Encounters*, 32.

[57] Lorimer, "The Failure of the English Guiana Ventures 1595–1667 and James I's foreign policy," (*The Journal of Imperial and Commonwealth History*, 21, no. 1 (1993: 1-30) 4.

[58] Williamson, *The Caribbee Islands*, 6-7

[59] Watts, *The West Indies*, 135.

[60] Williamson, *The Caribbee Islands*, 19.

[61] Andrews, *The Spanish Caribbean*, 242.

[62] British Library, Sloane MSS, 3662, f° 53.

[63] Otherwise, one of the depopulated islands in the northern Lesser Antilles or Barbados would have proved far more suitable for agricultural colonies and definitely less risky, which the British proved less than two decades later when they settled St. Christopher and Barbados.

[64] The seeds for the Jamestown colony came from Trinidad and Venezuela.

[65] Andrews, *The Spanish Caribbean*, 241. Beverley A. Steele, *Grenada: A History of its People* (Oxford: Macmillan Caribbean, 2003), 47, note 11, takes the "Grand Bay" literally and suggests it refers to Grand Anse or possibly "Grand Bay on the Point Salines peninsula." The often repeated site of Megrin, St. David as the settlement site of the British in 1609 is without foundation. There is no evidence other than what has been stated and absolutely no evidence that Megrin was that site.

[66] British Library, Sloane MSS, 3662, f° 53.

[67] British Library, Sloane MSS, 3662, f° 53.

[68] British Library, Sloane MSS, 3662, f° 53.

[69] The later successful French colony arrived in mid-March, but they were supported from Martinique, only a few days travel away. In the event of need they could readily get assistance.

[70] Robert Harcourt, *A Relation of a Voyage to Guiana* (London: The Hakluyt Society, 1926), 121.

[71] British Library, Sloane MSS, 3662, f° 53. The author identifies Sanchez de Mendoza as governor of Trinidad, but that is incorrect as Fernando de Berrío was governor though he would soon be replaced because of his contraband trade with foreigners.

[72] Lorimer. "The English Contraband Tobacco Trade," 140-141.

[73] British Library, Sloane MSS, 3662, f° 53.

[74] British Library, Sloane MSS, 3662, f° 53.

[75] Andrews, *The Spanish Caribbean*, 242. Harcourt notes that Hall's ships left a few days before the *Diana* and Andrews provides evidence that the *Penelope* and *Endeavour* clashed with three Spanish men-of-war off Cuba and the *Endeavour* was captured while trading at Cuba. In retaliation the *Penelope* captured a Spanish ship, taking it back to England. On

returning to England in 1610 the *Penelope* and its prize were confiscated by the Admiralty on suspicion of piracy. It was released but later impounded when the Spanish sued; Hall subsequently won. See Lorimer, "The English Contraband Tobacco Trade," 144-146.

[76] British Library, Sloane MSS, 3662, f° 53.

[77] Anonymous, *A True Declaration of the Estate Colonie in Virginia: With a Confutation of Such Scandalous Reports as Have Tended to the Disgrace of so Worthy an Enterprise* (London, 1610), 1.

[78] Andrews, *The Spanish Caribbean*, 242.

[79] The title of an address by George Arents, "The Seed From Which Virginia Grew," *The William and Mary Quarterly*, Second Series, 19, no. 22 (April 1939): 124-129.

[80] Edward D. Neill, *History of the Virginia Company of London, With Letters to and from the First Colony, Never Before Printed* (NY: Joel Munsell, 1869), 94.

[81] Wooley, *Savage Kingdom*, 212.

[82] Wooley, *Savage Kingdom*, 189.

[83] Karen Kupperman, *Roanoke: The Abandoned Colony* (NJ: Rowman & Littlefield, 2007), 7.

[84] Krupperman, *Roanoke*, 139.

[85] Wooley, *Savage Kingdom*, 208.

[86] Wooley, *Savage Kingdom*, 188.

Notes to Chapter 4: French Settlement & Island Carib Resistance

[1] James A. Williamson, *The Caribbee Islands Under the Proprietary Patents* (London: Oxford University Press, 1926), 4, on the Island Carib threat to European colonializers.

[2] There is some debate on the exact date of French colonists establishing some sort of settlement on St. Christopher. Though a "colony" may have been established before d'Esnambuc arrived, it is d'Esnambuc's date of arrival that is accepted.

[3] Established in 1635 following the collapse of its predecessor, the Company of St. Christopher, the Company of the Islands of America was a stock company that administered all French territories in the West Indies. Dating back to 1627, it laid claim, along with England, to much of the Lesser Antilles, including Grenada. Its organizers, especially Cardinal Richelieu, hoped that the new company would be more aggressive in colonizing the West Indies and extending French colonial trade.

[4] Nevis settled in 1628, Montserrat in 1632 and Antigua in 1632 by the British.

[5] De Bonnefoy possibly arrived at St. Christopher between 1635 and 1637, an official of the Company of the Islands of America, following its establishment in 1635.

[6] British Library, Sloane MSS, 3662, folio 53b-49b.

[7] Dutertre, *Histoire générale*, 1: 424 gives the date as 1638, but I suggest the year 1640 based on de Poincy's other colonizing venture; he assisted with establishing the French on Tortuga in August 1640. De Poincy did not arrive in the West Indies until February 1639 so his planned settlement of Grenada could not have been 1638, and this date must either be a misprint or an error.

[8] A number of historians, including Devas (page 42) and Brizan (19), have concluded that de Poincy actually sent an expedition to Grenada, but that is incorrect and may be due to misreading both Dutertre and Labat. When de Poincy did pursue new settlements in the late 1640s he looked at the smaller islands to the north of St. Christopher.

[9] Dutertre, *Histoire générale*, 1: 424. Petitjean Roget, in Anonymous (13), adds that Governor Houel had in fact "sent there a certain Potel who had failed on Saba," and Governor Aubert, in 1643, "sent Sieur Postel to examine the island, but this attempt was soon abandoned."

[10] Anonymous, *Histoire de l'isle de Grenade de Grenade*, 13-14. De Nouailly's name is sometimes rendered Philbert, and Novailly or Noailles.

[11] Boucher, *France and the American Tropics*, 94.

[12] Boucher, *France and the American Tropics*, 94.

[13] Anonymous, *Histoire de l'isle de Grenade de Grenade*, 13-14.

[14] Anonymous, *Histoire de l'isle de Grenade de Grenade*, 14; FR ANOM COL F² A¹³, F 65 10 July 1645.

[15] Anonymous, *Histoire de l'isle de Grenade de Grenade*, 14; FR ANOM COL F² A¹³, F 65, 10 July 1645.

[16] Cited in Bibliothèque nationale, *Quatres siècles de colonisation française* (Paris, 1931), 58-59.

[17] Jacques Petitjean Roget, *La société d'habitation à la Martinique: Un demi-siècle de formation, 1635-1685*, (Atelier Reproduction des thèses, Université de Lille III, 1980) v.1, 152. De Beaumanoir is possibly Louis Laboudat, Sieur de Beaumanoir who was a major and in 1680 commandant at St. Christopher.

[18] Moreau, Résidence des Missionnaires Jésuites, *Collection des procès-verbaux des assemblées générales du clergé de France depuis l'année 1560 jusqu'a présent rédigés par ordre de matière et réduits à ce qu'ils ont d'essentiel* (de l'imprimerie de Guillaume Desprez, 1770), T. 4, Assemblée de 1655 (19), 411-12.

[19] Petitjean Roget, *La société d'habitation à la Martinique*, 1: 152.

[20] Maurile de St-Michel remained in the French Antilles until 1647; in 1652 he published *Voyage des Isles Camercanes en l'Amérique qui font partie des Indes Occidentales...* (Le Mans: Hierôme Olivier, 1652).

[21] FR ANOM COL F² A¹³, F 73, and AN, MS 2f, 3X21, M.C. I, 122.

[22] A number of books do in fact record de Nouailly as having colonized "La Grénade et le Grenadines de cinq cents 'hommes de tout sexe'." See H. I. Priestley, *France Overseas Through the Old Regime: A Study of European Expansion* (Berkeley: University of California, 1939), 83; & Charles Germaine Marie Bourel de La Roncière, *Histoire de la Marine Française* (Plon-Nourrit, 1909), 666.

[23] Moreau, *Collection des procès-verbaux des assemblées générales du clergé de France...*, T. 4, 411-12.

[24] Boucher, *France and the American Tropics*, 86

[25] Crouse, *French Pioneers*, 209.

[26] See Pierre Margry, "Origines françaises de pays d'outre-mer," *Revue Maritime et Coloniale*, 58 (August 1878): 28-50, 276-305.

[27] See Crouse, *French Pioneers*, for a detailed telling of the early struggles in the French Caribbean.

[28] Anonymous, *Histoire de l'isle de Grenade de Grenade*, 48. La Rivière, a close friend of du Parquet, was in 1654 appointed the governor of St. Lucia, but he was killed by the Island Caribs soon thereafter.

[29] Anonymous, *Histoire de l'isle de Grenade de Grenade*, 14. An *ajoupa*, derived from the Island Carib, is a rudimentary shelter or hut made of sticks, vine and leaves, but here referred to a more sturdy building.

[30] Anonymous, *Histoire de l'isle de Grenade de Grenade*, 48. According to the Anonymous author, La Rivière "had been advised" to give this pretext, most probably by du Parquet.

[31] Anonymous, *Histoire de l'isle de Grenade de Grenade*, 48-49.

[32] Anonymous, *Histoire de l'isle de Grenade de Grenade*, 48.

[33] Dutertre, *Histoire générale*, 1: 424-25.

[34] The Anonymous author adds that the Island Caribs can be won over and kept loyal by giving gifts, and "they worship those who are good to them... [and] they often take their names to honor them and by affection," 57.

[35] Labat, *Nouveau voyage*, 3: 35; Devas, *History of the Island*, 45.

[36] Dutertre, *Histoire générale*, 1: 425.

[37] The 200 colonists given by Dutertre (and later Labat) appear to have been taken from the standard contract issued by the Company of the Islands of America to prospective colonists as in the one given to Philibert de Nouailly in 1645.

[38] Dutertre, *Histoire générale*, 1: 425.

[39] Dutertre, *Histoire générale*, 1: 425; Crouse, *French Pioneers*, 195.

[40] Labat, *Nouveau voyage*, 3: 35.

[41] Anonymous, *Histoire de l'isle de Grenade de Grenade*, 49. Dutertre, *Histoire générale*, 1: 425.

[42] Currently Victoria, St. Mark.

[43] Anonymous, *Histoire de l'isle de Grenade de Grenade*, 50.

[44] Anonymous, *Histoire de l'isle de Grenade de Grenade*, 50.

[45] Dutertre, *Histoire générale*, 1: 425; Labat, *Nouveau voyage*, 3: 36.

[46] Anonymous, *Histoire de l'isle de Grenade de Grenade*, 14-15.

[47] Is it in fact a "cover-up" or an error since St. Lucia was settled by du Parquet in June 1650? On 27 October 1650, at a cost of 41,500 *livres* ("the equivalent of the old £1,660 sterling"), du Parquet became the sole proprietor of these islands, and in August 1651 King Louis XIV appointed him governor-general and his lieutenant general of the islands. He returned to Grenada in October 1652 and took possession of the island for the second time, also taking the opportunity to get a pledge of loyalty from his offices and the colonists.

[48] See the analysis of the Leapers' Hill incident in Chapter 12 below.

[49] Anonymous, *Histoire de l'isle de Grenade de Grenade*, 51.

[50] According to Dutertre, *Histoire générale*, 1: 425, after the construction of the house du Parquet had "all his people busy cutting the woods so that to surround it with a strong fence at eight or ten feet distant. He had placed into [the fence] two pieces of cannon guns, and four rock throwers." This constituted the palisade fort. So named because it was completed on 25 March, the day of the Roman Catholic religious festival celebrating the Annunciation of the Virgin Mary

[51] Anonymous, *Histoire de l'isle de Grenade de Grenade*, 51-52.

[52] Anonymous, *Histoire de l'isle de Grenade de Grenade*, 54.

[53] Anonymous, *Histoire de l'isle de Grenade de Grenade*, 54-55.

[54] Anonymous, *Histoire de l'isle de Grenade de Grenade*, 55.

[55] Anonymous, *Histoire de l'isle de Grenade de Grenade*, 55.

[56] Anonymous, *Histoire de l'isle de Grenade*, 56.

[57] Dutertre, *Histoire générale*, 1: 424. As a matter of fact, Dutertre criticizes de Rochefort who claimed that du Parquet had taken control of Grenada by force of arms.

[58] Anonymous, *Histoire de l'isle de Grenade de Grenade*, 56.

[59] Anonymous, *Histoire de l'isle de Grenade de Grenade*, 56.

[60] Anonyomous, *Histoire de l'isle de Grenade de Grenade*, 52.

[61] Anonyomous, *Histoire de l'isle de Grenade de Grenade*, 91-92.

[62] Dutertre, *Histoire générale*, 1: 427.

[63] Though Le Comte is often referred to as governor, he was in fact the administrator, with Du Parquet the governor of Grenada. This was also the case under the Comte de Sérillac and Du Bu. Le Comte and Du Bu were deputies.

[64] Dutertre quoted in Devas, *History of the Island*, 45.

[65] Dutertre quoted in Devas, *History of the Island*, 45.

[66] Anonymous, *Histoire de l'isle de Grenade de Grenade*, 57.

[67] Anonyomous, *Histoire de l'isle de Grenade de Grenade*, 59.

[68] David Clyde, *Health in Grenada: A Social and Historical Account* (London: Vade-Mecum Press, 1985), 7.

[69] Labat quoted in Clyde, *Health in Grenada*, 5.

70 Dutertre, *Histoire générale*, 1: 426.

71 Anonymous, *Histoire de l'isle de Grenade de Grenade*, 59.

72 Anonymous, *Histoire de l'isle de Grenade de Grenade*, 57.

73 Anonymous, *Histoire de l'isle de Grenade de Grenade*, 57.

74 Anonymous, *Histoire de l'isle de Grenade de Grenade*, 57-59.

75 Anonymous, *Histoire de l'isle de Grenade de Grenade*, 56.

76 Boucher, *Cannibal Encounters*, 48.

77 Boucher, *Cannibal Encounters*, 86.

78 The Anonymous author fails to mention the exact dates of the attacks.

79 Anonymous, *Histoire de l'isle de Grenade*, 62. The author was incorrect of course, since an untold number of British colonists had lost their lives in 1609 at the hands of the Island Caribs.

80 Anonymous, *Histoire de l'isle de Grenade*, 62.

81 Anonymous, *Histoire de l'isle de Grenade*, 63.

82 Anonymous, *Histoire de l'isle de Grenade*, 63-64.

83 Anonymous, *Histoire de l'isle de Grenade*, 66.

84 Anonymous, *Histoire de l'isle de Grenade*, 67.

85 Anonymous, *Histoire de l'isle de Grenade*, 71. See Chapter 12 below for a detailed description of the Leapers' Hill incident and its legacy.

86 Dutertre, *Histoire générale*, 1: 431.

87 Le Fort has been identified as Yves Le Cercueil of Pont-l'Eveque, France who had been in the French Antilles since 1635. He is variously identified as related to du Parquet and married to the niece of Le Comte, but he was a close friend of the governor. He arrived in Grenada in 1650 after over 1½ years as the commander of Marie Galante. He would have been around 34 years old then. See Anonymous, *Histoire de l'isle de Grenade*, 72-73.

88 Anonyomous, *Histoire de l'isle de Grenade*, 87.

89 Anonyomous, *Histoire de l'isle de Grenade*, 92.

90 Anonyomous, *Histoire de l'isle de Grenade*, 100. Some 4-500 colonists under Balthazar Le Roux de Royville attempted to settle Cayenne in 1652. The expedition ran into problems even before they arrived, with Royville killed and his body dumped overboard during the voyage to Cayenne. At Cayenne the colonists fought amongst themselves and succumbed to attacks by the Amerindians. The survivors abandoned the colony.

91 Anonymous, *Histoire de l'isle de Grenade*, 97.

92 Anonymous, *Histoire de l'isle de Grenade*, 99-100.

93 Dutertre, *Histoire générale*, 1: 464-65.

94 Anonymous, *Histoire de l'isle de Grenade*, 99-100.

95 Anonymous, *Histoire de l'isle de Grenade*, 101-103.

96 Anonymous, *Histoire de l'isle de Grenade*, 103.

97 Anonymous, *Histoire de l'isle de Grenade*, 103.

98 Anonymous, *Histoire de l'isle de Grenade*, 103.

99 Anonymous, *Histoire de l'isle de Grenade*, 105.

100 Anonymous, *Histoire de l'isle de Grenade*, 118. Dutertre (*Histoire générale*, 1: 431) writes that the poison was brought to Le Fort by "a Savage who was in his service."

101 Anonymous, *Histoire de l'isle de Grenade*, 119-120; Dutertre, *Histoire générale*, 1: 431; Labat, *Nouveau voyage*, 3: 39.

102 Dutertre, *Histoire générale*, 1: 509.

103 Anonymous, *Histoire de l'isle de Grenade*, 150. *Caret* reffered to the hawksbill sea turtle, while *turtue* referred to the green turtle.

104 Anonymous, *Histoire de l'isle de Grenade*, 150.

105 Anonymous, *Histoire de l'isle de Grenade*, 150.

106 Jean III de Faudoas, comte de Sérillac, is also spelled Cérillac.

¹⁰⁷ Dutertre, *Histoire générale*, 1: 426.

¹⁰⁸ Figures calculated from information on deaths given by the Anonymous author, and does not include the additional deaths of the 56 soldiers or mercenaries who were hired between 1654 and 1655.

¹⁰⁹ Based on information in Anonymous, I have calculated that about 719 people arrived in Grenada as settlers between March 1649 and October 1659.

¹¹⁰ The case of the arrival of the 300 French from a failed settlement at Cayenne in 1654 is illustrative. They arrived in Grenada soon after the Island Carib attack and destruction of Beau Séjour (the smoke from the fires was still evident), but the Grenada colonists "decided under great threat" to deceive the 300 "because if they had known the truth they would not have wanted to stay." See Anonymous, *Histoire de l'isle de Grenade*, 100.

Notes to Chapter 5: Comte de Sérillac's Colonial Misadventures

¹ Nellis M. Crouse, *French Pioneers in the West Indies, 1624-1664* (New York: Columbia University Press, 1940), 231. The correct spelling of de Sérillac's name seems to be with an "S", but the spelling with the "C" may be more common because of its rendition as such in Dutertre.

² Crouse, *French Pioneers*, 230.

³ Dutertre, *Histoire générale*, 1: 499.

⁴ A. Latron, "Les mesaventures d'un gentilhomme colonial," (*Revue Historique des Antilles* 3 (June/October 1929): 1-14), 1-3.

⁵ Latron, "Les mesaventures," 2-3.

⁶ Latron, "Les mesaventures," 2-3.

⁷ Dutertre, *Histoire générale*, 3: 499.

⁸ Dutertre, *Histoire générale*, 3: 499.

⁹ Dutertre, *Histoire générale*, 3: 499-500.

¹⁰ Dutertre, *Histoire générale*, 3: 507.

¹¹ Dutertre, *Histoire générale*, 3: 509.

¹² See Anonyomous, *Histoire de l'isle*, 134-139 for the full contract.

¹³ Anonyomous, *Histoire de l'isle*, 134-139, 227-230. The *livre tournois* (l.t.) was a French accounting unit prevalent in contracts at the time.

¹⁴ Dutertre, *Histoire générale*, 3: 507-510.

¹⁵ Dutertre, *Histoire générale*, 3: 510.

¹⁶ Anonyomous, *Histoire de l'isle*, 140.

¹⁷ Anonyomous, *Histoire de l'isle*, 140. De Maubray, after falling-out with de Sérillac, traveled to Martinique in 1658 and becomes a confident of Madame du Parquet. Her relationship with him later caused her much trouble with the French on Martinique and he was forced to leave the island. See Crouse, *French Pioneers*, 238-240.

¹⁸ Dutertre, *Histoire générale*, 3: 510.

¹⁹ Anonymous, *Histoire de l'isle*, 132.

²⁰ Dutertre, *Histoire générale*, 3: 508. There were oysters at Tyrrell Bay, Carriacou, but no valuable pearls.

²¹ Boucher, *France and the American Tropics*, 103.

²² Dutertre, *Histoire générale*, 3: 499.

²³ According to the Anonymous author, 151-52, de Sérillac contracted with Le Vasseau of Dieppe for 1,000 *livres* to arrange the procurement of slaves. *La Fortune*, a flyboat under Captain Dubois, attempted to sail on 1 December 1657, but bad weather forced it back to port. It left a few days later and traveled to West Africa where a cargo of slaves was

purchased, but sank on its way to Grenada.

24 Dutertre, *Histoire générale*, 3: 511.

25 Dutertre, *Histoire générale*, 3: 511.

26 Dutertre, *Histoire générale*, 3: 512-514.

27 Dutertre, *Histoire générale*, 3: 514. On 25 May 1660 de Sérillac received a judgment from the Admiralty Court awarding him £241.00.

28 Dutertre, after learning that de Sérillac had made a secret deal with the Capuchins to minister in Grenada "in spite of the contract that he had signed with our superiors in Paris," was hesitant about continuing his trip to Grenada. Dutertre felt betrayed by de Sérillac and when the first opportunity arose after the ship ran aground in England, he took his leave of de Sérillac.

29 The spelling of du Bu's names varies, even by the Anonymous author. It is sometimes du But and du Buc. In his letter of 10 April 1658 to du Parquet de Sérillac mentions that he was about to "dispatch only eighty passengers," not 70 as stated by the Anonymous author who witnesed their arrival.

30 Anonymous, *Histoire de l'isle*, 163-167.

31 Anonymous, *Histoire de l'isle*, 163.

32 Anonymous, *Histoire de l'isle*, 168-9.

33 Anonymous, *Histoire de l'isle*, 172.

34 Anonymous, *Histoire de l'isle*, 172.

35 Anonymous, *Histoire de l'isle*, 168-182. See Anonymous, 227-230, for a list of the property, including *engagés* and slaves, that were handed over to du Bu.

36 Anonymous, *Histoire de l'isle*, 174-177.

37 Anonymous, *Histoire de l'isle*, 174.

38 Anonymous, *Histoire de l'isle*, 178.

39 Anonymous, *Histoire de l'isle*, 163.

40 See Anonymous, *Histoire de l'isle*, 25-35 for a discussion of the manuscript's authorship.

41 Anonymous, *Histoire de l'isle*, 35.

42 Anonymous, *Histoire de l'isle*, 201-2.

43 Anonymous, *Histoire de l'isle*, 152.

44 Anonymous, *Histoire de l'isle*, 174-75.

45 Dutertre, *Histoire générale*, 3: 86.

46 Dutertre, *Histoire de l'isle*, 1: 201.

47 See Anonymous, *Histoire de l'isle*, 181-210.

48 Anonymous, *Histoire de l'isle*, 167.

49 Anonymous, *Histoire de l'isle*, 180.

50 Anonymous, *Histoire de l'isle*, 179.

51 Anonymous, *Histoire de l'isle*, 206.

52 See Anonymous, *Histoire de l'isle*, 181-210.

53 Anonymous, *Histoire de l'isle*, 208.

54 Anonymous, *Histoire de l'isle*, 186.

55 Anonymous, *Histoire de l'isle*, 190.

56 Anonymous, *Histoire de l'isle*, 190.

57 Anonymous, *Histoire de l'isle*, 190.

58 Anonymous, *Histoire de l'isle*, 192-3.

59 Anonymous, *Histoire de l'isle*, 206.

60 Anonymous, *Histoire de l'isle*, 213.

61 Anonymous, *Histoire de l'isle*, 214-15.

62 Anonymous, *Histoire de l'isle*, 215.

63 Anonymous, *Histoire de l'isle*, 215.

64 Anonymous, *Histoire de l'isle*, 214.

[65] Dutertre, *Histoire générale*, 1 : 514.

[66] Labat, *Nouveau voyage*, 3: 288.

[67] Devas, *A History of the Island of Grenada*, 60-61.

[68] Labat, *Nouveau voyage*, 3: 288.

[69] Labat, *Nouveau voyage*, 3: 288.

[70] Anonymous, *Histoire de l'isle*, 182.

[71] Dutertre, *Histoire générale*, 1: 502.

[72] Anonymous, *Histoire de l'isle*, 24.

[73] Anonymous, *Histoire de l'isle*, 24.

[74] Anonymous, *Histoire de l'isle*, 24.

[75] Anonymous, *Histoire de l'isle*, 24.

[76] Anonymous, *Histoire de l'isle*, 86.

[77] Anonymous, *Histoire de l'isle*, 86.

Notes to Chapter 6: A Tenuously Held Colony

[1] James Pritchard, *In Search of Empire* , 59-60.

[2] Cayenne, though far from the other French colonies, received much attention because of its location on the South American continent, but its early development also proved problemic.

[3] It's a claim that Jean-Baptiste Labat would make when he visits around 1700.

[4] Mims, *West India Policy*, 45.

[5] FR ANOM COL C[8], 2nd Series, I Mémoire du Sr. Formont.

[6] See Mims, *West India Policy*, for a detailed discussion of the Dutch trade with the French colonies.

[7] Mims, *West India Policy*, 21.

[8] Dutertre, *Histoire générale*, 3: 87.

[9] Dutertre, *Histoire générale*, 3: 88.

[10] One of Tracy's new policies was to end the restrictions local governors had imposed on colonists from moving between French colonies.

[11] Dutertre, *Histoire générale*, 3: 88.

[12] Dutertre, *Histoire générale*, 3: 88.

[13] Dutertre, *Histoire générale*, 3: 89.

[14] Mims, *West India Policy*, 69.

[15] Médéric Moreau de Saint-Méry, *Loix et constitutions des colonies Francoises sous le vent...*, 1: 112.

[16] Crouse, *French Pioneers*, 267.

[17] Mims, *West India Policy*, 69.

[18] Latron, "Les mesaventures," 3.

[19] Dutertre, *Histoire générale*, 3: 87.

[20] Dutertre, *Histoire générale*, 3: 89. Tracy, according to Boucher (*The American Tropics*, 172), had done the same in "Guadeloupe, where he ended the endless quarrels between the sons of Houël and those of the latter's brother-in-law Jean de Boisseret d'Herblay by shipping them home." It appears that one of de Sérillac's sons, Jean, maintained property at "le Fond du Quesne," given by the Comte in 1663; he reportedly was still on the island as late as 1671.

[21] Dutertre, *Histoire générale*, 3: 89-90. The reference is to protestantism.

[22] Dutertre, *Histoire générale*, 3: 92.

[23] Dutertre, *Histoire générale*, 3: 89.

24 Dutertre, *Histoire générale*, 3: 90.

25 Mims, *West India Policy*, 83.

26 Dutertre, *Histoire générale*, 3: 90-91.

27 Dutertre, *Histoire générale*, 3: 91.

28 Dutertre, *Histoire générale*, 3: 91.

29 Dutertre, *Histoire générale*, 3: 91.

30 Dutertre, *Histoire générale*, 3: 92.

31 Nellis M. Crouse, *The French Struggle for the West Indies, 1665-1713* (New York: Columbia University Press, 1943), 21.

32 Dutertre, *Histoire générale*, 3: 150.

33 Dutertre, *Histoire générale*, 3: 150-152. Dutertre's qualification at the end makes one a bit skeptical: "This story was told to the public in an entirely different manner than what I said here, and I can only give you the word of M. Vincent, the governor of Grenada, who ordered this enterprise and who told me of it in his memoirs, that this is true."

34 C.S.P., America & West Indies, 1661-68, No. 1692, quoted in Crouse, *French Struggle*, 87.

35 C.S.P., America & West Indies, 1661-68, No. 1692, quoted in Crouse, *French Struggle*, 87.

36 Crouse, *French Struggle*, 95.

37 Crouse, *French Struggle*, 45.

38 Crouse, *French Struggle*, 95.

39 Dutertre, *Histoire générale*, 3: 94.

40 Dutertre, *Histoire générale*, 3: 94.

41 See FR ANOM, 13DFC2C, Fort Royal, Martinique. Accessed 20 May 2013 at http://anom.archivesnationales.culture.gouv.fr/sdx/ulysse/notice?qid=sdx_q0&n=1&id=FR%20ANOM%2013DFC2C&p=1.

42 BnF, Cartes et Plans, SHM, pf. 157 bis, div. 22, pièce 1 D.

43 Bibliothèque nationale de France, département Cartes et plans, GE D-15557; http://catalogue.bnf.fr/ark:/12148/cb40645383w (accessed 28 November 2012).

44 See Labat (*Nouveau Voyage*, 4: 418-419) for a detailed discussion of the incorrect orientation of Grenada on Guillaume De L'Isle's 1717 *Carte des Antilles Francoises et des Isles Voisines*, where he blames engineer Thimothée Petit for the error and not De L'Isle. It is not clear if De L'Isle or Petit had access to Blondel's earlier map thus duplicating his error, or created their own. It seems possible that this error was simply administrative as Petit just ran out of space and used what was there to complete his map.

45 Laurent Vidal and Émilie d'Orgeix, *Les villes françaises du Nouveau Monde: des premiers fondateurs aux ingénieurs du roi, XVIe-XVIIIe siècles* (Somogy, 1999), 159.

46 Louis de Canchy was an ensign, later promoted to lieutenant, in the Orléans Regiment which was commanded by Vincent, the governor of Grenada and his predecessor. Canchy is remembered in Carignan, Quebec with a street named after him.

47 FR ANOM G1 498 N° 28, Ile de la Grenada recensement du 22 octobre 1669. In the *Bulletin de la Section de géographie*, v. 14 (Paris: Imprimerie nationale, 1900), 281, n.2, it is recorded that de Canchy was the governor after 1668, but was not given provisions until 1671. See also Jean-Baptiste Colbert, *Lettres, Instructions et Memoires de Colbert* (1873), 3: 528.

48 Mims, *West India Policy*, 150.

49 Mims, *West India Policy*, 153.

50 Mims, *West India Policy*, 155-6.

51 Crouse, *French Struggle*, 95.

52 The 1669 policy called for "a complete census ..., classified according to localities, race, sex-this for the benefit of Colbert" for the individual territories, including Grenada. See Crouse, *French Struggle*, 95.

53 The 1669 census does not provide information on the types of plantations owned by

each family recorded as does the 1696 nominal census, but the format of the latter creates some confusion in the presentation of the data. Also, the 1696 census does not provide geographical data.

54 As a comparison, the French colony of Martinique in 1669, three times the size of Grenada and more developed, had a slave to white population of 60 to 40%; a male to female population of 39 to 28%; and the percentage of white children was almost equal (13.2%), but white women was only 7%. The French colony of St. Christopher, about half the size of Grenada, had a slave to white population of 59 to 41%; a male to female population of 40 to 29%, and the percentage of white children was almost equal (15%), but white women was only 7% in 1671.

55 Cole, *Colbert and a Century of French Mercantilism*, 2: 41.

56 This area was most assuredly due to the recent settlement of colonists and new land grants. Under de Sérillac there were only two quartiers which were increased to four, Palmistes being one of the new ones. In 1664 Dutertre reports that some "60 or 80 inhabitants of Guadeloupe and Martinique" arrived in Grenada with de Tracy. "He distributed land to the colonists who had accompanied him, of which the greatest part was communal land" most probably in the newly established quartiers of Beau Séjour and Palmistes. See Dutertre, *Histoire général*, 2: 87-88. Ten heads of household listed on the 1669 census, representing just over 10 percent, were listed on the 1664 census of Martinique.

57 The area, because of its flat and dry climate, has traditionally been used to raise livestock.

58 FR ANOM, COL C8A 1, Colbert to de Baas, 12 June 1669.

59 FR ANOM, COL C8A 1, Colbert to de Baas, 15 September 1669.

60 FR ANOM, COL C8A 1, de Baas to Colbert, 26 December 1669.

61 FR ANOM COL G1 498 N° 28, 22 October 1669, and C10A 1, 5 November 1669.

62 One other possible Jewish resident was Abraham Dodeman. Cole adds that the population issue was so important to Colbert that he insisted, despite protests, that Jews "must not be driven out" because they "had made considerable investments in the islands and were improving the cultivation of the land." Cole, *Colbert and a Century of French Mercantilism*, 2: 42.

63 Eric Williams, *From Columbus to Castro*, 114.

64 Jacques Petitjean-Roget and Eugène Bruneau-Latouche, *Personnes et familles à la Martinique au XVIIe siècle* ([Fort-de-France]; [Montreuil]: Désormeaux, 2000), 2: 481.

65 Dutertre, *Histoire générale*, 3: 87-88.

66 Many influential people like de Tracy and Colbert believed that Grenada had much potential.

67 R. C. Batie, "A Comparative Economic History of the Spanish, French and English on the Caribbean Islands During the Seventeenth Century" (Ph.D. dissertation, University of Washington, 1972), 194; Munford, *The Black Ordeal of Slavery*, 2: 513.

68 Mims, *West India Policy*, 31.

69 Mims, *West India Policy*, 32.

70 FR ANOM COL C10A 1, 5 November 1669.

71 Savary, *Le parfait négociant*, 2: 256.

72 FR ANOM COL C8A 1 F° 167, 1672.

73 Boucher, *Cannibal Encounters*, 77.

74 Pritchard, *In Search of Empire*, 281.

75 Boucher, *Cannibal Encounters*, 86.

76 Boucher, *Cannibal Encounters*, 86.

77 Boucher, *Cannibal Encounters*, 87; and FR ANOM COL C8A 2 F° 104.

78 Boucher, *Cannibal Encounters*, 87.

[79] Memoire jour d'huy, 27 août 1679, L'assembée faite au Cul-de-sac du Marin de cette isle Martinique par ordre de M. comte de Blénac....

[80] Boucher, *Cannibal Encounters*, 88.

[81] Archives Nationales. *Guide des sources de l'histoire de l'Amérique Latine et des Antilles dans les Archives Françoise* (Paris: Archives Nationales, 1984), 630. FR ANOM COL C8A 1 F° 107, 29 March 1671. Pierre Hincelin, king's lieutenant at Guadeloupe, was appointed to replace de Canchy, but there is no evidence that he actually took up the position before de Canchy returned in December 1671.

[82] FR ANOM COL E 61, 1673.

[83] FR ANOM COL B6 F° 146 v°, 30 May 1675.

[84] Henri Malo, "Prise et reprise de la Grenade, mars 1674," *Fueilles d'histoire du XVIIe au XXe*, 3, 5 (1911), 102-103.

[85] Pritchard, *In Search of Empire*, 282; Malo, "Prise et Reprise," 103; FR ANOM COL C8A 1 F° 322, 26 December 1674.

[86] Prichard, *In Search of Empire*, 103; FR ANOM COL C8A 1 F° 316, 20 January 1675.

[87] Malo, "Prise et reprise," 104.

[88] Malo, "Prise et reprise," 103-104.

[89] Malo, "Prise et reprise," 103-104; the area is presently called Grand Mal.

[90] Malo, "Prise et reprise," 106.

[91] Malo, "Prise et reprise," 108.

[92] Pricthard, *In Search of Empire*, 282.

[93] Boucher, *France and the American Tropics*, 197.

[94] Boucher, *France and the American Tropics*, 198.

[95] Boucher, *France and the American Tropics*, 199.

[96] Pierre de Vaissière, "Origines de la colonisation et la formation de la société Française a Saint-Domingue," *Revue des Questions Historique*, 79 (April 1906), 358.

[97] Malo, "Prise et reprise," 109; Pritchard, *In Search of Empire*, 304.

[98] Munford, *The Black Ordeal of Slavery*, 3: 769.

[99] FR ANOM COL C8A 4 F° 249: 486, 15 May 1687.

[100] Malo, "Prise et reprise," 109-10.

[101] Munford, *The Black Ordeal of Slavery*, 2: 769.

[102] FR ANOM COL C8A 5 F° 88: 158, 24 June 1688.

[103] FR ANOM COL B13 F° 90, 18 May 1689.

[104] Munford, *The Black Ordeal of Slavery*, 2: 768.

[105] Dessalles, *Histoire générale des Antilles*, 381-382

[106] Watts, *The West Indies*, 241.

[107] Watts, *The West Indies*, 241.

[108] FR ANOM COL C8A 9 F° 209.

[109] Pricthard, *In Search of Empire*, 328.

[110] Dutertre, *Histoire générale*, 3: 88.

[111] Pricthard, *In Search of Empire*, 59.

[112] FR ANOM COL C8A 1, Colbert to de Baas, 15 September 1669.

[113] Boucher, *Cannibal Encounters*, 74.

[114] Arthur P. Newton, *The European Nations in the West Indies, 1493-1688* (London: A&C Black, Ltd., 1933), 235, 317.

[115] Boucher, *France and the American Tropics*, 195.

[116] Mims, *West India Policy*, 192.

[117] Mims, *West India Policy*, 193.

[118] Newton, *European Nations*, 235, 317.

[119] "Memoire de S. Chambré pour les entreprises a faire a St. Domingue, Portobelo et Panama et les advantages d'un etablissement solids a la Grenade pour faciliter les

343

entreprises sur la terre firme." FR ANOM COL C10A, 1675.

120 "Mémoire concernant le commerce que peuvent faire les Français habitans de l'îsle de la Grenade en la terre ferme de l'Amérique en la rivière appelée par les Français Ouarabiche ou autrement dicte Monopado," FR ANOM COL C8A 1 F° 88, 20 November 1670.

121 FR ANOM COL C8A 1 F° 88, 20 November 1670.

122 FR ANOM COL C10A, 1675.

123 FR ANOM COL C10A, 1675.

124 Pricthard, *In Search of Empire*, 204.

125 Jean de La Mousse, *Les indiens de la Sinnamary: Journal du père Jean de La Mousse en Guyane, 1684-1691* (Paris: Chandeigne, 2006), 158.

126 FR ANOM COL C8A 6 F° 324: 601, 16 February 1691.

127 Abbe Raynal, *A Philosophical and Political History of the Settlements and Trade of the Europeans in the East and West Indies*, 5 vols., 70.

128 FR ANOM COL C8B 2 N° 73: 384, 1704.

129 FR ANOM COL C8B 2 N° 81: 450, 1705.

130 Pricthard, *In Search of Empire*, 367.

131 Boucher, *Cannibal Encounters*, 103.

132 FR ANOM COL C8B 3 N° 42: 355-360.

133 FR ANOM COL C8B 3 N° 42: 355-360, 8 March 1713; Pritchard, *In Search of Empire*, 59.

Notes to Chapter 7: Peopling Grenada's Slave Society

1 FR ANOM COL C8A 1, de Baas to Colbert, 26 decembre 1669.

2 Cole, *Colbert and a Century of French Mercantilism*, 2: 41.

3 According to Boucher, *France and the American Tropics*, 248: in the 17th century the British sent over 400,000 migrants to the Americas while the French sent less than 100,000 in the 17th and 18th centuries.

4 A. J. Pelletier, "Canadian Censuses of the 17th Century," *Papers and Proceedings of the Annual Meeting of the Canadian Political Science Association*, 2 (1931: 20-34), 21.

5 Boucher, *France and the American Tropics*, 237.

6 FR ANOM COL C10A 1, 1678.

7 Jean de la Mousse, *Les Indiens de la Sinnamaty: Journal du Père Jean de la Mousse en Guyane, 1684-1691* (Paris: Chandeigne, 2006), 160. Dessales, *Histoire générale de Antilles*, 2: 453, records nine Caribs as "slaves" in a footnote to the 1687 census data for the French Antilles, but uses "indentured" for a 2nd group of Caribs not free in the 1688 table.

8 Boucher, *Cannibal Encounters*, 40.

9 De la Mouse, *Les Indiens de la Sinnamaty*, 160.

10 Labat quoted in Devas, *Island of Grenada*, 64.

11 Labat quoted in Devas, *Island of Grenada*, 64.

12 FR ANOM COL C10A 1, No. 98, 3 September 1705; see Hulme & Whitehead, *Wild Majesty*, 174-177.

13 See Chapter 12 for the legacy of the Island Caribs in Grenada.

14 Éric Saugera, *Bordeaux, port négrier: chronologie, économie, idéologie, XVIIe-XIXe siècles* (Paris: Karthala, 2002), 39; Anonymous, *Histoire de l'isle de la Grenade*, 151-152.

15 Voyages Database. 2009. *Voyages: The Trans-Atlantic Slave Trade Database*. http://www.slavevoyages.org (accessed August 15, 2010).

16 Voyages Database. 2009. *Voyages: The Trans-Atlantic Slave Trade Database*. http://www.

slavevoyages.org (accessed August 15, 2010).

[17] FR ANOM COL C¹⁰ᴬ 1, 22 March 1670.

[18] Mims, *West India Policy*, 196-197.

[19] FR ANOM COL C8ᴬ 1 F° 279, 8 June 1674; Munford, *Black Ordeal of Slavery*, 2: 474.

[20] Munford, *Black Ordeal of Slavery*, 2: 382.

[21] Munford, *Black Ordeal of Slavery*, 2: 382.

[22] Munford, *Black Ordeal of Slavery*, 2: 478.

[23] Munford, *Black Ordeal of Slavery*, 2: 443.

[24] Malo, "Prise et reprise," 109.

[25] Munford, *Black Ordeal of Slavery*, 2: 447.

[26] Pritchard, *In Search of Empire*, 219.

[27] Adrien Dessalles, *Histoire générale des Antilles*, 348

[28] Scelle, *La traite négrière*, 2: 253.

[29] FR ANOM COL B 36 F° 304, 26 November 1714.

[30] FR ANOM COL C8ᴬ 17, 18 April 1709 in Munford, *Black Ordeal of Slavery*, 2: 485.

[31] Gwendolyn Midlo Hall, *Africans in Colonial Louisiana: The Development of Afro-Creole Culture in the Eighteenth Century* (Baton Rouge: Louisiana State University Press, 1992), 58.

[32] Hall, *Africans in Colonial Louisiana*, 62.

[33] Hall, *Africans in Colonial Louisiana*, 58-59.

[34] Hall, *Africans in Colonial Louisiana*, 64.

[35] Hall, *Africans in Colonial Louisiana*, 64, 69-70, 71.

[36] Jean Mettas, *Répertoire des expéditions négrières Françaises au xviiie siècle* (Paris: Société Française d'Histoire d'Outre-Mer, 1978), 1: 2.

[37] Hall, *Africans in Colonial Louisiana*, 160.

[38] David Eltis and David Richardson, "A New Assessment of the Transatlantic Slave Trade," in *Extending the Frontiers: Essays on the New Transatlantic Slave Trade Database*, eds., David Eltis and David Richardson (New Haven: Yale University, 2008): 51.

[39] Boucher, *France and the American Tropics*, 222.

[40] Munford, *Black Ordeal of Slavery*, 2: 382; see also FR ANOM COL C8ᴬ 15 F° 39, 18 August 1703, F° 339, 2 October 1704, and F° 425, 24 October 1705.

[41] One of the slave traders was René Bertrand de La Clauserie, a member of one of France's richest families involved in the slave trade, who was bringing slaves to Grenada as early as 1756. René Montaudouin has been associated with slave trade to Grenada since the early 1700s.

[42] Eltis, et al., "A New Assessment of the Transatlantic Slave Trade," 51.

[43] Gonzalez, Javier A. "'A Strange Discordant Mass of Heterogeneous Animals': The Role of Ethnic Divisions in British Grenada, 1763-1779." (Thesis (B.A.), Harvard University, Boston, MA), 25-26.

[44] See Voyages Database. 2009. *Voyages: The Trans-Atlantic Slave Trade Database*. http://www .slavevoyages.org (accessed August 15, 2010).

[45] Anonymous, *Histoire de l'isle de la Grenade*, 145, 157, 183.

[46] Anonymous, *Histoire de l'isle de la Grenade*, 118. Dutertre (*Histoire générale*, 1: 431) contradicts the Anonymous author when he writes that the poison was brought to Le Fort by "a Savage who was in his service."

[47] Dutertre, *Histoire générale*, 1: 508; Anonymous, *Histoire de l'isle de la Grenade*, 228.

[48] The Anonymous author (*Histoire de l'isle de la Grenade*, 160), records that Governor de Valminière offered compensation in goods worth about "500 *livres* for what was worth more than 4,000."

[49] Watts, *The West Indies*, 238.

[50] The French patois expression is derived from *Bois Nègre marron* meaning "Black maroon

woods," i.e. place where runaway slaves/maroons found refuge in the mountains.

[51] Munford, *Black Ordeal of Slavery*, 3: 934.

[52] The common term maroon is derived from the American Spanish *cimarrón* (<Sp. *cimarra*: "wild place"), with its reference to domesticated animals taking to the wild. The term was first applied to the escaped Amerindian captives in Hispaniola and by the 1530s to escaped African slaves. Runaway slaves throughout the region were thence referred to as maroons, with implications of "fierceness," "wild," and "unbroken."

[53] FR ANOM COL C^{10A} 1, 1732, or FR ANOM F134, 21 Lettre de Larnage du 23 mai 1732. It records that between 1702 and 1732 93 slaves escaped to Margarita.

[54] Neville A.T. Hall, "Maritime Maroons: *Grand Marronage* from the Danish West Indies," *William and Mary Quarterly*, 62, 4 (3rd Series, October 1985: 476-468), 482.

[55] FR ANOM COL C^{8B} 7 N° 115, 18 November 1721.

[56] Pritchard, *In Search of Empire*, 60.

[57] FR ANOM COL C^{8B} 7 N° 115, 18 November 1721.

[58] FR ANOM COL C^{8B} 8 N° 10, 30 January 1722.

[59] FR ANOM COL C^{8B} 8 N° 63, 12 June 1722.

[60] Between 1702 and 1732, 93 slaves were recorded by name as leaving Grenada for Margarita per F134/31 Lettre de Larnage du 23 mai 1732.

[61] Watts, *The West Indies*, 171.

[62] Hall, *Africans in Colonial Louisiana*, 64.

[63] Gabriel Debien, "Marronage in the French Caribbean" in *Maroon Societies: Rebel Slave Communities in the Americas*, ed., Richard Price (Baltimore: Johns Hopkins Press, 1979), 110.

[64] Dessalles, *Annales*, 1: 510-512.

[65] Debien, "Marronage in the French Caribbean," 109.

[66] FR ANOM COL C^{8A} 34 F° 354, 25 August 1725; C^{8A} 35 F° 197, 9 July 1726.

[67] Dessalles, *Annales*, 1: 512.

[68] Munford, *Black Ordeal of Slavery*, 3: 904.

[69] Dessalles, *Annales*, 1: 513-514.

[70] FR ANOM COL C^{8A} 53 F° 57, 22 mai 1741; C^{8A} 54 F° 13, 3 March 1742.

[71] FR ANOM COL C^{8A} 55 F° 11, no. 9 - 7 February 1743.

[72] There are still places in the interior of Grenada associated with the name Bwa Neg Marron, a reference to its occupation by runaway slaves as maroon camps. One such place name exists in the hills of Concord, St. John.

[73] FR ANOM COL C^{8A} 1, de Baas to Colbert, 26 December 1669.

[74] FR ANOM (Série B) Registres 1 à 37 (1654-1715), 1707 F° 451.

[75] FR ANOM COL C^{8B} 2 (1690-1709), 89-1708.

[76] The decreasing white population was a reoccurring feature of Caribbean plantation society following the establishment of large sugar plantations which were responsible for the decrease of the small, white, peasant farmer.

[77] There is most probably a direct correlation between the decreasing white female population and the increasing free (and enslaved) mixed-race population after the 1740s, due to consensual and nonconsensual (rape) sexual relationships between female slaves and free non-whites on the one hand and white men on the other.

[78] Labat quoted in Devas, *Island of Grenada*, 38.

[79] Dutertre quoted in Anonymous, *Histoire de l'isle de la Grenade*, 222.

[80] Dutertre, *Histoire générale*, 1: 45.

[81] Anonymous, *Histoire de l'isle de la Grenade*, 80.

[82] FR ANOM SOM, G^1 498, N° 28-53.

[83] FR ANOM COL C^{10A} 1, 2 April 1680.

[84] Jacques Petitjean Roget, "Les femmes des colons à la Martinique au XVIe et XVIIe siècle," *Revue d'histoire de l'Amérique française*, 9, no. 2 (1955): 211.

[85] Devas, *History of the Island of Grenada*, 66.

[86] FR ANOM COL C⁸ᴮ 5 N° 79, 30 November 1718.

[87] Georg Bernhard Depping, *Correspondance administrative sous le règne de Louis xiv...* (Paris : Imprimerie Nationale), 3: 664-665.

[88] Malo, "Prise et reprise," 109-110.

[89] Pritchard, *In Search of Empire*, 20.

[90] Pritchard, *In Search of Empire*, 20.

[91] FR ANOM COL C8ᴬ-6 - 1691 Fᵒ 300/324

[92] Christian Huetz de Lemps, "Indentured Servants Bound for the French Antilles in the 17th and 18th centuries," in *"To Make America": European Emigration in the Early Modern Period* (eds. by Ida Altman & James Horn. Berkeley: Univ. of California Press, 1991), 199.

[93] *Gens de couleur libre*, though originally applied to people of mixed racial heritage, is used here not only to refer to free coloureds but also free blacks who formed the free non-white group. The term *affranchise*, meaning "freeman," is also used to refer to both free blacks and mixed race.

[94] The term mulatto, now regarded as derogatory, is commonly accepted as deriving from the Spanish *mulatto* (<Am. Sp. 'young mule'; but may have derived originally from Sp. <Arabic *muwallad*: 'person of mixed race'). It gained prominence because of the prevailing belief that like the mule–the offspring of a donkey and a horse–the offspring of two different races, the mulatto, was a hybrid and therefore sterile. The mule's so-called lack of intelligence was also associated with the mulatto.

[95] Munford, *Black Ordeal of Slavery*, 3: 716.

[96] The 1683 figure appears inadequate. Clarence Munford (3: 723) characterized it as having "gaping holes" with regard to the count for many of the other islands. An important issue has to be addressed here which is who fell under the mulatto/free coloured grouping. Though these terms often referred to people of mixed racial heritage, blacks exhibiting 100 percent African racial heritage were often included in the general count because they both shared similar legal status, but socially the possession of a partial white racial heritage and physical manifestations–fair or white skin color, "straight" facial features and "straight" hair–often meant increased social prestige.

[97] Though their impact on the plantation society in French Grenada was minor, their large numbers under the British created some interesting social, economic and political dynamics that continued throughout slavery.

[98] Except Lorna McDaniels, "The Philips: A 'Free Mulatto' Family of Grenada," *Journal of Caribbean History*, 24, 2 (Nov. 1990): 178-194.

[99] See McDaniels, "The Philips"; Curtis Jacobs, "The Fédons of Grenada, 1763-1814" (http://www.cavehill.uwi.edu/ BNCCde/grenada/conference/papers/jacobsc.html), and Pierre Boulle, *Race et esclavage dans la France de l'Ancien Régime* (Perrin, 2007), 157, 183, 188.

[100] Francis MacMahon, *A Narrative of the Insurrection in the Island of Grenada, in the Year 1795* (Printed by J. Spahn, 1823), 26. The family name is still apparent in place names like Clozier, St. John and Chantemel, St. Patrick, places where the family owned plantations.

[101] In his will, Clozier Decoteaux left "to my freed woman Labeth 4,000 *livres* to be paid into any installments from the day of my decrease." In 1815, one of his sons, Francis Malhereux Decoteaux, requested of the British colonial government to be granted the slaves left by his father to Euphemie de la Perouse, a free black woman, and her five children. The "De Coteau" family name is still quite visible in Grenada.

Notes to Chapter 8: Production in Grenada's Slave Society

[1] Pricthard, *In Search of Empire*, 59-60.

[2] Arthur M. Wilson, *French Foreign Policy During the Administration of Cardinal Fleury, 1726-1743: A study in Diplomacy and Commercial Development* (Cambridge: Harvard University Press, 1936), 303.

[3] Richard Sheridan, *Sugar and Slavery: An Economic History of the British West Indies, 1623-1775* (Baltimore: The Johns Hopkins University Press, 1973), 417.

[4] Boucher, *Cannibal Encounters*, 31.

[5] Batie, "Why sugar…?," 51.

[6] Boucher, *Cannibal Encounters*, 31.

[7] Kenneth R. Andrews, *The Spanish Caribbean: Trade and Plunder, 1530-1630*, (New Haven: Yale University Press, 1978), 241.

[8] Dutretre, *Histoire générale*, 1: 425.

[9] Dutertre, *Histoire générale*, 1: 427.

[10] Watts, *West Indies*, 156.

[11] The initial French settlement on the banks of the lagoon in the area known today as the Ballast Ground was probably not heavily wooded and afforded easy clearing. Much of their early cultivation seemed to be in the area of the Ballast Ground and on le Morne de la Monnoye or Morne des Pendus, the hill on which once stood Monckton Redoubt, the Hotel Santa Maria/Islander Hotel/Butler House.

[12] Watts, *West Indies*, 156. Though much of the Caribbean tobacco production was by small farmers using little if any additional labor, there were some planters, because of their greater wealth who could afford to hire *engagés* or other white laborers, or own slaves, and cultivated a greater number of acres than the average one or two.

[13] In the first decade of the settlement of Grenada available land was constrained by the deadly attacks by the Island Caribs whose actions forced the settlers to farm together to be able to defend themselves.

[14] R. C. Batie, "A Comparative Economic History of the Spanish, French and English on the Caribbean Islands During the Seventeenth Century" (Ph.D. dissertation, University of Washington, 1972), 61.

[15] Batie, "A Comparative Economic History," 62.

[16] The Anonymous author talks of "the negroes and *engagés* [who] came back from the woods loaded with roole sticks to be sent to Martinique." See Anonymous, *L'Histoire de l'Isle de la Grenade*, 124.

[17] See footnote no. 16 above.

[18] Jacques Savary. *Le parfait négociant ou instruction général pour ce qui regarde le commerce de route sorte de merchandises, tout de France, que des pays estrangers …* Geneve: Chez J.H. Widerhold, 1675), 2: 256.

[19] Labat, *Nouveau voyages*, 3: 293.

[20] Watts, *West Indies*, 225.

[21] Mims, *Colbert's West India Policy*, 253.

[22] Mims, *Colbert's West India Policy*, 259.

[23] The majority of free holders, 89 percent, owned no slaves, *engagés*, or livestock and therefore had no resources to switch to other more lucrative crops. Only 11 percent of the free holders owned property, but those who owned greater than six slaves were only 28 percent.

[24] Batie, "Comparative Economic History," 78.

[25] Mims, *Colbert's West India Policy*, 269. It would be almost 200 years before nutmeg would become an economic crop in Grenada.

[26] Pricthard, *In Search of Empire*, 124.

[27] Batie, "Comparative Economic History," 77.

[28] César de Rochefort, *Histoire naturelle et morale des iles Antilles de l'Amérique*, (Rotterdam: R. Leers, 1681), 23.

[29] FR ANOM COL C^{10A} 2 , 18 July 1752. One quinteaux equals 48.95 kilograms.

[30] Louis Philippe May, *Histoire économique de la Martinique* (Paris: Librarie des Sciences Politiques et Sociales, 1930), 103.

[31] May, *Histoire économique de la Martinique*, 104.

[32] FR ANOM COL C^{8A} 5 F^o 22, 1688.

[33] Pritchard, *In Search of Empire*, 126.

[34] Batie, "Comparative Economic History," 72.

[35] Watts, *West Indies*, 159.

[36] Though *Indigofera suffriticosa* was native to the region, it was the Asian species which was cultivated.

[37] Batie, "Comparative Economic History," 70.

[38] Ratooning is a practice of allowing a second crop to grow from the previous crop's shoots. It is more commonly known in sugar cane cultivation because of the widespread practice in the eighteenth and nineteenth centuries.

[39] Batie, "Comparative Economic History," 70.

[40] Labat gives the dimensions of the vat as 20lX12-15hX3-4w in Batie, "Comparative Economic History," 70.

[41] Batie, "Comparative Economic History," 70.

[42] Batie, "Comparative Economic History," 70.

[43] Dutertre, *Histoire générale*, 2: 103.

[44] Dutertre, *Histoire générale*, 2: 103-104.

[45] The boucan used to dry coffee and cocoa later on were probably modeled on the drying houses for indigo which comprised an open shed with wheeled trays to afford easy access to and from the sun.

[46] Anonymous, *Histoire de l'isle de Grenade*, 226.

[47] Battie, "Comparative Economic History," 71.

[48] Batie, "Comparative Economic History," 71.

[49] Dutertre, *Histoire générale*, 2: 104.

[50] Indigo could be cultivated with a labor/land ratio of one slave per acre.

[51] Pritchard, *In Search of Empire*, 59.

[52] *Indigoterie* translates as indigo processing plant and is taken here as plantation though there may have been plantations without processing facilities.

[53] FR ANOM COL C^{10A} 2, 1761.

[54] The causes of the 19th century demise of indigo production, its death knoll, was, according to Bryan Edwards, due to the death of slaves from "vapors, ravages of the worm and the burdens of the duties imposed by the government." J. B. Dutertre did comment that bad odors from the processing of the plant caused the death of both French and slaves.

[55] Jacques Savary des Brûlons and Philémon-Louis Savary, *Dictionnaire universel de commerce: D'histoire naturelle, & des arts & métiers* (Copenhagen: chez les frères Cl. & Ant. Philibert, 1765), 5: 139.

[56] Bryan Edwrds, *The History Civil and Commercial of the British West Indies* (London, 1793), 1: 362.

[57] Hilary Beckles, 27. In 1687 Grenada had four sugar plantations.

[58] Batie, "Comparative Economic History," 73.

[59] Batie, "Comparative Economic History," 73; St. John's Time is 24 June.

[60] Batie, "Comparative Economic History," 73.

[61] Batie, "Comparative Economic History," 73.

[62] Batie, "Comparative Economic History," 74.

[63] Labat, *Nouveau voyages*, 3: 293.

[64] Purseglove, *Tropical Crops*, 344.

[65] Ideal conditions included rainfall of 40-60 in. and lots of sunlight. Purseglove, *Tropical Crops*, 348.

[66] Labat, *Nouveau voyages*, 3: 293.

[67] TNA: PRO T 1/423/277-278, "The amount of the produce of the island of Grenada exported in the year 1762," 19 January 1763. This probably does not account for all of the cotton produced in 1762 because the French continued to ship their produce to Martinique and the other French islands.

[68] Figures for 1764 are from Brizan, *Island of Conflict*, 42.

[69] See Mark S. Quintanilla, "The World of Alexander Campbell: An 18th Century Grenadian Planter," *Albion*, 35, 2 (2003): 229-256.

[70] Though the spelling "cacao" is usually used for the plant and its products, and "cocoa" used for manufactured products, I, like Purseglove, will use "cocoa" throughout.

[71] See Louis-Philippe May, *Histoire économique de la Martinique, 1635-1763* (Paris: Librarie des Sciences Politiques et Sociales, 1930), 95 for the history of cocoa's introduction into Martinique.

[72] The 1714 date had been incorrectly implied from Guillaume-Thomas Raynal, *Histoire Philosophique et Politique des Establissemens et du Commerce des Européens dans les Deux Indes* (Paris, 1781), 392 by Edward Drayton, *The Grenada Handbook, Directory and Almanac for the Year 1897* (London: Sampson Low, Marston and Company, 1897), 24.

[73] Ideal conditions for growing cocoa are elevations under 1,000 ft., 70-90° F with small seasonal and diurnal range, 40-100 inches of rainfall. See Purseglove, *Tropical Crops*, 57.

[74] Charles de Rochefort, *Histoire naturelle et morale des iles Antilles de l'Amerique*, 2: 38.

[75] May, *Histoire économique de la Martinique*, 95.

[76] Robin Dand, *The International Cocoa Trade*, 2nd edition (New York: Woodhead Publishing, 1999), 6.

[77] Dand, *The International Cocoa Trade*, 6.

[78] Paterson, *A Topographical Description of the Island of Grenada*, (London, 1780), 5.

[79] W. G. Clarence-Smith, *Cocoa and Chocolate, 1765-1914* (New York: Psychology Press, 2000), 174.

[80] According to C. Williams and F. James, "Comparative Epidemiology Study: Grenada," 93 (in *Disease Management in Cocoa: Comparative Epidemiology of Witches' Broom*, ed. S. A. Rudgard, A. C. Maddison and T. Andebrhan, London: Chapman & Hall, 1993), "The first record of cocoa being exported from Grenada was in 1763, when there were nearly 300 hectares [741 acres] of land under cocoa cultivation."

[81] Williams and James, "Comparative Epidemiology Study: Grenada," 93.

[82] TNA: PRO T 1/423/277-278, "The amount of the produce of the island of Grenada exported in the year 1762," 19 January 1763. This probably does not account for all of the cocoa produced in 1762 because the French continued to ship some of their produce to Martinique and the other French islands.

[83] Lowell J. Ragatz, *Statistics for the Study of British Caribbean Economic History, 1763-1833* (The Bryan Edwards press, 1927), 15.

[84] See George Brizan's *Island of Conflict* for a history of cocoa production in Grenada.

[85] Purseglove, *Tropical Crops*, 460.

[86] Michel-Rolph Trouillot, *Peasants and Capital: Dominica in the World Economy* (Baltimore: Johns Hopkins University Press, 1983), 143.

[87] With coffee requiring 3-4 years to bear its first fruits and 7-9 before full production, it would appear from the cultivation data, that it was introduced in Grenada around 1725.

[88] Trouillot, "Coffee Planters and Coffee in the Antilles," 124.

89 Trouillot, "Coffee Planters and Coffee in the Antilles," 124-125.

90 Trouillot, "Coffee Planters and Coffee in the Antilles," 128.

91 Munford, *Black Ordeal of Slavery*, 2: 513.

92 Watts, *West Indies*, 228-229.

93 Watts, *West Indies*, 238.

94 Watts, *West Indies*, 178-184.

95 Daniel Paterson, *A Topographical Description of the Island of Grenada*, 3.

96 Munford, *Black Ordeal of Slavery*, 2: 512.

97 Dutertre, *Histoire générale*, 2: 87-88.

98 It is also possible that predomantly former *engagés* arrived in Grenada seeking land grants, thus creating a large group of small, poor farmers without resources to develop the island.

99 A *quarré* or *carré* is equal to 3.2 acres.

100 FR ANOM, C10A 1, 1723.

101 Watts, *West Indies*, 297. As early as 1714 Governor de Maupeou complained that the size of concessions were too large and needed to be reduced (FR ANOM B 36 F 528, 23 August 1714). In 1718 and 1719 administrators in Grenada threatened to uphold the laws and confiscate concessions not cleared and return them to the *domaine du roi* so new concessions would be granted to attract new settlers; see FR ANOM C8B 5 N 79, 30 November 1718, C8A 26 F° 60, 20 June 1719; C8A 26 F° 77, 23 June 1719.

102 FR ANOM COL C10A 1, 1723.

103 Munford, *Black Ordeal of Slavery*, 2: 382.

104 Watts, *West Indies*, 238.

105 Munford, *The Black Ordeal of Slavery*, 2: 505.

106 Watts, *West Indies*, 238.

107 Watts, *West Indies*, 308-325.

108 The export data are from trade primarily between Grenada and France. It does not include the trade to the Spanish Main or the illegal trade with the British colonies, etc.

109 Stein, *The French Sugar Business*, 67.

110 Stein, *The French Sugar Business*, 68.

111 Williams, *From Columbus to Castro*, 130.

112 TNA: PRO T 1/423/277-278, "The amount of the produce of the island of Grenada exported in the year 1762," 19 January 1763. This probably does not account for all of the sugar produced between 1762 and 1765 because the French continued to ship their produce to Martinique and the other French islands.

113 British Library, Add. Mss. 38,202, f. 374.

114 Crouse, *French Pioneers*, 48-51.

115 Labat, *Nouveau voyage*, 3: 35

116 Anonymous, *L'Histoire de l'isle de la Grenade*, 57.

117 Anonymous, *L'Histoire de l'isle de la Grenade*, 57.

118 Boucher, *Cannibal Encounters*, 31.

119 Dutretre, *Histoire générale*, 1: 509.

120 Anonymous, *L'Histoire de l'isle de la Grenade*, 228-229.

121 Anonymous, *L'Histoire de l'isle de la Grenade*, 99-100.

122 Anonymous, *L'Histoire de l'isle de la Grenade*, 100.

123 It was common for the colonists to be attacked by the Island Caribs while out hunting. Sometimes the Island Caribs would set deliberate traps to catch the colonists like the rouse where a pig was allowed to run in view of the colonists who ran after it and were then killed by the Island Caribs. See Anonymous, *Histoire de l'isle de la Grenade*, 62-63.

124 Devas, *Island of Grenada*, 58.

125 Devas, *Island of Grenada*, 59.

126 Raynal, *Histoire Philosophique et Politique*, 5: 70

127 Watts, *The West Indies*, 57.

128 Munford, *The Ordeal of Black Slavery*, 3: 624.

129 Dutretre, *Histoire générale*, 3: 96.

130 Dutretre, *Histoire générale*, 3: 96.

131 Horses especially were in great demand in Europe because they were needed by the military and their exportation was often restricted or forbidden at various times.

132 Watts, *West Indies*, 197.

133 Watts, *West Indies*, 163.

134 The *Isle à Cochon* or Hog Island, located in the south just west of Calivigny, may have received its name because of the presence of wild hogs on the island or as a breeding place for hogs.

Notes to Chapter 9: Plantation Society

1 James Prichard, "Population in French America, 1670-1730: Demographic Context of Colonial Louisiana," in *French Colonial Louisiana and the Atlantic World*, ed. by Bradley G. Bond (Baton Rouge: Louisiana State University Press, 2005), 190.

2 Abbé Raynal, *A Philosophical and Political History of the Settlements and Trade of the Europeans in the East and West Indies* (Dublin: John Exshaw, 1784. 6 vols.), 5: 84-85.

3 Richard Sheridan, "The Development of the Plantation to 1750," 25.

4 Lowell Ragatz, *Fall of the Planter Class in the British Caribbean, 1763-1833: A Study in Social and Economic History* (New York: The Century Co. 1928), 3.

5 Ragatz, *Fall of the Planter Class*, 4.

6 Ragatz, *Fall of the Planter Class*, 4.

7 Data for this graph are taken from the *Extract From the Capitation Rolls* which identify most of the slave ownership based on type of crops produced. Some of the names were cross checked with *A Topographical Description of the Island of Grenada* to make as accurate and complete listing of all entries.

8 Jean-Baptiste-Pierre Le Romain, "Negroes," in *Encyclopédie ou dictionnaire raisonné des sciences, des arts et des métiers* by Denis Diderot and Jean le Rond d'Alembert (Paris, 1751-72), 2: 79-80.

9 Le Romain, "Negroes," 2: 79-80.

10 Le Romain, "Negroes," 2: 79-80.

11 FR ANOM COL C8A 37 F° 73, 20 April 1727.

12 FR ANOM DPPC G1 498, 1669/1755.

13 Matthew Mulcahy, *Hurricanes and Society in the British Greater Caribbean, 1624-1783* (Baltimore: JHU Press, 2005), 86.

14 FR ANOM COL C8A 42 F° 261, 9 September 1731.

15 FR ANOM COL C8A 42 F° 261, 9 September 1731.

16 Pritchard, *In Search of Empire*, 77.

17 Labat, *Nouveau voyage*, 6: 295.

18 FR ANOM COL C8B 2 N° 80, 31 March 1705.

19 Colin Chisholm, *An Essay on the Malignant Pestilential Fever Introduced into the West Indian Islands from Boullam, on the Coast of Guinea, as it Appeared in 1793 and 1794* (Philadelphia, 1799), 32-39.

20 FR ANOM COL B [35] Fo 528, 23 August 1714.

21 Sue Peabody, "A Dangerous Zeal: Catholic Missions to Slaves in the French Antilles,

1635-1800," *French Historical Studies*, 25, 1 (Winter 2002): 69.

[22] FR ANOM COL C8A 27 F° 25, 8 October 1720.

[23] FR ANOM COL C10A 1, 4 February 1700.

[24] Devas (*Conception Island*, 27) is somewhat misleading when he states that "The hospital, which seems to have been situated where the present cemetery lies, on top of the ridge (of Hospital Hill) above the Vicariate." The hospital was located on Hospital Hill, but further west than "above the Vicariate"; it overlooked what became known as Melville Street to its west and the St. John's River to its north.

[25] Labat, *Nouveau voyage*, 3: 287.

[26] Anonymous, *Histoire de l'isle de la Grenade*, 178.

[27] Prichard, *In Search of Empire*, 250.

[28] FR ANOM COL C8A 4 F° 249, 15 March 1687.

[29] FR ANOM COL C8A 5 F° 88, 24 June 1688.

[30] ANOM COL C8A 51 F° 394, 20 December 1740.

[31] FR ANOM COL C8A 1 F° 42, 3 March 1670; FR ANOM COL C8A 1 F° 279, 8 June 1674.

[32] FR ANOM COL C8B 3 N° 42, 8 March 1713.

[33] FR ANOM COL C8A 51 F° 158, 317-318, 20 June 1740.

[34] FR ANOM COL C8B 10 N° 88, October 1757.

[35] W. J. Eccles, *France in America*, 152.

[36] Dutertre, *Histoire générale*, 3: 512; David Bernard, *Le clergé: Dictionnaire biographique de la Martinique, 1635-1848* (Fort-de-France: Société d'histoire de la Martinique, 1984. 3 vols), 1: 81.

[37] Labat, *Nouveau voyage*, 1: 24.

[38] Raymund Devas, *Conception Island or The Troubled History of the Catholic Church in Grenada, BWI* (London: Sands & Co.), 11.

[39] Labat, *Nouveau voyage*, 1: 24.

[40] *Archivum Fratrum Praedicatorum*, 52: 329.

[41] Devas, *Conception Island*, 11-12.

[42] Bernard, *Le clergé*, 1: 163.

[43] Bernard, *Le clergé*, 1: 85.

[44] Jean de la Mousse and Gérard Collomb, *Les indiens de la Sinnamary: Journal du père Jean de La Mousse en Guyane, 1684-1691* (Editions Chandeigne, 2006), 159.

[45] Devas, *Conception Island*, 20-21. Devas adds that the church was constructed on land once owned by Labidade. His full name Dominique de la Bedade was first notary of the island who was exiled for his part in the trial and execution of du Bu in 1658.

[46] Devas, *Conception Island*, 21.

[47] FR ANOM COL C8A 6 F° 471, 29 October 1691.

[48] Labat, *Nouveau voyage*, 6: 293.

[49] FR ANOM COL C8A 15 F° 282, 19 October 1704.

[50] Munford, *The Black Ordeal of Slavery*, 3: 860.

[51] FR ANOM COL C8B 8 N° 102, 2 October 1722.

[52] FR ANOM COL C8A 19 F° 318, 21 February 1713.

[53] FR ANOM COL C8A 26 F° 60, 20 June 1719.

[54] Labat, *Nouveau voyage*, 6: 260.

[55] FR ANOM COL C8A 35 F° 161, 20 October 1726.

[56] FR ANOM COL C8A 55 F° 134, n° 91-15, December 1743. The northern half of the Quartier du Grand Marquis would have become the Quartier du Conférence with its own parish while the southern part would remain the Quartier du Grand Marquis with its parish center remaining at Grand Marquis.

[57] Peabody, "A Dangerous Zeal," 69.

58 *Le Code Noir ou recueil des reglements rendus jusqu'a present* (Paris: Prault, 1767) [1980 reprd. by the Societé, d'Histoire de la Guadeloupe], Trannslated by John Garrigus. Accessed 15 April 2012 at http://les.traitesnegrieres.free.fr/39_esclavage_code_noir_agl.html.

59 Munford, *The Black Ordeal of Slavery*, 3: 860.

60 Le Romain, "Negroes," 79-80.

61 Arnold Bertram, "Jamaican Higglers' Marketing System and the Future of Kingston, Part I," *The Gleaner*, Sunday 31 October 2010. Online edition; accessed 15 May 2011 at http://jamaica-gleaner.com/gleaner/20101031/focus/focus6 .html.

62 Le Romain, "Negroes," 11: 8-830.

63 Labat quoted in J. Gerstin, "Tangled Roots: Kalenda and Other Neo-African Dances in the Circum-Caribbean," *New West Indian Guide* 78, no. 1/2 (2004: 5-41), 7.

64 See Lorna McDaniel, *The Big Drum Ritual of Carriacou: Praisesongs for Re-memory of Flight* (Gainesville, Florida: University of Florida Press, 1998).

65 Prichard, *In Search of Empire*, 59-60.

66 Militia officers received renumerations in the form of exemptions from the capitation or head tax for some of their slaves. In 1722 the captain was exempted for 12 slaves, the lieutenant eight, and the ensign six.

67 FR ANOM COL C8A 1 F° 260, 8 February 1674.

68 FR ANOM COL C10A 1, January 1678; FR ANOM COL C10A 1, 10 February 1692.

69 FR ANOM COL C8B 2 F° 80, 31 March 1705.

70 Nicolas Binoist de Reteuil name sometimes appear as Binois. He replaced de Caylus in 1706 as chief engineer of the French Antilles, but in 1716 was appointed engineer and major at Grenada after taking up permanent residence there; he subsequently became king's lieutenant and died in Grenada in 1737.

71 Raynal, *Philosophical and Political History*, 5: 70.

72 Richard Pares, *War and Trade in the West Indies, 1739-1763* (New York: Frank Cass and Sons, 1963), 318.

73 Pares, *War and Trade*, 318.

74 Pares, *War and Trade*, 351.

75 Raynal, *Philosophical and Political History*, 5: 71.

Notes to Chapter 10: An Ending and a Beginning

1 Ellen H. Robbins, *Lord Macartney, Our First Ambassador to China* (London, 1908), 96.

2 Pointe des Cabrites: Goat Point, Morne des Pendus: future site of Monckton Redoubt, Morne de l'Hôpital: Hospital Hill, Richemont: future site of Fort Matthew; Morne Molière: Mount Cardigan, and Morne Latoniere: future site of Fort Adolphus.

3 Sir Julian Stafford Corbett, *England in the Seven Years' War: A Study in Combined Strategy* (London: Longmans, Green, 1907) 2: 177.

4 TNA: PRO CO 166/2/20 f. 78-79, 6 March 1762, Letter from [Brigadier General] Hunt[ington] Walsh in Grenada to Major General Monckton.

5 The ships were the *Vanguard* (70), *Temple* (70), *Devonshire* (64), *Modeste* (64), *Nottingham* (60), *Falkland* (50) and *Rochester* (50), frigates *Repulse* (32), *Lizard* (28) and *Actaeon* (28); and bomb-ketches Grenada and Thunder.

6 Adrien Dessalles, *Histoire générale des Antilles* (Libraire-éditeur, 1848), 276-277.

7 TNA: PRO CO 166/2/20 f. 78-79, 6 March 1762, Letter from [Brigadier General] Hunt[ington] Walsh in Grenada to Major General Monckton.

8 Robert Beaston, *Naval and Military Memoirs of Great Britain, From 1727 to 1783* (London: Printed for Longman, Hurst, Rees and Orme, 1804) 2: 527.

[9] TNA: PRO CO 166/2/20 f. 78-79, 6 March 1762, Letter from [Brigadier General] Hunt[ington] Walsh in Grenada to Major General Monckton.

[10] TNA: PRO CO 166/2/19 f. 72-77, "Monckton, St. Peters, Martinique, to Egremont," 18 March 1762.

[11] TNA: PRO CO 166/2/19 f. 72-77, "Monckton, St. Peters, Martinique, to Egremont," 18 March 1762.

[12] In negotiations with the British, the governor and military officials at Martinique proposed to be taken to Grenada, the only French colony of note in the region not captured, but were informed that they would have to be sent to France since Grenada was at that moment blockaded.

[13] TNA: PRO CO 166/2/19 f. 72-77, "Monckton, St. Peters, Martinique, to Egremont," 18 March 1762; See also CO 166/2/8 f.24-32, 9 February 1762 and CO 166/2/10 f. 37-42, [1762]; and Beatson, *Naval and Military Memoirs of Great Britain*, 3: 368-79.

[14] D. L. Niddrie, "Eighteenth-Century Settlement in the British Caribbean," *Transactions of the British Institute of British Geographers*, 40 (December 1966), 76.

[15] See TNA: PRO CO 101/28/33, ff. 121-123, 12 April 1788, State of Grenada; TNA: PRO, CO 101/1 f.18-31, *Extracts From the Capitation Rolls for the Quarters of Basse Terre, Maigrin, Marquis, Sauteurs, Grand Pauvre and Goyave, Grenada, and the Island of Carioacou*. The census of the slaves was probably carried out in late 1762.

[16] It is often repeated that the white population in Grenada at this time was 3,500, a figure recorded by Lieutenant Governor Scott in communication in 1763 (CO 102/1, f. 132), but this number was almost three times the number of French resident on the island in 1763 per his own correspondence. See Tables A, B and C in Appendix III.

[17] William L. Grant, "Canada Versus Guadeloupe: An Episode of the Seven Years' War," *The American Historical Review*, 17, 4 (July 1912): 735-743.

[18] Julian Stafford Corbett, *England in the Seven Years' War: A Study in Combined Strategy* (Cambridge: Cambridge University Press, 2010. 2 vols). The Neutral Islands comprised St. Lucia, Dominica and St. Vincent, with the British retaining Dominica and St. Vincent, together with Tobago; St. Lucia was returned to the French.

[19] Lowell J. Ragatz, *The Fall of the Planter Class in the British Caribbean, 1763-1833* (New York: Octagon Books, 1971), 112.

[20] Pares, *War and Trade in the West Indies*, 226.

[21] Grenada became the seat of the Government of Grenada of the Southern Caribbe Islands which comprised the Neutral Islands and Tobago.

[22] John Campbell, *Candid and Impartial Considerations on the Nature of the Sugar Trade; the Comparative Importance of the British and French Islands in the West-Indies: with the Value and Consequences of St. Lucia and Granada, Truly Stated, London: Printed for R. Balwin, 1763;* and Sir William Young, *Considerations Which May Tend to Promote the Settlement of Our New West-India Colonies: By Encouraging Individuals to Embark in the Undertaking*, London: Printed for James Robson, 1764.

[23] "The definitive Treaty of Peace and Friendship between his Britannick Majesty, the Most Christian King, and the King of Spain. Concluded at Paris the 10th day of February, 1763. To which the King of Portugal acceded on the same day." Retrieved 25 September 2010 from http://avalon.law.yale.edu/18th_century/paris763.asp.

[24] Javier A. Gonzalez, "'A Strange Discordant Mass of Heterogeneous Animals': The Role of Ethnic Divisions in British Grenada, 1763-1779" (BA Honors Thesis, Department of History, Harvard University, 1994), 8.

[25] M166. Ceded Islands (Grenada). [Oath of Allegiance]. Grenada, 1765. Beinecke Rare Book and Manuscript Library, Hamilton College, Hamilton, New York.

[26] Devas, *Conception Island*, 18.

[27] Clyde, *Health in Grenada*, 12, quoting Lt. Governor Scott in a letter to the Secretary of

State in London.
[28] Devas, *Conception Island*, 27-28.
[29] Clyde, *Health in Grenada*, 12.
[30] FR ANOM COL F³ 17, "Etat dupuis des habitations de la Grenade vendues aux anglois; la liste de M. D'Ennery du 24 avril 1765."

Notes to Chapter 11: ... and the Grenadines

[1] Thomas Jefferys, *The Natural and Civil History of the French Dominions in North and South America*, (London, 1760), 157.
[2] John Edward Adams, "Union Island, West Indies: An Historical and Geographical Sketch," *Caribbean Studies*, 18, 3/4 (Oct. 1978-Jan. 1979), 16.
[3] Pierre du Val d'Abbeville, "Isles d'Amérique dites Caribes ou Cannibales et de Barlovento," Geographe du Roy, Paris: Chez l'Auteur avec privilège du Roy, 1664.
[4] Adams, "Union Island, West Indies," 6.
[5] Frances Kay Brinkley, "An Analysis of the 1750 Carriacou Census," *Caribbean Quarterly* 24, no. 1/2 (1978): 44-60.
[6] The Registrar's Office, Supreme Court of Grenada, Registers of Records, 1764-1797.
[7] See Jean-Pierre Moreau, *Les Petites Antilles de Christophe Colomb à Richelieu* (Paris: 1992), 58.
[8] Granadillos is the diminutive form of Granada, illustrating the small sizes of the islands and islets that make up the chain, and their connection to the parent island of Grenada.
[9] The French often spelled Grenadines as "Grenadins," or it sometimes appeared as "Grenadilles."
[10] The spelling of the various islands have varied over the years with Bequia historically appearing as Becouya or Bekia; Carriacou as Cariaco, Cariouacou, Cariacou, Cariabacu and Cariobacou; and Canouan as Cannaouan. The other major island is Union.
[11] See C. Jessie, "Sold For a Song: Du Parquet Buys St. Lucia, with Martinique, Grenada, the Grenadines, In A.D. 1650, for £1,660 Sterling," *Caribbean Quarterly* 13, no. 4 (Dec. 1967): 44-52. See also "Lettres patentes par lesquelles le roi ratifie et confirme la validité du contrat conclu le 27 septembre 1650 portant vente par la *Compagnie des îles d'Amérique* à Jacques Dyel Du Parquet des îles de la Martinique, de la Grenade, Grenadines et Sainte-Lucie (août 1651), FR ANOM COL C⁸ᴮ 1 N° 2. ccessed on 15 April 2012 at http://anom.archivesnationales.culture.gouv.fr/ir?c=FRANOM_00010,1.03.1&num=20 &ir=FRANOM_00010&start=&q=grenade&geogname=&date=&from=&to=
[12] Dutertre, *Histoire général*, 2: 41.
[13] Dutertre, *Histoire général*, 2: 41-42.
[14] Jean-Baptiste Labat, *Nouveau voyage*, 4: 440-441.
[15] Dutertre, *Histoire général*, 3: 508. There were oysters but no pearls.
[16] It is not clear what evidence led to the reporting of the meaning of the word Carriacou as "Land of Reefs" or "Land surrounded by reefs," but around the mid-1980s it became popular.
[17] Thierry L'Etang, "Du nom indigène des îles de l'archipel des Antilles." Accessed 24 February 2011 at http://www.montraykreyol.org/spip.php?article62. The woodpigeon, ramier or red-necked pigeon (*Columba squamosa*) is quite common across Carriacou.
[18] Cesar de Rochefort, *Histoire générale des Antilles habitées par les Français* (Paris, 1667), 6.
[19] Adams, "Union Island, West Indies," 14.
[20] Thierry L'Etang quoting Hernando Colon, *Historia* (1984), 166.
[21] Roukema, "Some Remarks on the La Cosa Map," 16.
[22] Dutertre, *Histoire général*, 2: 41-42.

23 Dutertre, *Histoire général*, 2: 41-42.

24 Dutertre, *Histoire général*, 2: 41-42, 241.

25 De Rochefort, *Histoire générale des Antilles*, 7.

26 Adams, "Union Island, West Indies," 17.

27 FR ANOM COL C⁸ᴬ 5 F° 88: 156. The name of the island of Canouan is derived from the Island Carib/Kalinago *caouane* for turtle.

28 Adams, "Union Island, West Indies," 17.

29 Adams, "Union Island, West Indies," 17.

30 Archives Nationales, *Voyage aux iles d'Amérique catalogue de l'exposition organisée par la Direction des Archives de France du Ministère de la Culture* (Hôtel de Rohan : Archives Nationales, 1992), 32. Grenada was exporting *caret* to France as late as 1752.

31 Malo, "La perte et reprise de la Grenade," 104.

32 Malo, "La perte et reprise de la Grenade," 104.

33 FR ANOM COL C⁸ᴬ 23 F° 39, 10 December 1717; FR ANOM COL C⁸ᴬ 24 F° 143, 12 May 1718.

34 Some of the slaves and crew reached Martinique where the slaves were subsequently sold.

35 Guillaume De Lisle's controversial map of the *Antilles Françoises et les Iles Voisines* listed all the major islands of the Grenadines, but it recorded Grenada and the Grenadines upside down. De Lisle received his information from a plan by Petit, royal engineer in the islands.

36 FR ANOM COL C⁸ᴮ 5 N° 62, 30 October 1719. It should be noted that Cornette's request coincided with the signing of a treaty with the Island (Yellow) Caribs of St. Vincent which gave the French access to that island in return for protection from the so called Black Caribs.

37 Defoe, *A General History of the Pyrates* (New York: Dover Publications, 1999), 126.

38 FR ANOM COL C⁸ᴬ 27 F° 75: 149.

39 Campbell, *Candid and Impartial Considerations on the Nature of the Sugar Trade*, 193.

40 FR ANOM COL C⁸ᴬ 28 F° 157, 18 November 1721.

41 FR ANOM COL C⁸ᴬ 42 F° 98, 24 April 1731.

42 COL C8A 48 F° 218: 388-390, 15 July 1737.

43 Adams, "Union Island, West Indies," 17.

44 Adams, "Union Island, West Indies," 17.

45 Jean-Baptiste Le Blond, *Voyage aux Antilles et a l'Amérique Méridionale* (Paris : Chez Arthus-Bertrand, 1813), 249. It is possible that Le Blond's reference reflected development that took place under the British and not during the French period.

46 Reynal quoted in Devas, *A History of the Island of Grenada*, 181.

47 Jefferys, *Natural and Civil History*, 157.

48 Raynal, *Philosphical and Political History*, 4: 369.

49 Young, *Conditions Which May Tend to Promote the Settlement*, 7.

50 Boucher, *Cannibal Encounters*, 97.

51 Boucher, *Cannibal Encounters*, 104.

52 Adams, "Union Island, West Indies," 15.

53 Le Blond, *Voyage aux Antilles*, 249.

54 UK TNA CO 101/18 [Report from S.V. Morse on the Grenadines] to Lord McCartney, 22 July 1778.

55 See for example, Raymund Devas, *Conception Island* and *The History of the Island of Grenada*.

56 See FR ANOM COL F³ 17 "Recensement de Cariacou pris par le Sr. La Bourgerie du Sablon par ordre de M. de Poincy…," 27 January 1750; Brinkley, "An Analysis of the 1750 Carriacou Census," 44-60. The census was carried out between 19-20 January 1750 by the commanding officer of Carriacou, Lieutenant de La Bourgerie du Sablon, and sent

to Governor de Poincy on 27 January 1750.

⁵⁷ Maybe the final tally of "202" is in fact accurate because the census taker added in residents who may have been absent from the island even though he failed to record specific information regarding them.

⁵⁸ To compensate for the missing data on the eighteen slaves of the Marquis Delisle, the total population is reduced to 181 rather than 199 for analysis to reflect the population for which consistent data are available.

⁵⁹ This could be the basis of the subsequent identification of the slaves and their descendants from Carriacou being able to identify with specific African tribes/ethnic groups through their African Nation Dance or Big Drum Dance.

⁶⁰ Brinkley, "An Analysis of the 1750 Carriacou Census," 44.

⁶¹ FR ANOM COL C⁸ᴬ 59 F° 354, n° 71, 15 June 1752.

⁶² FR ANOM COL C⁸ᴬ 59 F° 354, n° 71, 15 June 1752. The season "*de l'hivernage*" was between mid-June and September, the hurricane season in the Caribbean.

⁶³ FR ANOM COL C⁸ᴬ 59 F° 354, n° 71, 15 June 1752. The roadstead was a reference to La Baye de la Gande Ance.

⁶⁴ FR ANOM COL E 97, 1765/81. St. Hilaire remained a proprietor on Carriacou until his death and his name became part of the local environment as he is remembered with the place name Point St. Hilaire in the east of the island, just south of Baye à l'Eau or Watering Bay where he had a plantation since the 1750s.

⁶⁵ FR ANOM COL C⁸ᴮ 10 N° 85, n° 264, 1 November 1756.

⁶⁶ FR ANOM COL C⁸ᴮ 10 N° 85, n° 264, 1 November 1756.

⁶⁷ Naddrie, "Eighteenth-Century Settlement in the British Caribbean," 67.

⁶⁸ John Byres, *Plan of the Island of Bequia Laid Down by Actual Survey Under the Direction of the Honorable the Commissioners for the Sale of Lands in the Ceded Islands*, London, 1776. Among the proprietors were [Jean Marie] Aquart, Fornease, Peter Servant, Brociette, Marianne Estancan, Louis Augier and Jean-Baptiste Pierre Chevally, Estancan, Joseph de St. Hillaire and Labord; Sir William Young had purchased two large plantations from the departing French. Most of the names were accompanied by Monsieur, thus making idntification easier. Sir William Young was President of the Commission for the Sale and Disposal of Lands in the Ceded Islands, himself purchasing plantations in St. Vincent, Bequia and Carriacou from the French.

⁶⁹ Young, *Conditions Which May Tend to Promote the Settlement...*, 7.

⁷⁰ Walter Fenner, *A New and Accurate Map of the Island of Carriacou in the West Indies*, [London, 1784], British Library.

⁷¹ TNA: PRO EXT 1/253/2, 1763, "Extracts from the Capitation Rolls of the Island of Carriacou for the Year 1763" in Extracts from the Capitation Rolls for the Quarters of Basse-Terre, Maigrin, Marquis, Sauteurs, Grand Pauvre and Goyave, Grenada, and the Island of Carioacou.

⁷² Young, *Conditions Which May Tend to Promote the Settlement*, 7.

⁷³ His name also appears as De Lisle and De l'Isle. According to Cindy Kilgore, *Adventure Guide to Grenada, St. Vincent and the Grenadines* (Edison: Hunter, 2003), 163: "His interest lay in the production of lime for construction, which involves the burning of coral in kilns. We do know that he died on Mayreau due to his cruelty. A woman, Nellie Ibo, knocked him from his horse and killed him with a hoe." The tale is uncorroborated. His full name was Louis Depressat Delisle, the father of John Hector DePressat De Lionel Delisle who inherited much of the Marquis' property.

⁷⁴ St. Hilaire's name is spelt incorrectly on the 1776 Bequia survey by John Byres where it's listed as "St. Hillary" (plot #3). The place name St. Hilaire Point is on the same

peninsula where his plantation was located; there is also a Point St. Hilaire/St. Hilaire Point, Carriacou.

75 Raynal, *Phisophical and Political History*, 4: 369.

76 TNA: PRO CO 101/16, State of the Island of Carriacou, 1 April 1772.

77 Rhodes House Library, Oxford, "The State of Carriacou and the Other Grenadine Islands, 1776."

78 Georges Lacour-Gáyet, *La marine militaire de la France sous le règne de Louis XVI* (Paris: H. Champion, 1905), 211.

79 Valentine Morris, *A Narrative of the Official Conduct of Valentine Morris: Late Captain General, Governor in Chief &c. &c. of the Island of St. Vincent and its Dependencies* (London: Printed by J. Walter and sold by S. Hooper, 1787), 7-8.

80 Should be St. Vincent not S. Lucia. Bedfordshire and Luton Archives and Record Service, Correspondence between Thomas Robinson, 2nd Baron Grantham, Foreign Secretary (1782-83), and Valentine Morris, L 30/14/260/1, 28 November 1782.

81 Slade, "Craigston & Meldrum Estates, Carriacou, 1796-1841," *Society of Antiquaries of Scotland*, 114 (1984: 481-537), 486 describes Carriacou's British influences by the 1770s thus, "More important to the island after it was lost to the French was the influx of British, or more accurately, and to use the eighteenth-century idiom, North British planters - Cumming, Reid, McKellar, McLean, Kirkland, Milne, Robertson and Urquhart, with their estates of Dumfries, Craigston, Meldrum. The names of their managers and apprentices, the Arbuthnots, Reids, Simpsons, Brands, Lauries, Grants, Cruickshanks, Robertsons, Bells and Mitchells all tell the same story: Carriacou was in a fair way to becoming a colony of North Britain, but especially that part of the northern kingdom that lies between the Dee and the Deveron."

82 TNA: PRO CO 101/31/25 f. 100-104, 7 January 1791, "Schedule of the Population of the Island of Carriacou, Taken the 1st September 1790."

83 Edward Drayton, *The Grenada Handbook, Directory and Almanac for the Year 1897* (London: Sampson Low, Marston & Co., 1897), 37.

84 Grenada issues postage stamps under the names "Grenada" and " Grenada Grenadines."

Notes to Chapter 12: Legacy of the Island Caribs

1 Kalinago man to Father Philippe de Beaumont, 1660.

2 See Boucher, *Cannibal Encounters*, for a detailed discussion of the European view of the Island Caribs.

3 The Anonymous author, *Histoire de l'isle de Grenade*, records at least 120 Island Carib deaths between 1649 and 1659, but it was difficult, almost impossible for the French to learn if they had killed Island Caribs who ohad run or were carried away wounded.

4 The interpretation center has been closed for some time now, but there are attempts to reopen it.

5 Derek Walcott, *Derek Walcott Collected Poems, 1948-84*, (New York: Farrar, Straus & Giroux, 1986), 281.

6 There are descendants of Island Caribs on the island of Dominica, predominantly Black Caribs who are the result of the mixing of Blacks/escaped slaves and Island Caribs. The Island Caribs of St. Vincent were removed from that island by the British in 1796 following their revolt. Their descendants presently live in Belize and are called Garifuna.

7 See Dutertre, *Histoire général des Antilles habitées par les François*; Anonymous, *Histoire de l'Isle de Grenade en Amérique, 1649-1659*; and Labat, *Nouveau voyages aux isles de l'Amérique*, which

differs little from Dutertre's which was his source.

[8] The 1651 date is in all books, articles, etc. published on Grenada. Even though Steele in *Grenada: A History of Its People* consulted Bresson's chronicle, she kept the 1651 date. Crouse, in *French Pioneers in the West Indies*, also used the manuscript tfor the information on Grenada in his book.

[9] Anonymous, *Histoire de l'isle de Grenade*, 70.

[10] Dutertre, *Histoire générale*, 429-430. It is interesting to note that Dutertre adds the story of the young Carib girl: "A young Savage girl, rather pretty, about twelve or thirteen years of age, was for a short time at issue between two officers, but while they discussed who will get her, a third came, who having fired a shot of pistol in the head of this poor girl, and having her fell down dead, put them both in accordance."

[11] Holdren, "Raiders and Traders," 59.

[12] Anonymous, *Histoire de l'isle de Grenade*, 68.

[13] Anonymous, *Histoire de l'isle de Grenade*, 70

[14] Anonymous, *Histoire de l'isle de Grenade*, 71.

[15] Anonymous, *Histoire de l'isle de Grenade*, 71.

[16] Anonymous, *Histoire de l'isle de Grenade*, 71.

[17] Anonymous, *Histoire de l'isle de Grenade*, 71.

[18] Anonymous, *Histoire de l'isle de Grenade*, 71.

[19] Anonymous, *Histoire de l'isle de Grenade*, 72.

[20] Anonymous, *Histoire de l'isle de Grenade*, 68

[21] Edwards, *The History, Civil and Commercial, of the British Colonies in the West Indies*, 1: 347.

[22] Anonymous, *Histoire de l'isle de Grenade*, 101.

[23] See Frank Kums, "Les Sauteurs à la Grenade, ou Ina la Caraibe," *New Era*, 12 June 1871, and Horatio Nelson Huggins, *Hiroona: An Historical Romance in Poetic Form*, 1937.

[24] Amerindian Heritage Day is celebrated in Trinidad & Tobago (Oct. 14 since 2000); Guyana celebrates Amerindian Heritage Month and Day (September 10, since 1976); Dominica has a Carib Model Village; and Surinam has a day also. Belize has a Garifuna Settlement Day (Nov. 19, since 1943).

Appendices

Appendix I: Tables

Appendix II: Colonial Administration

Appendix III: Populations

Appendix IV: La Ville du Fort Royal

Appendix V: Grenada Divided into Quartiers

Table 6.1

Geographic Distribution by Race,
Gender and Age of the Population, 1669

| | ------------------------------Quartiers------------------------------ | | | | |
	Grand Ance	Fort Royal	Beau Séjour	Palmistes	Total
Population of the Island					
Total	101	231	116	58	506
Total (%)	20	46	23	11	100
Men[3] (%)	57.4	57.6	47.4	53.4	54.7
Women (%)	25.7	26.4	27.7	27.6	26.4
Children (%)	16.8	16.0	25.2	19.0	18.6
White Population (percentage)					
Total[1]	48.5	41.6	90.5	58.6	56.1
Men[1]	25.7	25.5	41.4	34.5	30.2
Women[2]	12.9	9.1	24.1	12.1	13.6
Engagés	9.9	12.6	10.3	6.9	10.9
Children	9.9	6.9	25.0	12.1	12.3
Slave Population (percentage)					
Total	51.5	58.4	9.5	41.4	43.9
Men	61.5	54.8	63.6	45.8	24.5
Women	25.0	29.6	36.4	37.5	13.0
Children	13.5	15.6	0.0	16.7	6.3

Source: FR ANOM DPPC G[1] 498, no. 28, Dénombrement des hommes, femmes, enfants, blancs, nègres… dans l'île de la Grenade de la présente année 1669.

[1] Includes *engagés* who are all assumed to be white and male indentured servants.
[2] The women were all married ("*Femmes*"), except for one who most likely was a widow.
[3] Includes both whites and slaves; no children included.

Table 6.2

Family Structure, 1669

Categories	Number (Percentages)
Married couples	69 (68% of households)
Children	62 (12% of population)
Males	28 (5.5% of population)
Females	34 (6.7% of pop.)
Childless couples	40 (60% married couples)
Widows/widowers	1/2
Single householders	30 (30% of households)
No. of households	99
Mean no. of white men/woman	1.44
Mean no. of whites/household	2.89
Mean no. of white children	0.63
Mean no. of *engagés*/household	0.56
Mean no. of slaves/household	2.27
Mean no. of individuals/household	5.10

Source: See source for Table 6.1.

Table 6.3
Administrative Distribution by Race, Gender and Age of the Population, 1696

| | ----------------------Compagnies/Bourgs---------------------- | | | | |
	Colonnelle	La Blennerie	Vieux Bourg	Noveau Bourg	Total
Population of the Island					
Total	493	274	16	28	811
Total (%)	61	34	2	3	100
Men[1] (%)	37	40	37	35	58.2
Women[1] (%)	24	24	19	17	27.3
Children[1] (%)	29	27	44	25	28.6
Other	10	9	0	0	2.2
White Population (percentage)					
Total	43	45	4.5	7.2	40.0
Men	37	37	23	38	13.1
Women	28	25	23	29	9.5
Children	35	38	54	33	13.3
Slave Population (percentage)					
Total	72	26	1.1	1.3	55.0
Men	42	41	100	62.5	25.0
Women	27	28	0.0	37.5	15.0
Children	31	43	0.0	0.0	15.0

Source: FR ANOM DPPC G[1] 498, no. 39, Recensement de l'île de la Grenade de l'année 1669 (11 mars 1696).

[1] Includes whites and slaves.

Table 6.4
Family Structure, 1696

Categories	Number (Percentages)
Married couples	77
Children	107 (17% of population)
No. of households	103
Mean no. of white men/woman	1.12
Mean no. of whites/household	2.83
Mean no. of white children	1.04
Mean no. of slaves/household	4.33
Mean no. of individuals/household	7.87

Source: See source for Table 6.3.

Table 7.1

Population by Race and
Average Annual Rate of Change, 1669-1763

Year	Total Population	% Slaves	% White	% FNW[1]	Avg, Annual Rate of Increase Since Previous Census (%)			
					Total	White	Slave	FNW[1]
1669	506	44	56	--	---	---	---	---
1687	659	45	47	8	1.7	1.43	1.62	
1690	795	50	42	8	6.9	-2.75	9.51	5.23
1700	835	63	31	6	0.5	-2.71	2.85	-1.57
1704	1,365	71	26	3	15.9	7.93	14.16	-5.82
1707[2]	1,466	76	24	--	---			
1718	3,476	80	13	7	11.0			
1722	3,668	83	12	5	1.4			
1726	4,328	80	15	5	4.5	4.56	2.80	4.34
1731	5,275	83	14	3	4.4	2.83	4.60	-0.88
1735	6,406	83	13	4	5.4	2.37	4.79	6.51
1741	8,983	86	12	2	6.7	4.25	6.28	2.17
1745	9,986	88	10	2	2.8	-0.82	3.12	2.47
1749	9,965	87	11	2	(.1)	2.01	-0.13	2.37
1755	14,036	90	8	2	6.8	-0.86	6.18	9.27
1761	16,456	87	10	3				
1763[3]	13,846	88	9	3	(.3)	1.79	-0.71	3.87

Source: FR ANOM DPPC G[1] 498, Recensements, la Grenade, 1669-1755.

[1] FNW – Free Non-Whites.
[2] Figures for 1707 are only overall numbers of people taken from a correspondence by the governor; see FR ANOM COL C[8B] 2 N° 8.
[3] TNA, Key, UK. Colonial Office 101/1/6. This is the recorded total though it was a miscaluclation due to the undercounting by at least 1,400 slaves of the 14 year olds and under in the district of Grand Marquis (St. Andrew).

Table 7.2

Amerindians on French Censuses, 1678-1735

Year	Adult Females	Adult Males	Children	Total	% of Total	Census Descriptors
1678	3	1	3	7	---	Sauvages
1687	---	---	---	22	3.3	Sauvages
1690	15	---	5	20	2.5	Sauvages
1718	40	40	30	110	3.2	Caraïbes
1722	35	35	28	98	---	Caraïbes
1723	40	40	35	110	2.9	Caraïbes
1725	30	40	18	88	2.0	Caraïbes
1726	25	30	17	72	1.6	Caraïbes
1731	7	10	7	24	---	Caraïbes
1735	42	42	38	122	1.9	Caraïbes

Source: See source for Table 7.1.

Table 7.3

Recorded Arrival of Slave Ships at Grenada, 1669-1761

Year	Name of Ship	# of Slaves	Slaves Sold at Gda
1669	S. Franciscus[1]	337	25
1670	Reine Ester[2]	200	200
1670	Vredenberg[3]	110	95
1674	Unknown[4]		80
1691	Unknown[5]		~45
1709	Le César[6]	210	Part
1709	Le Duc de Bretagne[7]	452	
1710	Amsterdam[8]	500	500
1711	Le Jason[9]		
1714	L'Impudent[10]		
1717	Le Concorde[11]		
1719	L'Aurore[12]		
1721	La Méduse[13]	200	105
1721	L'Afriquain[14]		
1721	Le Duc du Maine[15]		
1721	Néréide		
1723	Le Courrier de Bourbon		
1725	La Mutine		
1726	L'Aurore		
1739	La Paix		260
1747	L'Aigle		50
1751	Le César		Part
1755	Cométe		145
1756	Courrier		
1756	Le Duc d'Aiguillon		
1756	Furteuse		
1758	Judith		259
1761	Sally		150

[1] Voyages Database. 2009. *Voyages: The Trans-Atlantic Slave Trade Database.* http://www.slavevoyages.org (accessed 15 June 2011).
[2] Voyages Database; FR ANOM COL C8A 1 F0 42, 91-2; COL C8A 1 F0 50, 95.
[3] Voyages Database.

Table 7.4

Slave Population, 1669-1763

Year	Slave Population	Total	Men	Women	Children	Infirm	Maroons
			---------------------- Percentages ----------------------				
1669	222	44	55.9	29.7	14.4		
1683	300		44.3	26.3	29.3		
1687	297	47	44.8	25.6	29.6		
1690	395	50	46.6	30.1	23.3		
1700	520	63	42.9	29.6	27.5		
1704	970	70	43.6	28.4	28.0		
1707[1]	1,116	76					
1715[2]	2,400						
1718	2,779	80	42.0	23.0	28.4	6.6	
1726	3,476	78	39.1	22.3	29.6	8.9	
1731	4,375	82	38.5	22.1	28.2	11.2	
1735	5,299	82	38.8	23.6	29.0	8.6	
1741	7,240	85	40.0	24.7	29.0	6.3	
1745	8,747	88	38.8	26.7	29.1	5.4	
1749	8,700	86	39.6	27.0	26.9	6.5	0.6
1755	12,608	90	37.5	28.0	30.0	4.5	
1761	14,308	87	38.5	31.5	24.5	3.5	2.1
1763[3]	15,200	90					

Source: See source for Table 7.1.

[1] Figures for 1707 are only overall numbers of people taken from a correspondence by the governor; see FR ANOM COL C8B 2 N° 8.
[2] Estimate of slaves by governor in correspondence; see FR ANOM COL C8B 3 N° 75.
[3] TNA, Key, UK. Colonial Office 101/1/6. Though the Capitation Rolls recorded 13, 846 slaves, it was an undercount by at least 1,400 slaves, with the under 14 year olds for Grand Marquis (St. Andrew) not counted. This number is a more accurate representation of the slave population.

Table 7.5

Number and Ratio of Slaves to Whites, 1669-1763

Year	Slaves	Whites	Ratio
1669	222	283	0.78:1
1687	350	366	0.96:1
1690	395	377	1.0:1
1700	520	250	2.1:1
1704	970	353	2.7:1
1707[1]	1,116	351	3.2:1
1718	2,779	461	6.0:1
1725	3,590	629	5.7:1
1731	4,375	765	5.7:1
1735	5,299	841	6.3:1
1741	7,725	1,085	7.1:1
1745	8,747	1,050	8.3:1
1749	8,700	1,138	7.6:1
1755	12,608	1,081	11.6:1
1761	14,308	1,574	9.0:1
1763[2]	15,200	1,225	12.4:1

Source: See Source for Table 7.1

[1] Figures for 1707 are only overall numbers of people taken from a correspondence by the governor; see FR ANOM COL C8B 2 N° 8.
[2] TNA, Key, UK. Colonial Office 101/1/6. Though the Capitation Rolls recorded 13, 846 slaves, it was an undercount by at least 1,400 slaves, with the under 14 year olds for Grand Marquis (St. Andrew) not counted. This number is a more accurate representation of the slave population.

Table 7.6

Age Composition and Fertility, 1669-1761

| Year | ------------Whites---------------- | | | --------------Slaves-------------- | | |
	Children (%)	Adults (%)	Children/ Woman	Children (%)	Adults (%)	Children/ Woman
1669	21.9	78.1	0.91	14.4	85.6	0.49
1687	36.3	63.7	2.11	29.6	70.4	1.16
1690	42.1	57.9	1.97	23.3	76.7	0.77
1700	46.0	54.0	2.02	27.5	72.5	0.93
1704	51.8	48.2	2.54	24.5	75.5	0.83
1718	51.8	48.2	2.39	28.4	71.6	1.23
1725	52.6	47.4	2.81	28.0	72.0	1.25
1731	57.0	43.0	3.10	28.2	71.8	1.28
1735	62.5	37.5	3.81	29.0	71.0	1.23
1741	62.0	38.0	3.36	29.0	71.0	1.18
1745	59.2	40.8	3.47	25.7	74.3	0.96
1749	64.1	35.9	5.00	26.7	73.3	1.00
1755	57.0	43.0	3.80	30.0	70.0	1.10
1761	52.5	47.5	3.00	24.5	75.5	0.78

Source: See source for Table 7.1.

Table 7.7

Sex Ratios, 1669-1761

| Year | ------------Whites---------- | | Slaves |
	Children	Adults	Adults
1669	0.82	1.44	1.88
1687	0.75	2.69	1.75
1690	1.96	1.24	1.55
1700	1.45	1.19	1.45
1704	1.78	1.32	1.54
1718	2.01	1.22	1.82
1725	1.71	1.53	1.84
1731	1.48	1.33	1.74
1735	1.58	1.18	1.65
1741	1.53	1.06	1.62
1745	1.41	1.39	1.46
1749	1.63	1.79	1.53
1755	1.64	1.87	1.34
1761	1.39	1.70	1.22

Source: See Source for Table 7.1.

Table 7.8

Geographic Distribution of the Population, 1749/1755

| Quartiers | Total Population (%) | ------------Racial Composition (%) ----------- | | |
		Slave	FNW	White
Fort Royal	19.3/16.3	84.4/89.8	9.6/7.7	3.7/3.7
Gouyave	11.1/10.9	82.5/82.8	20.4/11.3	3.1/5.9
Grand Pauvre	6.4/8.7	77.8/85.6	15.6/12.2	0.3/2.3
Sauteurs	21.0/24.1	85.8/92.9	10.5/5.4	2.6/1.7
Grand Marquis	29.3/26.0	89.0/91.2	10.0/7.7	0.4/1.0
Mègrin	12.9/12.8	86.9/89.4	8.8/7.5	3.0/3.0

Source: See source for Table 7.1.

Table 7.9

White Population, 1669-1763

Year	White Population	Total	Men	Women	Boys	Girls
			----------------Percentages----------------			
1669	283	56	34.6	24.0	9.9	12.0
1683	302	57	49.7	26.2	14.2	9.9
1687	366	58	46.4	17.2	15.6	17.2
1690	337	42	36.5	21.4	27.9	14.2
1700	250	48	31.2	22.8	27.2	18.8
1704	353	26	26.9	20.4	33.7	19.0
1707[1]	351	24	31.3	41.6	27.1 (children)	
1718	461	13	26.5	21.7	34.7	17.1
1726	664	15	30.0	17.3	33.0	19.7
1731	893	17	35.4	15.8	29.1	19.7
1735	841	13	21.0	16.4	38.3	24.3
1741	1,085	12	19.5	18.4	37.5	24.5
1745	1,050	11	23.7	17.0	34.7	24.6
1749	1,138	11	23.0	12.8	39.7	24.4
1755	1,081	8	28.0	15.0	35.4	21.6
1761	1,574	10	29.9	17.6	30.6	21.9
1763[2]	1,225	9				

Source: See source for Table 7.1.

[1] Figures for 1707 are only overall numbers of people taken from a correspondence by the governor; see FR ANOM COL C8B 2 N° 8. Boys and girls were grouped as children.
[2] TNA, Key, UK. Colonial Office 101/1/6.

Table 7.10

Engagé Population, 1669-1755

Year	Total	% of Population	Description
1669	55	9.0	Blancs
1671	55		Servantes blancs
1688	70	8.0	Forçats
1691	34	8.0	Forçats
1704	3		
1718	36	1	Engagés/domestiques blancs
1722	36		Engagés/domestiques blancs
1723	42		Engagés
1725	60		Engagés
1726	62	1	Engagés
1731	59	1	Engagés
1735	54	<1	Engagés
1741	39	<1	Domestiques
1743	62	<1	Domestiques
1745	64	<1	Domestiques
1747	100	<1	Domestiques
1749	42	<1	Serves
1755	19	<1	Serves

Source: See source for Table 7.1.

Table 7.11

Free Non-White (FNW) Population, 1683-1763

Year	FNW Pop	Total Pop	Total Free	Mulattoes M/F	Blacks M/F	FNW Children (M/F)
		------------Percentages------------				
1683				3		
1687	31			16/15		
1688	34	5.2	9.4	18/16		
1690	42	5.3	10.5	23/19		
1700	47	5.6	14.9	35/12		
1704	42	3.2	10.6	11/31		
1718	107	3.1		11/22	17/21	
1722	151			9/25	13/17	23
1726	116	2.6		16/28	20	26 26
1731	111	2.1		18/27	20	26 20
1735	157	2.4		21/29	23	30 41

Year	FNW Pop	Total Pop	Total Free	M/F	Children/Infants	Infirm
1741	164	1.8	12	40	112	
1745	181	1.8		55/74	52	
1749	189	1.9		54/74	61	
1755	347	2.5		85/132	130	
1761	574	3.5	26.7	160/137	222	55
1763[1]	455	3.3	27.1	236	219	

Source: See source for Table 7.1. M = Male; F = Female.

[1] TNA, Key, UK. Colonial Office 101/1/6.

Table 8.1

Number of *Indigoteries*, 1687-1761[1]

Year	Number of Indigoteries	Year	Number of Indigoteries
1687	21	1723	140
1690	34	1725	76
1696	47	1726	70
1700	58	1731	25
1704	86	1735	23
1718	152	1741	3
1722	159	1761	69 acres planted in indigo

Source: See source for Table 7.1.

[1] *Indigoteries* refer to indigo factories, plantations with the vats to process indigo; there may have been other planters who cultivated the crop but depended on the processing facilities of others.

Table 8.2

Coffee, Cocoa and Cotton Cultivation, 1718-1763

Year	*"Pieds de Coffee"*	*"Pieds de Cacao"*	*"Pieds de Cotton"*
1718		126,010	480
1722		182,800	1,500
1723		241,450	1,000
1725		140,014	400
1726		600,000	600
1731	11,300	11,300[1]	8,500
1735	951,855	39,520	
1738	1,816,300	17,350	139,500
1741	1,945,000	7,120	46,500
1745	1,771,900	109,200	1,771,900
1749	1,800,700	161,200	
1753	2,725,600	150,000	
1755	3,153,900	82,600	
1761	3,369,000	138,500	89,000
1762[2]	1,248,202	75,530	46,713
1763[2]	1,330,998	196,300	185,000

Source: See source for Table 7.1.

Pied: a linear measurement equaling a foot, but used here to mean "head," as in the number or heads of plants.
[1] Disease practically destroyed Martinique's cocoa crop and Grenada may have suffered a similar fate hence the low production in 1731. See Richard Sheridan, "The Development of the Plantations to 1750," 36.
[2] Reports exports for each crop in pounds.

Table 8.3

Geographic Distribution of
Coffee, Cocoa and Sugar Plantations, 1763

	Fort Royal	L'Ance Goyave	Grand Pauvre	Sauteurs	Grand Marquis	Megrin	Total
# Coffee	26	23	16	25	48	24	162
# Acres	4,218	2,747	2,023	3,124	8,517	3,294	23,923
Avg. Size	162	119	126	125	177	137	148
# Cf/Cc[1]	1	12	7	1	2	1	24
# Acres	57	1,748	1,279	225	207	281	3,887
# Cocoa	1	2	0	0	1	0	4
# Acres	114	656	0	0	160	0	930
# Sugar	13	10	6	18	23	11	81
# Acres	7,637	3,068	1,241	5,871	8,008	5,340	31,165
Avg. Size	588	307	248	326	364	485	385

Source: Daniel Paterson, *A Topographical Description of the Island of Grenada*, 3-9.

[1] Coffee/Cocoa plantations.

Table 8.4

Ranges of Slave Ownership
on Coffee/Cocoa Plantations by District, 1763[1]

	Fort Royal	Goyave	Grand Pauvre	Sauteurs	Mégrin	Total
1-5	1	16	2	13	6	38
6-10	10	15	5	16	7	53
11-15	7	13	13	8	6	47
16-20	11	6	1	4	6	28
21-30	6	7	4	6	8	31
31-40	2	1	5	6	4	18
41-50	0	3	2	0	2	7
>50	1	0	2	6	5	14
Total	38	61	34	53	44	236

Source: TNA, Key, UK. CO 101/1 f.18-31, Capitation Rolls for the Quarters of Basse-Terre....

[1] Grand Marquis is not included in this table because of incomplete data.

Table 8.5

Comparison Between the Number of Sucreries
(Sugar Factories) and the Total Number of Slaves, 1687-1763

Year	No. of Sucreries	No. of Slaves	Year	No. of Sucreries	No of Slaves
1687	4	350	1731	57	4,375
1690	4	395	1735	68	5,299
1700	3	520	1738	60	------
1704	6	970	1741	56	7,240
1707	6	1,116	1745	74	8,747
1718	9	2,779	1749	83	8,700
1722	15	3,045	1753	83	11,991
1723	17	3,106	1755	87	12,608
1725	18	3,590	1761	65	14,308
1726	20	3,476	1763	81	15,200

Source: See source for Table 7.1.

Table 8.6

Ranges of Slave Ownership
on Sugar Plantations by District, 1763

	Fort Royal	Goyave	Grand Pauvre	Sauteurs	Grand Marquis[1]	Mégrin	Total
26-50	2	1	0	0	5	3	11
51-75	3	4	4	2	6	1	20
76-100	5	3	1	4	6	1	20
101-125	2	2	0	3	1	3	11
126-150	0	0	1	1	0	2	4
151-200	0	0	0	4	2	0	6
>200	0	0	0	2	1	0	3
Total	12	10	6	16	21	10	75

Source: See source for Table 8.4.
[1] Numbers for Grand Marquis are undercounted due to error in compiling original data.

Table 8.7

Exports of Sugar, Sirop and Tafia, 1739-1752

Sugar (quintaux/lbs)

Year	Sucre Blanc[1]	Sucre Commun[2]	Sucre Têté[3]	Sucre Brut[4]
1739	3,730/373,000	3,233/323,300	2,659/352,200	
1746	3,522/352,200	6,887/688,700	984/98,400	206/20,600
1751	1,660/166,000	1,477/147,700	789/78,900	
1752	2,065/206,500	2,565/256,500	770/77,000	22/2,200

Sirop[5] (barrels)

1739	6
1741	130
1745	155

Tafia[6] (barrels)

1741	8
1744	80
1746	124

Source: FR ANOM COL C[10A] 2

[1] *Sucre blanc*: Non-refined "white" sugar, which was the highest quality clayed sugar and often mistaken for refined sugar.
[2] *Sucre commun*: Common sugar; which was a lower grade of "white" sugar, but higher than *sucre têté*.
[3] *Sucre têté*: A lower quality clayed sugar; so named because it was situated at the "head" of the clayed loaf.
[4] *Sucre brut*: Muscovado sugar; a brown, unrefined sugar; lowest quality.
[5] *Sirop*: Byproduce of sugar production; thick, dark syrup used to make rum.
[6] *Tafia*: Rum made from the lower grades of molasses.

Table 8.8

Production of Subsistence Crops, 1741-1761

Crops	Legumes	Cassava	Banana	Potato/Yams	Potato
1738		2.9m³	821,800²		
1741	3.336m	5.784m[1]	954,750²		
1744		4.423m[1]	934,350²		
1745		3.86m³		3.86m³	
1749		4.876 m³	1.54m[1]	165.5[4]	
1761		5.458m³	1.202m[1]		1,647[5]

Source: See notes to Table 7.1.   m = million

[1] *Pied*: A linear measurement equaling a foot, but used here to mean "head," as in number or heads of plants.   [2] *Costes*: Hill/mound; as in number of mounds planted.
[3] *Fossé*: Hole or ditch; as in number of holes planted.
[4] *Carré/quarré*: Land measurement equal to 1.29 hectares.   [5] *Acres*

Table 8.9

Livestock, 1669-1761

Year	Horned Cattle	Horse/ Mule	Sheep/ Goat	Pigs
1669	89	14		
1687	264	52		
1690	310	52		
1700	659	74		
1704	496	120	80	
1718	945	352	1062	1063
1725	1252	711	1856	667
1731	1848	530	3588	817
1735	2378	740	4385	1159
1741	2179	1536	4274	745
1745	1853	1466	3739	977
1749	2483	2002	5112	1251
1755	1969	1085	3184	186
1761	1830	1029	2229	999

Table 9.1

Number of Priests and Parishes in Grenada, 1651-1755

Year	No. of Priests	Orders	No. of Parishes	Names of Parishes
1651	1	Secular		
1656	2	C/D		
1657	2	C/D		
1665	2	Capuchin		
1674	2	Capuchin	1	St. Jacques, Basse-Terre[1]
1690	1	Capuchin	1	
1700	1	Capuchin	1	
1718	3	2C/1S	2	Notre Dame du Bon Secours, Sauteurs[2]
1722	3	2C/1S	3	Notre Dame de l'Assomption, Marquis[3]
1725	5	1C/3S/1D	3/1 NP	Ste. Rose, Grand Pauvre[4]
1726	5	1C/3S/1D	4/1 NP	Petit Marquis, Mégrin[5]
1733	5	2C/3S	5	St. Pierre, l'Ance à Goyave[6]
1741	6	3C/2D/1J	6	St. Jean-Baptiste, Mégrin[7]
1755	7	3C/3D/1J	6	

Source: See source for Table 7.1. Also Raymund Devas, *Conception Island*.
Key to Table
    C – Capuchin; Franciscan order.   **D** – Dominican; Dominican order; Jacobins.
    J – Jesuits; Society of Jesus.   **NP** – Non-parish; not a parish church.
    S – Secular (*preste seculier*); not monastic or belonging to particular religious order.

[1] The parish was officially created after 1674 when the island became a crown colony. In 1690 a sturdy church was built, but permanent church/presbytery were constructed after 1704 on the site of the current St. George's Anglican Church. The Anglicans appropriated this church/site in 1784, forcing the Catholics to use the presbytery to hold religious services. The structure was destroyed c. 1824 and rebuilt as the current Anglican Church.

[2] This chapel was constructed by 1718 on the site of the current Sauteurs Police Station. It was destroyed during Fédon's Rebellion, 1795-96.

[3] Chapel built after 1721; appropriated by the Anglicans in 1784; used for worship until 1789 then abandoned. By 1800 it had fallen into disrepair; walled ruins are still visible. In 1743 residents of the Quartier de la Conférence requested the new parish of Rivière d'Antoine to make it easier for them to attend services than at Marquis; not created.

[4] First chapel built in the 1720s and a more permanent one built in 1734. Until at least 1731 it was listed as *église non paroisnales*. See Devas, *Conception Island*, 9-15, for discussion.

[5] The parish was established in 1726, but the Jesuits were not installed until 1730. The church was destroyed by a hurricane in August 1731, rebuilt in 1733, but abandoned in 1736 for the new parish of St. Jean-Baptiste at L'Ance Père, Mégrin.

[6] The chapel was constructed in 1734. It is not clear where this first chapel was located since it was abandoned by the Anglicans after appropriation in 1784.

[7] Appropriated in 1784 and used by the Anglicans for worship. During Fédon's Rebellion it was the scene of fighting when the British used it as a fortress. Its ruins are still evident.

Table 9.2

Militia Strength, Arms/Ammunitions, 1704-1761

Year	Total[1]	Companies[2]	Officers	Muskets	Pistols	Swords	Powder (lbs)	No. Balls
1669[3]	>98	2	--	--	--	--	--	--
1688	>102	2	--	171	22	20	--	--
1690	120	2	--	136	38	18	--	--
1704	124	2	4	155	43	55	406	425
1707[4]	110	2	--	--	--	--	--	--
1713[5]	150	3/1	--	--	--	--	--	--
1718	230 (202/28)	3/1	13	255	124	102	848	795
1722	220 (198/22)	3/1	13	268	148	123	1497	826
1726	342 (306/36)	3/1	16	322	200	220	800	900
1731	343 (305/38)	4/2	35	387	249	253	1000	1446
1735	385 (341/44)	5/2	31	405	260	280	776	1514
1741	484 (402/82)	6/3	43	723	422	506	1882	2651
1745	518 (402/55)	6/3	55	831	499	584	1305	2678
1749	584 (530/54)	6/3	55	1068	501	648	1697	3044
1755	592 (507/85)	6/3	55	921	616	945	2409	3897
1757[6]	--	7/3	58	--	--	--	--	--
1761[7]	523 (363/160)							

Source: See source for Table 7.1.

[1] Total militia strength; after 1718 figures show (whites/free non-whites).
[2] After 1715 figures show the number of infantry/calvary companies.
[3] The 1669 census lists 98 white males who were capable of bearing arms; the males among the 55 *engagés* could also bear arms and were required to do so by this date. Except for 1741, the numbers of people serving in the militia are estimates based on the sum of white men, *engagés* and free blacks and coloureds listed on the censuses. Actual numbers could be less. Boys were usually listed as >12 yrs and <12 yrs, and those >12 yrs were considered capable of bearing arms.
[4] Figure from report by Governor de Bouloc in C^{8B} 2 N° 86, 1707.
[5] Figure from report of visit by Phélypeaux in 1713 in C^{8B} 3 N° 75, 15 October 1713.
[6] The seventh infantry company was formed on Carriacou.
[7] The census listed 255 men as "exempted and priviledged."

Table 9.3

Population by *Quartiers*, 1749

	Fort Royal	Mégrin	Grand Marquis	Sauteurs	Grand Pauvre	L'Ance Goyave	Totals
Slaves							
Men	655	434	1035	731	198	365	3418
Women	438	321	729	407	146	244	2335
Children	428	272	713	507	135	277	2322
Slaves (old)	110	98	137	165	20	35	563
Maroons	9	18	7	25	0	3	62
Totals	1640	1143	2621	1835	499	924	8700
Whites							
Men	50	16	49	40	11	31	193
Men (old)	1	3	9	6	6	2	27
Boys (>12)	36	41	89	52	24	53	295
Boys (<12)	29	9	38	28	14	39	157
Women	28	15	38	27	12	26	146
Servants	6	7	8	2	6	13	42
Girls (>12)	15	12	38	25	14	23	127
Girls (<12)	20	11	25	41	13	41	151
Totals	185	114	294	221	100	228	1138
Free Non-Whites							
Men	19	7	5	15	1	27	54
Women	35	14	3	6	1	5	74
Children	18	18	4	23	0	3	61
Totals	72	39	12	44	2	35	189
Totals	**1932**	**1294**	**2937**	**2110**	**641**	**1117**	**10021**

Source: See source for Table 7.1.

Table 9.4

Population by Quartiers, 1755

	Fort Royal	Mégrin	Grand Marquis	Sauteurs	Grand Pauvre	L'Ance Goyave	Totals
Slaves							
Men	698	617	1093	1075	368	482	4733
Women	580	414	1053	852	261	365	3525
Children	616	466	1429	991	352	329	3783
Slaves (old)	96	68	173	135	38	57	567
Totals	1990	1565	3748	3053	1019	1233	12608
Whites							
Men	57	29	60	34	21	46	247
Men (old)	6	5	9	2	6	5	33
Boys (>12)	11	31	73	56	50	20	241
Boys (<12)	28	13	46	18	17	20	142
Women	29	26	40	20	21	26	162
Widows	3	3	4	4	0	5	19
Girls (>12)	11	7	21	22	11	16	88
Girls (<12)	25	18	31	22	19	30	145
Totals	170	132	284	178	145	168	1077
Free Non-Whites							
Men	21	12	7	11	5	29	85
Women	31	16	17	21	11	35	131
Children	31	25	14	25	11	24	130
Totals	83	53	38	57	27	88	346
Total	**2243**	**1750**	**4070**	**3238**	**1191**	**1489**	**14032**

Source: See source for Table 7.1.

Table 9.5

Ranges of Slave Ownership by District, 1763

	Fort Royal	Goyave	Grand Pauvre	Sauteurs	Grand Marquis[1]	Megrin	Carriacou
1	11	8	8	10	4	5	7
2-3	32	16	11	24	23	19	18
4-5	25	18	4	11	12	9	15
6-10	29	14	5	17	13	16	12
11-20	19	19	14	12	24	13	14
21-30	9	7	4	6	11	8	3
31-40	2	1	5	6	7	5	3
41-50	3	4	2	0	4	3	0
51-75	3	3	6	6	7	5	0
76-100	6	4	1	4	7	1	0
101-50	2	2	0	6	0	6	0
>150	0	0	1	6	3	0	0
Total	141	96	61	108	115	90	72

Source: TNA, Key, UK. CO 101/1 f.18-31, "Capitation Rolls for the Quarters of Basse-Terre...."

[1] Numbers for Grand Marquis are undercounted due to error in compiling original data.

Table 10.1

Ranges of Slave Ownership by Type of Plantation, 1763

Range	Sugar	Coffee/Cocoa	Other	Total
1	0	4	43	47
2-3	0	18	108	126
4-5	0	21	62	83
6-10	0	51	51	102
11-20	0	88	18	106
21-30	4	38	3	45
31-40	3	23	1	27
41-50	6	11	0	17
51-75	20	11	0	31
76-100	21	1	0	22
101-150	13	3	0	16
>150	10	0	0	10
Total	77	269	286	632

Source: See source for Table 9.5.

Table 11.1 Geographic and Racial Distribution of Carriacou's Population, 1750

Districts (Quartiers)	Total Pop	House-holds	Total (%)	White Population (%)				Non-White Population (%)					
				Total	Males	Females	Children	Total	Slave	Free	Males	Females	Children
La Baye des Jufs[1]	21	3	10.6	47.6	50	10	40	52.4	72.7	27.3	54.5	18.2	27.3
La Baye à l'Eau[2]	58	11	29.1	51.7	36.7	20	43.3	48.3	60.7	39.3	25	21.4	53.6
La Grande Baye[3]	8	1	4.0	25	50	0	50	75.0	100	0.0	0.0	33.3	66.7
Ramier[4]	20	3	10.1	75	20	13.3	66.7	25	25	0.0	60	40	0.0
La Grande Ance[5]	37	7	18.6	37.8	42.8	28.6	28.6	62.2	95.7	4.3	34.8	34.8	30.4
La Breteche[6]	18	1	9.0	0.0	0.0	0.0	0.0	100	100	0.0	---	---	---
L'Ance Noire[7]	3	2	1.5	100	100	0.0	0.0	0.0	0.0	0.0	0.0	0.0	0.0
Le Grand Carenage[8]	8	1	4.0	100	50.0	25.0	25.0	0.0	0.0	0.0	0.0	0.0	0.0
Grand Carenage[9]	26	4	13.1	38.5	100	0.0	0.0	61.5	100	0.0	25	31.3	43.7
Total Population	199	33		46.2	47.8	16.3	35.9	53.8	69.2	30.8	>28	>25.2	>32.7

Sources: FR ANOM F³ 17; Francis Kay Brinkley, "An Analysis of the 1750 Carriacou Census," *Caribbean Quarterly*, 24, 1-2 (1978): 44-60.

1 Located on the NE coast, it bears its original French name as the English translation Jew Bay. The 1750 census records Jean Abraham, 21 years, of possible Jewish heritage living just north of Jew Bay at Bay à l'Eau.

2 Located on the NE coast, it still bears its original French name, or its English translation Watering Bay; also known as Windward.

3 Located on the E, it still bears the original French name, though Anglicized as Grand Bay.

4 From French meaning "woodpigeon"), a former name for Sparrow Bay on the NW, the only area unaccounted for after all areas have been assigned. Encompasses L'Ance la Roche area and Sparrow Bay.

5 Located on the W, it is currently known as Hillsborough Bay and encompassed the primary settlement/administrative center of the island.

6 Located on the SE, it still bears the original name from the French bretèche ("brattice: breastwork erected during a siege") for the "Old Redoubt."

7 Located on the SW, it bears part of its French name as Black Bay, from L'Ance Noire Joignant le Carenage ("Black Bay joining the Carenage").

8 Located in the S, it bears part of its French name as Manchineel Bay, from Manchenilliers Joignant le Grand Carenage (Manchineel Bay across from or joining Grand Carenage); name possibly derived from the abundance of manchineel trees (*Hippomane mancinella*) in the area.

9 Located in the SW, the area is currently known as Tyrrel Bay/Harvey Vale, the French name having disappeared.

Table 11.2

Age Distribution, Carriacou (N=181)[a]

	0-9	10-19	20-29	30-39	40-49	50-59	60-69	70+
	---------------------------Age in Years---------------------------							
% Pop	27.7	13.9	11.6	18.5	16.2	4.0	4.0	4.0
Ratio	1.2	1.6	1.0	1.3	3.0	6	0.4	0.4

Source: See source for Table 11.1.
[a] The total (N) is not 199 b/c the ages for the 18 slaves of the Marquis Delisle are not recorded.

Table 11.3

Family Structure on Carriacou, 1750

Categories	Number (Percentages)
No. of households	33
Children (white and mulatto)	45 (22.6% of pop)
Mean no. of white men per woman	2.9
Mean no. of whites/ household	2.8
Mean no. of white children/household	2.2
Mean no. of slaves/household	2.2
Mean no. of individual/household	6.0

Source: See source for Table 11.1.

Table 11.4

Age Composition and Fertility, Carriacou, 1750 (N=181)[a]

Whites/Free			Slaves		
Children (%)	Adults (%)	Children/ Woman	Children (%)	Adults (%)	Children/ Woman
42.1	57.9	2.2	21.7	72.3	0.8

Source: See source for Table 11.1.

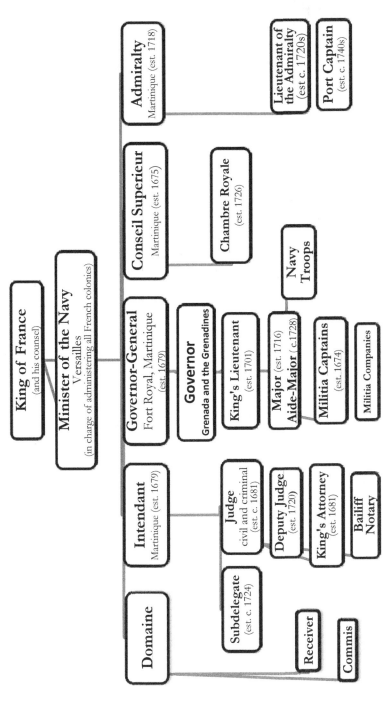

Hierarchy of French Colonial Administration in Grenada, 1674-1762

Appendix II: French Colonial Administration in Grenada

Before 1674 and Grenada's designation as a French crown colony, the island was under proprietary rule (1649-64), and administration under the government-organized Compagnie des Indies occidentales (West India Company, 1664-74). From thenceforth it fell under the governance of the French Crown and as such was part of the centralized administrative system of French colonialism in the region. Between 1674 and 1762 that structure witnessed some cosmetic changes, mainly additions of checks and balances, but Grenada remained a small part of a larger system that was designed for the exploitation of colonies for the benefit of France.

The structure of the French colonial system exhibited some divergence from its British counterpart like the absence of legislatures in its colonies. It was a top-down system directly controlled from the metropolis, though its effect on the ground was far from absolute, and local conditions played a vital role in the final outcome. The administrative hierarchy, as outlined in the figure above, began at the top in France with the French king, through the secretary of the Navy (*secretaire d'etat à la Marine*) which issued Royal edicts and ordinances for the day-to-day administration of the colonies. The secretary of the Navy was responsible for the administration of the Caribbean colonies, forwarding the Royal directives to its appointed authority. In the *Iles du Vent*, the headquarters of the French colonial authority was at Martinique where the governor-general, intendant and other officials resided.

The role of the governor-general was the management of the administration of all the colonies. Before 1713 the governor-general was in charge of the Islands of America (*Iles de l'Amerique*), comprising St. Domingue, Martinique, Guadeloupe, Grenada and a number of smaller islands. After 1713 St. Domingue formed its own government with its own governor-general, and the remainder of the islands fell under the Windward Islands (*Iles du Vent*) and administered from Fort Royal, Martinique. The post of governor-general was a military one, with command of all the militias and military forces in the colonies. As the official job description read, he was responsible for "All that concerns the dignity of authority and the military."[1] He had authority over defense of the colonies and as such supervised the planning and construction of fortifications. In the event of war he was the highest ranking officer in charge of the forces. Though he could freely make decisions, the governor-general was expected to seek the advice of the secretary of the Navy and his staff on many issues of governance, though that advice may be long in coming due to difficulties with communication.

His considerable authority was tempered by that of an intendant, a post which was established in 1678. The post of intendant, on par with the governor-general in many respects, was created to check the power of the governor-general. As the governor-general administered the external affairs of the colonies, the intendant was responsible for internal affairs– justice, finances (except in respect to fortifications and the military) and the police. The two were expected to work together, but more often than not were at odds over policy.

Under both the governor-general and intendant was the *Conseil Souverain* which was established in 1675 and composed of the latter two officials, along with the king's lieutenant, and about four to five principal citizens as councilors. Though it had no legislative authority and dealings with financial matters, it was the only participatory arm of government in the islands, disregarding the fact that its representation was limited to the island's elite. It also functioned as a criminal court while the Admiralty court, established in 1718 and seated in Martinique, dealt with civil cases.

From there, authority filtered down to the governor at Fort Royal, Grenada. Like the governor-general in Martinique, the governor was in charge of the island's military command. He was the highest authority on the island, and for many years possessed a great deal of authority as other structures of government were slow to be established. Financial and judicial authority were under a sub-delegate of the intendant and a royal civil and criminal judge, and other support staff. The governor was responsible for correspondence with both Martinique and Versailles. He was expected to work with the local officials, the governor-general and intendant at Martinique, but again conflicts arose between them.

Under the governor was the king's/royal lieutenant (*lieutenand du roi*) who was answerable to the governor and functioned as deputy governor; he often acted as interim governor or replaced him. Under the orders of the governor he was directly in charge of the company of Navy troops and militia until the creation of the post of major. Under him were the captains of the militia (*capitains des milice*) who were in charge of the individual militias or companies representing each administrative district.

Over time various positions were added to support the economic and demographic growth of the colony. These included the position of army surgeon (*chirurgien-major*), which provided an official medical officer for Grenada for the first time in 1714. The surveyor of roads and road officer (*voyer et arpenteur*) for each district took over the construction and maintenance of roads and bridges from the militia captains. They were appointed by the road overseer (*grand voyer*) who was responsible for the development and maintenance of public places, including roads, bridges and towns. The engineer was primarily responsible for the maintenance and improvement of the island's fortifications, but was also called upon to design other public buildings like the hospital and prison.

The following list of colonial administrators in Grenada between 1649 and 1762 (arranged by official positions) is an attempt to provide as much information as available on the individuals who held these various positions of authority in the colony. The list of the governors and their representatives, the king's lieutenants and majors are complete; dates and names are incomplete for many of the other positions.

Governors of Grenada, 1649-1762

<u>Lord Proprietors (*Seigneurs-propriétaires*), 1649-64</u>[2]
Jacques **Dyel du Parquet** (Mar 1649–Jul 1658)[3]
    1649, Mar–Jul 1654   Jean **Le Comte**[4]
    1654, Sep–Jul 1658   Louis de **Cacqueray de Valméniere**[5]
Jean de Faudoas II, Comte de Sérillac (Jul 1658–Nov 1664)[6]
    1658, Jul–Oct 1659   François **du Bu**[7]
    1660, Dec–Aug 1662 Jean de Faudoas II (father)
    1662, Aug–Nov 1664 Jean de Faudoas III (son)

<u>West India Company (Compagnie des Indes occidentales), 1664-74</u>
1664, Nov–1671   **Vincent**[8]
1671, Nov–May 1674   Louis de **Canchy de Lerole**[9]

<u>French Colony, 1674-1763</u>
1674, Oct–1679   Pierre **Sainte-Marthe de Lalande**[10]
1679, Oct–Jun 1680   Jacques de **Chambly**[11]
1680, Jun–Jun 1689   Nicolas de **Gabaret**[12]
1690, May–Dec 1695   Louis **Ancelin de Gémosat**[13]
1696, Oct–Jan 1700   Pierre de **Bellair de Saint-Aignan**[14]
1700, Nov–Dec 1708   Joseph de **Bouloc**[15]
1709, Jan–Sep 1710   Laurent de **Valernod**[16]
1711, Oct–1711   Paul-François de **La Grange,** Comte d'**Arquian**[17]
1712, Apr–Jul 1716   Guillaume-Emmanuel-Théodore de **Maupeou-Ribaudon**, Comte de L'Estrange[18]
1716, Oct–Oct 1717   François de **Pas de Mazen-Court,** Marquis de **Feuquières**[19]
1717, Aug–Nov   Alexandre de **Vaultier de Moyencourt**[20]
1717, Nov–Jan 1721   Jean-Michel de **Lépinay de la Longueville**[21]
1721, Apr–Aug 1722   Jean-Baltazar **du Houx**[22]
1722, Dec   Bonnaventure François de **Boisfermé**[23]
1723, Nov–Oct 1727   Robert **Giraud du Poyet**[24]
1727, Nov–Nov 1734   Charles Brunier, Marquis de **Larnage**[25]
1734, Nov–Feb 1747   Jean-Louis **Fournier de Carles de Pradines**[26]
1747, Mar–Oct 1757   Robert Phillipe de **Longvilliers de Poincy**[27]
1757, Nov–Mar 1762   Pierre-Claude-Antoine-François de Prulay de **Bonvoust D'Aulnay**[28]

Royal/King's Lieutenant (*Lieutenant du Roi*)[29]

1698, Apr–Dec 1700	De La Hogue[30]
1701, Dec–Jun 1711	Isle-Gilbert de Latouche[31]
1711, Jul–Mar 1712	Pierre La Rocheguyon, Chevalier de Guyon[32]
1712, Mar–Apr 1716	Philippe Bouvier de Quesnel de La Mothe[33]
1716, Apr–Nov 1734	Jean-Louis Fournier de Carles de Pradines[34]
1734, Nov–Sep 1737	Nicolas Binoist de Reteuil[35]
1738, Jul–Jun 1739	Jacques de Kearney[36]
1740, May–Nov 1757	Prulay de Bonvoust d'Aulnay[37]
1757, Nov–Mar 1762	Pierre Glapion, Chevalier de Glapion[38]

Counselors of the King in the *Chambre Royale*

1726- ?	Achallé[39]
1726–1731	Jean Rochard[40]
1726–1740s	Philippe Roume de Saint-Laurent[41]
	Antoine Delesgallery d'Apinat
1730–1746	Louis François de Gannes de Falaise[42]
1730–1750s	Jacques Lequoy de Mongiraud[43]
1740–1750s	Michel Ferdinand Ollivier[44]
1740–1750s	Jean des Fougeray de St-Martin de Traverni[45]
1750s	Charles Nicolas de Mesme de Chanteloup[46]

Major

1716, Oct–Nov 1734	Nicolas Binoist de Reteuil[47]
1735, Sep–May 1740	Prulay de Bonvoust d'Aulnay[48]
1739, Sep–1752	Léon-Alexis de Brémond d'Ars[49]
1753–1754	Jean-Gabriel de Cazenave de La Barrère[50]
	Simon de Gannes de la Chancellerie[51]
1757, Jul–Mar 1762	de Mange

Aide-Major (*Capitaine aide-major*)

?1728–1731	Jean Rochard[52]
1736–1742	Jacques de Brie de La Guérenne[53]
1743–1748	François Camille de Francesqui[54]
1746–1762	Jean Gabriel Fornier Carles de Pradines[55]
1748	Chevalier d'Élevemont[56]
1748–1757	Pierre Glapion, Chevalier de Glapion

Army Surgeon (*Chirurgien-major*)

Charles Houllier (1714-43)

de Bruere (1744-48)

Joseph Maillard (?-1762)

Judge *(Juge royal/ ordinaire civil et criminel)*

1688–1697	Théodore de Thallas[57]
1697–1723	Jean Rochard[58]
1723–1733, 1737	Julien Girard[59]
1733, Nov–Mar 1737	Jean-Joseph Doussan[60]
1737, May–1759	François Ollivier[61]
1759, Nov–Mar 1762	Jean-Louis Azémar[62]

Lieutenant/Deputy Judge *(Lieutenant de juge)*

1720–1723	Julien Girard[63]
1723–?	François Clozier de Beauleau[64]

Royal/King's Attorney/Prosecutor *(Procureur du roi)*

1704–?1713	Allou[65]
1714–1723	François Clozier de Beauleau[66]
1724–1729	Hérissier (d. Jul 1729)
1731-1733	Jean-Joseph Doussan
1734	Guillaume Hantot
1735	Joseph Rey (died upon arrival to take up post)
1748	Chaubet
1754 –1759	Jean-Louis Azémar[67]
	Michel Danglebermes

Subdelegate of the Intendant *(Subdélégué de l'intendant)*

1724–?1737	Philippe Roume de Saint-Laurent[68]
1738–1740	Julien Girard[69]
1740–1759	François Ollivier
1760–1762	Jean Pouzacq[70]

Lieutenant of the Admiralty *(Lieut. général de l'amirauté)*[71]

1718 –1731	Jean Rochard
1733–1740	Julien Girard
1740–1759	François Ollivier

Port Captain *(Capitaine de port)*

? –1748	Guillaume Lataste[72]
?1748–54	Louis d'Ailleboust d'Argenteuil[73]

Le Domaine

Nicolas Louis de Mesme de Chanteloup *(receveur du Domaine)*
Antoine Eustache de Louvigny *(commis du Domaine)*
Alquier *(sous-fermier du Domaine)*

Road Inspector & Surveyor (*Voyer et arpenteur*)

Joseph Cosquer Dupocard (?*Grand Voyer*)
Joseph Ronzier (for Grand Pauvre; d. 1753)
Antoine Bonis (for Grand Pauvre)
Collet de Cran[74]
Pierre Delpech de Laroque
Etienne Molinier[75]
Jean-Baptiste Pinel[76]
François d'Imbert[77]

Engineer (*Ingénieur*)

1699, 1716–1735	Nicolas Binoist de Reteuil[78]
1725–1748	Jean-Baptiste-Pierre Le Romain[79]
1750–1762	Barbier de Sassignies[80]

Companies of the Militia (*Campagnies de la Milice*)[81]
Captain / Lieutenant / Ensign (2) for each company

Captains

La Blenerie (c.1674–1704)
Du Meny (?–1678)
Jullien (1678–?)
De Lugerat (1692–95)
Robert Giraud du Poyet
Desouches (1696-1704)
René Des Vallées-Montrayer (1703–15)
Du Jardin (1715–16)
Joseph de Jarrier de La Chassaigne (1720–22)
Achallé (1720s)
Jean-Baptiste Pelet de Lautrec
Jean Baptiste Pichery[82]
Fouray d'Espagne (1752–)
Pierre Fauchier (1742–62)
Piché (1744–48)
Louis Le Jeune (1740s)[83]
Louis Papin (1740s)
Thomas-Daniel Rochard de L'Épine
Louis Alexandre Le Jeune Du Sablon (1740s)
Jean Baptiste Viette
Yves de La Tousche-Limouzinière de Mareuil
Philippe Charles Clozier (1750s–62)
Julien Le Jeune-Dugué (1759–62)

Notes to Colonial Administrators

1 Virginia R. Robeson and Patrick Douglas, *New France, 1713-1760* (Ontario: Ontario Institute for Studies in Education, 1977), 23.

2 The lord proprietors were the sole owners of the island and controlled most aspects of its administration, often through their deputies or lieutenant generals.

3 See Chapter 4 for details of du Parquet's ownership and settlement of Grenada. Though he sold the island in 1656, members of his family lived in Grenada in the 1700s. François-Pierre Dyel Duparquet, chevalier Desnambuc, served as *écrivain principal* and had requested a seat on the *Chambre Royale*; He owned a 224 acres coffee estate in Grand Marquis; he married in Grenada in 1745 and died there in 1759. Pierre Dyel Duparquet Desnambuc was captain of the *Compagnie des gens libre* in Grand Marquis in 1782. Jean-Claire Dyel Duparquet was captain aide-major in the militia in Grand Marquis in 1782. Both took part in Fédon's Rebellion, but surrendered; tried, respited and banished from Grenada in 1796.

4 Le Comte served as Governor du Parquet's lieutenant general or deputy, administering Grenada from its initial settlement in March 1649 to his accidental death by drowning in June 1654. He was married to du Parquet's niece. See Chapter 4 for details of his rule.

5 Valmenière replaced Le Comte as du Parquet's lieutenant general in September 1654 and was immediately confronted with a mutiny by some of the French colonists under Le Fort and Le Marquis. He administered Grenada until July 1657 when the island was officially transferred to the Comte de Sérillac via du Bu. He remained in Grenada for some time and caused problems when he took two slaves belonging to the Island Caribs. He left Grenada by 1658 and returned to Martinique where he later became a conselor on the conseil supèrieur. He died in 1682. See Chapter 4 and 5 for details of his rule.

6 See Chapter 5 for the details of de Sérillac's ownership of Grenada.

7 Du Bu served as Governor de Sérillac's lieutenant general or deputy, administering Grenada from July 1657 to his death by execution in October 1658. His administration of Grenada was consumed with political infighting and intrigue. See Chapter 5 for details of his rule and death.

8 Vincent was the captain of the Regiment of Orleans that accompanied Prouville de Tracy to take control of the islands for the Compagnie des Indies occidentales françaises. He arrived in November 1664 and installed as the new governor, replacing Jean de Faurdos III, de Cérillac's son who was ordered back to France. He was absent from Grenada after 1669, but was still officially the governor; it wasn't until November 1671 that he was replaced. See Chapter 6 for details of his rule.

9 Canchy probably arrived in Grenada in 1668 and was the commandant in the absence of the governor by at least 1669. He was officially made governor in November 1671, and dismissed in May 1674. See Chapter 6 for details of his rule.

10 Sainte-Marthe, son of the governor of Martinique, served as governor between 1674 and 1679. He later served as king's lieutenant at Guadeloupe and governor of Cayenne; he died in 1692. See Chapter 6 for details of his rule in Grenada.

11 Chambly served as captain in Canada, governor of Arcadia (1673), Grenada (1679) and Martinique (1680); died 1687 at Martinique.

12 Gabaret was a naval captain before serving as governor of Grenada (1680), Martinique (1689-73), lieutenant général to the governor of the *Îles de l'Amérique* (1703), and governor of St. Domingue (1711); died at Martinique in 1712.

13 Gemosat was engineer (1672) and king's lieutenant (1675) at Martinique before his appointment as governor of Grenada; he died on 24 December 1695 at Grenada.

14 De Bellair served as naval captain (1686) in France, governor of Grenada (1696); returned to the navy in 1700; died in France in 1701. See Devas, *A History of the Island of Grenada*, 62-63, for more on his career before Grenada.

[15] De Bouloc served as king's lieutenant at Port-au-Paix, St. Domingue (1699). He was appointed governor of Grenada in November 1700, but did not arrive there until January 1702. He died on 2 December 1708 at Grenada.

[16] Valernod was appointed in January 1709, but he did not take up position as he was appointed governor of St. Domingue in September 1710; he died in May 1711 at St. Domingue.

[17] It is not exactly clear when d'Arquian was appointed, but it may have been as early as September 1710 when Valernod was promoted to the governorship of Cap at St. Domingue. He did not arrive in Grenada until April 1711. In April 1712 his replacement at Grenada was appointed as he was promoted to the governorship of Cap at St. Domingue to replace Valernod. His brief time as governor was very contentious.

[18] Maupeou-Ribaudon served in a number of military positions in Canada before returning to France where he joined the navy, achieving the position of naval captain (1707) before his appointment as governor of Grenada (1711); Returned to France in 1716; died there in 1725.

[19] Feuquières spent a year in Grenada, as he was promoted to commandant of Martinique in July 1717, and within six months was governor-general of the *Iles du Vent* following a revolt in Martinique.

[20] Vaultier was named governor of Grenada to replace de Feuquières on 14 August 1717, but was appointed governor of Guadeloupe on 18 March 1718. Never took up position.

[21] Lépinay was the former governor of Louisiana; arrived in Grenada on 28 June 1720 from France, but took ill by the end of the year, supposedly suffering from dropsy. He was sent to Martinique because of the lack of adequate medical care in Grenada where he died on 2 January 1721.

[22] Governor du Houx (or du Hou) was appointed governor of Grenada on 23 April 1721; died at Grenada on 29 August 1722.

[23] Boisfermé was appointed governor of Grenada on 1 December 1722, but died at Martinique on 11 December that same year, without taking up his position; formerly governor of Marie Galante.

[24] Du Poyet requested the governorship of Grenada in September 1722, but it was given to Boisfermé who died within a week of his appointment. Du Poyet had served in Grenada as militia captain in the 1690s; later appointed governor of Guadeloupe.

[25] Though he left Grenada in 1734 for the governorship of Guadeloupe, Larnage continued to own two estates in Megrin, Grenada. He died in 1747, but his wife, the Dame de Larnage, remained in Grenada. In 1763 she and Birot owned 302 acres sugar estate with 63 slaves in Megrin; and 329 acres of unknown cultivation.

[26] De Pradines arrived in Grenada as king's lieutenant in 1716, and acted as governor on many occasions before becoming governor between 1734-47. Received the chevalier de St. Louis in 1718; died at Grenada on 4 February 1747. Depradine Street, Gouyave bears his name even today; De Pradines Street in the town St. George's no longer exists.

[27] Lonvilliers de Poincy, born in St. Christopher in 1681 to former Governor Robert de Poincy, worked himself through the ranks of the militia at Martinique before his appointment as major (1723), king's lieutenant (1725), governor (1729) at Marie Galante, and governor of Grenada (1748); he retired in 1757 and died in Grenada in 1761.

[28] Born 1698 in France, Bonvoust arrived in the French Caribbean c. 1725; in that year he married the daughter of the king's lieutenant at Grenada, de Pradines. He arrived in Grenada following his appointment as aide-major on 23 May 1735 where his father-in-law was governor since 1734. He had served as a captain at Martinique since 1729. Received the Order of St. Louis in 1742. Had requested the post of governor following the death of Governor de Pradines, but was passed over. In 1763 he owned a sugar estate of 342 acres

with a water mill in Basse-Terre. Though he wanted to resist the British in 1762, he had no choice but to capitulate, ending French rule on the island after signing the capitulation on 5 March 1762; most of the residents had signed the day before. Though he had to leave the island, his wife remained and complained in 1764 that she was ill-treated by the British lieutenant governor. He subsequently sold his property in Grenada; died 14 May 1785.

[29] The royal or king's lieutenant was second to the governor of the colony, acting as the lieutenant governor, especially in military matters. In the absence of the governor he automatically acted in his place. The position was not introduced to Grenada until 1701, but de La Hogue, king's lieutenant for St. Bartelemy, served in that capacity in Grenada between 1700 and 1701. The absence of the governor for various reasons, especially during the wars between 1698 and 1714, made the position necessary. In January 1737 the governor-general proposed that a second king's lieutenant position be created for the "Capesterre" because the island had seen extensive development, especially because of coffee cultivation, and it be given to Jacques de Kearney. Since the position became available following the death of Binoist later that year, the second post was never created.

[30] The king's lieutenant at St. Barthelemy, de La Hogue was given orders on 1 April 1698 to go to Grenada to serve in that capacity. He arrived in Grenada late in 1698. Following the departure of Governor de Bellair around January 1700 he became the interim commander of the government. He died at Grenada on 19 December 1700. So technically he was not the first king's lieutenant appointed for Grenada.

[31] Iles-Gilbert died at Grenada on 29 June 1711; formerly king's lieutenant at St. Barthelemy (1701) and major at Martinique (1701).

[32] Captain of a company of tropes of the Navy, he was in Grenada and asked to serve as commander in December 1701 for a year following the death of king's lieutenant de La Hogue. Due to the state of war in the region and the absence of a permanent governor, he was asked to serve as king's lieutenant on 11 July 1711 following the death of king's lieutenant Isle-Gilbert until his permanent replacement in 1712.

[33] De la Mothe retired in 1716.

[34] See Endnote 26 above.

[35] Arrived in Martinique in 1699 and served as engineer for Grenada; thereafter served throughout the French Windward Islands. He was made the chief engineer for the Windward Islands in 1706 following the retirement of Jean-Baptiste de Caylus. With the plans drawn up by de Caylus, Binoist supervised the upgrade of Fort Royal between 1706 and 1710. In 1715 he decided to permanently reside in Grenada after acquiring a sugar plantation there. On 1 October 1716 he was made the first major, resigning his position as engineer in chief. His primary duty was the completion of improvements to Fort Royal. On 13 November 1734 he was made the king's lieutenant; he died 27 September 1737.

[36] Born in Galway, Ireland in 1689, Kearney served in a number of positions in Martinique. In June 1737 he requested a transfer after purchasing land in Grenada. On 1 January 1738 he was appointed as king's lieutenant, but died at Grenada on 11 June 1739. One of his sons, Louis Claude de Kearney, was governor of St. Lucia in 1776.

[37] See Endnote 28 above.

[38] Chevalier de Glapion served in Grenada as ensign (1740), aide-major (1748), and king's lieutenant (1757-62). He received the Cross of St. Louis in November 1757. He was married to "a creole of the same island" and owned 275 acres sugar estate, with at least 54 slaves, and another 604 acres uncultivated in Grand Marquis in 1763. He died by 1771.

[39] Achellé, as captain of the militia, was appointed to serve on the newly created *Chambre Royale* in 1726.

[40] From La Rochelle, France, Rochard arrived in Grenada as early as 1697 as the judge of

the island, but it wasn't until December 1718 that he received his appointment as "juge royal" of Grenada. He married Margaurite Ferray, widow of the former judge Thallas. In 1723 he owned 429.5 *carres* at Grande Ance, Rivière Simon and Antoine, with 83 slaves. He retired in 1723, but was still involved in public life as a counselor on the newly created *Chambre Royale* in 1726, lieutenant of the admiralty, and aide-major in the militia. Probably died c. 1731 when an inventory of his property was carried out. He was the progenitor of the Rochard family in Grenada and Trinidad.

41 From the lesser nobility of Burgundy, France, Roume de St. Laurent arrived in Grenada via Martinique to serve as the sundelegate of the intendant. In 1726 he was appointed to the *Chambre Royale* as a counselor; he is subsequently listed as an honorary counselor on the *Chambre Royale*. He married Francisca le Clare; father of Laurent Philippe and grandfather of the well known Philippe-Rose Roume de St. Laurent. He died in 1747.

42 Born 1701 in Canada, and arrived in Grenada from Ile Royale in 1720/22. He registered his letter of nobility at the Conseil supérieur at Martinique in 1736. He was militia captain (1735) in Sauteurs, received the Cross of St. Louis; served as king's counselor on the *Chambre Royale*. Married Louise de Sainte-Marthe, a widow; died w/o children in 1746. He owned 433 acres La Plain sugar estate in Sauteurs.

43 He was resident in Grenada as early as the 1730s. In 1738 his 65 quarres (297 acres) Rivière Saint-Jean estate was bought to establish a sugar estate to support the new hospital; he owned 374 acres sugar estate in Basse-Terre in 1765 known as Tempe; father of François Jacques Lequoy de Montgiraud who served as administrator of Grenada (1779) and St. Lucia and commissioner at St. Domingue. He was councillor in the *Chambre Royale*.

44 The son of François Ollivier, he was a prominent resident. He was the father of Jean-Baptiste Ollivier of Julien Fédon fame. He died 13 December 1761. Owned 265 acres coffee estate with 82 slaves later known as Grand Mal; its subsequent sale and title remained embroiled in legal limbo for many years.

45 Native of St-Sulpice, France; married Angélique de Beltgens in 1742; died November 1757. Owned 115 acres coffee estate in Basse-Terre.

46 He was the son of Nicolas Louis de Mesme de Chanteloup, receiver of the Domaine. He owned 704 acres sugar estate at Beau Séjour. Advocated for the French under British rule and was appointed to the General Council in 1772 to represent them; died in 1773. Beauséjour River and Bay, bordering the estate, also bore the names Chantaloup River and Bay.

47 See Endnote 35 above.

48 Bonvoust was named major without appointment on 1 September 1735. See also Endnote 25 above.

49 While ship's ensign, he married in 1736 to Louise Faure de Fayolle, daughter of Élie Faure de Fayolle, merchant at St. Pierre, Martinique who owned property in Grenada; as a result he became established in Grenada pursuing business with his father-in-law, managing a sugar estate. He requested a position and in 1739 was made aide-major; promoted to king's lieutenant for Trinité, Martinique, but did not take up position. Owned 1,296 acres sugar estate with 68 slaves & watermill in Basse-Terre in 1763; also owned house plot in the Town of St. George in 1765; property sold in 1760s, and he died in 1779 in Geneva.

50 He served as lieutenant (1731) and captain (1735) in Grenada before moving to Martinique as aide-major (1740). He returned to Grenada as major (1753), but left for Martinique as king's lieutenant in 1754. He retired in 1757 and most likely returned to Grenada to manage two large sugar plantations: 620 acres with 108 slaves, and 1,338 acres with 145 slaves; both had water mills in Mégrin.

51 Born in Canada in 1707, de Gannes arrived in Grenada around c. 1720 as his brother, Louis de Gannes de Falaise; owned 220 sugar estate in Grand Pauvre in 1763. Progenitor of the De Gannes family of Trinidad.

52 See Endnote 40 above.

53 It is not clear when La Guérenne left the position. It appeared that he resigned in May 1742, but in November he was given leave to go to France. It also appeared he did not return because in January 1744 he was listed as having left without permission and the authorities were taking action to have him retired.

54 A native of Martinique, he served as a cadet in France, where he was recommended from Versailles for the position of aide-major in Grenada in 1743, arriving that year to take up the post. In 1747 he requested retirement and left the job in 1748. He married Marie Rose Achallé in February 1744 and they had four children. In 1757 he was charged with cruelty to his slaves following the deaths of six of them due to excessive punishment. Owned two sugar estates totaling 646 acres and powered by two watermills in Grand Marquis; he owned at least 188 slaves in 1763. He sold his estates and returned to France after the British takeover; died by 1774.

55 On the recommendation of his father Governor de Pradines, he was appointed aide-major for the *quartiers* of Sauteurs and Grand Marquis on 1 July 1746 following his return from France where he served as a *mousquetaire noire*. He married in 1759 to Elizabeth Marie-Margurite de Gannes de La Chancellier. Owned a 867 acres sugar estate with 122 slaves in Basse-Terre in 1763, and house plot in the Town of St. George in 1765. Assisted d'Estaign in 1779 when he captured the island from the British, with his estate used as a staging area/camp; distinguishing himself in this action and was hurt; awarded the Cross of St. Louis in June 1784. He remained in Grenada until at least 1786, but died soon after.

56 Appointed in March 1748, but by November there were many complaints against him so he was replaced in December.

57 Thalas served as notary until 1688 when he replaced the judge (1681) who was revoked that year. He may have served as the criminal and civil judge until 1697.

58 See Endnote 40 above.

59 Girard was from Vendôme, France, and served in Grenada as the lieutenant of the judge (1720), judge (1723), and retired in 1734; acted temporarily as judge in 1737. Upon his death in 1740 (at the age of 55 yrs) in Martinique he was listed as being the subdelegate of the intendant at Martinique and lieutenant general of the Amiralty of Grenada. He was also listed as an honorary counselor in the *Chambre Royale*.

60 Doussan served as king's attorney (30 Nov 1731) and juge (5 Nov 1733), but died on the job in March 1737.

61 Ollivier served as the king's attorney at Martinique before his appointment as judge at Grenada (1737) and subdelegate of the l'intendant (1740); he died c. 1759. He was the father of Michel-Ferdinand Ollivier and grandfather of Jean-Baptiste Ollivier who had a leadership role in Fédon's Rebellion and was bannished from the island as a result.

62 Azéma served as *commissaire de police et notaire royal* at Martinique before his appointment as king's attorney (1751) and judge royal (1759) in Grenada.

63 See Endnote 59 above.

64 Clozier was born c. 1692. He was appointed king's attorney in Grenada (1714) and notary (1720), but in 1721 was accused by the judge of illegal trade. Promoted to lieutenant of the judge (1723). The place name Clozier, St. John is derived from his family.

65 Allou/Alou/Dalou served as king's prosecutor and quartermaster by 1704, but may have been on the island as early as 1690. In 1704 he was accused of participating in illegal trade, but was rehabilated in 1705.

66 See Endnote 64 above.

[67] See Endnote 62 above.

[68] See Endnote 41 above.

[69] See Endnote 59 above.

[70] Pouzacq served as royal notary and subdelegate of the intendant. Owned 1,362 acres sugar estate, with 82 slaves in Basse-Terre; d. c. 1762.

[71] Judges served as the lieutenant of the Admiralty in Grenada.

[72] La Taste, a prominent resident, served as captain of the port; he owned what became known as La Taste estate, St. Patrick; died 1748. The place name of Lataste is after him.

[73] Moved from Martinique to Grenada c. 1747 to become port captain.

[74] Surveyor and road officer for Carriacou, de Cran owned a cotton plantaton on that island and remained there until the mid-1780s before returning to his native Redon, France by 1786.

[75] Molinièr was born in Millau, France in 1728 and arrived in Grenada c. 1754. He served as *arpenteur et voyer* and later captain of the *Voluntaires des les enfans perdus* by 1759. One of the many French who remained in Grenada under the British and played a promient role in the island for almost three decades. In October 1775 he was one of three French elected to the General Assembly for the parishes of St. George/St. John. During the French interregnum (1779-83) he was a councilor on the conseil superiuer and served as engineer in chief and commander of the district and battalion of Fort Royal. He was justice of the peace in the 1780s and took a very active role in the political struggles defending French rights; in May 1789 Governor Matthews reported to London that Molinier "seems to take the lead in all the French concerns in Grenada." He died by 1790. His residence and plantation at Bois Maurice bears the name Molinièr today.

[76] Pinel was from Bordeaux, France and served as *arpenteur royal et voyer* in Goyave, where he owned 160 acres coffee/cocoa estate with 14 slaves in 1763. He did the survey of Grenada in 1762 that resulted in the first detailed map of the island (see Illustration 10.2).

[77] Imbert was *arpenteur royal et voyer* for the district of Basse-Terre where had a 114 cocoa estate with 8 slaves in 1763, and a house plot in the Town of St. George in 1765. He was the author of "A plan of George Town in the Island of Grenada, 1765" (see Illustration 10.3).

[78] See Endnote 35 above.

[79] Le Romain was serving in Martinique when he was sent to Grenada in 1734 as assistant engineer to work on Fort Royal; he was promoted to chief engineer by 1748. He wrote about 70 articles for Diderot and Alembert's *Encyclopaédie* (1765) on the French Antilles, particularly slavery and the plantation environment. Le Romain is also the cartographer of "Plan de la Rade du Fort Royal," 1746 (see Illustration 9.4).

[80] Barbier served as engineer at Grenada (1750-62) and remained under British rule managing his 96 acres coffee/pasture estate in Gouyave until his departure in 1769.

[81] See Chapter 9 under "Colonial Conflicts and Defense" and Table 9.2 for more details on the development of the militia in Grenada.

[82] Arrived in Grenada c. 1722 and worked through the ranks of the militia to captain of the campany in Megrin (1742-52). He moved to Basse-Terre and served in a number of capacities for the governor. He owned 288 acres sugar and 160 acres pasture estates in Basse-Terre with 50 slaves in 1763. In 1762 he was appointed to the board of trustees for the hospital by the British. Left Grenada after he sold estates by 1772.

[83] Born c. 1710; member of the proprietory family long established in Grenada. Captain of the militia in Sauteurs, he received the Cross of St. Louis in 1749. He owned extensive sugar estates and slaves which he sold in 1764 and left Grenada; died 1770 in Martinique.

Appendix III: Populations of Grenada, 1669-1763

Table A

Slave Population, 1669-1763

Year	Total	Males	Females	Children	Infirm	Maroons
1669	222	124	66	32		
1687	297	133	76	88		
1690	303	184	119	92 (55/37)		
1700	525	223	154	143		
1704	925	423	275	227		
1707[1]	1116					
1715	2400					
1718	2779	1116	640	790	183	
1722	3045	1258	699	882	206	
1726	3476	1360	776	1030	310	
1731	4375	1683	965	1235	492	
1735	5299	2056	1249	1538	456	
1741	7725	3094	1906	2240	485	
1745	9986	3396	2332	2550	469	
1749	8700	3418	2335	2332	563	62
1755	12208	4333	3525	3783	567	
1761	14308	5505	4511	3500	496	296
1763[2]	13846	10531 (adults)		3315 (children)		

Source: Recensement de la population de la Grenade, 1669-1755. G[1] 498, Archives Nationales, Paris.

[1] Figures for 1707 are only overall numbers of people taken from a correspondence by the governor; see FR ANOM COL C8B 2 N° 8.
[2] The National Archives, Key, UK. Colonial Office 101/1, f. 6. The total slave population for 1763 was closer to 15,000 because of the ommission of slave children under 14 years in the largest district of Grand Marquis/St. Andrew.

Table B

White Population, 1669-1763

Year	Total	Men	Women	Children	Servants	Infirm
1669	283	98	68	62 (28/34)	55	
1683	302	150	79	73 (43/30)		
1686	299	123	86	90 (55/35)		
1687	311	170	63	133 (57/76)		
1690	337	89	72	142 (94/48)	34	
1700	250	78	57	115 (68/47)		10
1704	353	77	72	186 (119/67)		
1707[1]	351	110 (men/boys)	146 (women/girls)	95 (children/infirm)		
1718	461	78	100	332 (160/79)	36	13
1726	664	137	115	350 (219/131)	62	13
1731	893	257	141	446 (270/176)	59	11
1735	841	123	138	526 (322/204)	54	14
1741	1085	173	200	673 (407/266)	39	24
1745	1050	185	179	622 (364/258)	64	24
1749	1138	193	146	730 (452/278)	42	27
1755	1081	247	162	616 (283/233)	19	37
1761	1574	470	277	827 (482/345)		
1763[2]	1225	711 (males)		514 (females)		

Source: Recensement de la population de la Grenade, 1669-1755. G[1] 498, Archives Nationales, Paris.

[1] Figures for 1707 are only overall numbers of people taken from a correspondence by the governor: 110 men/boys bearing arms, 146 women/girls, 95 infirm/children; see FR ANOM COL C[8B] 2 N° 8.
[2] The National Archives, Key, UK. Colonial Office 101/1, f. 6.

Table C

Free Non-White Population, 1669-1763

Year	Total	Men	Women	Children	Infirm
1682	7				
1687	31				
1690	42	23	19		
1700	53				
1704	51				
1718	82	28	43	11	
1726	116	36	54	26	
1731	111	38	53	20	
1741	164	52	56	56	
1745	189	55	74	52	8
1749	189	54	74	61	
1755	347	85	132	130	
1761	574	160	137	222	55
1763[1]	455	236 (males)	219 (females)		

Source: Recensement de la population de la Grenade, 1669-1755. G[1] 498, Archives Nationales, Paris.

[1] The National Archives, Key, UK. Colonial Office 101/1, f. 6.

Appendix IV: La Ville du Fort Royal

The poor state of Grenada's economy prior to the 1700s meant that little or no resources went into the development of the island's infrastructure. It had to await the economic growth post-1713 which led to the building of the economic as well as the social infrastructure. Yet there was one feature of the plantation society that had to be addressed regardless of the prosperity of the economy. This was defense, and it was a constant preoccupation of the administrators and planters for much of the period of French occupation. The extent of the correspondence between the governor, the governor-general in Martinique and colonial authorities in France illustrated the preoccupation with the defense of the island, and in some cases for good reason.

The characteristics that contributed to the development of colonial towns in the French Caribbean were lacking or altogether absent from Grenada for decades following its settlement. The population was small and scattered, wealth non-existent, the church barely present, and government structures limited: a frontier environment. The Ville du Fort Royal was the only town (*bourg*) in Grenada for all of the seventeenth and the first two decades of the eighteenth centuries. It was even a stretch to call it a town; for its first sixty years it was a mere hamlet, with a few dozen rudely constructed houses, a place for ships to dock, and a chapel, all commanded by a small fort. Fort Royal, hence the name of the town, housed much of the colonial administration on the island for decades. The town nonetheless served as the center of economic and social life for the small population that made the island its home. Relative to the other towns in the Caribbean, the Ville du Fort Royal was inconsequential, and based on Watts' specifications it would have been considered a mere village.[1]

The Ville du Fort Royal had its beginnings in 1649 when the French established the settlement of Fort de l'Annunciation on a spit of land that enclosed a small lagoon within a protected bay on the western coast of the island. Visiting in 1656, Father Dutertre observed that:

> The fort, which is located between the Pond and the Haven, is a square frame dwelling...; it is surrounded at a distance of eight to ten feet from the building with a strong fence made of trees encircling it, at the two corners which face the sea are

two small frame lodges, in one is living the Commandant. The house of Mr. du Parquet is a large area which enclose the whole mountain [to the east] near the Haven, at the bottom of which are the warehouses, which are of one hundred or 120 feet of a building made of bricks and framework. The church is located on this place at a distance of about 300 steps from the Fort; but it is made of only pitchforks and reeds and is in very poor condition; the whole place is planted in manioc, potatoes and peas and set with orange-trees and other fruits.[2]

The settlement, also known as Grand Fort, protected the few houses, landing area, warehouses and chapel that lined the sandbar and the immediate area around the lagoon. Describing the bay and enclosed pond, Dutertre adds that "We have entered the Haven and found it very clean and in a condition to shelter fifty boats or canoes protected from every storm. Near the Haven is a big, round, very deep pond which is separated from it only by a sand dam; as wide as the causeway of your Pond, which if cut off, the Pond could contain a lot of ships and boats enclosed as in a box."[3] Under proprietary rule little changed for the small cluster of buildings, barely able to withstand attacks from the Amerindians.

The Compagnie des Indies occidentales françaises, following its takeover in 1664, made attempts to improve the island's infrastructure, the first of which was the construction of a fort capable of defending the settlement from colonial enemies. In 1667 François Blondel designed a small fort (Illustration 6.2) to the west of the initial settlement which he called Fort Royal, and the following year the stone structure was begun under Governor Vincent. Blondel recorded the bay as Port Louis after the reigning French King. His map of the settlement and planned fortification illustrated the crude cluster of about twenty or so buildings that the settlement comprised for the first three decades (Illustration 6.2). Fort Royal became the center of the growing town, a prominence that is illustrated by a c.1670s drawing of the settlement (Illustration 6.6). The new fort soon led to the expansion of the town west and north from its cramped beginnings to encompass the surrounding hills, with houses clinging to the hills rising from the water's edge.

In 1688 Father Jean de la Mousse visited, rendering a revealing description of the town: "After I said mass [at the church], the Governor [Gabaret] took me in his boat with the father Capuchin and carried us to the fort located on the mountain, where we dined. There is a town made up of only forty houses all frame and covered the essentials.... There are in Grenada few inhabitants, and the King maintains a company there of fifty men."[4] For the first time there is an idea of the population of the town, possibly between 80 to 120 people, mostly colonial officials, a few dozens French soldiers, a merchant or two, craftsmen, and farm families with their slaves and servants.

A decade later Jean-Baptiste Labat made a visit to the island at the turn of the seventh century and his description was rather scathing.[5] Labat states that "From the picture I have painted, it will be easy to see that on arrival from Barbados, I did not expect to enjoy myself in so dismal a place: I began to be tired of it before setting foot on land, so that there was no need for the ship's captain to press me to get through with my business upon which I had come."[6] Disappointed with what he saw, Labat summed up his unflattering view of the French efforts to date.

> The English are much better than us at putting any advantages they have to the best use, and if Grenada belonged to them it would long ago have changed in appearance and have become a rich and powerful colony. Instead of which we have not put to use a single advantage, as we could have done and for so many years now the country has been unexploited, sparsely inhabited, lacking amenities as well as trade, remaining poor; while the houses, or rather the huts, are badly built and even more badly furnished; in a word, the island is much the same as it was when M. du Parquet bought it from the savages.[7]

Despite his dismal picture of the island, he was able to ride a horse from Fort Royal all the way to Grand Pauvre some 17 miles away, a ride of about three hours. Considering that most transportation throughout the island was by ferry, the road along the western coast was, according to Labat "passable, and would be very good and suitable for every kind of vehicle, if it were possible to work on them a little."[8]

By the time the wars ended in 1713, the Ville du Fort Royal had seen some improvements—an upgraded fort, a stone church, military barracks—but nothing much to show for having been established six decades earlier. The colony had progressed from an outpost to a fairly stable colony, with many of the structures of French colonial government in place. After the construction of Fort Royal between 1706 and 1710 the center of the town had already shifted west, with the layout of the town occupying the arc around the fort (Illustration 9.5). The unique geography of the area led to the establishment of the small town on two sides of a ridge that ran from the fort north. To the west of Fort Royal, the small flat area was laid out on a grid system by de Caylus in 1705, with the center designated the *place d'armes*, and roads connected to primary arteries across the island, especially along the western coast and east inland. The eastern part of the town ran along a circular bay and proved ideal for a port and careening of ships, though few houses actually ringed the bay. A road over the ridge connected the two parts of the town and to the fort which sat on the southern height of the ridge.

By the mid-1700s the French had completed the complex that maintained the colonial administration of Grenada and its dependencies. The citadel of Fort Royal was at the center of this complex as it was the oldest permanent building, and everything emanated from it outwards. Along the *Rue du Gouvernment*, just off the glacis of the fort to the west were government buildings, including the residence of the governor since 1708 when Governor de Bouloc abandoned his residence in the fort; also present were the church (*l'eglise*), presbytery (*le presbytère*), and the Bureau de Domaine (tax office). Just below Fort Royal towards the bay and connected by *la Rue du Fort*, was located the court house (*palais de justice*) with an open area facing the *Rue du Fort* called the *place de palais*; underneath was the prison (*Geôle*). *Rue du Gouvernment* connected to the *Rue de l'Hôpital* that led to the hospital located just under the ridge that commanded Fort Royal and overlooking the Bay (Illustration 6.7).

Important to the economic development of the colony was the existence of adequate port facilities. Since all transportation to and from the colony was by ships, ports were very necessary if efficient and profitable trade in produce, merchandise and slaves were to be carried out. An adequate port had to meet a number of conditions, the most important being defense and protection from inclement weather. When the French arrived in Grenada in 1649 they immediately recognized the potential of the practically enclosed bay and established their settlement within. It was the island's most secure harbor, a great bay stretching inland from the sea and forming a lagoon and Carenage. By the 1670s the French settlers called it Port Louis after King Louis XIV. Formed from the erosion of a volcanic crater by the sea, the entrance is straddled by two hills on each side, ideal points for establishing defense positions; the French built Fort Royal on the western ridge and a redoubt on the eastern ridge. The entire bay is surrounded by hills which further protect it from storms and make it easily defensible though the French did not build extensive fortification in the initial period.

Notes to La Ville du Fort Royal

[1] Watts, *The West Indies*, 378-9.
[2] Anonymous, *Histoire de l'isle de Grenade en Amérique*, 224-225.
[3] Anonymous, *Histoire de l'isle de Grenade*, 225.
[4] Jean de La Mousse and Gérard Collomb, *Les indiens de la Sinnamary: Journal du père Jean de La Mousse en Guyane, 1684-1691* (Paris: Chandeigne, 2006), 157-158.
[5] Though Labat writes that he visited between 18-23 September 1700, he is incorrect. He claims that he met and stayed with Governor de Bellair, but the governor had already departed Grenada for France earlier that year.
[6] Labat quoted in Devas, *History of the Island of Grenada*, 63.
[7] Labat quoted in Devas, *History of the Island of Grenada*, 63.
[8] Labat quoted in Devas, *History of the Island of Grenada*, 65.

Appendix V: Grenada Divided Into Quartiers

The French colony of Grenada and the Grenadines had by the 1750s developed into a mature plantation colony. On the eve of its capture by the British, Grenada exhibited many of the signs that signaled its status as a developed plantation society: predominance of large plantations producing sugar, and a social, political and economic infrastructure that aided that production; a small land-owning elite which dominated the social and political realm, and a majority African/black slave population which was the predominant labor force. In common with the other plantation economies in the region, French Grenada could easily be considered a colony, if not highly developed, at least on its way to becoming a successful plantation society.

The island of Grenada and the largest of the Grenadines, Carriacou were fully settled by the mid-1700s. Much of the lands of these islands had been conceded to the *habitants* though large portions remained uncultivated. The French had gradually expanded their settlements across Grenada, establishing districts (*quartiers*) as they advanced, and by the middle of the eighteenth century had set-up six districts (Illustration 10.4). These *quartiers* were linked by a coastal road network that joined five hamlets or population centers to the main town (*bourg*) at the Ville du Fort Royal. The Grand Chemin du Fort Royal began in the Basse-Terre and connected to Sauteurs in the extreme north of the island via the western coast. The Chemin du Bas and Chemin des Hauteurs went south and east, joining at Canne Fonds and continuing east then north as the Chemin Royal des Hauteurs and Grand Chemin du Roy along the east coast, then inland until it connected at Sauteurs. Except for part of the southern section of the island and through Sauteurs, there were no transinsular roads.[1] There were no coastal roads in the northeast and southwest due to marshes and "barren soils," respectively. There were, however, many tracks across the island that connected to small ports or landings where canoes and ferries carried people and produce to the main ports.

The Quartier du Basse-Terre was the oldest district and encompassed much of the initial settlements of the French by 1669.[2] It contained the principal port, fortifications and troops, hospital, *bourg* du Fort Royal, the residence of the governor, and other government officials. Situated on the southwest of the island, it was bounded to the north by the Rivière Douce and east by the Rivière du Chemin, comprising 4,345 *carrées* (15,806 acres), or just under 21 percent (one fifth) of the island. Basse-Terre contained a number of rivers primarily in the north and east of the district, including the Grand Rivière du Beau Séjour and Grand Rivière des Mahots. The *quartier* contained 54 concessions, 35 of which were planted in coffee and cocoa, and 13 *sucreries*, with nine powered by watermills and four by cattle; it also produced a large portion of indigo (Table 8.2). In 1749 it had a population of 1,932, and 2,243 in 1755 (Tables 9.3 and 9.4), with slaves making up 86 and 89 percent respectively. The large southern part of the *quartier* was considered "dry, barren soil, and little inhabited." Along with Fort Royal, there were coastal batteries around the town and at Pointe de la Citerne, Pointe de Beau Séjour, Petit Havre and Pointe Jeudy. These were manned by the *troupes de la marine* and the militia companies.

Heading north along the Grand Chemin du Fort Royal the French established the Quartier de L'Ance Goyave.[3] It was the second smallest *quartier*, bounded on the south by the Rivière Douce and north by the Ravine Maran, with an area of 2,659 *carrées* (8,731 acres) and just under 13 percent of the island. Towards the interior it was dominated by a range of hills, including Hauteurs de L'Ance à Goyave, Montagne du Vauclain and Mont St. George. Major streams include the Grand Rivière de L'Ance Goyave, Grand Rivière des Palmistes and Rivière du Grand Roy. Being very hilly, its primary cultivation was tree crops like coffee and cocoa. It contained 49 concessions, 38 of which were planted in coffee and/or cocoa, and nine *sucreries*, the majority powered by watermills, none being considerable. It was the largest producer of cocoa. In 1749 it had a population of 1,117, and 1,489 in 1755 (Tables 9.3 and 9.4). The white population decreased, but free non-whites increased from just over 13 percent to 34 percent of the free population in that period. There was a small chapel (served by the Dominicans in the Parroise de St. Pierre) among the few houses in the tiny coastal Bourg de L'Ance Goyave. Port facilities were maintained at L'Ance Noire, Grand Roy and L'Ance Goyave, with coastal batteries at Pointe Noire and Palmistes. There was a *potterie* that made pots for clayed sugar processing and bulding bricks.

414

Just north of L'Ance Goyave was the Quartier du Grand Pauvre, the smallest *quartier*, with an area of 1,617 *carrées* (5,637 acres) and less than eight percent of the island; it was bounded to the south by the Ravine Maran and north by the Rivère Duquesne.[4] Large streams included the Grand Rivière du Grand Pauvre and the Grand Rivière des Escrevisses. Like Goyave it is hilly towards the interior, culminating in the Hauteurs du Grand Pauvre, the Pitons de Duquesne et du Grand Pauvre, and Morne St. Catherine, the island's highest peak. It was divided into 31 concessions, with 25 coffee/cocoa estates, and five *sucreries*, "three of which are considerable"; there were four watermills. Its population went from 641 to 1,191 between 1749 and 1755, with that of the slaves doubling. There were coastal batteries at Grosse Pointe and Pointe Duquesne. Both the *quartiers* of L'Ance Goyave and Grand Pauvre were described as "of little importance with regard to the number of its settlements," but there was a small chapel (served by the Dominicans at the Parroise du St. Rose), and a few houses at the Bourg du Grand Pauvre, which also maintained a small port for coasting trade.

Occupying the northern extreme of the island was the Quartier des Sauteurs that took its name from the mass suicide of a group of Island Carib men on the Morne des Sauteurs in 1650. It comprsied 3,078 *carrées* (10,624 acres), straching from the Rivière Duquesne in the west to the Rivière Antoine in the east; it constituted just under fifteen percent of the island. It was watered by a number of large streams, including the Grande Rivière des Sauteurs, Petite Rivière des Sauteurs and Rivière Sallée. A flat area in the eastern center was referred to as La Plaine. It was not hilly, except for the Hauteurs des Sauteurs in the south and the Piton de Levara in the northeast. There were two large lakes at Étang de Levara and Étang d'Antoine. The *quartier* was divided into 48 concessions, 18 of these were *sucreries*, with 12 powered by watermills and six by cattle; 30 were coffee/cocoa plantations. There was one *potterie* that produced pots for clayed sugar refining and bulding bricks. A lime kiln, located at Mt. Rodney, Sauteurs Bay, made white lime for sugar refining and mortar for building construction. With a population of 2,110 in 1749, and 3,238 in 1755, it was a very productive *quartier*, though the Bough des Sauteurs had about 21 houses as the majority of its *habitants* lived on their habitations scattered across the *quartier*. The *bourg* was linked directly to the Grand Chemin du Royal and at Duquesne via a transinsular road; it was connected to Grand Marquis via the transinsular Chemin Royal des Hauteurs. Like the other *quartiers*, it was organized through its militia, which was commanded by the *capitaine de la milice* and assisted by a lieutenant and an ensign. In the 1750s the militia captain was Louis Lejuene, a wealthy sugar planter. The Lejeune militia company had about 90 men and older boys who could be called upon to defend the district. Ports for coasting vessels were maintained at Sauteurs and Levara, both protected by coastal batteries; there was also a battery at Pointe David.

Occupying a huge portion of the less hilly, eastern part of the island was the Quartier du Grand Marquis.[5] It was the largest *quartier* at 6,212 *carrées* (20,356 acres), with just under 30 percent of the island. It was bounded by the Rivière Antoine to the north and the Rivière du Crochu to the south. Its higest points were Mont Simon in the northwest and the Hauteurs du Grand Étang in the southwest. It was watered by large streams, including the Grand Rivière, Rivière Simon, Rivière Antoine, Rivière du Grand Marquis and Rivière de la Baye. Its relative expanse led to the proposed breakoff of the Quartier de la Conférence in the upper third of the *quartier* in the early 1740s, but it did not remain by 1762. Of its 92 concessions, 23 were *sucreries*, 12 being considerable and powered by watermills; it also had 53 coffee/cocoa plantations. There were two *potteries* that produced pots for refining sugar and building bricks. In 1749 it had a population of 2,937, and 4,070 in 1755 (Tables 9.3 and 9.4). The small Bourg du Grand Marquis had a chapel (in the Paroisse de Notre Dame de l'Assomption) and few houses overlooking the port; there was a second port at Crochu. There were coastal batteries at Pointe Ducasse and Morne Cambala.

To the south from the Rivière du Crochu to the Rivière du Chemin was the Quartier du Megrin, occupying 3,000 *carrées* (10,987 acres), just over fourteen percent of the island.[6] Its 39 concessions comprised eleven *sucreries*, ten powered by watermills, and 27 coffee/cocoa plantations. In 1749 it had a population of 1,294, and 1,750 in 1755 (Tables 9.3 and 9.4). Its highest point is Mont Sanai, and watered by many streams, including the Rivière de la Tante, Grande Rivière du Requin and Grande Rivière du Petit Marquis. The small Bourg du Megrin had a few wooden houses, a small chapel (in the Paroisse de St. Jean Baptiste served by the Jesuits), and port; also port facilities at the Port du Requin.

416

Notes to Grenada Divided into Quartiers

[1] The road across Grand Etang was constructed by the British in the late 1700s.

[2] Basse-Terre is defined as "lowland," and was applied to protected areas on the western coast of islands in the Caribbean by the French. Though it is no longer a place name in Grenada, it remains as such in Guadeloupe and St. Kitts. The eastern portion of the island was called the Capesterre.

[3] The quartier takes its name from the fruit guava (<Fr. *goyave*). There was also a Quartier de la Goyave in Guadeloupe and Petit Goyave, Haiti. The British spelt it Gouyave, which is unique to Grenada.

[4] The *quartier* took its name from an Island Carib village chief the French called Grand Pauvre (<?Fr. "great poor").

[5] The *quartier* took its name from an Island Carib chief the French called Grand Marquis.

[6] The origin of the name Mégrin remains unclear; it is sometimes spelled Maigrin. Possibly with some reference to *maigre* ("thin"). Saint-Mégrin is a French family name, and there is a Saint-Maigrin in southwestern France, east of the port city of La Rochelle from where early colonists to Grenada departed.

Bibliography

Guides to Research

Archives de la Martinique. Archives départementales Martinique. *Conseil Souverain de la Martinique (série B) 1712-1791*. Inventaire analytique par Liliane Chauleau. Fort-de-France, Martinique, 1985.

Archives nationales. *Guide des sources de l'histoire de l'Amérique Latine et des Antilles dans les Archives Françaises*. Paris: Archives Nationales, 1984.

Boucher, Philip P. *The Shaping of the French Colonial Empire: A Bio-bibliography of the Careers of Richelieu, Fouquet and Colbert*. New York: Garland, 1985.

Dampierre, Jacques de. *Essai sur les souces de l'histoire de Antilles Françaises, 1492-1664*. Paris, 1904.

Gastmann, Albert L. *Historical Dictionary of the French and Netherlands Antilles*. Metuchen, N.J.: Scarecrow Press, 1978.

Krakovich, Odile. *Arrêts, déclarations, édits et ordonnances concernant les colonies, 1660-1779: Inventaire analytique de la série Colonies A*. Paris: Archives nationales, 1993.

Leland, Waldo G., ed. *Guide to Materials for American History in the Libraries and Archives of Paris*. Washington, DC: Carneigie Institution, 1932. Reprint N.Y.: Kraus Reprint, 1965.

Nadin, J. C. "The Old Records of Grenada" (Translated from an article published in the *Revue Francaise d'Histoire d'Outre-Mer* 49 (1962) in *Caribbean Archives Conference*. Mona, Jamaica: University of the West Indies, 1965.

Ragatz, Lowell J. "Early French West Indian Records in the Archives Nationales," *Inter-American Bibliographical Review* 1 (Fall: 1941): 151-190.

Rennard, Joseph. *Essai bibliographiqie sur l'histoire religieuse des Antilles Françaises*. Paris: Secretariat général, 1931.

Taillemite, Etienne. *Inventaire analytique de la correspondance générale avec les colonies, Départ, Série B, I : Registres 1 à 37* (1654-1715). Paris: Ministère de la France d'Outre-mer, 1959.

Taillemite, Etienne. *Inventaire de la série C⁸ᴬ, Martinique*. 3 vols. Paris: Imprimerie nationale, 1971-1984. Vol. 3 completed with assistance of Odile Krakovitch and Michèle Bimbenet.

Voyage aux iles d'Amérique catalogue de l'exposition organisée par la Direction des Archives de France du Ministère de la Culture. Hôtel de Rohan: Archives Nationales, 1992.

Wroth, Lawrence and Gertrude L. Annan. *Acts of French Royal Administration Concerning Canada, Guiana, the West Indies, and Louisiana Prior to 1791*. N.Y.: The New York Public Library, 1930.

Manuscript Sources

Anonymous [Bénigne Bresson]. *The History of the Island of Grenada in America, 1649-1650.* Translated from the French by Jacques Petitjean Roget. Unpublished, 1972.

Archives Nationales d'Outre-Mer (France). COL C¹⁰ᴬ 1 à C¹⁰ᴬ 4. Ile de la Grenade: General correspondances: Carton I-II (1654-1798).

Archives Nationales d'Outre-Mer (France). DPPC G¹ 498. Recensement de la population de la Grenade, 1669-1755.

Archives Nationales d'Outre-Mer (France). Sous-série C⁸ᴬ et Supplément – Sous-série C⁸ᴮ. Martinique et Iles du Vent: General correspondance, 1635-1815. Accessed 15 April 2012 at http://anom.archivesnationales.culture.gouv.fr/ark:/61561/zn401g720n.

Bibliothèque nationale de France, département Cartes et plans. Various maps of Grenada accessed at http://gallica.bnf.fr/.

British Library (London). Sloane MSS, 3662, fº 53. Description of Granada.

_____. Walter Fenner. *A New and Accurate Map of the Island of Carriacou in the West Indies.* [London, 1784].

Beinecke Rare Book and Manuscript Library, Hamilton College, Hamilton, New York. M166. Ceded Islands (Grenada). [Oath of Allegiance]. Grenada, 1765.

Library of Congress (US). Parallel Histories: Spain, the United States, and the American Frontier: Nicolás de Cardona. *Descripciones Geográficas e Hidrográficas..., en Especial del Descubrimiento de la California* (1632). Accessed 15 April 2012 at http://memory.loc.gov/cgi-bin/query/ h?intldl/esbib:@field%28DOCID+@lit%2 8asce sp000006%29%29.

New York Public Library, Schomburg Center. Manuscripts and Archives: Grenada Plantation Records, 1737-1845. SC MG 383.

Registers of Records, 1764-96, Registrar's Office, Grenada Supreme Court, St. George's, Grenada. Can also be accessed from the Family History Centers through microfilm loans.

Voyages Database. 2009. *Voyages: The Trans-Atlantic Slave Trade Database.* Accessed August 15, 2010 at http://www. slavevoyages.org.

The National Archive (Kew, UK): Public Record Office, CO 101/1: Grenada, Original Correspondence, 1762-92.

Maps and Plans Available Online

Bellin, Jacques Nicolas. "Port et fort royal de la Grenade." BnF, Cartes et plans, CPL GE DD-2987 (9141). Accessed 1 April 2013 at http://gallica.bnf.fr/ark:/12148/btv1b5902509q.

_____. "Carte de l'isle de la Grenade." BnF, Cartes et plans, CPL GE DD-2987 (9139). Accessed 1 April 2013 at http://gallica.bnf.fr/ark:/12148/btv1b5902507w.

_____. "Partie des isles Antilles." BnF, Cartes et plans, CPL GE DD-2987 (9122). Accessed 1 April 2013 at http://gallica.bnf.fr/ark:/12148/btv1b5902487k,

Blaeu, Willem. "Insulae Americanae in Oceano Septentrionali cum Terris adiacentibus," 1638. Accessed 3 January 2013 at https://www.raremaps.com/gallery/enlarge/27221.

Blondel, François. "L'isle de la Grenade," 1667. BnF, Cartes et plans, GE D-8808. Accessed 3 January 2013 at http://gallica.bnf.fr/ark:/12148/btv1b8493404h.

_____. "Veue du fort royal, bourg, estang et du fort Louis de l'isle de la Grenade: Plan du fort royal de La Grenade, 1667." BnF, P184789 [Vd-22 (1)-Fol.]. Accessed 1 April 2013 at http://gallica.bnf.fr/ark:/12148/btv1b6903931f.

Bryes, John. "Plan of the Island of Bequia, Laid Down by Actual Survey," London, 1776. Accessed 1 April 2013 at http://jcb.lunaimaging.com/luna/servlet/JCBMAPS~1~1.

De Caylus, Jean-Baptiste. "Plan du fort de l'isle de la Grenade." BnF, Cartes et plans, CPL
    GE DD-2987 (9142). Accessed 1 April 2013 at
    http://gallica.bnf.fr/ark:/12148/btv1b5902510c.
_____. "Plan of the Town and Fort of Grenada," c. 1705, in Thomas Jeffreys, *The
    Natural and Civil History of the French Dominions in North and South America*, London, 1760.
    Accessed 1 April 2013 at http://memory.loc.gov/cgi-
    bin/query/D?gmd:1:./temp/~ammem_IK8D::
De L'Isle, Guillaume. "Carte des Antilles Françoises et des Isles Voisines," 1717. BnF,
    Cartes et plans, GEBB565 (14,101). Accessed 3 January 2013 at
    http://gallica.bnf.fr/ark:/12148/btv1b5973125p. See also the updated (1769) version
    by Philippe Buache with Grenada oriented correctly. Accessed 1 April 2013 at
    http://gallica.bnf.fr/ark:/12148/btv1b84467258/f1.item.
Le Romain, Jean-Baptiste Pierre. "Plan de la Rade du Fort Royal," 1746. Universität Bern.
    Accessed 1 April 2013 at
    http://biblio.unibe.ch/adam/ryhiner/8004/Ryh_8004_38_B.jpg.
"L'Isle de la Grenade avec son fort." BnF, Cartes et plans, GE SH 18 PF 142 DIV 1 P 2.
    Acessed 1 April 2013 at http://gallica.bnf.fr/ark:/12148/btv1b59708433/f13.item.
Buache, Phillipe. "Isle de la Grenade," Paris, 1747. Universität Bern. Accessed 1 April
    2013 at http://biblio.unibe.ch/adam/ryhiner/8004/Ryh_8004_38_A.jpg.
"Plan du port, du fort et du bourg de la Grenade." BnF, Cartes et plans, CPL GE DD-
    2987 (9140). Accessed 1 April 2013 at
    http://gallica.bnf.fr/ark:/12148/btv1b59025089.
Powell, John. "Plan of Fort Royal in the Island of Granada with the Harbour and
    Environs," in John Campbell's *Candid and Impartial Considerations on the Nature of the Sugar
    Trade...*, Accessed 3 January 2013 at http://gallica.bnf.fr/ark:/12148/btv1b8442368d.
Jefferys, Thomas. "Carte de l'isle de la Grenade," in *The West-India Atlas...* (London,
    1775). Accessed 3 January 2013 at http://www.davidrumsey.com/maps6416.html.

Primary Printed Sources

Anonymous. *A True Declaration of the Estate Colonie in Virginia: With a Confutation of Such
    Scandalous Reports as Have Tended to the Disgrace of so Worthy an Enterprise.* London, 1610.
Anonyme [Bénigne Bresson]. *L'Histoire de l'isle de Grenade en Amérique, 1649-1650.* Edited
    and annotated by Jacques Petitjean Roget. Montréal: Les Presse de L'Université de
    Montréal, 1975.
Bouton, Jacques. *Relation de l'establissement des Français depuis l'an 1635 en l'isle de la Martinique.*
    Paris: Cramoisy, 1640.
Boyer, Paul. *Veritable relation ... de voyage ... que Monsieur de Brétigny fit á l'Amérique occidentale.*
    Paris: Rocolet, 1654.
Breton, Raymond. *La dictionnaire français-caraïbe meslé de quantité de remarques historiques.*
    Auxerre, France: Gilles Bouquet, 1665. Reprein Liepzig: B. G. Teubner, 1900.
Code de la Martinique, 2 vols. St. Pierre: Imprimerie P. Richard, 1767.
Colbert, Jean-Baptiste. *Lettres, instructions et mémoires de Colbert.* Pierre Clément, ed. 8 vols.
    Paris: Imprimerie impréiale, 1859-82.
De L'Isle, Guillaume. *Carte des Antilles Francoises et les isles voisines. Dressee sur les memoires
    manuscrits de Mr. Petit, Ingenieur du Roy, et sur quelques observations.* Paris: Guillaume De
    L'Isle, 1717.
Desalles, Pierre-Regis. *Annales du Conseil Souverain de la Martinique, ou Tableau Historique du
    Gouvernement de cette colonie depuis son premier établissement jusqu'à nos jours*, 2 vols. Bergerac:
    Chez J. B. Puynesge, 1786. Reprinted Fort-de-France, Martinique: Société des Amis des
    Archives, 1995; and Paris: L'Harmattan, 1995.

Dutertre, Jean-Baptiste. *Histoire générale des Antilles, habitées par les François*, 4 vols. Paris: T. Jolly, 1667-71.

France. *Le Code Noir ou recueil des règlements rendus jusqu'á present.* Basse-Terre, Guadeloupe: Société d'Histoire de la Guadeloupe, 1980.

Labat, Jean-Baptiste. *Nouveau voyages aux isles de l'Amerique, 1693-1705*, 6 vols. Paris, 1722.

Moreau de Saint-Méry, Mederic Louis Elie. *Loix et constitutions des colonies Françaises de l'Amérique sous le vent.* 6 vols. Paris: Quillau, Mequignon jeune, 1784-1790.

Jefferys, Thomas. *Explication du plan de l'isle de la Grenade. Fait par ordre de son excellence Monsieur George Scott, governeur pour sa Majesté, de la dite Isle et de ses dependances, 1760.* London: Thomas Jefferys, [1763].

Jefferys, Thomas. *The Natural and Civil History of the French Dominions in North and South America.* London: Thomas Jefferys, 1760.

Patterson, Daniel. *A Topographical Description of the Island of Grenada; Surveyed by Monsieur Pinel in 1763 by Order of Government, with the Addition of English Names, Alterations of Property, and Other Improvements to the Present Time.* London: Faden, 1780.

Plumier, Charles. *Description des plantes de l'Amérique.* Paris: Imprimerie Royale, by J. Annison, 1693.

Ralegh, Walter. *The Discovery of Guiana.* London: Robert Robinson, 1596. Reprinted Amsterdam: Da Capo Press, 1968.

Rochefort, César de. *Histoire naturelle et morale des iles Antilles de l'Amérique.* Rotterdam: R. Leers, 1681.

Rochefort, Charles de. *The History of the Caribby Islands: Barbados, St. Christopher, Nevis, St. Vincents, Antego, Martinico, Monserrat, and the Rest of the Caribby-Islands, in all XXVIII: In two books, the first containing a natural, the second, the moral history of those islands.* Translated by J. Davies. London: Printed for John Starkey and Thomas Dring Jr., 1666.

Savary, Jacques. *Le parfait négociant ou instruction général pour ce qui regarde le commerce de route sorte de merchandises, tout de France, que des pays estrangers...*, 2 vols. Paris: Chez J. H. Widerhold, 1675.

Savary des Brûlons, Jacques and Philémon-Louis Savary. *Dictionnaire universel de commerce: D'histoire naturelle, & des arts & métiers.* 5 vols. Copenhagen: chez les frères Cl. & Ant. Philibert, 1765.

Secondary Sources

Abenon, Lucien. *Guadeloupe de 1671 á 1759, étude politique, économique et sociale.* 2 vols. Paris: L'Harmattan, 1987.

Adams, John Edward. "Union Island, West Indies: An Historical and Geographical Sketch," *Caribbean Studies*, 18, 3/4 (Oct. 1978-Jan. 1979): 5-45.

Allaire, Louis. "On the Historicity of Carib Migrations in the Lesser Antilles." *American Antiquity* 45, no. 2 (1980), 238-245.

Allaire, Louis. "Visions of Cannibal: Distant Islands and Distant Lands in Taino World Image," in *The Lesser Antilles in the Age of European Expansion*, edts. by Robert L. Paquette and Stanley L. Engerm. Gainesville: University Press of Florida, 1997, 33-49.

Andrews, K. R., N. P. Canny, and P. E. H. Hair., eds. *The Westward Enterprise: English Activities in Ireland, the Atlantic and America, 1480-1650.* Detroit: Wayne State University Press, 1979.

Andrews, Kenneth R. *The Spanish Caribbean: Trade and Plunder, 1530-1630.* New Haven: Yale University Press, 1978.

———. "Caribbean Rivalry and Anglo-Spanish Peace," *History*, 59, no. 195 (1974): 1–17.

Arens, Willian. *The Man-Eating Myth: Anthropology and Anthropophagy*. New York: Oxford University Press, 1979.

Arents, George. "The Seed From Which Virginia Grew," *The William and Mary Quarterly*, 2nd Series, 19, no. 22 (April 1939): 124-129.

Baker, Patrick L. *Centering the Periphery: Chaos, Order, and the Ethnohistory of Dominica*. Montreal: McGill-Queen's University Press, 1994.

Banbuck, C. A. *Histoire, politque, économique et sociale de la Martinique sous l'ancien régime, 1635-1789*. Paris: Marcel Rivière, 1935.

Barclay, George W. *Techniques of Population Analysis*. New York: Wiley, 1958.

Batie, Robert C. "Why Sugar? Economic Cycles and the Changing of Staples on the English and French Antilles, 1624-54" in *Caribbean Slave Society and Economy: A Student Reader*, eds., Hilary Beckles and Verne Shepherd. Kingston, Jamaica: Ian Randle Publishers, 1991.

_____. "A Comparative Economic History of the Spanish, French and English on the Caribbean Islands During the Seventeenth Century." Ph.D. diss., University of Washington, 1971.

Beard, J. S. *The Natural Vegetation of the Windward and Leeward Islands*. Oxford: Clarandon Press, 1949.

Beaston, Robert. *Naval and Military Memoirs of Great Britain, From 1727 to 1783*. 3 vols. London: Printed for Longman, Hurst, Rees and Orme, 1804.

Beckles, Hilary. "Kalinago (Carib) Resistance to European Colonisation in the Caribbean," *Caribbean Quarterly* 38, nos. 2-3 (1992): 1-14.

Beckles, Hilary McD. *European Settlement and Rivalry in the Caribbean 1492-1792*. London: Heinemann, 1973.

_____. *White Servitude and Black Slavery in Barbados, 1627-1715*. Knoxville: The University of Tennessee Press, 1989.

Beer, George-Louis. *The Origins of the British Colonial System, 1578-1660*. NY: Peter Smith, 1933.

Bernard, David. *Le clergé: Dictionnaire biographique de la Martinique, 1635-1848*. 3 vols. Fort-de-France: Société d'histoire de la Martinique, 1984.

Bertram, Arnold. "Jamaican Higglers' Marketing System and the Future of Kingston, Part I," *The Gleaner*, Sunday 31 October 2010. Online edition; accessed 15 May 2011 at http://jamaica-gleaner.com/gleaner/20101031/focus/focus6.html.

Bibliothèque nationale. *Quatres siècles de colonisation française*. Paris, 1931.

Blackburn, Robin. *The Making of New World Slavery: From the Baroque to the Modern*. London and N.Y.: Verso, 1997.

Boromé, Joseph A. "The French and Dominica, 1699-1763," *The Jamaican Historical Review* 7 (1967), 9-39.

_____. "Spain and Dominica," *Caribbean Quarterly* 12, no. 4 (1966): 30-46.

Boserup, E. *The Conditions of Agricultural Growth*. Chicago: Aldine Press, 1965.

Boucher, Philip P. *France and the American Tropics to 1700: Tropics of Discontent?* Baltimore: The Johns Hopkins University Press, 2007.

_____. *Cannibal Encounters: Europeans and Island Caribs, 1492-1763*. Baltimore: The Johns Hopkins University Press, 1992.

_____. *Les Nouvelles Frances: France in America, 1500-1815*. Providence: The John Carter Brown Library, 1989.

Boulle, Pierre H. *Race et esclavage dans la France de l'Ancien Régime*. Paris: Perrin, 2007.

_____. "French Mercantilism, Commercial Companies and Colonial Profitability" in *Companies and Trade: Essays on Overseas Trading Companies During the Ancien Regime*, ed., Leonard Blussé and Femme Gaastra. Leiden: Leiden University Press, 1981.

Bridenbaugh, Carl and Roberta. *No Peace Beyond the Line: The English in the Caribbean, 1624-1690*. New York: Oxford University Press, 1972.

Brinkley, Francis Kay. "An Analysis of the 1750 Carriacou Census," *Caribbean Quarterly* 24, no. 1/2 (1978): 44-60.

Brizan, George. *Grenada: Island of Conflict.* London: Macmillan Caribbean, 1998.

Boomert, Arie. "The Cayo Complex of St. Vincent: Ethnohistorical and Archaeological Aspects of the Island Carib Problem," *Anthropologica* 66 (1986): 3-68.

Bromley, J. S. "The French Privateering War, 1702-13" in *Historical Essays, 1600-1750 Presented to David Ogg*, eds. H. E. Bell and R. L. Ollard. New York: Barnes and Noble, Inc., 1963.

Bullen, Ripley P. "The Archaeology of Grenada, West Indies." *Contributions of the Florida State Museum, Social Sciences*, no. 11. Gainesville: University of Florida, 1964.

Butel, Paul. "France, the Antilles, and Europe in the Seventeenth and Eighteenth Centuries; Renewal of Foreign Trade," in *The Rise of Merchant Empires, Long Distance Trade in the Early Modern World, 1350-1750*, ed. by James D. Tracy. N.Y.: Cambridge University Press, 1990.

Byres, John. *Plan of the Island of Bequia Laid Down by Actual Survey Under the Direction of the Honorable the Commissioners for the Sale of Lands in the Ceded Islands.* London, 1776.

Campbell, John. *Conditions Which May Tend to Promote the Settlement of Our New West-India Colonies.* London: James Robson, 1764.

Cardona, Nicolás de. *Geographic and Hydrographic Descriptions of Many Northern and Southern Lands and Seas in the Indies, Specifically of the Discovery of the Kingdom of California.* Baja, California: Dawsons Book Shop, 1974.

Chambers, Edward J. and Donald F. Gordon. 1966. "Primary Products and Economic Growth: An Empirical Measurement." *The Journal of Political Economy* 74, no. 4 (August): 315-eoa.

Châtillon, Marcel. *Le père Labat à travers ses manuscrits.* S.I.: s.n., 1979.

Chauleau, Liliane. *Dans les îles du vent: La Martinique (XVIIe-XIXe siècle).* Paris: Editions L'Harmattan, 1993.

_____. *Histoire antillaise: La Martinique et la Guadeloupe de XVIIe á la fin du XIXe siècle.* Élements d'histoire antillaise. Pointe-á-Pitre: Desormeaux, 1973.

Chisholm, Colin. *An Essay on the Malignant Pestilential Fever Introduced into the West Indian Islands from Boullam, on the Coast of Guinea, as it Appeared in 1793 and 1794.* Philadelphia, 1799.

Clarence-Smith, W. G. *Cocoa and Chocolate, 1765-1914.* New York: Psychology Press, 2000.

Clyde, David F. *Health in Grenada: A Social and Historical Account.* London: Vade-Mecum Press, 1985.

Cole, Charles W. *Colbert and a Century of French Mercantilism.* 2 vols. Hamden, Connecticut: Archon Books, 1964.

Columbus, Christopher. *The Spanish Letter of Columbus to Luis de Sant'Angel: Escribano de Racion of the Kingdom of Aragon, Dated 15 February 1493*, edited by Michael P. Kerney and Bernard Quaritch. G. Norman and Son, printers, 1893.

Conklin, Beth. *Consuming Grief: Compassionate Cannibalism in an Amazonian Society.* Austin: University of Texas, 2001.

Corbett, Julian Stafford. *England in the Seven Years' War: A Study in Combined Strategy.* 2 vols. London: Longmans, Green, 1907.

Cox, Edward L. *Free Coloreds in the Slave Societies of St. Kitts and Grenada, 1763-1833.* Knoxville: The University of Tennessee Press, 1984.

Courtenay, P. P. *Plantation Agriculture.* Rev. Ed. Boulder: Westview Press, 1980.

Crosby, Jr., A. W. *The Columbian Exchange: Biological and Cultural Consequences of 1492.* Westport, Connecticut: Greenwood Press, 1972.

Crouse, Nellis M. *French Pioneers in the West Indies 1624-1664.* New York: Octagon Books, 1977.

Crouse, Nellis M. *The French Struggle for the West Indies, 1665-1713*. New York: Columbia University Press, 1943.

Curet, L. Antonio and Mark W. Hauser, eds. *Islands at the Crossroads: Migration, Seafaring, and Interaction in the Caribbean* (Tuscaloosa: University of Alabama Press, 2011).

Curtin, Phillip. *The Atlantic Slave Trade: A Census*. Madison: University of Wisconsin Press, 1969.

Dampierre, Jacques de. *Essai sur les sources de l'histoire des Antilles françaises (1492-1664)*. Paris: A. Picard, 1904.

Dand, Robin. *The International Cocoa Trade*, 2nd edition. New York: Woodhead Publishing, 1999.

Davis, Dave D. and R. Goodwin Christopher. "Island Carib Origins: Evidence and Non-evidence," *American Antiquity* 55 (1990): 37-48.

Davis, David Brion. *Inhuman Bondage: The Rise and Fall of Slavery in the New World*. Oxford: Oxford University Press, 2006.

Davis, Ralph. *The Rise of the Atlantic Economies*. Ithaca, New York: Cornell University Press, 1973.

_____. *English Overseas Trade, 1500-1700*. London: Macmillan Publishing Co., 1973.

Debien, Gabriel. "Les engagés pour les Antilles, 1634-1715," *Revue de l'histoire des colonies Françaises*, 38, no. 1-2 (1951): 1-279.

_____. "Marronage in the French Caribbean," in *Maroon Societies: Rebel Slave Communities in the Americas*, ed. by Richard Price. Baltimore: Johns Hopkins University Press, 1979.

_____. *Les Esclaves aux Antilles, xviiᵉ-xviiiᵉ siècles*. Basse-Terre: Société d'histoire de la Guadeloupe, 1974.

_____. "La Christianisation des esclaves des Antilles françaises au XVIIe et XVIIIe siècles." *Revue de l'histoire des colonies Françaises*, 20, no. 4 (1967): 525-55; 21, no. 1 (1967): 99-111.

Debien, M. G. and J. Houdaille. "Les origines Africanes des esclaves des Antilles Françaises." *Caribbean Studies* 10 (1970): 5-29.

Deere, Noel. *The History of Sugar*. 2 vols. London: Chapman and Hall, 1949-50.

Defoe, Daniel. *A General History of the Pyrates*. New York: Dover Publications, 1999.

Demos, John. "Families in Colonial Bristol, Rhode Island: An Exercise in Historical Demography." *William and Mary Quarterly*, 3rd Series 25 (Jan. 1968): 40-57.

Denis , Serge, ed. *Nos Antilles*. Orleans: Luzeray, 1935.

Depping, Georg Bernhard. *Correspondance administrative sous le règne de Louis xiv...* 3 vols. Paris: Imprimerie Nationale.

De Rionegro, Fray Froylan. *Relaciones de las misiones de los PP. Capuchinos en Venezuela, 1650-1817*. Serville: Tip. Zarzuela, 1918.

Dessalles, Adrien. *Histoire générale des Antilles*. 5 vols. Paris: Libraire-éditeur, 1848.

Dessalles, P. F. R. *Les annales du conseil souverain de la Martinique*. 4 vols. Paris: Éditions L'Harmattan, 1995.

Devas, Raymund P. *The History of the Island of Grenada, 1650-1796*. St. George's, Grenada: Carenage Press, 1974.

_____. *Conception Island, Or the Troubled History of the Catholic Church in Grenada*. London: Sands & Co., 1932.

Donkin, R. A. "Bixa Orellana: The Eternal Shrub." *Anthropos* 69 (1974): 3-56.

Drayton, Edward. *The Grenada Handbook, Directory and Almanac for the Year 1897*. London: Sampson Low, Marston and Company, 1897.

Dundes, Alan. *The Blood Libel Legend: A Casebook in Anti-Semitic Folklore*. Madison: University of Wisconsin Press, 1991.

Dunn, Richard. *Sugar and Slaves*. Chapel Hill: University of North Carolina Press, Institute of Early American History and Culture, 1972.

Dunn, Richard. "The Barbados Census of 1680: Profile of the Richest Colony in English America." *William and Mary Quarterly*, 3rd Series 26, no. 1 (Jan. 1969): 3-30.

Dyke, Bennett. "La population de Northside dans l'Ile Saint-Thomas: Un isolat Français dans les Antilles." *Population* 25, no. 6 (1970): 1197-1204.

Eccles, W. J. *France in America*. East Lansing: Michigan State University Press, 1990.

Edwards, Bryan. *The History Civil and Commercial of the British West Indies*. 2 vols. London, 1793.

Elisabeth, Léo. *La Société martiniquaise aux XVIIe et XVIIIe siècles: 1664-1789*. Paris: Karthala, 2003.

_____. "The French Antilles," in *Neither Slave nor Free: the Freedmen of African Descent in the Slave Societies of the New World*, eds. by David W. Cohen and Jack P. Greene. Baltimore: Johns Hopkins University Press, 1974.

Eltis, David and David Richardson. "A New Assessment of the Transatlantic Slave Trade," in *Extending the Frontiers: Essays on the New Transatlantic Slave Trade Database*, eds., David Eltis and David Richardson. New Haven: Yale University, 2008.

Frampton, John. *Of the Tobacco and his Greate Vertues* (Translation of Nicholas Monardes' 1577 publication of *Joyful Newes from our Newe Founde Worlde*). New York: Alfred A. Knoph, 1925.

Franklyn, Omowale David. *Morne Sauteurs (Leapers' Hill): Encounter Between Two Worlds in Grenada, 1650-1654*. St. George's, Grenada: Talented House Pub., 1992.

Frostin. Charles. "Les Pontchartrain et la pénétration commerciale française en Amérique espagnole (1690-1715)," *RH*, no. 245 (Apr.-June 1971): 307-336.

Gaston-Martin, P. *Histoire de l'esclavage dans les colonies françaises*. Paris: P.U.F, 1948.

General History of the Caribbean-UNESCO. Vol. 1: *Autochthonous Societies*. Ed. by Jalil Sued-Badillo. London: Palgrave Macmillan, 2006.

_____. Vol. 2: *New Societies: The Caribbean in the Long Sixteenth Century*. Ed. by Pieter C. Emmer. London: Palgrave Macmillan, 2006.

_____. Vol. 3: *The Slave Societies of the Caribbean*. Ed. by Franklin Knight. London: Palgrave Macmillan, 2004.

Gerstin, J. "Tangled Roots: Kalenda and Other Neo-African Dances in the Circum-Caribbean," *New West Indian Guide* 78, no. 1/2 (2004: 5-41.

Gonzalez, Javier A. "'A Strange Discordant Mass of Heterogeneous Animals': The Role of Ethnic Divisions in British Grenada, 1763-1779." BA Honors Thesis, Department of History, Harvard University, 1994.

Goslinga, Cornelis. *The Dutch in the Caribbean and in the Guianas, 1680-1791*. Assen, Netherlands: Van Yperen, 1985.

_____. *The Dutch in the Caribbean and on the Wild Coast, 1580-1680*. Gainesville: University of Florida Press, 1971.

Gould, Clarence P. "Trade Between the Windward Islands and the Continental Colonies of the French, 1635-1763." *The Mississippi Valley Historical Review* 25, no. 4 (March 1939): 473-490.

Grant, William L. "Canada Versus Guadeloupe: An Episode of the Seven Years' War," *The American Historical Review*, 17, 4 (July 1912): 735-743.

Grenada, Country Environmental Profile. St. Michael, Barbados: Caribbean Conservation Association, 1990.

Griffith, N. E. S. and John G. Reid. "New Evidence on New Scotland, 1629." *William and Mary Quarterly*, Third Series 49, no. 3 (July 1992): 429-508.

Guitar, Lynne. "No More Negotiations: Slavery and the Destabilization of Colonial Hispaniola's Encomienda System," *Revista/Review Interamericana* 29, 1-4 (January-December 1999).

Gullick, C. J. M. R. *Myths of a Minority*. Assen, Netherlands: Van Gorcum, 1985.

Gullick, C. J. M. R. "Island Carib Traditions About Their Arrival in the Lesser Antilles." In *Proceedings of the Eight International Congress for the Study of the Pre-Columbian Cultures of the Lesser Antilles*, ed. by Susan M. Lewenstein. Anthropological Research Papers, no. 22. Arizona State University, 1980.

Hall, Gwendolyn Midlo. *Africans in Colonial Louisiana: The Development of Afro-Creole Culture in the Eighteenth Century.* Baton Rouge: Louisiana State University Press, 1992.

Harcourt, Robert. *A Relation of a Voyage to Guiana.* London: The Hakluyt Society, 1926.

Harlow, V. T. *Colonizing Expeditions to the West Indies and Guiana, 1623-1667.* 2nd Series, No. 56, 1925.

Hauser, Henri. *Recherches et documents sur l'histoire des prix en France de 1500 à 1800.* Paris, 1936.

————. "The Characteristic Features of French Economic History From the Middle of the 16th to the Middle of the 18th Century." *The Economic History Review* 4, no. 3 (Oct. 1933): 257-272.

Hayward, John. "The Arnold Lulls Book of Jewels and the Court Jewellers of Queen Anne of Denmark," *Archaeologia*, 108 (1986): 227-237.

Hecht, Irene W. D. "The Virginia Muster of 1624/5 as a Source of Demographic History." *William and Mary Quarterly*, 3rd Series 30 (Jan. 1973): 65-92.

Henige, David. "On the Contact Population of Hispaniola: History as Higher Mathematics." *Hispanic American Historical Review* 58, 2 (1978): 217-237.

Herman, Arthur. *To Rule the Waves: How the British Navy Shaped the Modern World.* New York: Harper Collins, 2004.

Higham, C. S. S. *The Development of the Leeward Islands Under the Restoration, 1660-1688.* Cambridge: University of Cambridge Press, 1921.

Holdren, Ann Cody. "Raiders and Traders: Caraibe Social and Political Networks at the Time of European Contact and Colonization in the Eastern Caribbean." Ph.D. diss., University of California, Los Angeles, 1998.

Honychurch, Lennox. "The Leap at Sauteurs: The Lost Cosmology of indigenous Grenada." http://www.uwichill.edu.bb/bnccde/grenada/conference/papers/LH.html

Houdaille, J., R. Massio, and G. Debien. "Les origines des esclaves des Antilles." *Bulletin de l'Institut Francais d'Afrique Noire ser. B* 25, no. 3/4 (1963): 215-265.

Huetz de Lemps, Christian. "Indentured servants bound for the French Antilles in the seventeenth and eighteenth centuries," in *"To Make America": European Emigration in the Early Modern Period*, eds. by Ida Altman & James Horn. Berkeley: University of California Press, 1991.

Hubbard, Lucius Lee. "Did Columbus Discover Tobago?", in *Essays Offered to Herbert Putnam by his Colleagues and Friends on his Thirtieth Anniversary as Librarian of Congress, 5 April 1929*, eds. by Herbert Putnam, William W. Bishop, Andrew Keogh. Ayer Publishing, 1967.

Huggins, Horatio Nelson. *Hiroona: An Historical Romance in Poetic Form.* Trinidad : Franklin's Electric Printery, 1930.

Hulme, Peter. *Colonial Encounters: Europe and the Native Caribbean, 1492-1797.* New York: Methuen, 1986.

Hulme, Peter and Neil L. Whitehead., eds. *Wild Majesty: Encounters with Caribs from Columbus to the Present Day, An Anthology.* Oxford: Clarendon Press, 1992.

Innis, Harold A. *The Fur Trade in Canada: An Introduction to Canadian Economic History.* New Haven: Yale University Press, 1930.

Innes, F. C. "The Pre-sugar Era of European Settlement in Barbados." *Journal of Caribbean History* 1 (1970): 1-22.

Jacobs, Curtis. "The Fédons of Grenada, 1763-1814." Accessed 15 April 2012. http://www.cavehill.uwi.edu/ BNCCde/grenada/conference/papers/jacobsc.html.

James, C. L. R. *The Black Jacobins: Toussaint L'Ouverture and the San Domingo Revolution.* New York: Vintage Books, 1963.

Jaquay, Barbara Gaye. "The Caribbean Cotton Production: An Historical Geography of the Region's Mystery Crop." Ph.D. diss., Texas A&M University, 1997.

Jessie, C. "Sold For a Song, du Parquet Buys St. Lucia, Together with Martinique, Grenada, the Grenadines, in A. D. 1650 for £1,660 Sterling." *Caribbean Quarterly* 13, no. 4 (Dec. 1967): 44-52.

Jessie, C.. "The Spanish Cedula of December 23, 1511, On the Subject of the Caribs." *Caribbean Quarterly* 9, no. 3 (1963): 22-32.

Keegan, William F. *The People Who Discovered Columbus: The Prehistory of the Bahamas.* Gainesville: University Press of Florida, 1992.

Kilgore, Cindy. *Adventure Guide to Grenada, St. Vincent and the Grenadines.* Edison: Hunter, 2003.

Kimber, Clarissa T. *Martinique Revisited: The Changing plant Geographies of a West Indian Island.* College Station: Texas A&M Press, 1988.

Kiple, Kenneth F. and Kriemhild C. Ornelas. "After the Encounter: Disease and Demographics in the Lesser Antilles," in *The Lesser Antilles in the Age of European Expansion,* eds. by Robert Paquette and Stanley Engerman. Gainesville: University Press of Florida, 1996.

Kupperman, Karen. *Roanoke: The Abandoned Colony.* NJ: Rowman & Littlefield, 2007.

Las Casas, Bartolomé de. *The Diario of Christopher Columbus's First Voyage to America, 1492-1493.* Translated by Oliver Dunn and James Edward Kelley. University of Oklahoma Press, 1991.

_____. *The Devastation of the Indies: A Brief Account.* Translated by Herma Briffault. Baltimore: The Johns Hopkins University Press, 1974.

_____. *Historia de las Indias.* Ed. by Augustine Millares Carlo. 3 vols. Mexico-Buenos Aires: Fondo de Cultura Economica, 1951.

Lacour-Gayet, G. *La marine militaire de la France sous le regne de Louis XV.* Paris, 1902.

Lafleur, Gérard. *Les Caraïbes des Petites Antilles.* Paris: Karthala, 1992.

La Mousse, Jean de. *Les indiens de la Sinnamary: Journal du père Jean de La Mousse en Guyane, 1684-1691.* Paris: Chandeigne, 2006.

La Roncière, Charles Germaine Marie Bourel de. *Histoire de la Marine Française.* Plon-Nourrit, 1909.

Latron, A. "Les mésaventures d'un gentilhomme colonial." *Revue Historique des Antilles,* no. 3 (June/Oct. 1929): 1-14.

Le Code Noir ou recueil des reglements rendus jusqu'a present (Paris: Prault, 1767) [1980 reprd. by the Societé, d'Histoire de la Guadeloupe], Trannslated by John Garrigus. Accessed 15 April 2012 at http://les.traitesnegrieres.free.fr/39_esclavage_code_noir_agl.html.

Le Romain, Jean-Baptiste-Pierre. "Negroes," in *Encyclopédie ou dictionnaire raisonné des sciences, des arts et des métiers,* eds. by Denis Diderot and Jean le Rond d'Alembert. Paris, 1751-72.

Le Blond, Jean-Baptiste. *Voyage aux Antilles et a l'Amérique Méridionale.* Paris : Chez Arthus-Bertrand, 1813.

L'Etang, Tierry. "Du nom indigène des îles de l'archipel des Antilles." Internet. Accessed on 15 April 2012 at http://www.manioc.org/gsdl/collect/recherch/index/assoc/HASH0177/ 0dab508e.dir/dunomindig.pdf.

Ligon, Richard. *A True and Exact History of the Island of Barbados.* London, 1657.

Lorimer, Joyce. "The Failure of the English Guiana Ventures 1595–1667 and James I's Foreign Policy," *The Journal of Imperial and Commonwealth History,* 21, no. 1 (1993): 1-30.

_____. *English and Irish Settlements on the River Amazon, 1550-1646.* London: Haklyut Society, 1990.

427

Lorimer, Joyce. "The English Contraband Tobacco Trade in Trinidad and Guyana, 1590-1617," in *The Westward Enterprise*, eds. by K. R. Andrews, N. P. Canny and P. E. H. Hairs. Detriot: Wayne State University Press, 1979.

MacMahon, Francis. *A Narrative of the Insurrection in the Island of Grenada, in the Year 1795.* Printed by J. Spahn, 1823.

Malo, Henri. "La perte et prise de la Grenade (mars 1675)," *Feuilles d'histoire du XIIe au XXe siècle* 3, 5 (1911): 102-110.

Margry, Pierre. "Origines Françaises des Pays d'Outre-Mer." *Revue Maritime et Coloniale* 58 (1878): 283-305.

Martin, John Angus. "L'Isle de la Grenade: French Settlement and Development, 1649-1762." Thesis (MA), Clemson University, 1999.

May, Louis-Philippe. *Histoire économique de la Martinique, 1635-1763.* Paris: Libraire des Sciences Politiques et Sociales, 1930.

McClelland III, James. *Colonialism and Science: Saint-Domingue in the Old Regime.* Baltimore: Johns Hopkins University Press, 1992.

McCloy, Shelby T. *The Negro in the French West Indies.* Lexington: University of Kentucky Press, 1966.

McCusker, John J. and Russell R. Menard. *The Economy of British America 1607-1789.* Chapel Hill: The University of North Carolina Press, 1991.

McDaniels, Lorna. "The Philips: A 'Free Mulatto' Family of Grenada," *Journal of Caribbean History*, 24, 2 (Nov. 1990): 178-194.

Mettas, Jean. *Répertoire des expéditions négrières Françaises au xviiie siècle.* 2 vols. Paris: Société Française d'Histoire d'Outre-Mer, 1978.

Mieville, China. *Between Equal Rights: A Marxist Theory of International Law.* Haymarket Books, 2006.

Mims, Stewart L. *Colbert's West India Policy.* 1912. Reprint, New York: Octagon Books, 1977.

Mintz, Sidney. *Sweetness and Power: The Place of Sugar in Modern History.* New York: Viking, 1985.

Miquelon, Dale. *Dugard of Rouen: French Trade to Canada and the West Indies, 1729-1770.* Montreal: McGill-Queen's University Press, 1978.

Moisy, Henri. *Dictionnaire de patois Normand.* Genève: Slatkine Reprints, 1969.

Moitt, Bernard. *Women and Slavery in the French Antilles, 1635-1848.* Bloomington, IN.: Indiana University Press, 2001.

Moore, Richard B. "Carib Cannibalism: A Study in Anthropological Stereotyping." *Caribbean Studies* 13, no. 3 (October 1979): 117-135.

Moreau, Jean-Pierre. *Les Petites Antilles de Christophe Colomb à Richelieu, 1493-1635.* Paris: Karthala, 1992.

Moreau, Résidence des Missionnaires Jésuites. *Collection des procès-verbaux des assemblées générales du clergé de France depuis l'année 1560 jusqu'a présent rédigés par ordre de matière et réduits à ce qu'ils ont d'essentiel.* Paris: de l'imprimerie de Guillaume Desprez, 1770.

Morison, Samuel E. *The Great Explorers: The European Discovery of America.* New York: Oxford University Press, 1978.

_____. *The Caribbean as Columbus Saw It.* New York: Little Brown, 1964.

_____. *Journals and Other Documents on the Life and Voyages of Christopher Columbus.* New York: The Heritage Press, 1963.

Morris, Valentine. *A Narrative of the Official Conduct of Valentine Morris: Late Captain General, Governor in Chief &c. &c. of the Island of St. Vincent and its Dependencies.* London: Printed by J. Walter and sold by S. Hooper, 1787.

Mulcahy, Matthew. *Hurricanes and Society in the British Greater Caribbean, 1624-1783.* Baltimore: JHU Press, 2005.

Munford, Clarence J. *The Black Ordeal of Slavery and Slave Trading in the French West Indies, 1625-1715*. 3 vols. Lewiston, New York: E. Mellen Press, 1991.

Myers, Robert A. "Island Carib Cannibalism," *New West Indian Guide/Nieuwe West-Indische Gids*, 58, ¾ (1984): 147-184.

Nardin, J. C. "The Old Records of Grenada," *Report of the Caribbean Archives Conference*, Mona, Jamaica: UWI (1965): 327-347.

Neill, Edward D. *History of the Virginia Company of London, With Letters to and from the First Colony, Never Before Printed*. NY: Joel Munsell, 1869.

Newson, Linda A. *Aboriginal and Spanish Colonial Trinidad: A Study in Culture Contact*. New York: Academic Press, 1976.

Newton, Arthur P. *The European Nations in the West Indies, 1493-1688*. London: A&C Black, Ltd., 1933.

Niddrie, D. L. "Eighteenth-Century Settlement in the British Caribbean," *Transactions of the British Institute of British Geographers*, 40 (December 1966): 67-80.

North, Douglas C. *The Economic Growth of the United States, 1790-1860*. New Jersey, 1961.

Ottley, C. R. *Spanish Trinidad: An Account of the Life of Trinidad, 1498-1797*. London: Longman Caribbean, 1971.

Oviedo de Y Banos, Don José. *The Conquest and Settlement of Venezuela*. Translated by Jeannette Johnson Varner. Berkeley: University of California Press, 1987.

Pares, Richard. *War and Trade in the West Indies, 1739-1763*. London: Frank Cass & Co. Ltd., 1963.

_____. "Merchants and Planters." *Economic History Review, Supplement* 4, no. 1 (1960): 1-91.

Parry, J. H., P. M. Sherlock, and A. P. Maingot. *A Short History of the West Indies*. 4th ed. New York: St. Martin's Press, 1987.

Peabody, Sue. "*Négresse, Mulâtresse, Citoyenne:* Gender and Emancipation in the French Caribbean, 1650-1848," in *Gender and Emancipation in the Atlantic World, 1650-1848*, eds. by Pamela Scully and Diana Paton. Raleigh: Duke University Press, 2005.

_____. "A Dangerous Zeal: Catholic Missions to Slaves in the French Antilles, 1635-1800," *French Historical Studies*, 25, 1 (Winter, 2002): 53-90.

_____. *"There are no Slaves in France": The Political Culture of Race and Slavery in the Ancien Régime*. N.Y.: Oxford University Press, 1996.

Pelletier, A. J. "Canadian Censuses of the Seventeenth Century." *Canadian Political Science Association* 2 (1930): 20-34.

Pérotin-Dumon, Anne. *La ville aux îles, la ville dans l'île. Basse-Terre et Pointe-á-Pitre, Guadeloupe, 1650-1820*. Paris: Editions Karthala, 2000.

_____. "French, English and Dutch in the Lesser Antilles: From Privateering to Planting, c. 1550-1650," in *General History of the Caribbean Volume II. New Societies: The Caribbean in the Long 16th Century*, ed. by P. C. Emmer. UNESCO, 1999.

Petitjean Roget, Jacques. *La société d'habitation à la Martinique: Un demi-siècle de formation, 1635-1685*. 2 vols. Atelier Reproduction des thèses, Université de Lille III, 1980.

_____. "Les femmes des colons à la Martinique au XVIe et XVIIe siècle," *Revue d'histoire de l'Amérique française*, 9, no. 2 (1955): 176-235.

Petitjean Roget, Jacques and Eugène Bruneau-Latouche. *Personnes et familles a la Martinique au XVII siecle: D'après recensements et terrier nominatifs*. 2 vols. Fort de France: Societe d'histoire de la Martinique, 1983.

Pitman, Frank. 1917. *The Development of the British West Indies, 1700-1763*. New Haven: Yale University Press.

Pollard, A. H., Farhat Yusuf, and G. N. Pollard. *Demographic Techniques*. New York: Pergamon Press, 1974.

Pomfret, Richard. "The Staple Theory as an Approach to Canadian and Australian Economic Development." *Australian Economic History Review* 21, no. 2 (1981): 133-146.

Posthumus, Nicholaas Wilhemus. *Inquiry Into the History of Prices in Holland.* 2 vols. Leiden, 1946-64.

Priestley, Herbert I. *France Overseas Through the Old Regime: A Study of European Expansion.* New York, 1939.

Pritchard, James. "Population in French America, 1670-1730: Demographic Context of Colonial Louisiana," in *French Colonial Louisiana and the Atlantic World,* ed. by Bradley G. Bond. Baton Rouge: Louisiana State University Press, 2005.

_____. *In Search of Empire: The French in the Americas, 1670-1730.* Cambridge: Cambridge University Press, 2004.

Puckrein, Gary A. *Little England: Plantation Society and Anglo-Barbadian Politics, 1627-1700.* New York: New York University Press, 1984.

Purseglove, J. W. *Tropical Crops: Dicotyledons.* New York: John Wiley & Sons, 1968.

Ragatz, Lowell L. *Fall of the Planter Class in the British Caribbean, 1763-1833: A Study in Social and Economic History.* New York: The Century Co. 1928.

_____. *Statistics for the Study of British Caribbean Economic History, 1763-1833.* The Bryan Edwards press, 1927.

Raynal, Guillaume-Thomas. *A Philosophical and Political History of the Settlements and Trade of the Europeans in the East and West Indies.* 6 vols. 1770. Translated by J. O. Justamond. Reprint, New York: Negro University Press, 1969.

Rennard, Joseph. *Histoire religieuse des Antilles Françaises des origines à 1914 d'après des documents inédits.* Paris: Société de l'Histoire des Colonies Françaises et Librairie Larose, 1954.

_____. *Le commerce aux Antilles, 1635-1860.* Fort-de-France, Martinique: Imprimerie du Service de l'Information, 1946.

_____. *Essai bibliographique sur l'histoire religieuse des Antilles françaises.* Paris: Secrétariat Général S.J., 1931.

Richardson, Bonham C. *The Caribbean in the Wider World, 1492-1992: A Regional Geography.* Cambridge: Cambridge University Press, 1992.

Riddell, William R. "Le code noir." *Journal of Negro History* 10, no. 3 (July 1925): 321-329.

Rionegro, Froylan de. *Relaciones de las Missiones de los Capuchines en Venezuela, 1650-1817.* Seville, 1918.

Robeson, Virginia, ed. *Documents in Canadian History: New France, 1713-60.* Toronto: The Ontario Institute for Studies in Education, 1977.

Robbins, Ellen H. *Lord Macartney, Our First Ambassador to China.* London, 1908.

Rogers, James E. T. *A History of Agriculture and Prices in England.* Oxford, 1887.

Roget, Henri Petitjean. *Archaeology in Grenada: A Report.* St. Michael, Barbados: Caribbean Conservation Association, 1980.

Rogozinski, Jan. *A Brief History of the Caribbean: From the Arawak and the Carib to the Present.* New York: Facts on File, 1999.

Roukema, Edzer. "Some Remarks on the La Cosa Map," *Imogo Mundi,* 14 (1959): 38-54.

Rouse-Jones, Margaret D. "St. Kitts, 1713-1763: A Study of the Development of a Plantation Colony." Ph.D. diss., Johns Hopkins University., 1978

Ryden, David Beck. "'One of the Finest and Most Fruitful Spots in America': An Analysis of 18th Century Carriacou." *Journal of Interdisciplinary History* 43, no. 4 (Spring 2013): 539-570.

Sainton, Jean-Pierre and Raymond Boutin, in *Histoire et civilisation de la Caraïbe: Guadeloupe, Martinique, Petites Antilles….* Paris: Maisonneuve & Larose, 2004.

Sauer, Carl. *The Early Spanish Main.* Berkeley: University of California Press, 1966.

Saugera, Éric. *Bordeaux, port négrier: chronologie, économie, idéologie, XVIIe-XIXe siècles.* Paris: Karthala, 2002.

Sheridan, Richard. *Sugar and Slavery: An Economic History of the British West Indies.* Baltimore: The Johns Hopkins University Press, 1974.

Sheridan, Richard. "The Development of the Plantations to 1750." In *Chapters in Caribbean History I*, ed. by Douglas Hall, Elsa Goveia and Roy Augier. Barbados: Caribbean Universities Press, 1970.

_____. "An Era of West Indian Prosperity, 1750-1775," *Caribbean Journal* (1970) 73-111.

Slade, H. G. "Craigston & Meldrum Estates, Carriacou, 1796-1841," *Society of Antiquaries of Scotland*, 114 (1984 : 481-537.

Smith, William. *The History of the First Discovery and Settlement of Virginia*. London, 1747.

Steele, Beverley. *Grenada: A History of Its People*. Oxford: Macmillan Caribbean, 2003.

Stein, Robert L. *The French Sugar Business in the Eighteenth Century*. Baton Rouge: Louisiana State University Press, 1988.

Stein, Robert L. "The French Sugar Business in the Eighteenth Century: A Quantitative Study." *Business History* 22, no. 1 (1980): 3-17.

_____. *The French Slave Trade in the Eighteenth Century: An Old Regime Business*. Madison: The University of Wisconsin Press, 1979.

Stephens, S. G. "Cotton Growing in the West Indies During the Eighteenth and Nineteenth Centuries." *Tropical Agriculture* 21 (February 1944).

Stevens, Robert D. and Cathy L. Jabara. *Agricultural Development Principles: Economic Theory and Empirical Evidence*. Baltimore: Johns Hopkins University Press, 1988.

Steward, J. H. "South American Cultures: An Interpretative Summary," in *Handbook of South American Indians*, ed. by J.H. Steward. 6: 669-672.

Stinchcombe, Arthur L. *Sugar Island Slavery in the Age of Enlightenment: The Political Economy of the Caribbean World*. Princeton: Princeton University Press, 1995.

Taylor, Douglas. "Kinship and Social Structure of the Island Carib: Past and Present," *Southwestern Journal of Anthropology* 2, no. 2 (1946): 180-212.

Taylor, Douglas R. and Berend J. Hoff. "The Linguistic Repertory of the Island Caribs in the Seventeenth Century: The Men's Language—A Carib Pidgin?" in *International Journal of American Linguistics* 46, 4 (Oct. 1980): 301-312.

Taylor, Peter J. *Political Geography: World-economy, Nation-state and Locality*. New York: John Wiley & Sons, Inc., 1989.

Ternan, J. L., A. G. Williams, and C. Francis. "Land Capability Classification in Grenada, West Indies." *Mountain Research and Development* 9, no. 1 (1989): 71-82.

Thornton, A. P. "Some Statistics of West Indian Produce, Shipping and Revenue, 1660-1685." *Caribbean Historical Review* 4 (1954): 215-280.

Tomich, Dale W. *Slavery in the Circuit of Sugar: Martinique and the World Economy, 1830-1848*. Baltimore: The Johns Hopkins University Press, 1990.

Trouillot, Michel-Rolph. "Coffee Planters and Coffee Slaves in the Antilles: The Impact of a Secondary Crop," in *Cultivation and Culture: Labor and the Shaping of Black Life in the Americas*, ed. by Ira Berlin and Philip D. Morgan. Richmond: University Press of Virginia, 1993.

_____. *Peasants and Capital: Dominica in the World Economy*. Baltimore: Johns Hopkins University Press, 1983.

Turner, Christy and Jacqueline Turner, *Man Corn: Cannibalism and Violence in the Prehistoric American South West*. Salt Lake City: University of Utah, 1999.

Vaissière, Pierre de. *Origines de la colonisation et la formation de la société Française a Saint-Domingue*. Paris: Aux Bureaux de la Revue, 1906.

Val d'Abbeville, Pierre du. "Isles d'Amérique dites Caribes ou Cannibales et de Barlovento." Geographe du Roy. Paris: Chez l'Auteur avec privilège du Roy, 1664.

Vazquez de Espinosa, Antonio. *Description of the Indies*. Smithsonian Miscellaneous Collections, v. 102. Translated by Charles Upson Clark, Washington, DC: Smithsonian Institution Press, 1968 [c. 1620].

Vaughan, William. *Directions for Health*. London, 1626.

Verin, Pierre. "Carib Culture in Colonial Times," in *Proceedings of the Second International Congress for the Study of the Pre-Columbian Cultures of the Lesser Antilles*, St. Ann's, Barbados.

Vetterli, W. A. 1951. "The History of Indigo." *Ciba Review* no. 85 (April 1967): 3066-3087.

Vidal, Laurent and Émilie d'Orgeix. *Les villes françaises du Nouveau Monde: des premiers fondateurs aux ingénieurs du roi, XVIe-XVIIIe siècles.* Somogy, 1999.

Vignols, Léon. "Les Antilles Françaises sous l'Ancien Régime: Aspects économiques et sociaux: L'institution des engagés, 1626-1774." *Revue d'Histoire Economique et Sociale.* 16, no. 1 (1928): 12-45.

Walcott, Derek. *Derek Walcott Collected Poems, 1948-84.* New York: Farrar, Strass & Giroux, 1986.

Wallerstein, Immanuel. *The Modern World-system II: Mercantilism and the Consolidation of the European World-economy, 1600-1750.* New York: Academic Press, 1974.

Ward, J. R. "The Profitability of Sugar Planting in the British West Indies." *Economic Historical Review, 2nd Series* 31 (1978): 197-213.

Watkins, Melville H. "A Staple Theory of Economic Growth." *The Canadian Journal of Economics and Political Science* 29, no. 2 (May 1963): 141-158.

Watts, David. *The West Indies: Patterns of Development, Culture and Environmental Change Since 1492.* Cambridge Studies in Historical Geography No. 8. Cambridge: Cambridge University Press, 1987.

Weaver, P. *Forest Development, Grenada.* Technical Report: Planning and Management Activities. FAO Tech. Coop. Prog., tech. report. FO: TCP/GRN/8851. St. George's Grenada, 1989.

Webster, Jonathan H. "The Merchants of Bordeaux in Trade to the French West Indies, 1664-1717." Ph.D. diss., University of Minnesota, 1973.

Wells, Robert V. *The Population of the British Colonies in America Before 1776: A Survey of Census Data.* Princeton: Princeton University Press, 1975.

White, Tim. "Once More Cannibals," *Scientific American* (August 2001): 58-65.

Whitehead, Neil L. "Carib Cannibalism – The Historical Evidence," *Journal de la Société des Américanistes*, 70, 1 (1984): 69-87.

Williams, C. and F. James. "Comparative Epidemiology Study: Grenada," in *Disease Management in Cocoa: Comparative Epidemiology of Witches' Broom*, eds. S. A. Rudgard, A. C. Maddison and T. Andebrhan. London: Chapman & Hall, 1993.

Williams, Eric. *From Columbus to Castro: The History of the Caribbean, 1492-1969.* New York: Harper and Row, 1970.

————. *Capitalism and Slavery.* New York: Capricorn Books, 1966.

Williamson, James. *The Caribbee Islands Under the Proprietary Patents.* London: Oxford University Press, 1926.

Wilson, Arthur McCandless. *French Foreign Policy During the Administration of Cardinal Fleury, 1726-43: A Study in Diplomacy and Commercial Development.* Cambridge: Harvard University Press, 1936.

Wilson, Samuel M., ed. *The Indigenous People of the Caribbean.* Gainesville: University Press of Florida, 1997.

————. "The Cultural Mosaic of the Indigenous Caribbean," *Proceedings of the British Academy*, 81 (1993): 37-66.

Wooley, Benjamin. *Savage Kingdom: The True Story of Jamestown, 1607, and the Settlement of America.* New York: HarperCollins, 2007.

Wynne, John Huddlestone. *A General History of the British Empire in America.* London, 1770.

Young, William. *Considerations Which May Tend to Promote the Settlement of Our New West-India Colonies: By Encouraging Individuals to Embark in the Undertaking.* London: Printed for James Robson, 1764.

Index

Illustrations and tables identified in **bold**.

Made in the USA
Middletown, DE
01 September 2024

60233387R00255